The Meanings of Rights

Does the apparent victory, universality and ubiquity of the idea of rights indicate that such rights have transcended all conflicts of interests and moved beyond the presumption that it is the clash of ideas that drives culture? Or has the rhetorical triumph of rights not been replicated in reality? The contributors to this book answer these questions in the context of an increasing wealth gap between the metropolitan elites and the rest, a chasm in income and chances between the rich and the poor, and walls which divide the comfortable middle classes from the 'underclass'. Why do these inequalities persist in our supposed human-rights-abiding societies? In seeking to address the foundations, genealogies, meaning and impact of rights, this book captures some of the energy, breadth, power and paradoxes that make deployment of the language of human rights such an essential but changeable part of so many of our contemporary discourses.

COSTAS DOUZINAS is Professor of Law and Director of the Birkbeck Institute for the Humanities. He is a leading scholar in the field of the critical study of human rights.

CONOR GEARTY is Professor of Human Rights Law at the London School of Economics and Political Science and Director of LSE's Institute of Public Affairs. He is a specialist in UK human rights law, as well as in terrorism law and civil liberties.

D1089192

The Meanings of Rights

The Philosophy and Social Theory of Human Rights

Edited by

Costas Douzinas and Conor Gearty

 CAMBRIDGE
UNIVERSITY PRESS

CAMBRIDGE
UNIVERSITY PRESS

University Printing House, Cambridge CB2 8BS, United Kingdom

Cambridge University Press is part of the University of Cambridge.

It furthers the University's mission by disseminating knowledge in the pursuit of education, learning and research at the highest international levels of excellence.

www.cambridge.org
Information on this title: www.cambridge.org/9781107679597

First published 2014

Printed in the United Kingdom by Clays, St Ives plc

A catalogue record for this publication is available from the British Library

Library of Congress Cataloging in Publication data
The meanings of rights : the philosophy and social theory of human rights / [edited by] Costas Douzinas, Conor Gearty.
    pages   cm
ISBN 978-1-107-02785-5 (Hardback) – ISBN 978-1-107-67959-7 (Paperback)
1. Human rights–Philosophy.   2. Human rights–Social aspects.   I. Douzinas, Costas, 1951- editor of compilation.   II. Gearty, C. A., editor of compilation.
K3240.M395 2014
323.01–dc23   2013040409

ISBN 978-1-107-02785-5 Hardback
ISBN 978-1-107-67959-7 Paperback

Contents

v

Notes on contributors

PHENG CHEAH is Professor of Rhetoric at the University of California, Berkeley, where he has taught since 1999. He is the author of *Inhuman Conditions: On Cosmopolitanism and Human Rights* and *Spectral Nationality: Passages of Freedom from Kant to Postcolonial Literatures of Liberation* and co-editor of *Cosmopolitics: Thinking and Feeling Beyond the Nation*.

DRUCILLA CORNELL is a Professor of Political Science, Comparative Literature, and Women's and Gender Studies at Rutgers University. Her books include *Beyond Accommodation: Ethical Feminism, Deconstruction and the Law*; *The Philosophy of the Limit*; *Transformations: Recollective Imagination and Sexual Difference*; *The Imaginary Domain: Abortion, Pornography, and Sexual Harassment*; *Symbolic Forms for a New Humanity* (with Kenneth Panfilio).

COSTAS DOUZINAS is Professor of Law and Director of the Birkbeck Institute for the Humanities, Birkbeck, University of London. His books include *Justice Miscarried*; *The End of Human Rights*; *Critical Jurisprudence* (with Adam Gearey); *Nomos and Aesthetics*; *Human Rights and Empire*; *Resistance and Philosophy in the Crisis*. He has edited *The Cambridge Companion to Human Rights Law* with Conor Gearty.

CONOR GEARTY is Professor of Human Rights Law at the LSE Department of Law, Director of LSE's Institute of Public Affairs and a founding member of Matrix Chambers. His books include *Freedom under Thatcher* (with K. D. Ewing); *Terror*; *Can Human Rights Survive?*; *Civil Liberties*; *Liberty and Security*. He is the editor with Costas Douzinas of *The Cambridge Companion to Human Rights Law*.

PAUL GILROY is Professor of American and English Literature at Kings College, University of London. His many books include *There Ain't No Black In the Union Jack: The Cultural Politics of Race and Nation*; *The Black Atlantic: Modernity and Double Consciousness*; *Against Race: Imagining Political Culture Beyond the Color Line*; *After Empire:*

Multiculture or Postcolonial Melancholia; Darker Than Blue: On The Moral Economies of Black Atlantic Culture.

WALTER D. MIGNOLO is William H. Wannamaker Professor of Literature at Duke University. His books include *The Darker Side of the Renaissance: Literacy, Territoriality, Colonization; The Idea of Latin America; The Darker Side of Western Modernity: Global Futures, Decolonial Options.*

JOHN MILBANK is Professor in Religion, Politics and Ethics at the University of Nottingham. His many books include *The Monstrosity of Christ: Paradox or Dialectic?* (with Slavoj Žižek); *The Suspended Middle: Henri de Lubac and the Debate concerning the Supernatural; Truth in Aquinas* (with Catherine Pickstock); *Theology and Social Theory: Beyond Secular Reason.*

CHANTAL MOUFFE is a Professor of Politics at Westminster University. Her books include *Hegemony and Socialist Strategy: Towards a Radical Democratic Politics* (with Ernesto Laclau); *The Democratic Paradox; On the Political; Agonistics: Thinking The World Politically.*

SAMUEL MOYN is the James Bryce Professor of European Legal History at Columbia University. His books include *Origins of the Other: Emmanuel Levinas Between Revelation and Ethic; The Last Utopia: Human Rights in History;*

JEAN-LUC NANCY is a Professor Emeritus at the University of Strasbourg and an invited Professor in several other Universities. His books include *The Experience of Freedom; Being Singular Plural; The Creation of the World or Globalization; Dis-Enclosure: The Deconstruction of Christianity.*

PAUL PATTON is Scientia Professor of Philosophy at The University of New South Wales in Sydney, Australia. He is the author of *Deleuze and the Political* and *Deleuzian Concepts: Philosophy, Colonization, Politics.* He has edited *Nietzsche, Feminism and Political Theory; Deleuze: A Critical Reader; Between Deleuze and Derrida* (with John Protevi); *Deleuze and the Postcolonial* (with Simone Bignall).

BRUCE ROBBINS is Old Dominion Foundation Professor of the Humanities in the Department of English and Comparative Literature at Columbia University. His books include *Perpetual War: Cosmopolitanism from the Viewpoint of Violence; Upward Mobility and the Common Good; Feeling Global: Internationalism in Distress; The Servant's Hand:*

English Fiction from Below; *Secular Vocations: Intellectuals, Professionalism, Culture*.

JOSEPH R. SLAUGHTER is Associate Professor of English and Comparative Literature at Columbia University, where he teaches and publishes in postcolonial and twentieth-century ethnic and third world literature and theory and human rights. His *Human Rights, Inc.: The World Novel, Narrative Form, and International Law* was awarded the 2008 René Wellek prize for comparative literature and cultural theory.

ILLAN RUA WALL is an Associate Professor at the Warwick School of Law. He is the author of *Human Rights and Constituent Power: Without Model or Warranty* and has edited *New Critical Legal Thinking: Law and the Political* (with Costas Douzinas and Matthew Stone).

ROWAN WILLIAMS was Archbishop of Canterbury from 2002 until 2012. He is Master of Magdalene College Cambridge, and holds many honorary doctorates. He is the author of a number of books, is a noted poet and translator of poetry and, apart from Welsh, speaks or reads nine other languages. His books include *Dostoevsky: Language, Faith and Fiction*; *Grace and Necessity: Reflections on Art and Love*; *Writing in the Dust: Reflections on 11 September and Its Aftermath*; *Christ on Trial*.

SLAVOJ ŽIŽEK a Hegelian philosopher, a Lacanian psychoanalyst and a communist political activist, is international director at the Institute for Humanities, Birkbeck College, University of London. His books include *Less Than Nothing*; *The Year of Dreaming Dangerously*; *Demanding The Impossible*; *The Event*.

Introduction

Conor Gearty and Costas Douzinas

Human rights are an inescapable fact in the world. They bring together the North and the South, the left and right, church and state. Street activists look to them while armed forces adopt codes of conduct ostensibly on their basis. They are the ideology after 'the end of ideologies', the only set of values left now that we have arrived at 'the end of history'. Of course, such pervasiveness comes at a price of intellectual promiscuity. Human rights are used as a symbol or synonym for liberalism, capitalism or individualism by some and for development, social justice and/or peace by others. In the South, rights are seen as primarily collective rather than individual, social and economic rather than civil, associated with equality rather than with liberty. In the North, they can reflect commitments to solidarity and social justice as well as to political freedom – but they have also been used to underpin invasion and military brutality.

This volume captures and reflects the variegated nature of the meaning of human rights in contemporary scholarship and in public discussion. It brings together an eclectic group of leading philosophers, lawyers and social theorists to examine the foundations, meaning and impact of human rights on the world, and the dynamic inherent in the phrase's use today. The term itself is a combined one: the 'human' refers to morality and ethics and to the treatment that individuals are entitled to expect from public and private powers 'Rights' refers to their legal provenance. The hybridity of human rights introduces a number of paradoxes at the heart of society, which this volume explores in a way that is inquisitive, critical and above all inter-disciplinary. Let us introduce the volume by looking at four in particular.

Finding foundations

A first paradox underpinning this volume is the need to identify a set of truths for human rights against a background of a confident awareness on the part of most contributors of the improbability of the discovery of truth anywhere. It is clear that controversies around cultural relativism, humanitarian wars, the conflict between liberty and security and the most appropriate means for the protection of rights indicate that the proclamation of rights is not enough. As Catholic philosopher Jacques Maritain observed in *Man and the State*, we agree on the rights, providing we are not asked why. With the 'why', the dispute begins. But the fear of dispute should not put intellectual enquiry beyond the realm of discussion. Our volume reflects the tension not only in various versions of rights but even in the fact of having this discussion about origins.

In Chapter 1, Jean-Luc Nancy's two 'simple' remarks capture in their 'simplicity' a most profound philosophical reflection on human rights. The 'human' of rights carries in it the ambiguities and problems of humanism. Humanism is deeply implicated with power, capitalist domination, a restricted conception of freedom and the hierarchies of philanthropy. 'Rights', on the other hand, are the products and carriers of legal history. At the same time, right expresses a certain flexibility that inhabits the solidity of positive law. Right goes to the boundary of the legal domain and expresses law's mission to render justice. But justice cannot be founded or justified. Justice must be rendered to the singularity of existents and is therefore infinite. Human rights inscribe in law and remind law of its necessary and impossible commitment to an unconditional justice.

To Conor Gearty in Chapter 2, the power of the idea of human rights is driven by a very particular paradox: it craves a basis in truth but at the same time it needs to fail to have one in order to maintain its hegemonic power as the progressive ideal of the post-political age. Nature is the latest in a long line (which includes religion, reason and law) to tantalise us with a certainty that must forever remain impossible. The way to cope with this craving is to embrace it as a thirst for justice which is itself a kind of truth. Building on the work of American pragmatists as deployed by the philosopher Philip Kitcher in his effort to identify and describe mankind's ethical project, Gearty presents a vision of human rights which is half-truth, half desperate longing for a better life.

John Millbank in Chapter 3 offers a fascinating account of the genealogy and philosophy of human rights from medieval theological debates to our contemporary humanitarian wars. Human rights encourage a 'slide of neo-liberalism towards a fully-fledged totalitarian capitalism'. This drift is enabled by the ontology of human rights based on the isolated individual and by the abandonment of the Judaic and Christian conception of the 'person'. Millbank argues that a type of revisionist history and theology has tried to justify this distortion of Western identity by linking subjective rights with Christianity and justice. Reviewing in detail the long and complicated history of the emergence of rights, Millbank sides with Michel Villey and against Brian Tierney, arguing that the foundation of human rights must be sought in the nominalism of William of Ockham and Duns Scotus and their turn towards theological voluntarism and atomising metaphysics. This ontology persists in contemporary human rights, which combine extreme individualism with a sovereign omnipotence which regularly trumps rights. Millbank believes that we must abandon 'absolute' foundations for a relational conception of rights. An alternative modernity that abandons liberal capitalism for the egalitarian Christian legacy can achieve that. The foundation of self is not dignity and liberty but the sacredness of the person; the only effective rights are those of communal belonging and solidarity. In this sense, only a God can save us.

Taking up where Millbank leaves off, Rowan Williams' starting point in Chapter 4 is a reflection on what it means to be human and on the valuable contribution a religious perspective offers us as a source for 'resources for grounding the discourse' of human rights. An early breakthrough offered by Christianity is its rejection of the inequality of the master–slave relationship or, rather, its assertion that both are equal under God. The idea of the humanness of the body means that it is not reducible to an object among others and nor is it something which depends on the successful negotiation of pre-conditions for entry: Williams argues strongly against making dignity dependent on an actor's 'self-conscious' capacity as an 'organiser of experience into patterns of continuity through time, past and future'. Rather 'the irreducible core of human rights is the liberty to make sense as a bodily subject; which means that 'the inviolability of the body itself is where we should start in thinking about rights'.

Law, rights and revolution

Our second underlying paradox lies in the fact that the ideological power of human rights lies largely in their ambiguity, the oscillation between real and ideal, is and ought, community and humanity. When human rights are part of the law, as with the UK Human Rights Act 1998, such legislation invariably includes a principle of self-transcendence, which pushes against the law's settled state. A legal system that includes human rights is therefore not truly equal to itself, since human rights call the whole of law to account. In this sense, human rights become the latest expression of a human urge to resist domination and oppression and to dissent from the intolerance of public opinion. This was the case in the great revolutions of the eighteenth century, in the post-Second World War 'never again' declarations, in popular uprisings against fascist and communist rule. Viewed in this way, human rights are idealist, parts of a philosophy and practice of emancipation, the last great utopia of our age.

In Chapter 5, Costas Douzinas examines 'philosophy's hesitant exploration of the link between revolution and right'. The question is whether philosophy can explain the 'eternal return' of resistance despite law's persistent attempts to ban it'. A thorough reading of Kant, Hegel and legal philosophy explores the connection between revolution as the motor of modernity and rights as a key part of its ethical make-up. For modern philosophy, there can be no right to revolution as such – this would be an 'affront to the positivism and formalism of law'. Rather it is success, 'a question of fact', that determines the legal position: 'Whether one is a great criminal or a hero is decided by the outcome of the rebellion. The *is* reverses the *ought*.' The legal foreclosure of revolution and its philosophical justification has been regularly set aside by the *event* of revolution, which inexorably leads to a radical change of constitution and law and the retrospective legitimation of revolution and its right. Douzinas concludes that these opposed rights, the right to the existent and the right to what does not exist according to current legality, indicate perhaps that two types of will mobilise the language and practice of rights. A right to revolution exists despite the reservations of philosophers and lawyers. In this sense, the obligation to obey the law 'is absolute only when accompanied by the judgement that the law is morally just and democratically legitimate'.

Following a similar line of thought, Illan Rua Wall in Chapter 6 addresses the radical potential of human rights. Wall sketches the contours of the idea of *right-ing*, an imaginative re-conceptualisation of rights that mobilises a resistant core that lurks in human rights. Right-ing describes the practices of groups, which exceed the rights given to them by law in order to re-construct the 'institution of society'. The philosophical basis of right-ing is found in the theory of constituent power and the critiques of humanism, propriety and authenticity. However, insisting on the excess of human rights, in a philosophical sense, is not enough. It is necessary to begin to think about how right-ing engages with law in order to generate such moments of rupture. The chapter examines conceptions of critical legal strategy and constituent power in order to develop a vocabulary of right-ing. It argues that right-ing may entail the use of existent rights through the activation of an immanent torsion and confrontation or the generation of new rights. The question is ultimately *not* about the preservation of a fetishised body of rights, but about the unlocking of the radical potential which lies within rights discourse.

Frantz Fanon is a driver of two chapters. Drucilla Cornell in Chapter 7 is determined to emphasise his work as a route back to traditions of

African and Afro-Caribbean revolutionary thought that have served greatly to enrich our contemporary understanding of human rights. Her account shows how necessary the denial of the human was to the colonial project: '[I]f the colonized are recognized as human, then they of course have their own culture, their own intellectual traditions, their own values, because human beings never live outside not only language but the "symbolic forms" in which they are constituted. But if one is thrown off the register of the human, then such creatures, by definition, do not have a culture worth taking into account.' It is, therefore, 'the violent struggle' that 'must self-consciously grasp itself as part of the creation of a new national culture', something 'which is inseparable from the becoming of a people out of their own self-mobilization'. As Cornell shows, the way this is worked through in the mind of Fanon puts him at odds with some of the more orthodox of successful national liberation leaders of the 1960s, but who is to say that he was not right to be on the wrong side of that particular history?

Like Cornell, Paul Gilroy in Chapter 8 draws inspiration from the work of Frantz Fanon for his reflection on 'Race and the value of the human'. It is this writer's consistently expressed commitment to imagining a new kind of humanism that appeals to Gilroy, a version in other words of what it is to be alive which is not contaminated with the baggage of past meanings driven by the powerful. To Gilroy this involves a search for a 'reparative' humanism that, properly understood, can 'help to clarify a number of problems that characterise the *postcolonial* world'. This humanism is, however, 'stubborn' because so much of the structuralist and post-structuralist movements of recent times have 'converged around the idea that humanism was, at best, an anachronism'. Gilroy's chapter is a good example of the unceasing power of the language of human rights and of humanism to rejuvenate old discourses, filling terms grown stale with new possibilities, a project driven by frank acknowledgement of the 'costs of antihumanism'. Getting behind the human despite the debilitating effects of colonial and racial impositions is what is at the core of Gilroy's chapter, a bold effort to think through the 'elusive, reparative element in Fanon's thinking'.

Rights, justice, politics

In advanced western societies, we can see our third paradox in the way that human rights have mutated, expanded and turned into a vernacular touching every aspect of social life while resisting any kind of pinning down that can explain or support such pervasiveness. Secure in their ambiguity, human rights are seen as key concept in morals, politics, individual and collective identities. Claiming rights has become the main form of morality. Responsibility, virtue and duty, on the other hand, have been confined to religious or communitarian backwardness, with dire consequences. Similarly, rights recognition is the main tool and target of politics. Group claims and ideological positions, sectional interests and global campaigns are routinely expressed in the language of rights for individuals. But when rights become a 'trump card' that defeat state policies and collective priorities, allegedly to support the liberty of the individual, society starts breaking up into a collection of atoms indifferent to the common good. This way politics is depoliticised. Both liberty and security suffer in this process.

Walter D. Mignolo's Chapter 9 is concerned with justice, and in particular with the potential of human rights to rectify the injustices and wrongdoings of past eras. As with Gilroy and many other contributions in this volume, the 'splendour of human rights' lies in its capacity to force fresh thinking onto a stage that has been desiccated by the twin facts of state and corporate abuse. We must embrace the new language of 'thinking otherwise', and – echoing the famous challenge to this effect posed by Albert Einstein and Bertrand Russell in 1955 – Mignolo presents his subject as one in which there are three major shifts: from human rights to the right to life; from the saviours of the victims to the victims themselves; and from the politics of rights to an ethic of survival. As with Gilroy and Cornell, the spectre of colonialist and imperialist exploitation hangs over Mignolo's themes – decolonial thinking and thinking otherwise can manage, as in the Bandung Conference, to articulate a future that is expressed neither as 'capitalism nor communism, that is, life regulated by the economy or by the state'.

Chantal Mouffe in Chapter 10 starts with a brief presentation of political and agonistic democracy, her well-known theory of politics. Social order is the hegemonic articulation of contingent practices that temporarily pacify antagonism. From that position, Mouffe finds problems both in the standard liberal version of cosmopolitanism, which universalises European ideas of democracy, dignity and rights, and in the various subaltern cosmopolitanisms of Homi Bhabba, Walter Mignolo and Paul Gilroy. Such writers might prioritise diasporas, immigrants and refugees, but their 'pluralist universalism' fails to recognise the conflictual character of democracy. Mouffe proposes the creation of a multipolar world organised around regional units with their different cultures and values. The same perspective applies to human rights. Rights are usually presented as both universally valid and uniquely European in origin. In a multipolar world, however, non-European conceptions of selfhood, dignity, the good and democracy would be as acceptable as European individualism. Equivalent but different notions of dignity and selfhood would create an 'agonistic' version of human rights.

Samuel Moyn has already written an important book debunking the mythological foundationalism of the 1948 Universal Declaration so far as the contemporary human rights movement is concerned. Here, in Chapter 11, he turns his attention via the German scholar Bruno Snell to the supposed classical origins of the idea of humanity. Moyn argues that it is 'certainly wrong to conscript the Greeks into an invention of tradition', that while they knew what 'humanity' might entail, the real issue was 'living up to its implications'. On his reading, humanity 'is a simple discovery rather than an epoch-making breakthrough', something which being 'common in the annals of human affairs' inevitably takes many shapes (multiple universalisms), one of which has recently been that of 'human rights'. With the ground cleared, Moyn's chapter then produces an absorbing account of the interrelationship between sovereignty and human rights: 'The alliance with state and nation was not some accident that tragically befell the rights of man; it was their very essence, for the vast bulk of their history.' For Moyn, we should be careful not to mislead ourselves by the current meanings of human rights into believing that the universalisms they signify today were ever thus: 'It is now the order of the day to supplement [the] state forum for rights, but until recently the state was their sole and essential crucible.'

Rights and power

The very success of human rights produces our fourth and final paradox: the term's value as a guide to complex arenas of meaning depends in part on an overly simple approach to its subject, one that militates against a true understanding of that which the phrase purports to explain. In short, rights talk has become an easy and simple way of describing complex historical, social and political situations, a type of 'cognitive mapping' and the main tool of identity politics. In post-modern societies 'I want X' or 'X should be given to me' easily mutates to 'I have a right to X'. This linguistic inflation weakens the association of rights with significant human goods. Our volume explores the dangers inherent in too reckless a deployment of the term in pursuit of goals that are beyond the realm of the language being deployed to achieve them.

Pheng Cheah in Chapter 12 takes an iconoclastic approach to comfortable assumptions about the necessity of the protection of economic and social rights and how this is mediated through traditional international human rights law. The chapter provides an alternative reading rooted in a biopolitical analysis of the sort pioneered by Michel Foucault, Gilles Deleuze and Giorgio Agamben. Utilising a formidable philosophical erudition combined with detailed empirical socio-legal analysis, Cheah points to the Janus-like character of socio-economic rights. Far from being an enthusiast for the multiplication and proliferation of rights, Cheah sees the inevitable juridification that it entails as necessarily inimical to 'the biological or natural dimension of human life' that such rights should rightly encompass. Like Moyn, Cheah can get to this point because of his clear location of human rights in the power of the state: 'both the bourgeois liberal conception of human rights and the Marxist reformulation of human rights presuppose sovereignty'. The 'dynamic of simultaneous freedom and constriction' of human capacities that this approach foregrounds illuminates our condition much better than the tired and repeated orthodoxies of mainstream social theory.

The Left has developed, since Marx, a number of critiques of the abstract and formal character of rights. At the same time, rights claims are a main weapon mobilised by social and protest movements. Paul Patton in Chapter 13 starts from this paradox and focuses on the work of Michel Foucault and Giles Deleuze with Felix Guattari, philosophers who have been extensively utilised by the critics of rights. But, as Patton argues, the position is more complicated than it might seem. Both Foucault and Deleuze/Guattari agree that rights are not a-historical, a-cultural or absolute. They are embedded in relations of power and in structures of popular belief and action. Deleuze and Guattari reject the idea that rights are grounded on universal human characteristics such as freedom or rationality. On the contrary, rights operate within immanent modes of existence. In this sense, it is not law or judges but 'jurisprudence' that creates rights. Deleuze defines jurisprudence as the process of 'becoming-right', the variety of macro- and micro-political means by which new ways of acting become established. Foucault, on the other hand, reminds us that rights must be justified by discursive frameworks widely accepted. Citizen resistance against governmental actions, for example, draws on principles that inform governing. For Patton, Foucault argues that the necessary justification of rights depends on the available forms of public political reason, including conceptions of the nature and functions of government. The necessary justification of rights is not moral and universal but historical and political. In this sense, some of the standard critiques of rights are refuted and their positive political function affirmed.

Bruce Robbins in Chapter 14 agrees that traditional histories of human rights exhibit the problems that Patton has identified. Many historians (Micheline Ishay, Lynn Hunt, Aryeh Neier) take an idealist approach. They present human rights as either the end product of a progressive sequence that started in antiquity or as timeless. Critics, such as Samuel Moyn, can be problematic in reverse. They argue that rights are determined by the historical and political conditions of their emergence. But as all major political projects are conditioned by ideologies and structures of power, critics tend to undervalue their significance and contribution. The 'discourse of the beneficiary', which Robbins traces in texts by George Orwell, Jean-Paul Sartre and Wallace Shaun, has similar problems. This type of discourse denounces the system of power and exploitation to which the critic belongs and cannot escape while at the same time enjoying its benefits and privileges. Jacques Rancière's work is an example of this idealistic and at the same time somewhat cynical position. Pictures of suffering in remote lands create fear and pity but cannot lead to the 'impossible identification' with the 'cause of the other' that is the mark of politics. Rancière has based his political philosophy on a strong claim to equality. However, his belief that inequality is eternal and that support for the cause of the other emerges only in domestic politics means that his powerful appeal for change cannot recognise change when it occurs. All humanitarian action can lead to intervention and occupation and human rights do depoliticise politics. But if we abandon an impossible and exaggerated idealism, we have to recognise the tangible improvements that human rights, solidarity and development have achieved.

Joseph Slaughter, too, takes issue with the teleological histories of human rights. In Chapter 15 he focuses instead on the history of the person, the artificial subject of human rights, and its complex relationship with humans and corporations. This relationship is examined in legal history and jurisprudence and through a reading at Daniel Defoe's *Robinson Crusoe*, that is compared with the emergence of the corporation as a domestic and international legal person with legal and human rights. Standard histories see corporation rights as extensions of individual rights based on the personification of the company. Slaughter reverses this narrative. The genealogy of the human rights person and human rights law are intertwined with the legal life of the corporation and imperial and colonial capitalism. The business corporation preceded the human being in human rights. Basic provisions of human rights law were first given to the colonial charter company and articulated in so-called free-trade agreements. Capitalism and imperialism had a pivotal role in the formation and perpetuation of human rights and international law.

Slaughter's detailed reading shows that Crusoe bears a surplus of personality and has the characteristics of the colonial charter company.

Crusoe becomes a sovereign through the forced recognition of Man Friday; he is a castaway subject to sovereignty and, finally, he personifies the corporate enterprise. Crusoe's oaths, diaries and formalities follow the actions of the colonial charter company. When he grants human rights to his subjects, he imitates the rights corporations claimed for themselves and then spread to the world as part of the colonising and civilising mission. Crusoe prefigures the development of corporations. When the corporation finally became a full legal person in the nineteenth century, it acquired also international personality and international human rights well before the human became a subject of human rights and an international person in its own right. This re-writing of the history of legal personality changes contemporary political priorities in international human rights and economic law.

Slavoj Žižek starts his Chapter 16 with a number of examples illustrating his theory of ideology. Žižek's trademark approach bridges a number of fields: from opera to film and literature, from the French Revolution to North Korea and China and from *The Sound of Music* to cigarette advertisements to Berthold Brecht and documentaries about atrocities in Indonesia. The philosophical trajectory is similarly dizzying, moving from Hegel to Marx, Lacan and Rancière. Žižek argues that explicit ideology is sustained by a series of implicit obscene injunctions and prohibitions, teaching the subject how not to take certain explicit norms seriously and how to implement a set of publicly unacknowledged prohibitions. This analysis is then generalised: the law can only sustain its authority if people hear in it the echo of an unconditional and absolute assertion of power.

Applying a similar analysis to human rights and humanitarianism, Žižek argues that depoliticised humanitarianism acts as the ideology of military intervention serving specific economic–political interests. This supposed defence of the innocent and the powerless against power, questions the opposition between universal, a-political human rights and the political rights of citizens. Adopting a standard ideology critique, Žižek argues that no a-historical human rights above politics exist. However rights should not be dismissed either as the reified fetish of concrete historical processes. The Marxist critique of the gap between the ideological function of the universal legal form and the particular interests that effectively sustain it is not enough; it neglects the emergence and operation of the form of universality itself. When abstract universality emerged as a form, like all forms, it started affecting social life. Following Rancière's analysis, Žižek argues that the bourgeois 'formal' freedom allowed the emergence of 'material' political demands and practices, from trade unions to feminism.

Renewing language

This volume reaches beyond the legal perspective that informed our recent, co-edited *Cambridge Companion to Human Rights Law*, in the process asking some fundamental questions about the field. It is offered as a set of fresh reflections on human rights theory from a range of different perspectives and disciplines. We are asking here a number of questions critical to the future of human rights. Can we find a common foundation for human rights that can justify the liberal claims? Is the proclaimed universality of rights founded on eternal values or does it result from agreements among governments and lawyers? Do rights, dignity and equality represent the ineliminably religious element of law? Why is the gap between declarations of right and their application and enforcement as wide as ever? Is it better to impose rights from above or to foster their gradual evolution in the morals and ethos of communities?

And then, further, there are the questions provoked by the success of rights-talk. Does the apparent victory, the universality and the ubiquity of the idea of rights indicate that such rights have transcended all conflicts of interests, indeed have moved beyond the presumption that it is the clash of ideas that drives culture? Have rights become a common horizon uniting Cardiff and Kabul, London and Lahore? Or has the rhetorical triumph of rights been anything but replicated in reality – as would seem to be suggested by the increasing wealth gap between the metropolitan lands and the rest, the yawning chasm in income and chances between the rich and the poor, the ever new and strictly policed walls which divide the comfortable middle classes from the 'underclass' of immigrants, refugees and undesirables, all the pockets of 'third world' that persist in our human rights-abiding societies?

In seeking through its various contributors to address these issues, the overarching aim of the book is to capture some of the energy, breadth, power and paradoxes that make deployment of the language of human rights such an essential but at the same time chameleonic part of so many of our contemporary discourses.

This volume is partly the outcome of a research project on 'Cosmo-politanism or Empire' by Costas Douzinas and Patrick Hanafin funded by the Leverhulme Trust. Valerie Kelly administered the project and helped organise at Birkbeck in November 2011 the conference 'Being-In-Human' where many of the chapters in this collection originated. A longer version of John Milbank's chapter was published in the *Oxford Journal of Law and Religion*, 1(1) (2012), 203–234. We thank Oxford University Press for permission to reprint the article.

Part I

Finding foundations

1   On human rights: two simple remarks

Jean-Luc Nancy

First remark

Today, political correctness demands that we say in French *droits humains* (human rights) when we used to say *droits de l'homme* (rights of man).[1] This demand, which also occurs in other areas, is made because the French *homme*, like '*man*' in English, does not distinguish between the human race and the male gender. German is better equipped, differentiating between *Mensch* and *Mann*. Latin distinguishes between *vir* and *homo*, Greek between *anêr* and *anthrōpos*, etc.

We could discuss the reasons for this. However, it is also important to note the introduction of another ambiguity. The adjective 'human' in French has a value that corresponds to the usual meaning we now give to the term 'humanist' and, more generally, to the moral qualities of 'care' (a word which has recently been imported unchanged from English into French), 'compassion' or 'charity'. The English language attributes this value to the word 'human', further ascribing to it a more specific term, 'humane'. German has introduced, along with *menschlish*, the words *human*, *humanitär*, and *Humanität* as terms of ethical evaluation. In other words, human rights can be seen as rights basking in the aura of humanity, since this term, in its currently impoverished and rather ridiculous sense, has taken on the meaning of a 'love of mankind' or 'friendship' (in French, this is the meaning frequently ascribed to *philia*). Now philanthropy – which was actually a secular displacement of the ostensibly all-too-Christian charity – is based upon a more or less hidden axiom of condescension: it is the act of the rich, cultivated and dominant, who feel benevolence, compassion and pity for the social misfortune of others. For all that, philanthropists have never sought to challenge the social order, except in minor ways.

---

[1] Translator's note: *droit(s)* and *loi(s)* have been consistently translated as right(s) and law(s) respectively, unless otherwise indicated.

Philanthropy contains an implicit negation of the respect for the unconditional dignity of all human beings, which appears at the beginning of the Universal Declaration of Human Rights of 1948 (hereafter referred to as 'Declaration') and is repeated further on. It can even be said to represent an interpretation of dignity that is conservative, selfish and gushing with sentimentality.

Without arguing against the use of the term 'human rights', it is necessary to draw attention to the extent of its ambivalence. For whatever the term used, human rights are marked by a certain degree of philanthropy mixed with a promise of 'social progress', which is always linked to a 'larger freedom'. In this sense, freedom prevails over social justice through the resonance, tone and emphasis of the text.

Moreover, the Declaration affirms that 'the advent of a world in which human beings shall enjoy freedom of speech and belief and freedom from fear and want has been proclaimed as the highest aspiration of the common people'.[2] But what is proclaimed here and cannot be challenged should not be considered the 'highest aspiration'. One can and must think that freedom (of speech and belief) does not limit the aspirations of the common people (*hommes*). It would not be wrong to say that the people can expect and want different things – engagements, collaborations, relations – things that are larger, infinitely larger and more, than freedoms. Being 'free from fear and want' is not the only reality of freedom; there are other stakes that lie beyond any human freedom. Spinoza, for example, who can hardly be accused of being inhuman or an enemy of freedom, considered 'freedom' to exist only as the freedom of the entire world (which he called 'nature or god'). The independence and autonomy of persons has a long way to go before it reaches its limits, if limits exist. Autonomy should be conceived in relation to the sense of existence or, more exactly, in relation to existence itself – of each, of all and of the world as sense.

Some will object, 'What do you expect from a declaration of rights? You're not considering the extent to which your words go beyond the predetermined sphere that constitutes a kind of minimum necessary to free humanity from oppression. You're departing the realm of right for philosophy, if not for dreams or speculation.'

My response is that it is indeed necessary to enter a philosophical register since the text of the Declaration – and the huge body of texts inspired by it and by the defence of 'human' rights – carries an implicit

---

[2] Translator's note: In this section of the Universal Declaration of Human Rights, the French text uses the word *hommes*, while the English text uses the expression 'common people'.

or latent ideology that should be brought to light. In fact, this is the price to be paid in order to avoid the self-righteous inanity of such 'rights'. The self-righteousness here is that of a 'humanism' of European origin, which one must always remember 'does not think the *humanitas* of man high enough', as Heidegger wrote.

Pascal, another European, said the same thing much earlier but in a different way: 'Man infinitely surpasses man.' Pascal was a Christian. Heidegger, on the contrary, believed that he could find the force of re-foundation in an anti-Christian direction. Today, all these references are written off, and human rights float more or less on the surface of the 'icy water of egotistical calculation'.[3]

Second remark

The Declaration is based – as a declaration of rights, that is to say, as a juridical production or *juris-dictio* – on the following sentence:

Whereas it is essential, if man is not to be compelled to have recourse, as a last resort, to rebellion against tyranny and oppression, that human rights should be protected by the rule of law.

This is the third of seven *'considérants'* ('whereas') after which the text proceeds with the actual declaration. The French text reads:

Considérant qu'il est essentiel que les droits de l'homme soient protégés par un régime de droit pour que l'homme ne soit pas contraint, en suprême recours, à la révolte contre la tyrannie et l'oppression.

We will pass quickly over the complex and fragile character of a proposition that seeks to avoid a resort to rebellion. It is clear that this resort is seen as something 'compelled' and that this compulsion can engender 'tyranny and oppression.' In 1948, in a text drafted by a committee of nine members whose political and intellectual composition calls for lengthy analysis,[4] tyranny and oppression focused on the fascisms that had just been defeated. In a sense, the Declaration is part of the general movement that, somehow nebulously, fosters the condemnation of 'fascism' and what this word would, over a long period, ignominiously signify. However, any questioning of the underlying reasons for the rise of fascisms is relegated to the background, if not even further. There

---

[3] Marx–Engels in the *Communist Manifesto*.

[4] It comprised a Soviet ambassador, a scholar and diplomat from China (China, with the help of the Soviet Union, would soon pass from Chiang Kai-shek to Mao Zedong) together with seven other members (American, Australian, Canadian, Chilean, English, French and Lebanese) who clearly all belonged to the space of democratic humanism.

is no examination, from the perspective of democracy and twentieth-century capitalism, of what could have facilitated or even caused the emergence of fascisms. There is, therefore, no opportunity to consider other possibilities of oppression – and consequently of rebellion – like those represented by the abominable figure of a Head of State or Leader flanked by party apparatus, police and mythology.

Here, again, some will protest. The preceding sentences will be criticised for being unacceptably suspicious of the virtuous words of the Declaration. I was careful above to write, '[i]n a sense', and to limit myself to pointing out the absence of examination, nothing more. In all sincerity, I am not trying to construct a machinery of denunciation. Yet it is difficult to dispute that the question of 'humanism' has been continually refined or deepened, according to different views. This has occurred along the road from the defeat of fascism to the unbridled expansion of capitalism, which is undermining human rights in an increasingly obvious way. It is a road that passes through the other collapse of so-called 'socialisms' and, today, through the various tensions in religious and/or communitarian movements. 'Humanism' is strictly coeval with mercantile civilisation, techno-scientific development and democracy. 'Human rights' are not absolutely pristine, as their pre-history in Roman law (*droit*) after a certain period already shows. They derive from Roman legal culture, transported first out of Roman civil religion and then out of Christianity to fertilise the spirit of modern law (*droit*) and especially so-called 'natural' law (*droit*).

Now, it is here that we must consider the other clause of this 'whereas'. The French version provides a striking statement: Human rights must be protected by the rule of law (*régime de droit*). The English distinguishes rights and law, the Italian distinguishes *diritti* and *norme giuridiche*, whereas other languages (e.g. Greek or German) repeat, like the French, the same term. Perhaps the Latin translation best clarifies the distinction in stating that: *hominum jura civitatis forma quae justa est tegi* (human rights must be covered by a just civil form).

This is much more than a linguistic curiosity. Repeating a single term (*droit*) or distinguishing two terms (rights and law), indicates the same difficulty: do rights (*droits*) exist that have not been established by law (*droit*)? Here the Declaration declares its own necessity: it is not just a formulation, words solemnly declared. The Declaration is the legal institution of the rights it declares. If we leave aside the well-known American and French antecedents that paved the way, prior to the Declaration only factual rights and not legal rights (*droits de droit*) existed. At most, some of these rights pre-existed as rights of certain States, the United Kingdom, the United States and France in particular. But what are 'factual' rights or national rights with regard to international law? These two distinct questions are in part intertwined.

These questions share a concern about the foundation of a right in general. The idea of 'human rights' brings to light the extraordinary difficulty of founding right, if not the impossibility of such a foundation. We have sought to dismiss the idea of 'natural rights', which represents an internal contradiction because their non-positive (in the legal sense) character prevents legal enforcement and sanction. Yet we have invoked a 'minimum norm' (Rawls) that is necessary for the constitution of a just state or the state of the rule of 'law' (*État de 'droit'*) as it is popularly called today.[5] This is no less lacking in foundations, in the fullest sense of the word, than 'natural' rights. Hannah Arendt also showed how the national appropriation of 'human rights' gave rise to categories of persons without rights (refugees, displaced and stateless persons). It follows from these analyses that forms of non-right have not stopped imposing their iron law within positive rights, with the help of economic, technical and political chaos.

Undoubtedly, the 'right to have rights', as Arendt formulated it, is plain to see: we can recognise neither the quality of the human being, nor, perhaps, that of the existent in general, without the involvement of this right. However, this again says nothing about the nature of this singular 'right' or about the possibility of its recognition, which should be universal and prior – if not superior – to any determined legal institution.

It is well known that the powerlessness of international law (*droit*) – of what passes under this name – or perhaps the basic impossibility of such a law (*droit*) (yet called for, desired and proclaimed by philosophical humanism for more than two centuries and formally *declared* in the twentieth century) impedes its effective implementation. But as Hegel says, what is well known is not known at all. What remains here unknown is nothing other than the absence of foundation of right in general. This absence is not temporary or contingent: it is constitutive, I would even say that it is 'constituent' of right.

Indeed, right can only exist or be guaranteed by a divine authority, whatever that may be. In such a case, it is not a question of right, if something worthy of this name requires the continuing possibility of recovery, transformation and re-creation in the various practical circumstances – technical, political, cultural and spiritual – to which it must respond. Both the history of legislated rights of the Roman type as well as the customary rights of the Anglo-Saxon type clearly show that an essential plasticity of right exists within the fixity that the law, no less essentially, requires.

---

[5] Since, by definition, a state cannot but possess its law or laws, even if they are laws of oppression, exploitation, discrimination, and even exclusion.

Both the interminable ascent to the 'basic norm' in a pyramid of norms (Kelsen) and the recourse to an ultimate power to decide the exception (Schmitt), the right to exceed right, converge towards a passage to the limit. Right can only be exposed to such a passage; it is by nature the institution of what cannot be instituted, in other words of justice in the non-legal sense of the word. And it is not by seeking a categorical legal imperative that we can hope to found such a justice since the universal can be found neither here nor in a Kantian imperative, where it is reduced to the representation of 'nature' as a 'type' or non-deterministic model of morality.

In a sense, which itself passes on to the limit of sense, justice consists in *rendering* justice. This is not 'to render *the* justice' – which assumes a determined or instituted justice. This is rendering to someone or something the justice that this person or thing – event, work, any form of existent – deserves.[6] But what does each X deserve? Each X deserves an infinite recognition of its singularity. In other words, the justice that must be rendered to X is a justice whose nature and extent or non-naturalness and incommensurability only X can determine.

This justice must be effectively rendered, given back, returned to any X. This justice must be recognised for every X. Justice must be done to X and yet it is not it – whatever *it* is, tree or man (*homme*) – that can produce its due and present it as 'justice' or as 'right'. This justice rests on the unfound-able certainty that it is *just* that *that* exists. On the certainty, therefore, that it is just that the world exists even though nothing can justify its existence.

Unjustifiable justice,[7] far from founding any kind of rights – as extensive as these may be – opens up instead an infinite perspective that exceeds all possibility of right. From this infinity and to this infinity, all things and every singularity proceed and return. This perspective must remain present beyond the horizon of right; for without an appeal or a sign towards it, right can only fall back into its inevitable fragility, whether of impotence, arbitrariness, relativity or rigidity. The greatest merit of 'human rights' is to bring out all these difficulties and all these exigencies. The aim of these two simple remarks was, within their narrow limits, to draw attention to this.

Translated by Gilbert Leung.

---

[6] Immediately, the very idea of 'rendering justice' raises a difficulty in describing what is needed to render it, for it involves all 'things' without exception, and the world in its entirety. From the outset, 'human' rights are exceeded.

[7] Jacques Derrida speaks in this sense of the undeconstructability of justice.

2　Human rights: the necessary quest for foundations

*Conor Gearty**

Introduction

In *The Ethical Project*[1] the distinguished philosopher and historian of science Philip Kitcher attempts an ambitious project: to bring together post-Darwinian fatalism about the self with human reason's not unreasonable desire to keep itself at the centre of our species-story. The first – rooted in the idea that we are what our genes tell us to be; nothing less and certainly nothing more – has ridden off the back of recent neurological breakthroughs to grab the attention of mass audiences (via Pinker,[2] Dennett[3] *et al.*) with its seductive tale of hard-wired brains predisposing each of us to this or that, practically pre-determining (albeit in a general sense) what we do. The latter, though, having human vanity and centuries of learning on its side, is not proving that easy to dislodge: Kant, Hegel and the rest of us are not just the products of lumps of interconnections behind our foreheads. Doing right, behaving properly, leading a good life are qualities we get to, not the side-effects of genetic composition. Reasoning matters in a way that is different from wanting food or not wanting to be cold or needing sex, or even cleverly using our thumbs.[4] Sociologists are not slow to join in the critique as well, seeing in the

---

* My thanks to Tim Besley, Helena Cronin, Oliver Curry, Costas Douzinas, Bernard Keenan, Luke McDonagh, Claire Moon, Paul O'Connell, Aoife Nolan and Barry Sullivan for uniformly helpful comments on earlier drafts of this chapter.
1 P. Kitcher, *The Ethical Project* (Cambridge, Mass., Harvard University Press, 2011). I first came across this book in the *London Review of Books* where it is the subject of a highly informative review by Amia Srinivasan, *London Review of Books*, 34(23) (2012), 17–18.
2 For a very good introduction to Pinker see his website at http://stevenpinker.com/. A superb recent work is *The Better Angels of our Nature. The Decline of Violence in History and Its Causes* (London, Allen Lane, 2011).
3 See Dennett's informative home page at http://ase.tufts.edu/cogstud/incbios/dennettd/dennettd.htm for a full introduction to this stimulating thinker.
4 See P. Singer, *The Expanding Circle: Ethics, Evolution and Moral Progress* (first published 1981, reissued with a new Afterword by the author, Princeton University Press, 2011).

Darwinian perspective a challenge to the assumptions upon which their specialism may seem to depend.[5]

Kitcher says about reason, society and our genes words more or less to the following effect, 'Hey relax, we can have all of this.' And – this is the Houdini trick – you don't have to turn all those 'is' things you find in nature into a bunch of 'oughts' simply because they are part of our evolutionary story, helping us to get our genes through another generation. What we ought to do is part of what we are but not all of what we are is what we ought to do; '[t]here is ... no such thing as *the* naturalistic fallacy'.[6] There have been other Houdinis of course; as Oliver Curry demonstrates in his excellent discussion of the topic, the father of is/ought scepticism is David Hume, for whom the passions were a guide to conduct with this term including moral passions. This was the idea of sympathy or later empathy or – after Darwin and to adopt Curry's contemporary description – 'evolved motivational systems for co-operation'.[7] Reason was neither here nor there so far as these (or any of the passions) were concerned: 'Morals excite passions, and produce or prevent actions. Reason itself is utterly impotent in this particular.'[8] While Kitcher is certainly building on the foundations put down by others,[9] the house he seeks to construct is vaster than any attempted hitherto.

On his analysis (and to begin – as he does – at the very beginning), there was the sound of what we had grown used to calling 'good conduct' even as our primitive ancestors roamed wherever they roamed tens of thousands of years ago. They didn't just kill each other casually. Nor was it merely that the brighter of them played at being nice (feigned altruism) in order to make the social gains necessary to their survival. Rather like de Waal's bonobos[10] they liked each other, weren't afraid to show it, and early worked out that showing it (co-operating) often had advantages that went beyond merely minding their back (laughing was fun; there was some-one to do their hair, exchange songs and grunts with, paint walls with).

---

[5] H. Rose and S. Rose, 'Darwin and After', *New Left Review*, 63 (2010), 91–113. Cf. A. Komter, 'The Evolutionary Origins of Human Generosity', *International Sociology*, 25(3) (2010), 443–464 for a creative argument about what social scientists working in this area can learn from the linkages between altruism and human generosity.

[6] Kitcher, above n. 1, 253 (emphasis in the original).

[7] O. Curry, 'Who's Afraid of the Naturalistic Fallacy?', *Evolutionary Psychology*, 4 (2006), 234, at p. 235.

[8] Hume, cited by Curry, ibid., 237.

[9] Further examples follow in the text – and for a recent overview see M. Tomasello and A. Vaish, 'Origins of Human Cooperation and Morality', *Annual Review of Psychology*, 64 (2013), 231–255.

[10] See F. de Waal, *Our Inner Ape: The Best and Worst of Human Nature* (London, Granta Books, 2005). For more details about these fascinating Great Apes see www.bonobo.org/ [last accessed 27 February 2013].

But how could you tie everyone into this really handy but fragile trick of collegiality? Looking at religion's grip on culture, a few years ago Pascal Boyer came up with the notion of 'a commitment gadget', something (in his context, a belief in a watchful God) to keep you on the straight and narrow when temptation beckoned.[11] Kitcher calls his version of this pre-commitment to good behaviour 'normative guidance' and our capacity for it from the very earliest times, our (natural) openness to tying our hands for our own good is what marks us out as ethical beings. We don't have to spend ages grooming after some untowardly naughty event like a bunch of barely consolable chimpanzees. We have rules that prevent such naughtiness occurring in the first place.

As I have said, Kitcher is not breaking new ground here. Key work pointing in the same direction, so far as the very early humans are concerned, has already been done by Robert Boyd and Peter Richerson. In articles and books, they had sought to solve the 'evolutionary puzzle' that is set by the 'scale of human cooperation'.[12] In particular in their more recent work they ground this amazing attribute enjoyed by our species in cumulative, non-genetic evolution (via cultural adaptation) which in turn (and on their view inevitably) leads to great variety between groups on the ground, with the more effectively combining communities doing better. It is in these 'culturally evolved cooperative social environments' that 'social selection within groups' comes to favour 'genes that gave rise to new, more pro-social motives'.[13] Of course these 'new tribal social instincts did not eliminate ancient ones, favouring self, kin and friends'[14] but they did throw a new way of engaging into the frame, one that embedded itself via culture into what we gradually were to become. Boyd and Richerson note that 'evolutionary thinkers typically explain human cooperation as resulting from the "three Rs": reputation, reciprocation and retribution'[15] (although of course on their analysis the interactions between the two are more complex than simple cause and effect). Thus to start with, it was fear of shame or hope of a 'good turn' or the meting out of just punishment that kept selfish freeloaders to a minimum As culture progressed, more sophisticated ways of creating social solidarity became manifest: authority

---

[11] P. Boyer, *Religion Explained: The Human Instincts that Fashion Gods, Spirits and Ancestors* (London, Heinemann, 2001).

[12] R. Boyd and P. J. Richerson, 'Culture and the Evolution of Human Cooperation', *Philosophical Transactions of the Royal Society*, 364 (2009), 3281–3288. And see their 'seminal' (Kitcher, above n. 1, 109, n. 5) analysis in *Culture and the Evolutionary Process* (University of Chicago Press, 1985) and their *Origins and Evolution of Cultures* (Oxford University Press, 2005).

[13] Boyd and Richerson, 'Culture and the Evolution of Human Cooperation', above n. 12, 3281.

[14] Ibid., 3287.   [15] Ibid., 3283 where the literature is cited.

figures who were either natural (the tribal leader) or divine (this is where Boyer's account of religion fits in); exemplars whose conduct could and should be emulated; and eventually whole ranges of behaviour mandated by frameworks of social rules that we would today call moral codes.

It is clear from all this that, as Curry reminds us 'there is more to ethics than evolution'.[16] Like Boyd and Richerson, Kitcher sees these early advances as the result of the interaction between how our ancestors were (genetically) constructed and how they engaged with each other. On his and their account there is no gulf between how we are made and what we become: our sense of what we are and what we ought to do is a consequence of both. Kitcher then goes further, creating a timeline from this pre-history direct to the present. Drawing from American pragmatism's distaste for *a priori* truth and its favouring of experiment over assertion,[17] Kitcher see ethics as a bit like learning to repair a faulty machine that you know you'd like to have working: altruism is great, that is obvious, but it doesn't always work, so let's try to fix it; woops, look what our repair work has caused, need to manage that now; and so on and so on, from those roaming hunter-gatherers through to today's varied and often sophisticated ethical perspectives: all reflecting 'the ethical project' of Kitcher's title. And so far as today is concerned, perhaps 'over-sophisticated' would be the best summary of Kitcher's concluding remarks about the contemporary state of ethics – there is too much that is technical, too much that is rendered immutable by oversanctification, too much that is reified by over-reverence in today's approach to what ethics entails. It has become a specialism and not a community practice. We need more flexibility about what doing the right thing might entail today, and consequently more public deliberation and less reliance on yesterday's rules, reflecting as they may do on a common sense now past In short, ethics should get out of the ivory tower and the pulpit and back down into the market square.

Using human rights

Now it seems reasonably clear that those proponents of human rights who hinge their approach to the subject on moral certainties should hate all this stuff. Kitcher calls himself a 'pragmatic naturalist' and for him '[e]thical truths are those acquired in progressive transitions and

---

[16] Curry, above n.7, 240.

[17] For a good summary of this strand of thought see the entry in the *Stanford Encyclopedia of Philosophy*, http://plato.stanford.edu/entries/pragmatism/ [last accessed 27 February 2013].

retained through an indefinite sequence of progressive transitions'.[18] On an orthodox reading, human rights are in contrast an example *par excellence* of moral realism, the idea that there are independent truths out there that we can see almost and certainly grasp if we try hard enough and which, once discovered, can tell us how we should behave.[19] Once upon a time it was our religious leaders who told us what was right and wrong, plucking their guidance from a spiritual ether opened up to them by brain- and prayer-power. Later it was simply the human mind, or clever speculations derived from a state of nature that, conveniently, it was agreed needed never to have existed to do its moral good now. Various renditions of human rights that have done important ethical work have been launched on each of these various premises, all now however subject to strong criticism from many quarters.[20] An alternative structure – the law, and in particular international human rights law – seems more promisingly solid, all those eternal rights 'found' by the drafters of human rights codes and acknowledged (rather than created) in this or that heroic ethical instrument. But of course the substance only survives so long as its flimsy foundations are ignored: where exactly did this or that right come from? What about the rights to A and B (which are absent) as opposed to C and D which somehow made it in? And how can rights documents vary so much if they are doing what they say, capturing a set of immutable truths?

For all its ostensible certainty, until quite recently very little serious attention was paid to the foundations of human rights. The subject was too mired in high politics or the specifics of this or that legal charter. As a result its realism had very rarely to work out how to accommodate Darwinian-inspired determinism or (as we can now call it) Kitcher's brand of pragmatic naturalism.[21] But this changed after the end of the

---

[18] Kitcher, above n. 1, 7.

[19] I am somewhat caricaturing such an orthodoxy: certainly many writers in the liberal tradition today have found space for an approach to rights which is more constructivist than the text would suggest, for example Jeremy Waldron and Jack Donnelly. As regards the former see, most recently, 'Is Dignity the Foundation of Human Rights?', *NYU School of Law, Public Law Research Paper No. 12–73* (3 January 2013). For the latter see *Universal Human Rights in Theory and Practice*, 2nd edn (Ithaca, NY, Cornell University Press, 2003).

[20] E.g. A. MacIntyre, *After Virtue: A Study in Moral Theory*, 3rd edn (University of Notre Dame Press, 2007).

[21] There have however been recent moves towards understanding the bioethical dimension: D Keane, 'Survival of the Fairest? Evolution and the Genetization of Rights', *Oxford Journal of Legal Studies*, 30(3) (2010), 467–494. Cf. N. Rose, '"Screen and Intervene": Governing Risky Brains', *History of the Human Sciences*, 23(1) (2010), 79–105. And for an imaginative treatment of the effect of insights from evolutionary thinking and psychology on public law see D. Oliver, 'Psychological Constitutionalism', *Cambridge Law Journal*, 69(3) (2010), 639–675.

Cold War in 1989 and with this new human rights hegemony has come a new level of importance for the subject, and consequently a greater responsibility to think through seriously what the term actually means, to ask questions about the term's place in mankind's ethical project. Foundations now matter because human rights matter – and they matter more than ever not only because they are no longer a religious imposition or a political tool but because there are precious few other examples of commitment gadgets and/or normative guidance around in today's world.

To an extent the range of security offered to the whole people in western democratic states, and which had seen a gradual improvement in the living standards of all and a narrowing of the gap between rich and poor, had always been something of a tactical rather than strategic (much less ethical) move, the *de facto* social democracy of western states (whatever the nominal colour of their political leaders) being the tribute defensive capital paid to the seriousness of its communist enemy. But with the opponent off the pitch, and religion largely disengaged from liberal public culture, there was no need to concede so much of the midfield. Neo-liberalism emerged as a way of describing this new kind of transnational model in which the state served as a guarantor (both nationally and supernationally) of a society otherwise organised on the basis that the right answer to the challenge of living together would always be delivered by the operation of the market; that – going even further – whatever the market produced was by definition the right answer. The newly emerging post-Soviet states were also designed along these market-friendly lines. Traditional democratic states competed with each other to sell assets which had previously been thought to be inherently public goods (gas; electricity; rail services; airports; banks; hospitals; schools) but which were now seen as much better left to the supposedly benign (albeit invisible) hand of market forces. The last couple of decades has seen an explosion of inequality around much of the developed world, and in large parts of the developing world as well.[22] Far from releasing the state from its regulatory role, the neo-liberal experiment has depended heavily on the state both to ensure the protection of the assets of the rich so as to make certain that the market playing field is never level and thereafter by dint of policies advantageous to power to skew it further in the direction of the already affluent and well entrenched. The banking collapse of 2008 was merely the culmination of a process which had started well before, one in which the neo-liberal

---

[22] OECD report, 'Divided We Stand: Why Inequality Keeps Rising (December 2011), www.oecd.org/document/51/0,3746,en_2649_33933_49147827_1_1_1_1,00.html [last accessed 10 June 2012].

ideology was merely a cover for a much cruder activity than this label suggests: the reassertion by the privileged of their power over the poor.

With compassion-oriented churches in decline and social democracy badly affected by the association its enemies made with defeated communist ideas, there have been few opportunities for the altruism of our ancestors to find any kind of ethical traction. Bereft of the support that would have been offered by being underpinned by religious enthusiasm or democratic activism, the role of human rights in the neo-liberal shift we have been describing has been disturbing. The rights which have advanced over the decades since 1989 have tended to be the rights most amenable to a neo-liberal point of view, i.e. the rights which do not involve interferences with individual property rights or large amounts of public expenditure (education, healthcare, etc.). Neither of the two primary shapes that the term has taken in the years after the collapse of communism have offered effective 'normative guidance' or a powerful 'commitment gadget' against the excesses of the market. First there is that meaning of human rights which sees the idea it represents as a cultural value in the possession of this or that tribe as opposed to an enemy 'other'. This has been most prominent in the minds of those who have seen in what they have called 'the war on terror' (or to its more scrupulous adherents 'the war on terrorism') a clash of civilisations, a battle between good and evil in which good belongs to the defenders of democracy, the rule of law and human rights, and bad to those who would destroy these principles, fundamental though they are to the effective functioning of the 'good' (and therefore superior) society. On this analysis – and it might be thought incredibly – human rights stops being an inhibition on wrong conduct and become a positive accelerator of brutal behaviour, justifying inhuman and degrading treatment, coercive interrogation, even military invasion, as 'lesser evils' with which the superior civilisation's carnivorous defenders protect their herbivorous peoples from the horrors of what defeat in the terror war would inevitably entail.[23] This is human rights as the ethical accessory of a successful culture, one not afraid to kill and instrumentalise 'the other' to secure what it judges it needs, a place where water-boarding is morally neutral and targeted assassination applauded rather than subjected to legal proceedings. The spill-over effect is to take the human out of human rights and render even the poor and impoverished within a culture invisible to those who loudly proclaim their society's human rights supremacy, a technique of denial that was familiar to the late Stan Cohen, whose

---

[23] See M. Ignatieff, *The Lesser Evil: Political Ethics in an Age of Terror* (Princeton University Press, 2004).

States of Denial[24] detailed how the privileged can have it both ways like this – be rich, and good too.

Law has no primary role in this first version of what human rights means today but it plays a central part in the second of the two manipulations with which we are confronted at the present time. Here the fragile nature of the law's underpinnings of rights is all too apparent. After 1989 the shift to neo-liberalism was accompanied by a move on the part of Russia and all post-Soviet republics and their erstwhile Cold War allies as well to democracy, the rule of law and the constitutional protection of human rights. The same had already happened in Africa when post-colonial polities invariably set themselves up along these lines immediately upon securing their independence. Indeed it seems these days that nowhere is without its constitution guaranteeing human rights and/or fundamental rights.

We can distinguish three kinds of human rights 'protection' of this legal/constitutional sort. The first are the genuine democracies, places where the role of elections is to determine who should govern, where an independent judiciary impose checks on officials in the name of law and the underlying idea behind the human rights guaranteed in some fashion or other by the state's constitution remains universalist in reach and compassionate in content. Historically this kind of authentic democracy – a refined staging-post on the ethical project (as we shall shortly see) – has been most embedded in social democratic societies, so it is little surprise that it has thrown down deep roots in western and northern Europe (and to some extent as well in the United States) during the social democratic years after the war and before the collapse of communism (albeit as we have earlier noted gaining much of its traction from the spectre of communism that lay behind it). At the other extreme – and Belarus is a good example, though sadly there are others – are those places where the representation of government as popular is a self-evident sham – Belarus' constitution screams 'The State for the people!' on its masthead in a way that even Borat might have ruled out as too unreal for inclusion in his satirical movie.[25] In the middle, between these two exemplars – the first positive, the second negative – is an increasingly crowded space in which are to be found the 'neo-democracies'.[26] This is where there is the appearance but not the reality of democracy, with human rights proclaimed as rights but then departed from in practice, either because there are so many

---

[24] S. Cohen, *States of Denial* (Cambridge, Polity Press, 2001).
[25] http://president.gov.by/en/press10669.html [last accessed 22 February 2013].
[26] C. A. Gearty, *Liberty and Security* (Cambridge, Polity Press, 2013).

exceptions to the rights that they have little impact, or because there is no real commitment to their application. Such countries sign up to international human rights instruments, welcome human rights monitors, appoint national human rights commissions but feel able *at the same time* to dispense secret justice, assassinate political opponents and critical members of the media, fix trials of their opponents, launch military assaults on dissident parts of their countries, and even (as in one case, in 2008) invade a neighbouring state without much of a response from the human rights body to which both belonged.[27] In recent years traditional democracies have been dressing down in the direction of neo-democracy (Guantánamo; secret justice; terrorism prevention and investigation measures) while pseudo-democracies have been dressing up – if we are not careful they will soon be meeting in a depressing middle where human rights will have been transformed into a constitutional fashion accessory designed to hide a culture's brutality from itself.

A pragmatic rescue

With this groundwork done, it is time to return to ethics. If we acknowledge the legitimacy of the search for foundations but turn away from the two problematic meanings frequently ascribed to human rights today we have just been discussing (which we can summarise here as the cultural and the legal), we open ourselves to an encounter with a third idea that keeps bubbling tenaciously to the surface – the *popular* understanding of human rights. This alternative story has a high level of altruism within it of the sort that Kitcher would surely recognise (though his book nowhere refers to human rights). Acknowledging it can help us get to a new kind of foundationalism, one that puts giving and compassion – and courageous taking on behalf of others – at the heart of the human rights story and as such is better able to resist the manipulations of the cultural and legal versions of the term that we have been discussing. Stephen Hopgood from SOAS has written a fine book about that iconic human rights movement Amnesty International, *Keepers of the Flame*, in which he finds the analogy with a religious movement to be a strong one.[28] Certainly human rights has its Holy Days (for example, 10 December), its saints (Eleanor Roosevelt, Peter Benenson, the various UN special rapporteurs), its martyrs (Serge di Mello; Archbishop Romero; Rachel Corrie;

---

[27] The invading country was Russia, the invaded state Georgia – both members of the Council of Europe.
[28] S. Hopgood, *Keepers of the Flame* (Ithaca, NY, Cornell University Press, 2006).

too many, sadly, to mention all) and its missionary orders (Amnesty itself, Human Rights Watch, many smaller movements). But proponents of human rights of this sort do not follow a religion. Jesus is not their guide, nor is Mohammed, nor any other of the great leaders of any of our world faiths. These are people who reach past law and culture to put the poor, the disadvantaged and the oppressed at the centre of their human rights concern. If we view the human rights movement in this way, not as a cultural or legal exercise but as a visibility project, we can see that its goal is to get us to *see* people truly *as* people and therefore – *each of them* – as *entitled* to right treatment *on account of their humanity*. It is surely in this sense that Tom Stoppard was using the term when he said that 'human rights simply endorse a view of life and a set of moral values that are perfectly clear to an eight-year-old child'.[29] Respect for the human in each and every one of us is what drives the champions of human rights in this sense to fight hard to protect the vulnerable from abuse and to work to secure opportunity for all, and not just those advantaged by family, good fortune or social standing. Perhaps this is a kind of post-Enlightenment humanism, drawing from without been dominated by the religious and intellectual traditions of the past.

This is where Kitcher comes back into our discussion. For all that he did not mention human rights, he has effectively written a pragmatist's account of the subject. Consider the highlights of his narrative, starting with pre-history:

Equality, even a commitment to egalitarianism, was important in the earliest phases of the ethical project. In formulating the code, the voices of all adult members of the band needed to be heard: they participated on equal terms. Moreover, no proposal for regulating conduct could be accepted unless all those in the group were satisfied with it ... Around the campfires, they reached agreement on precepts, on stories of model behaviour, on ways of training the young, on practices of punishment, on sanctioned habits, perhaps occasionally on changes in the concepts hitherto employed.[30]

---

[29] *The Observer*, 21 September 2008. Cf. Tomasello and Vaish, above n. 9, 240: 'Although young children are of course selfish in many situations, in many other situations they subordinate their self-interests in order to do such things as collaborate with others, sympathise with and help others, and share resources with others. They also evaluate others in terms of such cooperative behaviours and begin to help and share with others more selectively as a result.'

[30] Kitcher, above n.1, 6–97. Cf. Tomasello and Vaish, above n. 9, identifying (at 240) a 'collective morality emerging from group-mindedness, one 'in which individuals regulated their actions via the morally legitimate expectations of others and the group – morally legitimate by their own assessment – engendering what some have called normative self-governance', citing C. M. Korsgaard, *The Sources of Normativity* (Cambridge University Press, 1996).

A bit later came a further dramatic advance:

The earliest law codes provide the clearest indications of the evolution of ethical codes that occurred late in prehistory. Ancient Near Eastern texts include stories embodying ideals of behaviour, myths about the afterlife, and partial codes of law ... [M]ost obviously, the lists of rules found in the Mesopotamian codes, from the Lipit–Ishtar code of the early second millennium, through the code of Hammurabi (a century later) and beyond provide us with a sense of the conduct requiring explicit prohibition and of the relative importance of various social breaches.[31]

And to complete this triangle of ethical corners that makes up Kitcher's progress is 'the emphasis on compassion introduced by Christianity'.[32] For Kitcher, a key to moral improvement is the idea of ethics as involving an 'expanding circle' of humans seen as fellow creatures and therefore attracting solicitude and (it further follows) support, via not just behavioural but psychological altruism as well.[33] Indeed while it is 'relatively easy to understand how many examples of ethical progress are functional requirements achieved by widening the scope of existing ethical precepts,'[34] it would be foolish to take too mechanistic a view of the inevitability of assumed human progress. 'Progressive changes of a particular type – those offering new ideas of the human being and of human life – remain problematic.'[35] It is when Kitcher reaches our modern times that his account most closely comes to resemble that of the human rights activist, covering the battle for the emancipation of the slaves, for the liberation of women from male servitude, for racial equality and (most recently of all and by way of clearest illustration) the role played by empathetic solidarity in the gay rights movement:

When homosexuality is no longer characterised as a vice, the framework of appraisal is modified. Instead of focusing on the sexes of the partners (or on the anatomical organs brought into context), actions are judged on other grounds: whether they are coercive, exploitative, in violation of prior promises, and so forth. In consequence, people who had fought to curb desires that often arose with great violence within them, people who were compelled to seek transient expressions of their sexual passions in clandestine and unsatisfactory encounters, people who constantly feared exposure of their secret lives, people whose central love for someone else could never be fully developed in arrangements that openly expressed it, are succeeded by similar people for whom all these problems are overcome. It is hard not to view that as ethical progress.[36]

And reading this magnificent piece of controlled passion, it is hard not to see its author as a human rights proponent *de nos jours*.

---

[31] Kitcher, above n. 1, 118.   [32] Ibid., 140.   [33] Ibid., 236 and also 213–217.
[34] Ibid., 236.   [35] Ibid., 237.   [36] Ibid., 162–163.

Ethical fuel

Echoing Kitcher, we can see that across time and across cultures, this project – of the 'expanding circle'[37] of *care* because of what is *seen* – has gone under – continues to go under – different labels, protected by the benign power of God, or reason, or custom, or law, or (these days in many places, using the term in this third sense) 'human rights'. But all these structures and terms and arguments and habits are not reasons to care or explanations of why we care, rather they are *ex post facto* rationalisations of a propensity to care that precedes them, part of Kitcher's tinkering with the machine to get it to work better. We are not persuaded by our brains to care; we care because of what we are and have become/ are becoming, not because of what we think. We start with feelings and end with reason rather than the other way round. Jonathan Haidt has the brilliant analogy of an elephant of feeling being controlled by the rider of reason.[38] Nature gives us the first draft of our lives and reason, experience and plain luck do the rest.

Which natural predispositions matter for human rights? It has long been evident that the way we are is not all self-oriented: as Adam Smith put it in 1759, 'How selfish soever man may be supposed, there are evidently some principles in his nature, which interest him in the fortune of others, and render their happiness necessary to him, though he derives nothing from it, except the pleasure of seeing it'.[39] What the Darwinian breakthrough allows us to do is to locate an insight of this sort within science and then to see it as part of an animal (rather than uniquely human) approach to living. As the great primatologist Frans de Waal put it in his Tanner lectures 'the building blocks of morality' are 'evolutionarily ancient'.[40] Tom Stoppard was conceding too much when he thought the child needed to be as old as eight, even that it needed to be a child, as opposed to a gorilla, a chimpanzee, a dolphin or an elephant. Here are some more provocative words from the printed version of de Waal's lecture, echoing Kitcher and providing a new angle of support for what I am calling here the popular approach to human rights:

The evolutionary origin of this inclination is no mystery. All species that rely on cooperation – from elephants to wolves and people – show group loyalty and helping tendencies. These tendencies evolved in the context of a close-knit social life in which they benefited relatives and companions able to repay the favour.

---

[37] And cf. Singer, above n. 4.
[38] *The Happiness Hypothesis* (London, William Heinemann, 2006).
[39] Quoted in F. de Waal, *Primates and Philosophers: How Morality Evolved* (Princeton University Press, 2006), 15.   [40] Ibid., 7.

The impulse to help was therefore never totally without survival value to the ones showing the impulse. But, as so often, the impulse became divorced from the consequences that shaped its evolution. This permitted its expression even when payoffs were unlikely, such as when strangers were beneficiaries. This brings animal altruism much closer to that of humans than usually thought, and explains the call for the temporary removal of ethics from the hands of philosophers.[41]

Following the logic of this, de Waal asserts that 'empathy is the original pre-linguistic form of inter-individual linkage that only secondarily has come under the influence of language and culture'.[42] The way empathetic tendencies like these influence our behaviour is not conscious in the sense in which we ordinarily use that term. Pascal Boyer describes it[43] as being 'the same as "deciding" how to stay upright. You do not have to think about it, but a special system in the brain takes into account your current posture, the pressure on each foot and corrects your position to avoid a fall. In the same way, [do] specialised cognitive systems register situations of exchange, store them in memory and produce inferences for subsequent behaviour, none of which requires an explicit consideration of the various options available.'[44] The intuition to help others that is the product of this evolutionary dynamic, and its offshoot into a more general empathy and outreach to the other that de Waal describes, is clearly close to the desire to help that drives so many human rights activists and volunteers.

But of course there are other feelings that burst through the human subconscious into our active selves. The ethical project is not a story of unavoidable, Whiggish success. These are merely the *better*, not the *only*, angels of our nature.[45] We have already seen that Kitcher is careful to distance himself from the unavoidability of success. There are and have always been other propensities at work too, powerful ones that assert the primacy of the in-group over the other, that may start with kin-support but then move quite quickly into hostility to the stranger. In fact as we know all too well, even today this sense of the solidarity of the group frequently collides with efforts to engage a wider empathetic response to the plight of others. (What we earlier described as the cultural approach to human rights may be thought to fit neatly into this category.) It may even be right to say that the universalistic tendency is a weak one in comparison with that which directs our attention and solicitude in the direction of those we know or at least know of – our family, our kin, our community –and

---

[41] Ibid., 15.   [42] Ibid., 24.
[43] In Boyer's innovative *Religion Explained*, above n. 11.
[44] Ibid., 209.   [45] Pinker, above n. 2.

consequently which underpins and reflexively legitimises our hostility to others. Indeed it may well be that we learned morality by bonding with those we knew, thereby rooting such mutuality at least partly in a shared antipathy to the outsider: if so, then as de Waal puts it 'the profound irony is that our noblest achievement – morality – has evolutionary ties to our basest behaviour – warfare'.[46]

The disposition towards empathy for the outsider will always be delicate and fragile, perpetually at risk of being overridden. To maintain a commitment to others even within communities is not easy. The reach towards the other is certainly at its strongest where close family is concerned but gets progressively weaker as it move away from our direct relations into wider kin and then into community. How has the wider impulse survived? Here is Philip Kitcher again stating his theories in an earlier contribution, focusing on the emergence of language:

there began a process of cultural evolution. Different small bands of human beings tried out various sets of normative resources – rules, stories, myths, images, and more – to define the way in which 'we' live. Some of these were more popular with neighbours and with descendent groups, perhaps because they offered greater reproductive success, more likely because they made for smoother societies, greater harmony, and increased cooperation. The most successful ones were transmitted across generations, appearing in fragmentary ways in the first documents we have, the addenda to law codes of societies in Mesopotamia.[47]

The law codes mentioned here are another example of one of Pascal Boyer's 'commitment gadgets'.[48] The point here is about a spin-off from mutual reciprocity that then develops a new head of steam as society evolves and the attractiveness of harmony and smoothness over perpetual violence becomes apparent. This has a strong explanatory power so far as Hobbes and indeed the authority of law are concerned – but neither of these speaks necessarily on behalf of the outsider: mutual reciprocity and smoothness more easily produce walled cities than open societies. To look for a commitment gadget that ties us to that better part of our nature marked 'empathy', we need to look elsewhere. We have already mentioned religion as having fulfilled an obvious function here: Rowan Williams has written in this volume about how early Christianity undermined the classical hierarchies[49] and that particular belief system was rooted in the nobility of dying to redeem others and (at a more practical level) stopping to help others: not only Christ on the cross but the Good Samaritan as well in whose unintended reproachful shadow many of us of a certain age lived out our childhoods. Literature too – as the late Richard

---

[46] Kitcher, above n. 1, 55.   [47] In de Waal, above n. 39, 136–137.
[48] Boyer, above n. 11, 211.   [49] Chapter 4.

Rorty believed (with his suggestions about the need for a sentimental education), and as recent work on the Victorian novel has claimed, good writing has 'helped us to evolve into nicer people'.[50] And also custom: in a recent book, *Moral Relativism*, Steven Lukes speculated that 'Perhaps when we are in the "grip of custom", we are motivated by moral emotions that are indeed "natural", or innate, which developed because they helped individuals spread their genes: they sounded alarm bells, offering reliable, immediate responses to recurring situations'.[51] And then Lukes says this: 'Perhaps we "prop up" these emotional responses by elaborating deontological rationalizations with talk of the Moral Law and "rights" and with categorical and inflexible moral rules.'[52] On this reading, philosophy is reduced to the status of a mere flying buttress for the cathedral of feeling, the reins held by the rider of Jonathan Haidt's elephant. Is this where Ted Honderich's principle of humanity[53] comes from, or even the capabilities approach of Amartya Sen and Martha Nussbaum[54] – control gadgets put in place by clever people, and believed by other clever people, as reflections not only of their brain power but also less consciously of the ethical fuel that makes their brains work in the particular way they do?

When people talk of common humanity, Steven Lukes says, '[t]hese days they will speak the language of human rights'.[55] Maybe once they would have been evangelical Christians bent on saving souls and later socialist idealists intent on global government. Those days have passed. In our contemporary culture, human rights is the best 'commitment gadget' available to those whose life project or immediate ethical task is the generalisation of the propensity to help the other into something beyond kin, beyond immediate community, beyond nation even, into the world at large. It is the habit of mind that flows from the far-seeing activist's capacity to grasp that in our shrunken world we are all affected by actions in a way that requires us all to be seen: the island people whose homes are destroyed by an inundation precipitated by first-world greed and recklessness are the contemporary equivalent of the newly arrived neighbour whom some grunting but imaginatively wired pre-linguistic human types thought it better to befriend and help rather than to kill.

The term 'human rights' works so well to capture this feeling because it is multi-purpose: making sense at the level of philosophy ('here is why

---

[50] As the *Guardian* report succinctly put it (15 January 2009, 4).

[51] S. Lukes, *Moral Relativism* (London, Profile Books, 2008), 47.

[52] Ibid.

[53] See T. Honderich, *After the Terror* (Edinburgh University Press, 2002).

[54] See M. Nussbaum, *Frontiers of Justice: Disability, Nationality, Species Membership* (Cambridge, Mass., Harvard University Press, 2006).

[55] Lukes, above n. 51, 20.

you ought to help the stranger'), at the level of politics ('they have a human right to this or a human right to that – therefore arrangements must be made for them to get it'); and at the level of law ('the right is set out in the Charter or the covenant or in the constitution that our forefathers created to guide our decision-making and keep us in check'). Of course as we have seen already of some of these, each can spin off in the wrong direction – philosophy into analytical aridity; politics into an inflation of rights' claims or the promotion of one kinship community over another; law into an over-reliance on litigation or a too-easily-abused rights' charter – but these wrong turnings into cul-de-sacs are inevitable in a journey as ambitious as this – an effort to persuade the world that it is indeed a village and that the unknown stranger is as worthy of my care as my blood brother. Kitcher is right to say that we need always to be prepared to tinker with the machine we have created – ethics is a subject which never comes to an end.[56]

Conclusion

Costas Douzinas describes the 'human rights movement' as 'the ongoing but failing struggle to close the gap between the abstract man of the Declarations and the empirical human being'.[57] It is difficult and will never be perfect, might well not succeed, but surely we must believe that it does not *have* to fail. The word 'struggle' is important here and introduces a further but crucial dimension to human rights of which explicit account must be taken, a fourth layer of meaning (after the legal,

[56] Boyd and Richerson put it beautifully: 'Social learning allows human *populations* to accumulate adaptive information over many generations, leading to the cultural evolution of highly adaptive behaviours and technology. Because this process is much faster than genetic evolution, human populations can evolve cultural adaptations to local environments, an especially valuable adaptation to the chaotic, rapidly changing world of the Pleistocene. However the same psychological mechanisms that create this benefit *necessarily* come with a built in cost. To get the benefits of social learning, humans have to be credulous, for the most part accepting the ways that they observe in their society as sensible and proper, and such credulity opens up human minds to the spread of maladaptive beliefs. This cost can be shaved by tinkering with human psychology, but it cannot be eliminated without also losing the adaptive benefits of cumulative cultural evolution. Culture is a little like breathing. One could reduce the chances of respiratory infections by breathing less, but the costs of doing so would curtail other essential activities. One could learn less from other people in order to avoid getting bad ideas from them. In humans, the optimum in these tradeoffs has led to lots of breathing and lots of cultural transmission': 'Culture and the Evolution of Human Cooperation', above n. 12, 3286 (emphasis in the original).

[57] 'Who Counts as Human?', Guardian Unlimited 1 April 2009, www.guardian.co.uk/commentisfree/libertycentral/2009/apr/01/deconstructing-human-rights-equality [last accessed 25 February 2013].

the cultural and the popular). Human rights would not have succeeded in the way they have (as concrete rights; as central to discourse; as shapers of culture) if all that they were was the law and practice of niceness, of Comtean altruism.[58] The human rights story is not all about givers, it is about takers, too: there is a large-scale subaltern tradition to take into account, a tradition of solidarity, of resistance to the abuse of power and of the assertion of right in the face of immoral might. The 'visibility project' is about the powerless stepping into the light as well as about getting the powerful to have better eyesight.

This is why Magna Carta is so often appropriated as a human rights achievement: the chief barons stood up to King John. It casts a new light too on parts of the human rights story that we have earlier suggested might have led the subject down various wrong turnings. For example, we can regard Kant's reworking of the Christian ethic into secular shape as a breakthrough for human rights – notwithstanding our earlier criticisms, not to mention the various differentials in the status of many humans that he rather coldly contemplated (active and passive citizens; the ones able to make life plans against the second division ones who can't; and so on). This is not embarrassing because Kant's innovation can be read as being mainly about power: wresting authority from the church in favour of the people. This revolutionary dimension to human rights becomes explicit with the American Declaration of Independence in 1776 (not even the fact that some of its signatories were slave-owners has been able to dampen the enthusiasm of later generations) and then of course – and quintessentially – the French Declaration of the Rights of Man and of the Citizen, a document still celebrated as a founding text despite not only its vacuities but also the violence which the new regime sanctified by it very soon unleashed. For all that it led into tragedy the Haiti bill of rights can be read in the same way.

This connection with agitation, protest, destabilisation, even violence has always been part of the human rights story. The Universal Declaration of Human Rights in 1948 acknowledges as much when in its preamble it might not explain where human rights come from but it does announce the necessity of their protection by the rule of law 'if man is not to be compelled to have recourse, as a last resort, to rebellion against tyranny and oppression'. This perceived necessity drove the anti-colonial insurgents of the 1950s and 1960s, just as it does many of the climate protectors and eco-warriors of today. There is a connection between this idea of human rights as linked to struggle and the popular version of

---

[58] See T. Dixon, *The Invention of Altruism: Making Moral Meanings in Victorian Britain* (London, British Academy, 2008).

human rights as doing good for others that we have been earlier discussing. Revolution is rarely a sensible option for a person whose DNA is made up only of selfish genes. Resistance, and even political violence, in pursuit of the rights of all can be a dramatic example of ethics in action. So too is a march in support of an occupied people whom most have never met, or a gathering outside an embassy in the name of the disregarded citizens in the country of which that building is a part. Our understanding of what it is to be human makes sense of the affront we feel at an abuse of power, whether directed at our own community, or at a people whom we merely know of – it is what legitimises our anger, possibly even (as the Universal Declaration saw) our violence.

The power of the idea of human rights is driven by a paradox: it both craves a basis in truth but at the same time it needs to fail to have one in order to maintain its hegemonic power as the progressive ideal of the post-political age. The 'human rights movement' can capture a lot of idealist space across the globe even in quite different societies from our own while of course having to have some substantive content without which it risks total subversion – another paradox. And so must human rights be true? As Kitcher says of the followers of religion, the 'fact that these people have presupposed massively false beliefs about the universe does not undermine their status as ethical agents'.[59] Nature is the latest in a long line (which includes religion, reason and law) to tantalise us with a certainty that must forever remain impossible. The way to cope with this craving is to embrace it as a thirst for justice which is itself a kind of truth. Right at the end of *The Descent of Man*, Charles Darwin wrote this:

We must acknowledge ... that man with all his noble qualities, with sympathy which feels for the most debased, with benevolence which extends not only to other men but to the humblest living creature, with his god-like intellect which has penetrated into the movements and constitution of the solar system – with all these exalted powers – Man still bears in his bodily frame the indelible stamp of his lowly origins.[60]

And a good thing, too, for this is our salvation, the reason for our ethical project.

---

[59] Kitcher, above n. 1, 81. See F. de Waal, *The Bonobo and the Atheist: In Search of Humanism Among the Primates* (New York, W.W. Norton, 2013).

[60] Accessible free at www.gutenberg.org/ebooks/2300.

3 Against human rights: liberty in the western tradition

John Milbank

Prelude: liberalism, sovereignty and political economy

Political economy, the most developed form of liberalism, was, in the longest perspective, built upon two specifically modern concepts: first of all rights, and secondly sympathy. The notion of sympathy is in many ways in tension with the notion of rights and even derives from sources resistant to ideas of subjective right and cognate concepts of social contract as founding the political order.[1] Indeed, for the most part a direct, interpersonal exercise of sympathy was relegated by Adam Smith and other thinkers of the Scottish Enlightenment to the sphere of 'civil society' which lies outside the economic order, even though the latter was still crucially regarded as embedded within it – an assumption later lost to view within a later, more drastic elaboration of the liberal *credo*. Already for Smith, within the order of the properly 'economic', sympathetic, mutual goals are to be achieved indirectly, through a 'providential' and unintended co-ordination of sheerly egotistic purposes, politically legitimated in terms of ideas of subjective entitlement.

Such a notion of 'right' grounds the politically economic idea of person, property and contract. But here one can claim that, whenever the notion of sympathy was subordinated through indirection – or, in other terms, the idea of a reciprocalist pursuit of common ends is denied to be constitutive of the political foundation – then the idea of individually based natural rights, appealing to the normativity of negative freedom, was from the outset correlated with an absolutist account of

---

[1] On sympathy in distinction from earlier notions of *agape*, see John Milbank, 'The Invocation of Clio', in *The Future of Love* (Eugene, Oreg. and London: Wipf and Stock/SCM, 2008–2009), 175–220. For a later qualification of this view in terms of a greater continuity of sympathy with *agape* in certain respects and in certain enlightenment authors, plus a new recognition of a Christian residue in Hume, see John Milbank, 'Hume versus Kant: Faith, Reason and Feeling', *Modern Theology*, 27(2) (2011), 276–297.

the sovereignty of the centralised state.[2] In the case of Scots political economy this link re-emerges with James Stewart, who gave a more honest account than Adam Smith of the role that the state, empire and military conquest must play in processes of primacy accumulation. He explicitly stated that 'the Republic of Lycurgus [ancient Sparta] represents the more perfect plan of political economy – anywhere to be met with, either in ancient or modern times'.[3]

This issue of the hidden alliance between liberalism and political absolutism is of enormous contemporary importance, given that we are faced by the spectre of an Asiatic totalitarian capitalism and by the possible temptation for Germany (against the very reverse example which it has set, partly under Catholic influence, since the end of the Second World War) to repeat in a new way its past un-Roman (and so equally un-Byzantine) errors,[4] and impose an equivalent of this twin-headed hydra upon Europe. For totalitarian capitalism only seems like a contradiction in terms if we ignore the proximity of liberal philosophy, and practice upon which its rests, to a paradoxically authoritarian drift.

Against any such claim it might seem that, while the notion of alienable natural rights – private property held only under an eminent loan, and a purely provisional, not normative allowance of capitalist practice, as in China today – is compatible with an absolutist regime, the notion of inalienable natural rights – involving structures of property and contract that the state cannot legally suspend – is not.

But this is to miss the complex dialectic of rights and alienability. For William of Ockham, already in the late Middle Ages, the paradigm of subjective *ius* lay in the free ownership of property, regarded as a given fact independent of questions of right *usus* and objective *finis*.[5] The mark, therefore, of such inalienable right to possession is paradoxically its

---

[2] See Jean Bethke Elshtain, *Sovereignty: God, State and Self* (New York: Basic Books, 2008). This connection had earlier been variously pointed out by John Neville Figgis and Leo Strauss – besides several other historical analysts.

[3] Sir James Stewart, *The Works* (New York: Augustus M. Kelley, 1967), vol. I, 51, 97–98, 344–346, 352. See also Michael Perelman, *Classical Political Economy: Positive Accumulation and the Social Division of Labour* (Totowa, NJ: Rowman & Allenheld, 1984).

[4] As part of the long-composted intellectual soil of Nazism one should most certainly include the embrace of an impersonal 'oriental' metaphysic (including a reading of the 'original' Greece as oriental), stemming from a distorted and one-sided later exaggeration of certain themes in German romanticism (Schlegel, Hölderlin, etc., who are not themselves to blame) by Schopenhauer, Richard Wagner – who was nonetheless pulled in opposing directions here – Nietzsche and Heidegger. This turn to Greece and then to Asia has to be complexly related both to the German Reformation and the eventual lapse of the Holy Roman Emperorship whose legacy had earlier ensured a 'South-' rather than 'East'-looking Germanism.

[5] For Ockham, see further below.

absolute alienability: the property may be transferred and sold unconditionally and *ad libitum*, whereas an 'inalienable' property, held under a certain grant and condition within bonds of mutual obligation, *cannot* be simply shrugged off or exchanged for abstract equivalence by the owner at all times and under whatsoever circumstances.

This dialectic clearly haunts later liberalism supremely with respect to the relationship of the individual person to the sovereign power. How far may free subjects freely alienate to the state their original natural rights to self-protection and self-sustenance? Since the exigencies of fear are more absolute than those of comfortable living Hobbes, who focuses on the former, allows for a greater alienation of original right than does Locke, who focuses on the latter.[6] But Leo Strauss was right to assert that this does not render Locke the more clearly liberal thinker.[7] For if it is only 'self-ownership' that is absolutely inalienable (or ownership of the will itself by itself, as Rousseau and Kant later saw, in an Ockhamist lineage) then this is compatible with more or less any actual bondage – provided there is consent, which may well be taken to be tacit, since this is assumed to be sufficient by all known polities (to some degree absolutely, and in certain circumstances contingently). But in point of fact, even Hobbes did not think that private freedom of opinion and property entitlement could normally be alienated, since they follow directly from that self-possession upon which his contractual and biopolitical theory of politics is (aporetically) built: 'where there is no *Own*, that is, no Propriety, there is no Injustice; and where there is no coercive power erected, that is, where there is no Common-wealth, there is no Propriety, all men having Right to all things.'[8] Hence in the case of Hobbes, inalienable rights of freedom and property *are* held to support an absolutist regime, since this regime exists for Hobbes precisely to secure private freedom and property against religious enthusiasm and against any realist 'fairytale' metaphysics which underwrites collective ends.

These modern, Hobbesian structures and dilemmas were already articulated in William of Ockham's legal theology: in a monastic corporation the powers to elect a Prior and to sell collectively owned property could be alienated, but not the ownership prerogatives of non-resident by resident canons. Likewise, property rights could not be alienated to the

[6] Thomas Hobbes, *Leviathan*, (ed.) Richard Tuck (Cambridge University Press, 1991), 125, 225, 228.

[7] Leo Strauss, *Natural Right and History* (Chicago University Press, 1953), 165–251.

[8] Hobbes, *Leviathan*, 101; John Locke, *Two Treatises of Government*, (ed.) Peter Laslett (Cambridge University Press, 2000), 195–199, 350–351.

emperor, but the people's power of election could be so alienated. And though the emperor's authority originally derived from the people, there were no mechanisms to ensure their continuing participation in government, even if the emperor should in theory act only for 'common utility', which includes first and foremost the protection of subjective property and contractual rights.[9]

Much later than Ockham and considerably later than Hobbes, but essentially in their wake, the father of German absolute idealism, J.G. Fichte, elaborated arguably the first somewhat totalitarian political programme on strictly liberal premises, by arguing that absolute freedom of movement and decision can only be guaranteed by a continual and all-penetrating 'police', ensuring protection of travel, physical safety and reliable information as regards health and other matters. For where no shared implicit agreements guarantee personal security, no tacit and embedded horizons, then it can only be guaranteed by a centralist *surveillance*.[10] And since new risks always multiply, this control must become ever more precise. So when we forget the 'association' in the crucial Christian political legacy of 'free association' (which is far older and more fundamental for western liberty than any of the notions of liberalism), then a perverted solipsistic freedom will always require alien and draconian enforcement.

Liberalism and absolutism are further compatible, because the right of the absolutist monarch (or of any unrestricted sovereign power) is itself inalienable for just the same reason that individual right is inalienable. For the sake of order and security, all has been taken into his possession and therefore legality now flows from his own self-ownership, even though this implies (as Carl Schmitt rightly argued, though with perverse approval) that he may 'exceptionally' violate all the laws that he ultimately underwrites, and even 'sell off' his own sovereign jurisdiction – in the way that the UK has effectively done in terms of foreign policy (at least) to the United States since 1948, and the way that the leaders of modern Russia increasingly act like *rentier* rulers, subordinating her interests to their own private, cosmopolitan ones. In the case of either the individual subject, or of 'Leviathan', the artificially collective, absolutely sovereign subject, the subject's fundamental moral standing is defined in formal, voluntarist terms that sidestep any questions of normative goals or

---

[9] See Brian Tierney, *The Idea of Natural Rights: Studies on Natural Rights, Natural Law and Church Law 1150–1625* (Grand Rapids, Mich: Eerdmans, 1997), 170–194.

[10] J.G. Fichte, *Foundations of Natural Right*, (trans.) Michael Baur (Cambridge University Press, 2000), 254–263

substance and therefore imply the performative contradiction that the true test of freedom's exercise is one's right to abandon it altogether.

Indeed, given this strictly nominalist logic of liberty, it can appear logical to conclude that all and any 'democratic' expression of collective will – whether by specific freely associating group, or by the freely associating people as a whole – violates the neutrality of the state organ, whose own absoluteness exists in order to underwrite the equal absoluteness of the inviolable will of the 'self-owning' and property-owning individual. Here the long-standing liberal suspicion of semi-autonomous corporate bodies below the level of the state is remorselessly extended to a 'de-corporatisation' of the state itself, a removal of any taint of realism hovering over its corporate personhood that would legitimate it in terms of emergent notions of the common good and its collective continuous discernment.

In this way, the more that doctrines of human rights are seen as the normative basis of all politics, then the more they covertly encourage a slide of neo-liberalism towards a fully fledged totalitarian capitalism, by passing over the democratic in the name of freedom as well as efficiency – given that, without the restoration of mutualist bonds of trust, centralist micro-organisation is the only barrier against anarchy and the violation of rights by an individual liberty appealing back through exception to the *bios* component of its dual bio and political foundation (as witnessed by the quotation already given from Hobbes which speaks of a pre-political right of nature). Here Chinese despotism would seem to be the only alternative to the enthronement of mafia rule, as in northern Mexico, and yet there is clearly a certain resemblance between the two – as witnessed, perhaps, by the diabolical Russian synthesis.[11]

The drift to a new despotism is therefore, in a strange-seeming way, partially enabled by an excessive stress upon the isolated individual. But at the same time, it is important to see that this is in reality a dethronement of a true western valuing of the individual, derived from the Judaic and Christian (and to a degree Islamic) valuing of 'the person', with its double understanding that the person is shaped through all her interrelationships and yet as a unique 'character' is transcendently of more value than any conglomerated whole. By contrast, liberalism parodies this legacy, because when irreplaceable 'personality' is reduced to an inviolable but inscrutable abstract interiority of negative will, then the *social manifestation* of the individual person can be no more than that of an always replaceable and

---

[11] For Mexico, see Ed Vulliamy, *Amexica: War Along the Borderline* (London: Vintage, 2010).

disposable atom, component of an impersonal machine. Here 'alien-ability' which, as we have already seen, is constitutive of the subjective notion of right, ironically metamorphoses into the dispensability of the bearer of rights, who is imminently redundant. In this way the 'exceptional' suspension of human rights by the super-subjectivity of the sovereign state proves the inevitably proper destiny of human rights themselves – as we have seen in the case of the defence of western liberalism through processes of 'special rendition'.

And while contemporary China may, for the moment, ignore crucial aspects of 'human rights', there is nothing in its agenda of over-riding the natural justice of procreation or of consigning masses of people to misery in the name of economic and political progress which is essentially out of keeping with the principles of liberalism, nor its past manifestations in the west in terms of various (subtle as well as unsubtle) eugenicist procedures, besides processes of primary accumulation that have commodified land, labour and value, whose extra-equivalent integrity can alone secure the human pursuit of a sacred 'characterised' identity.[12]

If, therefore, liberal individualism does not lie at the core of the real western legacy and yet capitalism is founded upon it, then capitalism also must be viewed as an aberrant product of the west – which may indeed, partially explain why it has proved so readily translatable outside western norms. To underscore this claim, one would have to show how capital-ism was born from the later corruption of the emergent medieval market system which, as has recently been demonstrated, was thoroughly 'sympathetic' or reciprocalist in character, always seeking to keep the monetary economy in line with an 'economy of esteem', or an economy of honour. The operation of supply and demand only became detached from the offer and grateful reception of the ethical through the break-up of Christendom; the fatally exemplary reduction of the English peasantry to wage-labour; the seductive example of oriental despotism (Islamic and further Eastern) as a salve against anarchic crisis; the equally seductive lures of African slave economies, along with new, seemingly inexhaust-ible supplies of gold – encouraging a switch to capital accumulation as the prime objective, and even (arguably, despite ostensibly expressed horror) the sacral political economies of forced labour linked to absolute noble ownership in Meso-America. Rampant capitalist appropriation can be seen as in part a contamination of the western political economy by alien notions of eminent domain (as grasped so well by Deleuze and

[12] On this triple commodification, see Karl Polanyi, *The Great Transformation* (Boston Mass.: Beacon, 2001).

Guattari),[13] fused with new western sacralisations of the will and abstract value, and capitalist proletarianisation of agricultural and industrial workers as a new, more subtle enslavement and sacrificial calculus to prove either a 'Catholic' advance in merit or the Protestant presence of unmerited providential blessing.[14]

Today this perversion of the western legacy has proved exportable in terms of the combination of western technocracy (detached from Francis Bacon's link of technology to charity and the eschatological redemption and perfecting of nature, which resonated down the British Protestant inheritance)[15] with the more impersonal Asiatic religious legacy that is so often a kind of 'technology of the spirit' – aimed at the ironically perfect achievement of control through indifference or submission. This is why Slavoj Žižek is so precisely right to speak of the dangers of 'Western Buddhism' – which one could equally describe as an 'Eastern mystique of the technological'.[16]

I would submit, therefore, that promotion of personhood and free association are essential to the defence and revival of the western legacy and that the promotion of human rights will, by comparison, tend to hasten its collapse.

But obviously this claim is wildly at variance with the views that now dominate western public discourse. The assumption here is that the notion of human rights is the high mead, the finest distillation of the western tradition – the very point where it fulfils itself by denying its specificity and opening up to the universal. Those who have

---

[13] Gilles Deleuze and Felix Guattari, *A Thousand Plateaus*, (trans.) Brian Massumi (London: Athlone, 1987), 424–500.

[14] See Martha C. Howell, *Commerce Before Capitalism in Europe: 1300–1600* (Cambridge University Press, 2010). To these dialectical complexities of imperialist corruption American-originated 'postcolonialist' theory is largely oblivious.

[15] See Charles Webster, *The Great Instauration: Science, Medicine and Reform 1626–1660* (London: Duckworth, 1975). As the great Anglo-Catholic Sinologist Joseph Needham (who was earlier himself aware of just the dimension later discussed in detail by Webster) stressed, native Chinese natural philosophy was both encouraged and tempered by Taoist mysticism which, like Christianity, tended to give it that practical, technological bias which rendered it a genuine mode of experimental 'natural science'. Yet the subordination of physical purpose to interpersonal communion and the hope for an entirely transfigured cosmos are not quite arrived at in this perspective, whose geomantic awareness has been in any case drastically abandoned by the modern communist and post-communist sensibility.

[16] Slavoj Žižek, *The Parallax View* (Cambridge Mass.: MIT 2006), 383–384. The novels of Haruki Murakami sometimes convey this tendency very well, besides its tension with western individualist influences, both genuine and debased. However, I am by no means wishing to deny here that there are other potentials within Eastern religion, nor that Christianity cannot further develop some of its own insights in dialogue with Mahayana Buddhism, Shin Buddhism, modern Hinduism, Taoism and Confucianism.

challenged this view – Leo Strauss, Michel Villey, Alasdair MacIntyre – have tended to be historians of thought, but more recently their interventions have faced resistance from alternative appeals to history which seek to show that the idea of subjective right is truly well grounded in the medieval, Patristic, Biblical and even, to a degree, ancient Roman legacy.

In what follows I shall try to show why their revisionist histories are erroneous, and therefore why the notion of 'human rights' is indeed an historical aberration in terms of our genuine western identity.

Wolterstorff and the history of rights

The claims of the historical revisionists have now been ably summed up and most coherently developed by Nicholas Wolterstorff in his book *Justice: Rights and Wrongs*.[17] This camp consists largely of American Christians who wish to defend the deep consistency of the American legacy with their Christian commitment, and who take Americanism to imply a commitment to liberalism and to liberal democracy (rather than to 'civic republicanism' in the French style – although this difference is problematic). They wish, as Wolterstorff puts it, to defend the idea that justice is most fundamentally derived from subjective rights, and also to argue that this notion is entirely compatible with Christianity. In Wolterstorff's case he wants further to argue that it is *derived* from Christianity, and becomes incoherent when not grounded in Christian theology. Hence he wishes to claim that modernity, properly understood, is the consummation of Christian practice.

The American Christian liberal camp therefore oppose the idea that justice is grounded in cosmic 'right order', as it was for the ancient Greeks, John Chrysostom, Augustine and Aquinas. If Christians supposed for a long time that this was the case then, according to Wolterstorff, this was because their thinking was not sufficiently Biblical or de-Hellenised.

To think of justice as 'right order' is supposedly to have an insufficient sense of human personal dignity, of equality and the primacy of freedom. It follows that a just polity must be explicitly based upon the primacy of individual subjective rights which will have its concomitant in the negatively free capitalist market, however tempered this may be by state welfarism that ensures equality of opportunity, and therefore a level playing field for economic competition – on a roughly Rawlsian model,

---

[17] Nicholas Wolterstorff, *Justice: Rights and Wrongs* (Princeton University Press, 2008). In the Wolterstorff camp, see also John Witte, Jr., *The Reformation of Rights: Law, Religion and Human Rights in Early Modern Calvinism* (Cambridge University Press, 2010).

for which Wolterstorff indeed claims (with much plausibility) to be providing a better philosophical basis.[18]

Wolterstorff's allegation is that a polity based upon right order will tend to involve an arbitrary hierarchy and not to recognise the full personhood of all its members. The reverse allegation of proponents of right order (like myself), as already indicated, is that a foundation of politics in human rights is indissolubly linked with an augmentation of arbitrary will that applies as much to the sovereign political centre as to the individuals on the periphery who directly confront this centre, without an intervening network of mediating organic relationships. These individuals may be taken either one by one or *en masse:* in either case, it is claimed, there is a logical slide of liberalism into a nihilism of the enthroned will. The Straussian version of this charge tends to see the ancient *polis* as the model of human perfection and to be half-resigned to liberalism as a second best within a modern mass society, apart from the glorious enclave of the American university campus. Wolterstorff is in more or less negative agreement in recognising these two ideal types as the real alternatives.

Such a typology might, nevertheless, be challenged by Wolterstorff's own question as to whether we should mainly characterise the history of *ius* and so of Western justice in terms of *rupture*. The Straussians claim that objective *ius* is decisively replaced by subjective *ius* only with Thomas Hobbes.[19] Michel Villey and his followers claim, to the contrary, that this decisive shift happened earlier with the work of William of Ockham in the fourteenth century, whose position itself had significant intellectual antecedents.[20] The revisionists to whom Wolterstorff mainly refers claim, much more drastically, to discover subjective *ius* back in the twelfth-century canonists and even in the Justinian code itself, thereby implying that liberalism is not especially derived from the *via moderna*,

---

[18] Wolterstorff, *Justice*, 14–17.

[19] For a defence of the Straussian position against Brian Tierney, see Ernest L. Fortin, 'On the Presumed Medieval Origin of Individual Rights', in his *Classical Christianity and the Political Order; Reflections on the Theologico-Political Problem* (Lanham Md.: Rowman Littlefield, 1996), 243–264. Fortin rightly argues that Tierney offers no real case for considering the ascription of rights to subjects in the Middle Ages to be 'subjective rights'. On this, see further below.

[20] See Michel Villey, *La formation de la pensée juridique moderne* (Paris: PUF, 2006); *Le Droit et les Droits de L'Homme* (Paris: PUF, 1983). Villey has more contemporary defenders regarding his reading of Ockham than Wolterstorff allows. See for example Michel Bastit, 'Michel Villey et les ambiguités d'Occam', in Michael Garcin, (ed.), *Droit, nature, histoire* (Aix-en-Provence/Marseilles: Presses Universitaires D'Aix-Marseilles, 1985), 65–72; Daniel Gutmann, 'La question du droit subjective chez Guillaume D'Occam', in *Le droit des modernes (XIVe –XVIIIe siècles)*, (ed.) Stéphane Rials (Paris: Droit, 1998), 11–29. There are several other examples, both French and German.

but is rather rooted in both Christianity and in Roman thought and practice, perhaps under Stoic influence.[21]

However, an *alternative* group of revisionists (tending to have emerged from the Cambridge school of the History of Political Thought) to whom Wolterstorff refers far less, discover a different continuity. Not the ancient roots of liberalism, but rather the persistence in mainstream legal thought and practice of antique ideas of justice as rooted in right order as far as the late eighteenth century.[22] Even though much more importance is given in the early modern period and the eighteenth century to the primacy of personal self-possession and ownership of property, rights still remained fundamentally located within reciprocal relationships and therefore were usually correlated with duties.[23] This was true, for example, in the case of the self-theorisation of eighteenth-century Scots law, though far less so for the self-theorisation of eighteenth-century English law.[24]

Wolterstorff himself is not in the end denying a rupture – even if he sees this as a slow rending. For clearly he thinks that a supposedly Christian grounding of the politico-economic order in subjective rights gradually won out over the dominance of 'right order'.

---

[21] Besides Tierney, see mainly Charles Reid, Jr., 'The Canonistic Contribution to the Western Rights Tradition: An Historical Inquiry', *Boston College Law Review*, 33 (1991), 37–92; *Power over the Body: Equality in the Family: Rights and Domestic Relations in Medieval Canon Law* (Grand Rapids, Mich: Eerdmans, 2004). For a good summary of the entire debate in the wider context of the history of all notions of law in connection with notions of nature, see Francis Oakley, *Natural Law, Laws of Nature, Natural Rights: Continuity and Discontinuity in the History of Ideas* (New York: Continuum, 2005), 87–109.

[22] For this (loosely defined) 'second group of revisionists', see Annabel S. Brett, *Liberty, Right and Nature: Individual Rights in Later Scholastic Thought* (Cambridge University Press, 2003) and Knud Haakonssen, *Natural Law and Moral Philosophy: From Grotius to the Scottish Enlightenment* (Cambridge University Press, 1996)

[23] See mainly Haakonssen, *Natural Law and Moral Philosophy*.

[24] See James, Viscount Stair, *The Institutions of the Law of Scotland* (1693) (Edinburgh and Glasgow: Edinburgh University Press and Glasgow University Press, 1981): 'the first principles of right are obedience [to revealed and natural law], freedom and engagement [being held to voluntary contract]', 90; 'Obligation is that which is correspondent to a personal right', 93; 'liberty standeth in the midst betwixt obligations of obedience, which are anterior, and of engagements, which are posterior', 94. Contrast Sir William Blackstone, *On the Laws and Constitution of England* (1796) (London: Elibron, 2005): 'The absolute rights of men ... may be reduced to three principal or primary articles; the right of personal security, the right of personal liberty and the right of private property.' Whereas Stair, the Roman lawyer, offers an eclectic mix of objective natural law and subjective natural right, stressing reciprocity of right and duty and the partial legitimation of contract by natural equity, Blackstone, the common lawyer, grounds his legal hermeneutic on naked possessive individualism. This contrast is noted by Alasdair MacIntyre in *Whose Justice? Which Rationality?* (London: Duckworth, 1998), 228.

However, this may oddly mean that Wolterstorff himself does not take continuity seriously enough, as indicated by his relative ignoring of the second group of revisionists.

What is perhaps crucial here is the history of events rather than the history of ideas. To suppose that the basic theoretical issue is one of foundational rights versus the 'ancient liberty' of the *polis* is to look at things either through American or French eyes. That is to say, through *revolutionary* eyes – and it is very important to point out that the two revolutions, though so different, were still variants upon the same liberal principles. But the question to be raised here is whether the revolutionary paradigm, the paradigm of explicit formal foundation of constitutional liberty upon subjective right, is the only decisive modern alternative to either the ancient pagan polity or to a medieval feudal variant?

One can argue that it is not, because the political practice of other countries with relatively 'liberal' (upholding free association and the constitutional rule of law) and egalitarian traditions deeply rooted in the far past – Iceland and the Scandinavian nations, Switzerland, The Netherlands, England, Scotland (plus the British imperial derivatives), parts of the Germanic world and certain Italian cities – owe little to the liberal revolutions which they long pre-date, and only certain aspects owe to the influence of liberal ideology.[25] (Even though all these terrains contributed to the history of this ideology – the last six, massively – it has been heavily contested within those regions, and often does not adequately describe their own constitutional practice – which to this day often notably includes monarchy.)

In all these cases, a long-standing constitutionalism is rooted in the Middle Ages. Magna Carta is famous, but there were equivalents in Scotland and Sweden. Christian republicanism existed in several medieval Italian city-states. The question is, how is one to regard this continuity – in terms of the first revisionism as the *longue durée* of liberalism, or in terms of the second revisionism as the evolving persistence of 'right order', able to develop in its own terms certain more subjective emphases, even if one would have to allow that from early modern times onwards this too often gets perverted in a truly liberal 'possessive individualist' direction?

I would argue that it is more the latter. The ancient pagan *polis* was monolithic and the social there coincided with the political. But the medieval social polity was characterised by a plethora of complex

---

[25] See Wilhelm Roepke, *The Social Crisis of Our Time*, (New Brunswick: Transaction), 37–82; Augustine Thompson, *Cities of God* (University Park, Pa.: Penn State University Press, 2006).

and complexly overlapping 'free associations', as Otto von Gierke emphasised.[26] In consequence, it is not surprising if both civil and canon law came to talk much more than pagan antiquity about *iura* that attached to individual subjects and groups, and were rights to exercise a certain power or *facultas* in relation to other individuals and social formations.[27] Nor that the law tried further to define what one person might legitimately *demand* from another – who therefore had a reciprocal *duty* – in certain circumstances.

On top of this one can thoroughly agree with Wolterstorff that Christianity gave a new prominence to the notion of unforced consent, which is evidenced, for example, in the legal consideration of marriage. However, this does *not*, as Wolterstorff and the first group of revisionists claim, mean that the Middle Ages usually possessed precisely our modern liberal notion of a subjective civil right, never mind of a subjective natural right. Subjectivisation does not necessarily mean subjective grounding. Michel Villey in point of fact never denied that even ancient Romans, but more frequently medieval Christians, 'had rights'. Although he rightly insisted that a *ius* was anciently a 'thing' in the sense that it denoted justice as such, *id quod justum est*, he further stressed that the 'object of justice' was, according to Ulpian, *ius suum cuique tribuere*. Here the *ius* is 'owned' in the sense that each person has a proper 'share' in the distribution of things (material and ideal) according to justice, in order that they can perform acts appropriate to their assigned roles (following Gaius' tripartition of the concerns of justice into 'persons, things, actions'), not in the liberal sense that what 'belongs' to one can be known outside this architectonic act of distribution.[28] Yet Villey never denied, as Wolterstorff alleges, that such a share in *ius* belonged to the subject, nor that in this sense one can speak of a subject as 'having a right'. Hence Charles Donahue's indication, supposedly against Villey, of the 191 cases where Justinian's *Digest* speaks of *ius habere*, and the 103 where it speaks of *ius esse alicui*, merely begs the question at issue.[29]

For Villey's point was *not*, as Wolterstorff imagines, after Tierney and Reid, that a *ius* was anciently a 'thing' on our modern model of thing as *object* that could only be shared in terms of literal partition. To the contrary, it was a 'thing' in the sense of an objective ideality that could be *participated* in, just as, for Plato, a good man who shares in the Good can

---

[26] See John Milbank, 'On Complex Space', in John Milbank, *The Word Made Strange: Theology, Language, Culture* (Oxford: Blackwell, 1997), 268–292.

[27] See Ernest Fortin, 'On the Presumed Medieval Origin of Natural Rights'.

[28] Villey, *Le Droit et Les Droits de L'Homme*, 70–74.

[29] Wolterstorff, *Justice*, 58–59.

still be good 'in his own right'. Nor did Villey suppose that 'objective right' meant that rights are, as Wolterstorff has it, 'incorporeal realities attached to corporeal realities'[30] – to objects, like a piece of land, rather than to subjects, but rather that all *iura* were 'objective' in the sense that they reflected a 'right distribution', a correct placing. 'Incorporeality' in Roman law, following the Stoic sense of this term, denotes a certain meaningful 'interval' between *either* different things *or* different persons, *or* again between things and persons, that binds them together with the obligatory force of the ideal, although this binding has an instantiation in material practice. Examples according to Villey would be 'inheritance' 'usufruct', 'servitude' 'obligation' or 'ownership'.[31]

It is because (as Villey mentions, though I here elaborate) Aquinas thinks of ownership as the ownership *not* of land itself, but of an incorporeal dimension of land, that he can say that humans in general own not the essence but merely the usage of things (ST II.II. Q. 66 a.1 resp.). Equally it is for this reason that he can say that, based upon such a generic sense of usage, individual humans can more specifically 'own' a tract of land or other objects in so far as they procure, dispense with and take care of them, but *not* as regards the ultimate total usage of this property which *remains* a common possession (ST II.II Q. 66 a.2 resp.).

Therefore individual human beings *do not own* usage, but human beings in general *only* own usage. This is because Aquinas did not think of the right to buy, sell and manage as material, 'thingy' processes, which the law later legitimises (after the dualistic, biopolitical manner of modern liberalism), but rather saw these rights (outside any such dualism of nature and culture) as incorporeal relations in which we stand to things which are instrumentally subordinate to a more general and guiding incorporeal relationship of humanity as a whole to corporeal things as a whole. This relationship is *auto-legitimating* in accordance with natural law and is merely endorsed and interpreted by civil codes.

Hence one can have the 'right to claim' something because of the objective relation in which one is deemed to be situated: child with respect to parent, for example. Charles Reid has correctly stressed that the Middle Ages newly developed the rights of children.[32] However, they did so because they regarded such rights as the correlates of the duties of parents towards children, and indeed one could argue that, precisely because children's rights are mostly a dead letter if someone else is not performing their duties, that it was *easier* for the Middle Ages to develop notions of children's rights than for modernity, whose paradigm for the

---

[30] Wolterstorff, *Justice*, 48.   [31] Villey, *Le Droit et Les Droits de L'Homme*, 74–76.
[32] Reid, *Power over the Body*, 153–210.

possession of rights is the free, fully rational autonomous adult (and with historical precedence male) human subject.

In this instance, the foundation of the right of one party and the duty of another lies in objective *ius* and not in the sheerly subjective right of the claimant. Even the right to marry freely is only the right to enter into a relational bond with certain categories of persons and not others, and is furthermore the right to enter into a state of continuing reciprocal rights and duties.[33] And it is only a right of self-disposal because the New Testament had deemed that marriage was one of two valid ways for the individual to deal with their own sexuality—the other being celibacy. Therefore such a right is not finally traceable to one's own subjectivity standing in isolation, or else to certain merely conventional and contractual (even 'covenantal') relationships in which one stands to other fundamentally monadic subjects. Yet this *is* what distinguishes specifically liberal subjective rights, or else the concept becomes meaningless and we are arguing about nothing.

Indeed, for all that he is a fine legal historian, Charles Reid remarkably misses the real philosophical implication of his researches concerning the right to *contract* marriage in the Middle Ages.[34] Such was the high sacramental view of marriage in the west as signifying the union of Christ with his Church, that it was regarded as primarily a *de facto* state of free mutual union between a man and a woman. It was precisely the theologically grounded canon law which upheld the rights of women not to be coerced, and insisted (to the *chagrin* of so many noble parents) upon the legitimacy of even clandestine marriage. But in the Reformation and Counter-Reformation era, clandestine marriage became mostly illegal, and it may well be that that radical reactionary William Shakespeare is mounting an already nostalgically romantic protest against this bleak legal modernism in *Romeo and Juliet*. Indeed, England never followed

---

[33] Not respect for homosexual people, but fully consistent liberalism leads many in the United States to argue that marriage must be a contract that can be enacted between any adult human being and any other. The exclusion of incestuous relationships from this view is inconsistent and perhaps will not survive, unless on medical grounds. By comparison, most Europeans (up till very recently) have been content with 'civil partnerships' for gay people, and a large body of gay opinion itself prefers this option, because they still have a non-liberal preparedness to make judgements about what kinds of relationships between what kinds of people in what circumstances are 'essentially' right. The earlier European view had the advantage that it avoided creating an 'equal rights to marriage law' that is never likely to command the general assent of almost all, despite the fact that this is the necessary basis for good law. The generation of 'culture wars' around legal options in the United States is therefore a good illustration of the way in which foundational subjective rights, rejecting all essentialisms (even relatively 'liberal' ones) tend to foster irresolvable civil conflicts.

[34] Reid, *Power over the Body*, 55–66.

the requirements of continental reformers here, and the practice of clandestine marriage lingered on until 1753 (and beyond to the twentieth century up till the 1960s, if young persecuted couples could make it to the disputed Scots–English border town of Gretna Green). So if modernity in this fashion restricted the rights of the young to marry, then that was exactly because young people and especially young women came to be regarded as *more* under the quasi-possession of parents within a liberal outlook. Hence the greater medieval freedom of the individual to marry was only a freedom of two persons of opposed genders *mutually* to enter into what was regarded as an objective ontological condition. What Reid does not seem to realise is that the tolerance of clandestine marriage shows that medieval rights of the subject were *not* grounded in self-possession, and therefore were not in any degree tending in the direction of 'modern human rights'. Rather the reverse: once one has the latter, the 'right' of the adult over the child can cancel out the reality of secret nuptials.

Besides rights to claim and to enter into contract, the Middle Ages also recognised rights of exercise. Generally speaking, a *ius* to exercise freely a power as a manager or a judge over certain people or property was regarded, in the phrase still used by Ockham, as a *potestas licita*.[35] But it was not, as in Ockham's later theorisation of the notion, a right *derived* from *de facto* power, constitutionally legitimated for reasons of guarding the free power of each and everyone. This is precisely the liberal model. The medieval attribution of an 'exercise right' was rather a grant to the right kind of person to exercise according to right judgement a certain restricted authority in specific circumstances and with respect to certain *intrinsic relationships* in which he or she stood to certain other people.

So as Ernest Fortin puts it, medieval rights of subjects 'were by no means unconditional. They were contingent on the performance of prior duties and hence forfeitable. Anyone who failed to abide by the law that guarantees them could be deprived of everything to which he was previously entitled: his freedom, his property and in extreme cases his life.' By contrast, modern subjective rights, as Fortin says, are seen as 'absolute, inviolable, imprescriptible, unconditional, inalienable or sacred'.[36] Even murderers now often retain their estates, and some powers of disposal under the operation of civil rights, while natural rights to life, ownership, belief, welfare (and even, increasingly, the plebiscite) are regarded as non-suspendable in any circumstances whatsoever.

[35] Villey, *La formation*, 257; Wolterstorff, *Justice*, 48.
[36] Fortin, 'On the Presumed Medieval Origin', 247.

Subjective rights now cannot be lost because they are held to derive from the very nature of the isolated subject. But such was not the practical (or normally the theoretical) case in the Middle Ages.

Ignoring these considerations, the first group of revisionists, and Wolterstorff in their wake, talk far too much as if the mere attachment of a *ius* to a person was proof of the presence of a 'subjective right' in something approaching the modern liberal sense – even if they sometimes equivocate over this assimilation.[37] By contrast, Villey's observation remains entirely valid: *ius* in ancient and medieval law could betoken a valid power to claim, a permission or a right to exercise, but it could equally, when attached to a subject, denote a *restriction* on what he was allowed to do.[38] For *ius* up till at least the thirteenth century meant always the 'objectively right', that which was just, and it was linked to a notion of justice as distribution which meant always measuring the proper situation of persons and things in relation to each other. This was exactly why, as Villey also pointed out, law in this period was a branch of practical philosophy, a matter of exercising *juris-prudentia*, and not a matter of deduction from foundational principles or of applying positive prescriptions in the light of a rigid attachment to precedent.[39] It was indeed authentically *liberal* in the root sense of exercising a generous flexibility of discernment according to both circumstance and a sense of the transcendent good. But modern liberal law, by comparison, is rigid both in terms of its contractualist norms and its obeisance to what has been positively prescribed by central sovereign legislation.

In opposing judgement as discernment and imposition of 'right order', Wolterstorff is commendably thorough. He realises that he must also oppose the notion of morality as the search for true human happiness which is equivalent to human beings finding their right way to be within the cosmos. Accordingly, he denies that the Christian imperative to love can be validly regarded as eudaimonistic. This means that charity should rather be regarded as a sympathetic and benevolent concern for the other human being in their irreducible singularity and dignity of freedom. For this reason he explicitly endorses sympathy as an entirely valid later translation of *agape* regarded as 'compassion', and therefore signs up to a non-teleological 'sympathy' which tends to add imaginative projection to private utility along with 'rights' as the other founding dimension of modern political economy which is the essence and heart of fully

---

[37] See Reid, 'The Canonistic Contribution', 38, n. 3.
[38] Villey, *Le Droit et les Droits de L'Homme*, 57–104.
[39] Villey, *La formation*, 100–106, 149–176.

developed liberalism.[40] Indeed, it would appear that sympathy and rights belong for him in a mutually confirming circle: through projective or imaginative sympathy with others we accord them rights; but the 'right' of the free other should command our compassionate concern.

The coherence of all this I leave in suspense for the moment. What matters initially is that Wolterstorff's 'contest of narratives', or his opposition to the Strauss and Villey theses, is the very heart of his book. He is too subtle a thinker to fall into the trap of certain others in his camp of imagining that even to engage with it seriously is to fall into the supposed 'genetic fallacy'. For the question at issue is in part whether modern liberalism either depends upon, or is in hostage to certain unacknowledged theological positions. No one today would be able to see this by pure exercise of the power of reason, because this theological founding is a contingent fact, the result of people thinking in terms which are indebted to a certain religious heritage, linked to certain events, writings and claimed revelations. And all the more does one require a genealogy, even as a liberal, if one claims, like Wolterstorff, that we *still* require a Biblical, revealed foundation for liberalism.

Hence he commendably does not shirk the genealogical issue without quite conceding that his whole case stands or falls in relation to it. But given my above reasonings it must so stand or fall. Therefore I will now expand my critique of Wolterstorff and his camp with a more detailed account of his attack upon Villey's view that modern liberal subjective rights are rooted in Ockham's nominalism. I am defending Villey rather than Strauss because I agree with the former that modern subjective rights do have a medieval root in the (mainly) Franciscan tradition and do not only emerge with Hobbes and his epoch.

Defence of the Villey thesis

Wolterstorff concludes that, in the light of the evidence, Michel Villey's account can now be said to be 'indisputably false'.[41] Yet he never once cites Villey's (untranslated) texts and he omits or distorts several things: the fact that Villey execrates the entire Franciscan tradition of theological–jurisprudential reflection, and not just Ockham; the fact that he sees Renaissance Stoicism as also a contributing influence to

---

[40] Wolterstorff, *Justice*, 218. However, 'sympathy' as first reinvoked in modern times by Benjamin Whichcote and the Cambridge Platonists remained linked to an imaginative and interpersonal search for discernment of the true human end: here Stoic 'sympathy' was still yoked to Platonic *eros*. It is even arguable that this remains somewhat the case for David Hume. See n. 1.

[41] Wolterstorff, *Justice*, 62

liberalism alongside nominalism; the fact that he does, albeit briefly, mention the increasing recognition of 'subjectivity' in Canon Law, and finally the fact, already mentioned, that he does not see the objectivity of rights in quite the 'thingy' sort of way that Wolterstorff supposes.[42]

More specifically: Wolterstorff, along with other critics of Villey, fails to mention that the French scholar recognised that Thomas Aquinas himself, even though clearly free of all taint of juridical subjectivism, nonetheless learnt from the canonical glossators to emphasise human freedom and interpersonal relationship in a way that exceeded the Aristotelian and Roman juridical traditions.[43] Hence, for example, in their wake he allows greater religious and familial rights to slaves and allows also that the objective *ius* to food and shelter can be exercised as a subjective claim. (Wolterstorff's argument that this *ius* is in part subjectively derived even back in Chrysostom lacks any evidential and argumentative warrant.)[44]

As Villey says, after Jacques Maritain, these developments accord with a new sense of the 'person' as irreducible to the mere part of a totality. But if the person is now regarded as 'more than the whole', then this is nonetheless consistent with understanding the person (as, paradigmatically, in the case of the divine Trinity) as only constituted through the series of relationships in which he stands. For it is the insertion of the individual in such a chain, extending to his link with God himself, which ensures the *essential* place of the individual within the whole series, since this chain is itself only made up of uniquely characterised links. If, by contrast, as with nominalism, the individual is himself seen as a self-sufficient 'sovereign' entity, abstractable from his social insertion, then conversely he is not essential to the composition of any social aggregate. In that case his very ontological isolation ironically ensures his substitutability, and in consequence his autonomy proves to be less of a self-defence than that provided by inherent relational dependency against the arbitrary sovereignty of God, nature or the state. So by virtue of his personalism, as Villey argued, Aquinas was already 'modern' in a non-liberal sense which pointed towards a later increased recognition of the rights of subjects as objectively justifiable according to their social fittingness rather than a right of entitlement accruing to an absolute subjective will.

Therefore Villey recognised here a *third* sort of continuity in the history of right. Even though he considered that liberalism has developed greater freedom and equality in a distorted fashion (including the case of the

---

[42] Villey, *La formation*, 132–148, 394–432.   [43] Villey, *La formation*, 194–195.
[44] Wolterstorff, *Justice*, 59–62.

Iberian Second Scholasticism) he still thought that such a development was partially in keeping with the thought of Thomas himself, who had further Christianised the Aristotelian and Roman legacy in the path of Gratian.

So Wolterstorff has badly caricatured his main academic opponent, whom he has apparently not read, despite the fact that articulating this opposition is crucial for his own enterprise. Surely, in justice, he can expect no mercy . . .

Among the first group of revisionists, it is the work of Brian Tierney which is paramount, as Wolterstorff agrees.[45] Tierney has led the way in arguing that 'subjective rights' in something like our modern sense were already prevalent as far back as the twelfth century.

In assessing this claim, one should begin by acknowledging, in accordance with much that has already been said, that Tierney is justified in claiming that the terminological and conceptual history here is more complex than has often been allowed. Richard Tuck originally (he has now changed his mind following Tierney's intervention) saw the crucial distinction as lying merely between passive and claim rights on the one hand, and 'active rights' (*ius ad rem*) on the other. A passive right in general is the mere inactive counterpart of someone else's duty. A claim right is more specifically a particular right correlated with a more fundamental duty of the community (or its appropriate representatives) to provide whatever the *ius* alludes to (property exercise of a particular social role, etc.). It allows for active insistence by the possessor of the right, but is still reciprocally speaking passive and so objective: a legal entitlement held to be intrinsically just. An active right (*ius in rem*), by contrast, is a possessed right freely to exercise a certain role, wield a certain power (*potestas*) and fulfil a certain presumed capacity (*facultas*). Tuck thought that, on the whole, the early to high Middle Ages did not speak of active or subjective rights which he linked, following Michel Villey and many others, to nominalism–voluntarism. They sometimes but rarely, according to Tuck, spoke of claim rights. (It should therefore be clear that Tuck's original position was somewhat less complex than that of Villey.)[46]

Against the earlier Tuck, Tierney shows that, already in the twelfth century, civilian glossators linked *ius* with *potestates* and spoke of the right to election of the emperor as both a *facultas* and a *ius*; while Gratian

---

[45] Tierney, *The Idea of Natural Rights*.

[46] Richard Tuck, *Natural Rights Theories: Their Origin and Development* (Cambridge University Press, 1979); John Milbank, *Theology and Social Theory* (Oxford: Blackwell, 2006), xxxii, 9–25.

himself had spoken of the *ius* of the Pope to establish laws.[47] They even mentioned *ius naturale* as a faculty or power inherent in human nature's rational capacity, in a manner later echoed by Nicholas of Cusa.[48] Tierney points out that Villey was not unaware of this, but thought that Aquinas, by confining *ius* to mean *quod iustum est*, had rectified a Patristic confusion between divinely commanded *lex* and intrinsically just *ius*. He quite rightly says that such an absolute contrast of *lex* and *ius* would have been alien to the Middle Ages – even though one should mention that Aquinas, *contra* to John Finnis' reading, does place *ius* as dialectically arrived-at equity above *lex* seen as posited and formulated disposition expressing such equity: 'right is the object of justice' says Aquinas, and 'law is not the same as right but an expression of right' (ST 2.2 q.57 a.1 resp. and ad 2).

Yet in medieval usage, in the phrases *ius civile* and *ius gentium*, *ius* itself certainly meant inscribed 'law'. And although Aquinas never spoke of *ius naturale* in a subjective sense (this is for him a question of an objectively 'fair pattern of relationships' as Tierney puts it, which the practical intellect apprehends as pertaining in terms of accordance with indemonstrable first principles of the *lex naturalis*, which is only secondarily a habitually exercised mental capacity), Tierney points out that he does speak of *ius domini* (S.T. 2.2.q.62.a.1) and *ius possendi* (S.T. 2.2.q.66.a.5).

Tierney's interpretation of all this important evidence which he has carefully disinterred is, however, confusing. Really he is involved in a common Christian–American doublethink.[49] For in the end he wants to say that 'human rights' as understood by the United States today (or indeed much of Europe today, under French and American influence) are compatible with Catholic natural law theory. At times this seems to mean that the canonists were really already liberals and proto-moderns (as in his entirely debatable assertion that their juridical notions of rational human nature were separable from theological ideas of cosmic harmony, participation and divine grace.) But at other times this seems to mean, quite correctly, that their notion of 'right' remained a non-liberal one embedded in corporatist constitutionalist thinking. The true implications of this alternative then get much muddied by Tierney's curious view of the period of history intermediate between the High Middle Ages and later modernity ('the long early modernity', as it were.) Here he claims that Ockham's version of subjective *ius* had nothing to do

[47] Tierney, *The Idea of Natural Rights*, 13–77; Reid, 'The Canonistic Contribution'.
[48] Tierney, *The Idea of Natural Rights*, 234–235.
[49] Tierney is British by birth, but has worked in American universities for a long time.

with his philosophy; Hobbes was an isolated strange aberration, while Locke remained loyal to the main lines of medieval constitutional thought, innocent of Hobbes' proto-nihilism. All these conclusions are demonstrably erroneous.

It seems to me that one can theoretically save the appearances of Tierney's diligent and admirable researches better than he himself does. Tentatively I would suggest that one can discriminate four different moments regarding medieval *ius*.

First, ecclesial and political administrative anarchy somewhat forced in practice an increasing drift (accelerated after 1300) towards a more formal and absolute sense of ownership which affected the juridical meaning of 'right' – as indeed Michel Villey himself suggested.[50]

Secondly, however, the mere presence of concepts of claim and active exercise does not amount to a fully fledged doctrine of subjective rights, as we have already seen. It is actually obvious that one can have a power or faculty to do something that is socially conferred for objective reasons that are still to do with *ius* as partition, and the attribution of an object- ively 'incorporeal' quality of right possession, as Villey diagnosed.[51]

Thus the language of the glossators of Gratian's *Decretals* is sometimes echoed by Aquinas himself, whom no party to this debate save John Finnis suspects of having a subjective rights doctrine.[52] So, for example, because of one's position and recognised capacity, one could have a *ius* to establish laws, but it would be assumed (as indeed Tierney agrees) that one would exercise this capacity according to one's rational recognition of the law of nature. So it is not the case that free activity alone is sufficient to define subjective rights. Rather, such (modern) rights are *subjectively grounded* – that is to say, they take their sense not from social recognition in accordance with natural equity, but rather from a supposedly natural pre-moral fact, such as the claimed fact of self- ownership, or the contingent *de facto* circumstance of property ownership upon which legitimacy is then positively conferred. Here the right derives *solely* from the *facultas* or *potestas*, as is not the case for the glossators.

As Villey stressed, right is only subjective right when it ceases to be a *relational* matter and becomes something grounded in an isolated indi- vidual capacity. And the problem here, as he also suggested, is that such a right, precisely as non-relational, is infinite – we generally ascribe now a human right to adequate healthcare, but truly to fulfill that right to the maximum for each and every person would be *impossible*. This rights

---

[50] Villey, *La formation*, 248–251.   [51] See previous section.
[52] John Finnis, *Natural Law and Natural Rights* (Oxford University Press, 1980).

doctrine therefore tells us nothing about how healthcare is to be justly allocated and provided, even though these are the really crucial issues.

And once one projects a right from an individual to humanity as a whole, then the question becomes – who does humanity have rights against? The answer must be either a voluntarist, arbitrarily covenanting God, which helps no one save religious fanatics, or else (and *always* in practical terms) humanity itself. Humanity as such would then have the obligation, or rather the collective right, to fulfill an in principle infinitely expanding number of rights – rights to education, work, holidays, leisure, access to the countryside, even 'rights to sunshine', as Villey laconically noted – infinitely, in all perpetuity. So this notion of human rights clearly provides us with no practical ethical guidance. In reality it leads to a state of anarchy which is only ended by an authoritarian power which will arbitrarily promote one set of rights over another – liberal capitalist states the right of property; state socialist authorities the rights to food, health, work and culture. The former will be at the expense of majority economic well-being; the latter at the expense of people's rights of free association and the free choosing of roles and an order of existential priorities.

In the third place, there is the question of theological influence prior to the nominalists. Here Tierney cites links of earlier realist Franciscan theology and the Franciscan-linked thought of Godfrey of Fontaines and Henry of Ghent with subjective rights theory in order to qualify or even challenge the nominalist connection. He does not however seem to realise that the obvious riposte to this would be an argument, which indeed Villey already put forward, locating Ockham, etc. within a longer-term Franciscan (including their intellectual fellow travellers) drift towards voluntarism, logicism and individualism, often undergirded by notions of the univocity of being (latent already in Bonaventure) which allow a perfect rational grasp of finite realities in their now supposedly replete reality as finite.

Hence somewhat like Abelard already in the twelfth century, Franciscan theologians did tend to stress the role of the inward conscience in ethics and to regard motivation and intention as private possessions of the inner self. Bonaventure, for example, as Georges de Lagarde noted, reduced the Aristotelian doctrine of distributive justice to an assignment of what is due to each individual *according to their merits*.[53] He thereby 'de-juridified' the notion of distribution itself, which for the Aristotelian–Roman tradition was at the very heart of the

---

[53] Georges de Lagarde, *La naissance de l'esprit laïque au déclin du Moyen Age, III Secteur Social de la Scolastique* (Paris: Éditions Beatrice, 1942), 116–145.

definition of justice. This already opened up the way to regarding 'right' as a matter of obedience to divine precept and after that merely to the obligations consequent upon the agreements which human beings have artificially entered into with each other. And indeed Bonaventure (anticipating biopolitical dualism) saw human society as a work of art *rather than* a work of nature, in a manner that is quite different from the spirit of Aquinas who rather saw it as both at once.[54]

The Franciscans had a similarly subjective approach to the question of economic needs, seeing these more as divinely legitimated 'private usages' than did the Dominicans. For the latter, since poverty was a socially recognised state, and all ownership was derived from socially legitimated *usus*, the Dominican minimal and collective use of material goods was a certain form of ownership which therefore entered into public exchanges and could be considered a legal *ius*. The Dominican friar's poverty was not simply 'his', since it was made possible by certain social allowances for certain socio-religious purposes, and was moreover not so much a closed univocal finite achievement as a 'way' that opened up the participation of the finite in the infinite. Nor was it a poverty entirely without property since, as we have just pointed out, following Aristotle and Roman law, any legalised usage is a form of *ius* as *dominium*. Jesus in a minimal way owned the bread he ate and the things he was temporarily lent, while the disciples collectively owned the purse which Judas carried.

But, by contrast, the Franciscan friar's merely occasional usage was paradoxically, even though it was a refusal of 'possession', more purely 'his own', according to a supposedly direct divinely mediated grant, since it was regarded as his minimal self-provision for his material needs – outside all social, political and so juridical allocation. Just as, later for Ockham, a *de facto* property owner might 'claim' the recognition of the law as to licit usage,[55] so, already for Bonaventure, the friar might 'claim' from the Pope a right to material support, since he already, through self-ownership under God, possesses this quasi-right prior to ecclesial recognition.

For this reason Bonaventure, unlike Aquinas, did not regard such bare *usus* as a mode of legal *dominium* (= ownership). Everything the Franciscans apparently owned had to be nominally defined as lent, according to their novel idea of a *simplex usus facti*, a merely factual, rather than legally sanctioned usage. But this apparently more radical dispossession conceals an assumption that they absolutely owned in a directly and

---

[54] de Lagarde, *La naissance*, 116–147.
[55] Gutmann, 'La question du droit subjective', 11–29.

unmediated supernatural way by divine grant, outside social exchange, themselves, their bodies, and their own *dispossession* or poverty.

As many have noted, the dialectical development of Franciscanism is bizarre, and perhaps proffers the most extreme example one could give of the fate of Hegel's 'beautiful soul', who wrongly imagines that it is 'ethical' to set up an ideal too divorced from reality. Francis taught that his followers should be uneducated and own nothing whatsoever, refusing all power and domination. But when those followers entered the schools, they perforce had to deploy reasoning in favour of Gospel simplicity and they perforce had to settle down in one place and therefore required property in order to do so.

This led them into curious depths of double hypocrisy. An extreme rationalist reductionism is used to prove the absolutism of the supposedly 'simple' will, in a way that undoes all classical Christian ideas of metaphysical participation and objective natural law. Equivalently, the dubious idea that poverty is the absolute Christian virtue and proof of love (rather than being a way into charity, as Aquinas taught) is only upheld through the ruse that really the Pope owns the Franciscans' property which is not after all property since they merely use it.

Clearly this fiction is an incitement to corruption – for if poverty is guaranteed not by measured teleological use, but merely by using what is not your own, one can deceive oneself that one is poor even if the friaries get ever more commodious and the meals increasingly sumptuous. And that is in part what happened.

But much more crucial than this is the full dialectical twist in the story: if use is detached from ownership, then ownership will be seen as absolute and as legitimate apart from good usage, which previously underwrote both legitimate *dominium* and the *ius utendi*.

This development, along with other Franciscan tendencies to think of the person in terms of power over oneself, as already described, finally gives birth in Ockham to the modern notion of absolute ownership. Here one can do whatever one likes with one's own – whereas in the earlier Middle Ages there were many different degrees and modes of ownership, all linked to what the property was to be used for. As Villey pointed out (see the previous section), subjective *ius* of exercise over property was certainly known in antiquity, but it was always mixed up with objective elements of specific duties and responsibilities. And even though there were anarchic drifts towards contractualism in the Middle Ages, this mixture still in large part held – so, for example, the right to enjoy a manorial property came along with the obligation to run the manorial court.

In this way, even prior to the turn towards nominalism, Franciscan thought does indeed foreshadow a fully modern sense of subjective right.

This is the consequence of their tendency to divide will from reason and so to inaugurate a doctrine of choice, independent of the lure of truth. Such a sundering eventually encourages a fully fledged voluntarism which, in turn, by reducing the given ontological order to randomness, encourages the notion that every intellectual distinction that we can make points towards a certain distinction in reality. This (primarily Scotist) bias towards 'formal' distinctions of kind, and 'modal' distinctions of degree, eventually leads to a scepticism about the reality of universals, formal unity and real relations, thereby engendering a fully fledged nominalism, which is the ontological support for an outright social individualism.

As an example of this essential Franciscan continuity, one can discern, well before Ockham, as Tierney himself points out, the dialectical link between an inalienable but formal power of the will as such and alienability as to possessed content. Thus the Franciscan master Peter John Olivi already saw right as the confirmation of prior absolute possession, marked by the unrestricted power of alienability – free of the trusts and entails which legitimated most medieval property (and still does much modern property beyond any liberal theoretical accounting).[56] Olivi's position demonstrated already the dangerous contradiction lurking in any notion of absolutely inviolable subjective rights: namely that, since they are based upon the indefeasible right of the will, this right, taken in abstraction, can always be appealed to in order to *over-ride and abolish* any specific customary right whatsoever. In this way, as Edmund Burke partly realised, it is actually liberalism that poses the direst threat to all the real inherited and complexly negotiated *actual* liberties that people really care about.

But if such nascent liberalism already posed a tyrannical threat to real liberty, then it already posed an anarchic threat to true individual responsibility. Thus the question of the limits of alienability already intruded in medieval discussions of a classically inherited prisoner's dilemma: might even a guilty man condemned to death legitimately try to escape according to the natural law of self-preservation? Aquinas said 'no' – since real self-concern is tied up with one's position in society and the cosmos (although he allowed that a man *falsely* committed might rightly attempt to flee: ST II.II. Q.69 a.4). Henry of Ghent said 'yes', since he had already begun to espouse a subjective rights doctrine.[57] He was not a nominalist, yet his outlook was nurtured by the philosophical family to which nominalism belongs. For equivocity of being (as affirmed by Henry), just like its dialectical opposite, univocity,

[56] Tierney, *The Idea of Natural Rights*, 39–42.
[57] Tierney, *The Idea of Natural Rights*, 78–89.

encourages the sense that one's existence is entirely one's own by right, while the separation of reason from will encourages the sense that there is a 'raw' freedom independent of ends, of which one can never be legitimately robbed.

The fourth moment is the Ockhamist one, where *ius* is explicitly grounded in subjective power and capacity. Ockham put the capstone upon his Oxford Franciscan predecessor Duns Scotus' earlier conventionalist modification of the *bonum commune*, namely his derivation of the second table of the Decalogue as both natural and revealed law from divine willed imposition and, just as crucially, his pre-elaboration of the 'social contract' in his view that an *arbitrary* and merely consensually agreed-upon human division of property is permitted by the will of God after the Fall.[58] It is again typical of the extreme dialectic of the Franciscan 'beautiful soul' that it conceives of the situation in Eden in communistic rather than justly distributist terms as compared with Aquinas (or even, I would argue, Augustine), but then conceives of the legitimate post-Fallen situation in far more liberal and proto-capitalist terms than did the Dominicans.[59]

In Ockham's case, as in Scotus', it is entirely untrue, as Tierney alleges, that his theological reflections on reason and will are not transferred to questions of law and politics. To the contrary, it is completely clear, as Villey argued, that Ockham derived human entitlement based on prior power and possession from a divine entitlement based on absolute power and possession. This tends to legitimate economic and political tyranny even if, to be sure, the divine will in which humans *should* share is for Ockham a charitable will. Thus even though individual *dominium proprium* proceeds from natural *de facto* possession, in accordance with Ockham's metaphysical foregrounding of power (more fundamental for him that either 'nature' *or* 'will'), an unqualified *ius utendi* as *potestas licita* with respect to ownership proceeds from its recognition by the state to whom an over-riding divine power has been delegated.[60] The absoluteness of three sovereignties – divine, personal and political – are here seamlessly conjoined in terms of an ontology of pure power which ensures an embrace, well before Hobbes, of biopolitical duality and contradiction.[61] Right is at once entirely natural and

---

[58] Villey, *La formation*, 229–234.

[59] In this respect one can now see that Hilaire Belloc and G.K. Chesterton were political thinkers of genius in seeing that 'distributism' was the Thomist opposite of both capitalism and most forms of socialism, since the latter pair have a common Franciscan root. Their work can no longer be in any sense regarded as eccentric.

[60] See Gutmann, 'La question du droit subjective', 21, 24.

[61] See once more Elshtain, *Sovereignty*, 1–55.

yet operable only by a political will which entirely suspends and over-rides the natural, given order.

It may be insisted that human self-sovereignty as *facultas* or subjective *ius* is still for Ockham to be exercised according to right reason in pursuit of natural justice. However, the latter is itself no longer conceived by him in a teleological fashion, and is instead confined to the recognition and upholding of prior conventional contract. This is undergirded either by purely positive human law, or else by purely positive 'covenanted' divine law, since for Ockham even the first table of the Decalogue, never mind the second, is derived from the authority of divine willing in the last instance. On this point the rightly renowned medievalist Francis Oakley agrees with Lagarde and Villey against revisionist readings like that of Marilyn McCord Adams.[62]

Even the exhaustive citing of the Canonists which Tierney mentions as evidence of Ockham's dependence on them rather than on his own theology and philosophy itself shows, as Villey noted, a specifically *nominalist* obsession with positive precedent. More crucially, Ockham's actual literary deployment (as opposed to mere definition) of terms like *ius, dominium* and *usus* does show a nominalist and voluntarist excess beyond anything which the Canonists usually envisaged.[63]

Furthermore, Tierney loses sight of Villey's most decisive point at this juncture. In continuity with Bonaventure and the entire Franciscan political tradition, Ockham starts to *remove* ecclesiastically juridical matters from the sphere of canonical competence and to transfer these to the competence of the moral theologian.[64] He does this by insisting that the only theologically relevant aspect of law concerns the divinely instituted *ius poli* which are the positive commands of revelation, plus the indisputable dictates of natural reason, themselves in the end positively grounded in the divine will, as we have already seen. These dictates require us to obey the commands of God our master, to follow the instincts of *oikeiōsis* (self-preservation) in the natural state, and finally to observe the legitimacy of artificial contracts in the Fallen human state. But natural reason does not for Ockham suggest that we can infer from natural *relations* between people, and between people and things, the *ends* of these relationships and the proper way of composing them according to a 'right distribution' that is not founded in mere mutual agreement.

---

[62] Francis Oakley, *Natural Law, Laws of Nature, Natural Rights: Continuity and Discontinuity in the History of Ideas* (New York: Continuum, 2005), 87–109.

[63] Oakley, *Natural Law*; Villey, *La formation*, 251–269; William of Ockham, *Opus nonaginta dierum*, (ed.) Goldast, *Monarchia*, 2, 993–999.

[64] Villey, *La formation*, 229 ff.

Yet just this exercise of natural reason was precisely that which, for Aquinas, issued in 'natural law' in the most crucial sense as regards the practice of justice.[65]

This absence of the inherited sense of *ius naturale* is what tends to remove the function of the Canonists, which was a *hermeneutic* one: they had to interpret the bearing of doctrine, doctrinal writings and papal decrees upon the practical life of the Church. This was why their function was more than that of simply preaching the word or theologically expounding it according to its correct literal sense (to which Ockham now reduced Biblical exegesis). But within Ockham's perspective, the theological–juridical task must end at this point of mere declaration of the divinely revealed will. Beyond the exposition of the *ius poli* lies the *ius fori* of human law. Yet the latter, given Ockham's social metaphysics, concerns merely the upholding of positive conventions. Hence human law is thoroughly secularised: even within the Church there is no *participation* in divine wisdom through legal enactment. This means that all the relatively worldly aspects of church life – regarding property and the response to crime, for example – should fall under ordinary legal control. A spiritualised Church can have no rule for the ancient Canonic function.

Such a conclusion can be supported by a consideration that belongs to the 'second school of revision' with respect to historical theories of rupture in the understanding of *ius*. As Michel Bastit points out, canonical legal practice continued to work under older philosophical assumptions, uninflected by nominalism, until at least the sixteenth century.[66] When *ius* started to take on a more liberal subjective meaning beyond that point, one of the two decisive influences at work (the other being neo-Stoicism) was indeed theological, *rather than* canonical. And this theological influence unquestionably had its roots in Franciscan tradition, whose social metaphysics was brought to an extreme point of development in Ockham's writings.

One can add to this analysis four further ways in which Ockham's political theory was, *contra* Tierney, definitely informed by his metaphysical positions. First, in direct accordance with his nominalism, he denies in the *Opus nonaginta dierum* that a group of persons forms any more than a merely fictional unity: it is a sheer aggregate of *multi homines congregati in unum*.[67] From this it follows, in keeping with Duns Scotus, that

---

[65] Villey, *La formation*, 233.

[66] Michel Bastit, 'Michel Villey et les ambiguités d'Occam'.

[67] Bastit 'Michel Villey et les ambiguités d'Occam'; William of Ockham, *Opus nonaginta dierum*, in *Opera Politica*, vol. I, (ed.) H.S. Offler (Manchester University Press, 1956), 366.

political society emerged only after the Fall through divinely permitted artificial establishment. In direct anticipation of Rousseau even more than Hobbes, Ockham considered that, under a lapsarian dispensation, all power was consensually transferred to an absolutely sovereign centre which then accorded a right of 'licit usage' to the prior factuality of private property. Given the sheer fictionality of the human legal sphere, it became possible, as we have seen, for the Franciscans to claim abstinence from involvement in it, and to exercise a simple *usus facti* of things, even though this claim in itself had to be recognised and authorised by the Pope as a kind of right, in a shadowy sort of simulacrum of the political process.

Under this nominalist dispensation, the mediation of material things has ceased to carry juridical weight. This accords with a typical position of Franciscan metaphysics, also assumed by Ockham, and which provides a second additional point of metaphysical–political linkage in his thought. For many Franciscan thinkers, including Duns Scotus, unlike for Aristotle and Aquinas, matter possessed a 'quasi-form' independently of its shaping by spiritual form itself. This drastic qualification of hylomorphism allowed one to think of 'merely material' things whose form was fluid and in consequence detached from any intrinsic value or purpose.[68] These things were already objects and paradigmatically objects of possession. Hence the Franciscans might 'use things' without forming any bond of shaped, formal attachment to them, while the ephemerality of this usage falls short of any true seizure of a material thing which would take full advantage of its proferred 'objectivity'.

Here we come to the third, additional point of connection between Ockham's metaphysics and his politics. For the usual Papal, canonical and Dominican outlook, the use of something (whether 'using something up' like food or money, or using something replenishable like land) was a continuous process in time involving an action defined by its teleological completion (e.g. nourishment of the body, purchase of goods or alternatively the farming of a piece of owned or rented property). In consequence *usus* involves a certain distinct connectedness of person with an inherently purposeful thing which, if this link be licit, one has to describe in terms of ownership, of whatever kind. But for Ockham, who regarded time nominalistically as but a sequence of isolated moments, one can consider the act of using a now non-teleologically inflected *res* in punctual fashion, free from any continuity or teleology. Hence its licitness is not derived from the end in view, which must fall within a pattern of

---

[68] Bastit, 'Michel Villey et les ambiguités d'Occam', 71.

communal distribution, but rather from its instantiation of a pre-existing natural potential – for example, to eat or to dominate and defend a segment of the earth.[69] This natural power of appropriation can then be authorised as *unqualified* ownership – the right to do what one one likes with one's own, irrespective of communal ends. Here lies the overdetermination of factual ownership by rightful use. In other words, since legal possession is merely an enacted fiction, one can allow the purely punctual Franciscan use without possession that is regarded as having no sequentiality, no teleology and no co-determination within a network of human relationships.

Fourthly, Ockham subscribed to the Franciscan notion of a charity exercised by a will sundered from reason. This is a more unilateral, less reciprocal and 'bonding' conception of charity which tended to become instrumentalised as 'discipline' and eventually encouraged the rise of the biopolitical control of populations by an absolutely sovereign state.[70] A utilitarian 'do-gooding' is an eventual upshot of the Franciscan bias in ethical ontology.

Failure to appreciate these subtle points of continuity between Ockham's metaphysics and his politics is less the result of supposed scholarly rigour than of a certain metaphysical 'tone-deafness' of the modern (but not the authentic) Anglo-Saxon mentality.[71]

The historical case linking nominalism–voluntarism and modern subjective rights can still therefore stand. Ockham was the first to make fully explicit what had previously been but partially sketched out in earlier Franciscan theory.

The meaning of 'right' today

The above reflections indicate that we should also take seriously Michel Villey's hesitancy in the face of contemporary talk of 'human rights'. Their buried foundation lies in a questionable theological voluntarism and a questionably atomising metaphysic. In either case the same logic upholds both the absolute negative liberty of the individual and the

---

[69] Bastit, 'Michel Villey et les ambiguités d'Occam'; Ockham, *Opus nonaginta dierum*, vol. II, (ed.) Offler (Manchester University Press, 1956), 573, 586.

[70] See Pierre Rousselot, *The Problem of Love in the Middle Ages*, (trans.) Alan Vincelette (Milwaukee,Wis.: Marquette University Press, 2006), 155–211; Michel Foucault, *The Birth of Biopolitics*, (trans.) Graham Burchell (London: PalgraveMacmillan, 2008).

[71] I strongly agree with the intuition of thinkers like Coleridge, Newman, Ruskin and Chesterton that the true English spirit has for many reasons been suppressed. It is far more shown in English literature than in English philosophy, which is often much more *philosophically* sophisticated.

unrestricted formally grounded power of the sovereign political power. And only the latter can render the former *operable*, only the latter can effectuate positively the supposedly 'natural' character of rights, whether this naturalness is taken to be 'Fallen' (Ockham) or innocent (Rousseau).

However, the current *internationalising* of the idea of 'subjective right', so that it becomes more emphatically 'human right', can appear to obscure this biopolitical duality. Samuel Moyn has rightly pointed out that this development is both recent and a relative rupture with the discourse of rights since the seventeenth century, for which their very possibility was reliant upon an equal espousal of absolute state sovereignty.[72] Therefore to speak of sheerly 'human rights' as a matter of entirely pre-political natural law would seem at once to break with both the pessimistically realist and the optimistically civic–republican (Rousseau) versions of modern rights-talk in a newly cosmopolitan utopian direction and to detach the individual from the state, besides the *bios* from the *politeia*.

Moyn, however, for all the bracing stringency of his historical analysis, seems somewhat to play down the natural rather than the political side of subjective rights, especially in the case of the Lockean legacy. Conversely, he underestimates the political side of the new international human rights discourse. Surely the rise of the latter is co-terminous with the era of neo-liberalism, even where it poses as a negative and essentially individualist reaction against its ravages? Neo-liberalism can be said, in the shortest possible summary, to involve both an anarchic new reach of the global market outside political processes and yet, at the same time, the rise of 'the market state' which redefines the political in terms of meeting the wishes of citizens as consumers.

In the first case it can be said that human rights are not just a 'utopian project' to the degree that possessive individualism, on which subjective rights are predicated, is a philosophical pre-condition for the operation of the supposedly free, capitalist market. Hence if human rights may appear to be newly a-political, they are certainly not an-economic.

In the second case it can be said that the new 'economic anarchy' nonetheless continues to require the consent of the various national laws and their recent processes of deregulation of finance, restrictions of the rights of labour, etc. In this way 'the market state' itself involves the gradual build-up of a tacit international capitalist polity which encourages and permits individual liberty to the degree that accords with its purposes, but is also corrosive of democracy and of all free associating

[72] Samuel Moyn, *The Last Utopia: Human Rights in History* (Cambridge, Mass.: Harvard University Press, 2010).

around any sort of 'thick', non-abstract identity or purpose. Seen in this context, human rights remain tied to the political – it is just that the political is internationalising itself, moving (unpredictably and problematically) beyond its nation-state idiom. But if the 'market state' has thereby broken with the politics of the Romantic era, it has also reverted, though in a new way, to a seventeenth-century political idiom, which, as we have seen, has older roots in a Franciscan Middle Ages.

Let us hope then that soon we can revive doctrines of objective *ius* that will better protect, and also help to discriminate and mediate between those various more-or-less good causes of human dignity and freedom of action which we now try to protect through incoherent notions of 'human rights'. Then, perhaps, the Dominican Middle Ages of just partition related to the architectonics of virtuous usage can resume its quest for an alternative modernity that can retrieve, and repeat differently, the authentic legacy of the west which is Christian and equitably egalitarian rather than simply 'emancipatory' (from *everything* positive, towards the void . . .). Without this retrieval, as I tried to suggest in the first section of this chapter, it could well be that the cause of the West, in secular time, might be lost.

4   Religious faith and human rights

Rowan Williams

Twenty-seven years ago, Alasdair MacIntyre in his seminal work on the foundations of moral discourse, *After Virtue*, declared that human rights did not exist. 'Rights which are alleged to belong to human beings as such and which are cited as a reason for holding that people ought not to be interfered with in their pursuit of life, liberty and happiness' are a fiction: 'there are', he says, 'no such rights, and belief in them is one with belief in witches and in unicorns'.[1] The language of rights emerges, MacIntyre argues, at a time when people need a fresh moral compass in the wake of the dissolution of much traditional morality; like the concept of 'utility', which is another characteristic notion developed in the modern period as a touchstone for moral decision, the idea of 'rights' is meant to act as a trump in moral argument. The trouble is, MacIntyre argues, that rights and utility do not get along very well together in argument: one is essentially about the claims of the individual, the other about the priorities of administration. The result is the familiar modern standoff between the individual and the bureaucratic state. The state is both the guarantor of rights – more clearly than ever with the emergence of the 'market state' in which the most important reason for recognising the legitimacy of a state is its ability to maximise your choices, as Philip Bobbitt has demonstrated[2] – and the authority that claims the right to assess and on occasion overrule individual liberties. Hence the tension between the state and civil society which has been so explosive a theme in twentieth-century politics. The lack of mediating concepts to deal with this tension was identified by Hannah Arendt, echoed more recently by Gillian Rose, as one of the roots of totalitarianism.[3] But Rose notes also

---

[1] Alasdair MacIntyre, *After Virtue: A Study in Moral Theory* (London, Duckworth, 1981), 66–67.

[2] See Philip Bobbitt, *The Shield of Achilles: War, Peace and the Course of History* (London, Allen Lane, 2002), esp. Book I, Part III.

[3] Among Rose's many difficult and essential essays, 'Athens and Jerusalem: A Tale of Three Cities' and 'The Comedy of Hegel and the *Trauerspiel* of Modern Philosophy', in *Mourning Becomes the Law: Philosophy and Representation* (Cambridge University Press, 1996), are a good place to start.

the same problem identified by MacIntyre, the way in which the stand-off between rights and utility leaves the path open to an exclusively *managerial* account of political life, in which 'expertise' about process is allowed to short-circuit proper discussions of corporate human goals.

MacIntyre's point is not, therefore, to deny the reality of human rights in the name of some kind of absolutism; quite the contrary. He is anxious that the language of rights and the language of utility are, as typically used in the modern world, no more than assertion – stop-gap notions to avoid complete relativism in public morality. This is one of the undoubted complexities in contemporary discussion of rights. On the one hand, 'human rights' is habitually used as a discussion-stopper, as the way in which we speak about aspects of social morality that are not up for negotiation or compromise. 'Human rights abuses' are widely seen as the most damaging weaknesses in a state's claim to legitimacy, and in extreme cases may be used as part of an argument for direct intervention by other states. On the other hand, what is often discussed in connection with both the Universal Declaration of Human Rights and the specifics of current human rights legislation is in fact a hybrid mass of claims to be decided by the state through its legislative apparatus; it is a quintessentially bureaucratic or managerial business, weighing various supposed entitlements against each other. If we speak without qualification of the right to life, the right to a fair trial, the right to raise a family and the right to a paid holiday under exactly the same rubric, it is very hard to see how this language can plausibly be understood as dealing with moral foundations. Fundamental issues blend with reasonable contractual expectations in a confusing way, and the idea of a list of entitlements dropped, as it were, into the cradle of each individual is deeply vulnerable to the charge of arbitrariness. MacIntyre's scepticism is well placed.

But if we are to salvage something from this, what do we need? Salvaging is important, if only for the reason that, if the language of rights is indeed the only generally intelligible way in modern political ethics of decisively challenging the positive authority of the state to do what it pleases, the only way of expressing how the state is itself under law, then this language needs to be as robust as it can be. In this chapter, I want to propose two ways in which a particular religious tradition may offer resources for grounding the discourse. There is now an abundant literature on religion and human rights, and a certain feeling in some quarters that there is a tension between rights and religious belief. It has been a good deal discussed in the context of Muslim critiques of the Universal Declaration, but Christian theologians have also voiced some unease about a scheme of ideas that places claims ahead of duties or even dignity. But I do not believe that this supposed tension is as serious as it is made out to be – so long, that is, as there is some recognition that rights have to be more than pure assertion or, as some would now have it, necessary fictions to secure a maximal degree of social harmony.

As Roger Ruston has argued in a very important study of the development of rights language,[4] the idea of irreducible or non-negotiable liberties for human beings has a strong theological basis in medieval thought. Paradoxically, it is in part the result of Christianity's confused and uneasy relationship with the institution of slavery. As is often pointed out, slavery as such is not condemned in Scripture, and is taken for granted – with varying degrees of regret – as an unavoidable social institution by most if not all Christian thinkers of the first millennium and a half of Christian history. However, from the first, the Christian community included both slaves and slave-owners; the Letter to the Ephesians in the New Testament touches briefly on their relationship (6.5–9), as does the First Letter of Peter (2.13–25). The slave must give service as if freely to the Christian slave-owner, not as a response to compulsion, and being willing to serve the harsh master as willingly as the kind one; and the slave-owner must remember that s/he and the slave are alike bound in 'slavery' to one master. This last point relates to a passing remark made by St Paul in Romans 14.4 about refraining from judging another believer: you are not entitled to assess the satisfactoriness of the behaviour of someone else's slave.

The point is that the slave-owner's relationship to the slave is severely complicated by the baptismal relationship. The slave is no longer simply the property of the master or mistress, but 'belongs' to the one divine Master and is ultimately answerable to him, in exactly the same way as is the Christian slave-owner. As the Christian community develops and reflection about these issues continues, some implications are tentatively spelled out. In a world in which the slave-owner had powers of life and death over the slave, the Church determines that it is sinful to kill a slave (though the penitential tariff for this does not seem appropriately high to a modern reader). In a context where the slave-owner was assumed to have unlimited sexual access to slaves, sex with a slave is treated on the same basis as any other sexual misdemeanour; and marriage between a slave and a free person is recognised by the Church.

Stoic writers like Seneca had made it a commonplace that the master had no power over the mind of the slave; but no philosopher attempts to limit what ownership of the body might entail. The Christian attempt to think through the implications of slave and slave-owner as equal members of the same community inevitably qualified what could be said

---

[4] Ruston, *Human Rights and the Image of God* (Oxford University Press, 2004).

about absolute ownership, and offered minimal but real protection to the body of the slave. So it is not surprising that Thomas Aquinas, discussing the limits of obedience to earthly masters or sovereigns,[5] says explicitly that while 'a human being is bound to obey another in matters external to the body, in those things that affect the nature of the body, no one is bound to obey another human being, but to obey God alone – for instance, in matters to do with the body's sustenance or the begetting of children'. A slave cannot be commanded – for example – to starve to death; nor can he or she be prohibited from deciding on marriage or celibacy.

The principle that has been established is that the human body cannot in the Christian scheme of things be regarded as an item of property. It is not just that I have an 'ownership' of my body that is not transferable, though some moralists (including a few recent Christian writers) have tried to argue something like this; it is rather that the whole idea of ownership is inappropriate. I may talk about 'my body' in a phrase that parallels 'my house' or 'my car', but it should be obvious that there is a radical difference. I can't change it for another, I can't acquire more than one of it, I cannot survive the loss of it. The body – and this is where Aquinas and the tradition associated with him significantly refuses to accept a separation of 'soul' and 'body' as entities existing side by side – is the organ of the soul's meaning: it is the medium in which the conscious subject communicates, and there is no communication without it. To protect the body, to love the body, is to seek to sustain the means of communication which secure a place within human discourse. And so a claim to control the body absolutely, to the point where you could be commanded to deny your body what is needed for its life, would be a refusal to allow another to communicate, to make sense of themselves. The ultimate form of slavery would be a situation in which your body was made to carry the meanings or messages of another subject and never permitted to *say* in word or gesture what was distinctive for itself as the embodiment of a sense-making consciousness.

My own relation to my body is not that of an owner to an object; and to recognise another material thing as a human body is to recognise that it is not reducible in this way to an object among others. In that it is a means of communication, it cannot be simply instrumental to another's will or

---

[5] *Summa Theologiae* IIaIIae 104.5. Aquinas does not begin from a blank slate. For an excellent recent discussion of the implications of Christian teaching for the practice of slavery, see David Hart, *Atheist Delusions: The Christian Revolution and its Fashionable Enemies* (New Haven, Conn.: Yale University Press, 2009), particularly 77–81 on a significant sermon by the fourth-century bishop and philosopher, Gregory of Nyssa.

purpose. It is significant that Aquinas uses the examples he does. The nurture of the body is, for humans, more than an instinctive business; it requires thought and a measure of liberty. And the sexual involvement or non-involvement of the body is a primary locus for the making of sense; denial of this liberty is the denial of something absolutely fundamental (which is why sexual abuse is indeed a prime instance of rights being violated, the body becoming an instrument for someone else's 'meanings', a tool for the construction of another person's sense-making). The recognition of a body as a human body is, in this framework, the foundation of recognising the rights of another; and to recognise a body as a human body is to recognise that it is a vehicle of communication. It is not a recondite point. The state of mind in which someone is unable to grasp that another's body is a site of feeling and so of consciousness and so of communication is routinely regarded as seriously distorted, whether we are talking of the difficulties of the extreme end of the autism spectrum or of the plainly psychotic. Our ordinary human interchange simply and straightforwardly depends upon understanding any apparently human body we encounter as in some sense a potential communicator with me. And when in the past people have sought to justify slavery or other forms of institutionalised dehumanising, it has been necessary to restrict, often expensively and dramatically, their opportunity to communicate and to belittle their ability to do so. In George Steiner's extraordinary story 'The Portage to San Cristobal of A.H.', in which a group of Jewish agents have been given the task of kidnapping an aged Hitler from his South American hideaway, they are strictly instructed not to allow him to speak to them, because that will force them to see him as a human like themselves.[6]

One advantage of putting the issue in these terms is that it takes us away from the more unhelpful aspects of those rights theories that stress the grounding of rights in human dignity but then associate human dignity with a particular set of capacities. The danger of these is that, by trying to identify a list of essential capacities, it becomes possible to identify criteria according to which full claims to human rights may be granted or withheld. The right of the imperfectly rational person – whether the child or the person with mental disabilities – may be put in question if we stipulate a capacity for reasoned self-consciousness as a condition for acknowledging rights. And to speak of the right of the body as such casts a different light on the sensitive issue of the right of the unborn; the unanswerable question of when embryonic material becomes a 'person',

---

[6] In George Steiner, *The Deeps of the Sea and Other Fictions* (London, Faber, 1996).

let alone when it acquires a soul, still assumes a basic dualism about the body and its inhabitant or proprietor – whereas the way in which we ought to be framing the question is in terms of what counts as bodily continuity and what can be said about the 'communicative' dimension of the organic life of the unborn; how even the foetus requires to be seen and understood as expressing something to us in its character as an individual material human organism.

But that is a complex set of arguments, and my aim for now is simply to establish that recognising the human body as a human body, that is as a system of communication, by no means exclusively rational, let alone verbal, is fundamental for understanding why we should want to speak of rights at all, of equal liberties that are rooted in the liberty to 'make sense', that is to engage in communication. As I have said, it is in one way only to spell out the act of faith we make every time we engage in human communication at all. Yet behind that routine act lies something else, given that many human societies have in practice assumed that some human bodies are not worth communicating with or receiving communication from. Hence the point of excavating the theological insights that have moved us irreversibly in the direction that leads towards universal doctrines of right. Grasping that the body cannot be an item of property is one of the things that is established by the Christian doctrine of communion in Christ and shared obedience to Christ. The doctrine affirms that the body of every other individual is related to its maker and saviour before it is related to any human system of power. This in turn implies that there is a level of human identity or selfhood that cannot be taken over by any other person's will – a level of human identity both bodily and subjective or interior. And this belongs with the recognition that the body *speaks*, that it is the way I make myself present to myself and to others. This holds true even for the most inarticulate, or those whose communications are hardest to decode: to put it as vividly as I can, they still have *faces*. Over against those who want to locate human dignity in the distinctive structure of the human self, a position which still skirts the risks of setting *conditions* for dignity, I want to propose that the character of the body as the vehicle of language is what is basic here.

Michael Zuckert, in a careful and interesting essay on 'Human Dignity and the Basis of Justice' in a special issue of *The Hedgehog Review* (2007)[7] makes a strong case for beginning from the character of the self as a mental structure allowing human beings to understand themselves as

---

[7] *The Hedgehog Review*, 9.3 (special issue on Human Dignity and Justice, Fall 2007), 32–48.

agents with an identity that continues through time and a capacity for envisaging future situations as resulting from present decisions. This is surely what is most irreducibly unique about us, and thus what grounds a universal moral code. But I believe he weakens his case by speaking of the self – following Locke – as proprietor of its experiences: 'The relation of the rights-bearer to his property is remarkably parallel to his relation to his self.'[8] The embodied self as communicator, I suggest, is more than the self-conscious organiser of experience into patterns of continuity through time, past and future; it can survive the absence of this sort of self-awareness without forfeiting its claim to be treated as possessed of equal liberty in the basic sense defined earlier. Given the much-chronicled history of the abuse, psychological, physical and sexual, of the mentally challenged, of small children or of sufferers from dementia, it is crucial to clarify our grounds for regarding them as protected from being made the carriers of the desires and purposes of others; if we begin from the recognition of them as embodied in the same sense that we are, we have such a clear foundation, in a way that I am not sure we can have even on so sophisticated a version of capacity theory as Zuckert's.

If this is correct, the irreducible core of human rights is the liberty to make sense as a bodily subject; which means that the inviolability of the body itself is where we should start in thinking about rights. 'Man is "created equal"', wrote the poet and artist David Jones in the early 1940s, 'in the sense that all men belong to a form-creating group of creatures – and all men have unalienable rights with respect to that equal birthright';[9] and that form-creating character is anchored most simply and primitively in the character of what we mean by the very notion of a body (as opposed to an object). It is true, of course, that while the sort of Christian thinking represented by Thomas Aquinas laid the foundations for this, it still accepted extreme physical punishment, including death, for transgression, and of course did not understand the necessary freedom to determine the pattern of one's sexual life as a charter for everyone to shape their own destinies irrespective of the Church's teaching. The implications of Aquinas' view still allow the state to say that it will limit the bodily freedom of some of its citizens when that freedom threatens the freedom of others – though, centuries on from Aquinas, we have taken on board more fully the need for punishment both to respect the essential physical dignity of the punished, and to be capable of rational communication to the punished. The basic concept of right with which Aquinas works itself puts in question capital punishment or humiliating

---

[8] Ibid., 47.
[9] David Jones, *Epoch and Artist. Selected Writings* (London, Faber, 1959), 90.

and damaging physical penalties. It is what grounds the modern refusal of legitimacy to torture, degrading or humiliating punishment or even indefinite detention without charge; significant markers in the age of Guantánamo or Abu Ghraib, and at least a significant part of the argument about the time limits for detention regularly discussed in the UK legislature. Likewise, this view allows the Church to say that there is a limit on morally acceptable options for sexual life; although we would not now understand this as licensing a restriction by law on the decisions people may make in this area. We are free to make bad or inadequate sense of our bodily lives, and the legal restriction of this, beyond the obvious protections of the vulnerable, would have to be seen as outside the powers of rulers. If the state legislates against sexual violence and abuse, as it must, it is because of the recognition that this is an area in which the liberty to make sense of or with one's own body is most often put at risk by predatory behaviour on the part of others.

So: equal liberty is at root inseparable from the equality of being embodied. Rights belong not to the person who can demonstrate capacity or rationality but to any organism that can be recognised as a human body, at any stage of its organic development. If the body cannot be property, it will always be carrying meanings or messages that are inalienably its own. And this opens up the second area in which aspects of Christian theology offer a foundation for a discourse of universal rights. Thus far, the emphasis has been upon the view from within, as it were – the body as carrier of the soul's meaning, the body as 'formed', given intelligible shape, by the continuing self called into being by God. But the process by which the body realises its communicative nature, by which it becomes concretely and actively a locus of meaning is a process in which the body *receives* and digests communication. The individual communicates meaningfully when s/he is decoding and responding to the meanings that are present to him or her; the full development of the particular body's freedom to communicate is realised in the process of understanding and managing and responding to the communications that are being received.

The human other is thus essential to my own growth as a communicative being, a bearer of meaningful messages that cannot be silenced; my own liberty not to be silenced, not to have my body reduced to someone else's instrument, is nourished by the equal liberty of the other not to be silenced. And, in the framework we have been using, this is identified as the central feature of the community created by the Christian gospel. Slave and owner are not merely bound to a common divine Master, they are bound in a relation of mutuality according to which each becomes the bearer of necessary gifts to the other. The relation of each to the Master is such that each is given some unique contribution to the common life, so that no one member of the community is able fully to realise their calling and their possibilities without every other. Not killing or not abusing the slave is for the slave-owner the necessary implication of recognising that the slave is going to be his or her benefactor in ways that may never be visible or obvious but are nonetheless vital.

The dignity accorded to the human other is not, then, a recognition that they may be better than they seem, but simply a recognition that what they have to say (welcome or unwelcome, intelligible or unintelligible, convergent or divergent) could in certain circumstances be the gift of God. Not every human other is a fellow-member of the Body of Christ in the Biblical sense; but the universal command to preach the gospel to all prohibits any conclusion that this or that person is incapable of ever hearing and answering God's invitation, and therefore mandates an attitude of receptivity towards them. Not silencing the other or forcing their communication into your own agenda is part of remaining open to the communication of God – which may come even through the human other who is most repellent or opaque to sympathy. The recognition of a dignity that grounds the right to be heard is the recognition of my own need to receive as fully as I can what is being communicated to me by another being made by God. It compels that stepping back from control or manipulation of the other that we so often seek for our security, so as to hear what we cannot generate for ourselves. And it should be clear, incidentally, that this is an argument that also grounds whatever we might want to say about the 'right' of the non-human world to have an integrity not wholly at the mercy of human planning.

To found human rights on the body's liberty to express its own message and the need for all embodied human beings to receive each other's meaningful communication in order for them to be who and what they are removes from the argument those elements of conditionality which can creep in if we speak too glibly about capacities, whether rational or moral. Nicholas Wolterstorff, in the special issue of *The Hedgehog Review* already quoted, notes the way in which some other contributors insist that the discourse of human rights and dignity expresses simply 'an explication of what it is to treat humans as humans'; but he very reasonably goes on to ask why in particular circumstances I should treat *this* human being as a human being, if, for example, I conclude that s/he is a poor or inadequate specimen of humanity. If the appeal to treating humans as humans is not to be purely assertive or tautologous, we need more.[10] Something related

---

[10] *The Hedgehog Review*, 9.3, 68–69.

to language about the image of God seems called for – but we need also to be aware that this language cannot just be 'mentioned' as if it instantly provided a clear rationale for rights as we understand them.[11]

My purpose in these reflections has been to suggest precisely what might be involved in doing more than 'mentioning' the Biblical themes. Is this, then, to argue that we simply cannot talk about human rights intelligibly if we do not have a religious or even a Christian foundation for doing so? Given that there is already more than one essay in grounding human rights in traditions other than Christianity (Abdulaziz Sachedina's work is a case in point, as seen in his contribution to *The Hedgehog Review* symposium already quoted), it may be rash to make excessive claims for Christianity here. But the fact is that the question of foundations for the discourse of non-negotiable rights is not one that lends itself to simple resolution in secular terms; so it is not at all odd if diverse ways of framing this question in religious terms flourish so persistently. The uncomfortable truth is that a purely secular account of human rights is always going to be problematic if it attempts to establish the language of rights as a supreme and non-contestable governing concept in ethics. MacIntyre's argument, with which we began, alerts us to the anxiety and the tension that is hidden within the classical Enlightenment discourse of rights, the sense of having to manage the effects of a moral bereavement; and the development of that discourse in the ways we have witnessed in the late twentieth century does little to diminish the anxiety or resolve the tension. The question of whether there is anything at all that is quite strictly non-negotiable about human dignity – whether, for example, we might be permitted to revisit the consensus about torture when faced with the 'captured terrorist and ticking bomb' scenario beloved of some political ethicists – is not academic. Our instinct seems to be that something has to be secured over against the claims of *raison d'état* in the name of a common human 'culture' of mutual recognition intuited as beyond choice and convenience.

Sabina Lovibond, in her brilliant essay on *Realism and Imagination in Ethics*[12] has some pertinent reflections on Wittgenstein's remark that 'justification comes to an end' – i.e. that there comes a point where we have to stop arguing and accept that we have reached a level that is recognised as basic for any kind of human thinking. 'Justification', producing reasons for doing this rather than that, comes to an end, she argues, 'not because we get bored with it, but because rational discourse unfolds within a setting not chosen by ourselves' – a setting which she,

[11] Ibid., 65.
[12] Sabina Lovibond, *Realism and Imagination in Ethics* (Oxford, Blackwell, 1983).

with both Wittgenstein and Hegel, associates with the fact of embodiment.[13] When we grasp that our embodied state is the condition of everything else we might want to say about thinking in general and ethics in particular, we have arrived at the point where it no longer makes sense to ask for 'justification'. To speak of non-negotiable rights is to attempt some explication of this 'not chosen' dimension of our reality. And to be able to assess or even prioritise the wildly varied entitlements that are currently called 'rights' means developing some means of seeing how far – in a specific social context – this or that claimed entitlement reflects what is required for participation in the human conversation as such; how far it is inseparable from the imperative to allow the body the liberty to say what it means to say. We may, for instance, feel instinctively that the right to a paid vacation belongs to a different order from the right to fair trial; yet in certain economic conditions, guaranteed freedom for leisure is an intelligible aspect of possessing adequate bodily/ communicative liberty.

The idea of a pattern of embodied interaction in which every body, literally, is equipped to 'say' what it has in it to say, in intelligible exchange (which means more than a chorus of individual self-expressions) – this is, for Lovibond, the heart of an ethic that can seriously claim universality and objectivity, 'realism'. I would only add that, while this is an absolutely accurate account of the formal shape of a universal ethic – and thus one that can do justice to the language of inalienable right – it still leaves some unfinished business. I have interpreted the New Testament texts about slavery so as to suggest that the recognition that it is impossible to own a human body is rooted not only in the recognition of how the body works as a communicative organism but in the conviction that the bare fact of embodied reality 'encodes' a gift to be offered by each to all, a primitive communication by the creator; the inviolability of the body is ultimately grounded in the prior relation of each embodied subject to God. And, as I have hinted here, this has some application for the rest of the material order as well.

Political and legal philosophy is unlikely to arrive at complete convergence with theology in any imaginable future; but the way in which a theology may propose a frame for political and legal questions is not the less important for that. The theological perspective as I have tried to outline it here is – at least – a way of insisting that we should not pretend that the discourse of universal ethics and inalienable right has a firmer foundation than it actually has. If the Enlightenment has left us in some

---

[13] Ibid., 215.

measure bereaved, it is important to accept that, and to ask what are the most secure foundations that can still be laid for our universalist aspirations. We should beware of looking for easy refuge in bare assertion or brisk functionalism about rights: but it is also important to grasp that universalism itself is not a simple and self-evident idea and that there are various ways of conceiving it outside the strict Enlightenment framework. Among those ways will be the various religious modes of imagining universal destiny or equal human dignity. These, I suggest, need to be engaged with, rather than dismissed as irrational or regressive. It may be that the most important service that can be offered by religious commitment where human rights are concerned is to prevent any overlooking of the issue of how to establish a 'non-negotiable' foundation for the whole discourse. As in other areas of political or social thinking, theology is one of those elements that continue to pose questions about the legitimacy of what is said and done in society, about the foundations of law itself. The secularist may not have an answer and may not be convinced that the religious believer has an answer that can be generally accepted; but our discussion of social and political ethics will be a great deal poorer if we cannot acknowledge the force of the question.

© Rowan Williams, Magdalene College, Cambridge.

Part II

Law, rights and revolution

5   Philosophy and the right to resistance

Costas Douzinas

The end of history and the dawn of a 'new world order' was announced in 1989. If it was a 'new' order, it was the shortest in history. It came to an abrupt end in 2010. Protest, riots and uprisings have erupted all over the world, both in authoritarian and in democratic places.[1] Neither the mainstream nor the radicals had predicted the wave. This has led to a frantic search for historical precedents and to hyperbolic comparisons. Paul Mason reports that a former director of Britain's Secret Intelligence Service thought that 'it's a revolutionary wave, like 1848'.[2] Mason agrees: 'There are strong parallels – above all with 1848, and with the wave of discontent that preceded 1914.'[3] Alain Badiou diagnoses a 'rebirth of history' in a new age of 'riots and uprisings' that may bring the 'intervallic' period that follows major revolutionary upheavals to an end. In the intervallic period, the revolutionary idea is 'dormant'.[4] For Badiou, this earlier period closed after May 1968, the religious turn of the Iranian revolution and the end of the Chinese cultural revolution. The interval is coming to an end. Resistance and revolution are in the air. What causes their cyclical return? This chapter examines philosophy's hesitant exploration of the link between revolution and right. Can philosophy explain the eternal return of resistance despite law's persistent attempt to ban it?

If for Kant Enlightenment is 'man's emergence from his self-incurred immaturity', an immaturity caused by 'lack of resolution and courage', revolution is the condition of modernity and the autonomous individual its foundation.[5] Political revolutions have determined modernity's history; science and technology are in permanent upheaval; the artistic avant-garde

---

[1] Costas Douzinas, *Philosophy and Resistance in the Crisis* (Cambridge, Polity, 2013).

[2] Quoted in Paul Mason, *Why it's Kicking off Everywhere: The New Global Revolutions* (London, Verso, 2012), 65.

[3] Ibid.

[4] Alain Badiou, *The Rebirth of History: Times of Riots and Uprisings* (London, Verso, 2012), 38.

[5] Immanuel Kant, 'What is Enlightenment?', in *Political Writings*, H. S. Reiss, (ed.) (Cambridge University Press, 1991), 54.

keeps revolting and re-defining the *Zeitgeist*. Philosophy has dealt extensively with revolution and right. But the relationship between the two has
been rather superficially examined.

Let me start with a clarification of the relationship between resistance
and revolution. Most revolutions start with acts of individual disobedience, followed by collective resistance and insurrectional activities; a
multitude with common political purpose takes to the streets and persists
despite attacks by the forces of 'law and order'. We define 'resistance' as
mass popular action, which rejects and challenges ideologies and structures of power supporting domination or oppression.[6] Whether it results
in radical socio-political change – the formal definition of a successful
revolution – depends on the balance of forces, the existence of a political
subject prepared to take power and on contingent events. Individual
disobedience, collective resistance and revolution form an uneven
continuum. Irrespective of outcome, the emotional, physical and normative pressure people feel when they stand up to power are similar even
though the form and outcome of action may differ.

Revolution was all the rage in the twentieth century and dominated
philosophical debates. Recently, legal philosophers and judges have
extensively debated acts of civil disobedience.[7] Resistance precedes
revolution; but normative considerations rarely distinguish between the
two. Generally speaking, the duty to obey the law is absolute only when
accompanied by a free judgement that the law is morally right and
democratically legitimate. The autonomous citizen does not just obey
the law; she also judges the 'legitimacy' of the law and its relationship with
justice. If that was not the case, Hannah Arendt sarcastically comments,
Kant's categorical imperative would read: 'Act as if the principle of your
actions were the same as that of the legislator or of the law of the land.'
It would be the perfect maxim 'for the household use of the little man'.[8]
This is of course the *credo* of legal positivists, passive citizens and failed
governments.

The right to revolution is a strange right and a cause of philosophical
embarrassment. Let us take a brief tour through its landmark philosophical examinations. The liberal John Locke supported a limited right to
revolution based on the right to property. Private property rests on the
natural possession of our properties (body and labour). 'The reason why

---

[6] Jocelyn Hollander and Rachel Einwohner, 'Conceptualizing Resistance', *Sociological
Forum*, 19(4) (2004), 533–552. A companion piece to the current article discussing the
legal aspects of the topic and entitled 'Is there a Legal Right to Resistance?' is forthcoming.
[7] Costas Douzinas, *Philosophy and Resistance*, Chapters 5 and 6.
[8] Hannah Arendt, *Eichmann in Jerusalem: A Report on the Banality of Evil* (London:
Penguin, 1994), 136.

men enter into society is the preservation of their property.'[9] Property acts as a quasi-transcendental pre-condition of the socio-political order. It supplies the conceptual and material structure of constitution and law. Property was the first right and the model for all rights. As Michael Hardt and Antonio Negri have argued 'property, which is taken to be intrinsic to human thought and action, serves as the regulative idea for the constitutional state and the rule of law. This is not really a historical foundation but rather an ethical obligation, a constitutive form of the moral order.'[10] Locke was instrumental in this process. Attacks on property endanger not just individual rights but the order of the world and justify revolution. This 'appeal to Heaven', as Locke calls the revolution, becomes active, for example, when the legislature plans 'to invade the property of the subject, and to make themselves, or any part of the community, masters, or arbitrary disposers of the lives, liberties or fortunes of people'.[11] The people have the right to create 'a new legislative, when their legislators have acted contrary to their trust, by invading their property'.[12]

But only the propertied possess this right. As C. B. Macpherson puts it, 'it does not seem to cross [Locke's] mind here that the labouring class might have the right to make revolution ... The labouring class was an object of administration ... incapable of rational political action.'[13] The poor have no right to rebel in order to reduce their poverty or institute a society of equal or common property. As long as property is protected, Locke suspects and suspends the drive to revolt against the injustices of the world. In Illan Rua Wall's superb analysis of the 'withdrawal of the radical' from the tradition of human rights, Locke is pivotal. 'Locke's conception of the right to revolt is fundamentally prefigured by the question of property. This precondition sets property beyond the revolution.'[14]

Locke's right to revolution, which initially looked as a continuation of the medieval *jus resistentiae*, turns out to be a way for protecting property. According to Domenico Losurdo, the right to resistance is 'so little a recognition of a bottom-up initiative that, as far as the relationship between the people and the legislature, Locke not only denies the people

[9] John Locke, *Two Treatises on Government* (Cambridge University Press, 1988), vol. II, para. 222.
[10] Michael Hardt and Antonio Negri, *Commonwealth* (Cambridge, Mass., Harvard University Press, 2009), 7.
[11] Locke, *Two Treatises*, paras. 220 and 221.   [12] Ibid., para. 226.
[13] C. B. Macpherson, *The Political Theory of Possessive Individualism: Hobbes to Locke* (Oxford University Press, 1962), 224.
[14] Illan Rua Wall, *Human Rights and Constituent Power* (Abington, Routledge, 2012), 30. See Illan Rua Wall, 'On a Radical Politics for Human Rights', Chapter 6 in this volume.

any right to resistance, but even the right to abolish or modify, in structure or function, the Parliament'.[15] The philosophical justification of resistance is reactive and defensive, a limitation placed by law on attempts by the majority to restrict, regulate or tax property. The right to resistance turns out to be an insurance policy for the social order. In late modernity, property has become naturalised and passes as a commonsense about human nature. If for Locke revolution was invented in order to protect property, today revolution has been banned in order to keep it intact. This is why the right to resistance returns whenever wealth inequality and capitalist injustice come to the fore.

Edmund Burke answered Locke in his *Reflections on the Revolution in France*. The 1688 English revolution, Burke's model, unlike the French, was not an attempt to change polity. The glorious revolution was conservative, it preserved the organic nature and gradual evolution of the state. The revolutionaries did not abolish the monarchy and altered minimally the line of royal succession by settling for the Protestant line and upholding the pre-existing rights of the rulers represented in Parliament. The acceptance of William 'was not properly a *choice*; ... it was an act of *necessity*, in the strictest moral sense in which necessity can be taken'.[16] If for Locke, revolution is a right and a power of the propertied against the dangers of oppressive government, Burke's revolution is not a popular right but a correction, as a matter of 'grave and overruling necessity', of the King's breach of the 'original contract' with his subjects.[17] Its leaders realised historical necessity and acted as its representatives.

Locke and Burke represent opposed philosophical positions. For Locke, revolution expresses popular will against autocratic rulers who do not respect property rights. The American revolution was such a case. For Bourke, revolution consummates historical necessity and has little to do with individual or collective will. For both, however, the purpose of revolution is to protect the established order of property or monarchy. We must turn to Germany for a more radical version of (the right to) revolution.

Kant's paradox

German idealism welcomed the revolution. For Kant, Fichte, Schelling and Hegel, the French revolution was a sign of humanity's progress. It incarnated freedom into history and moved humanity to a higher level.

---

[15] Domenico Losurdo, *Hegel and the Freedom of the Moderns*, Marella and Jon Morris, (trans.) (Durham, Md., Duke University Press, 2004), 89.

[16] Edmund Burke, *Reflections on the Revolution in France* (London, J. Dodsley, M.DCC.XCI (1791), 24, emphasis in the original.

[17] Ibid., 39, 38.

At the same time, a combination of philosophical idealism and legal positivism led the Germans to reject the right to revolution. It would be a contradiction in terms, since no law or constitution can allow its own overthrow.

Nobles and lords had exercised regularly the medieval *jus resistentiae*, the right to resist and even rebel against Kings.[18] These rebellions removed usurpers or tyrants and returned legitimate rulers to the throne. Rebellions were justified by the violation of covenants and agreements between nobles and Kings or of legal limitations rulers had voluntarily accepted. The broad balance of forces between central and peripheral powers meant that feudal lords were able to enforce violated Kingly undertakings. The *jus resistentiae* was the legal gloss of a multi-polar world. Unlike classical *stasis*, however, medieval rebellions did not promote democratic rule. As Hannah Arendt put it, 'while the people might be admitted to have the right to decide who should *not* rule them, they certainly were not supposed to determine who *should*, and even less do we ever hear of a right of people to be their own rulers or to appoint persons from their own rank for the business of government'.[19]

The great revolutions changed that. The third estate or the 'common man' entered politics by revolting against the established social order of aristocratic and royal elites. The modern willing, acting subject and his rights could emerge only through revolution. The American and French Declarations, the manifestos of modernity, brought together, unsteadily and provisionally, the double source of right: equality and resistance: 'Men are born and remain free and equal in rights' states the first article of the French Declaration and adds that 'these rights are liberty, property, security and resistance to oppression'. Kant welcomed the American and French revolutions as well as the Irish resistance against the British. His revolutionary enthusiasm 'earned him the unenviable epithet "the old Jacobin"'.[20] It was even reputed that he was about to go to Paris to advise Abbé Sieyès. But while Kant retained his enthusiasm for the revolution, he went to great lengths to dismiss disobedience and the idea of a 'right to revolution'. 'All resistance against the supreme legislative power, all incitement of the subjects to violent expressions of discontent, all defiance which breaks out in rebellion, is the greatest and most punishable crime in a commonwealth, for it destroys its foundations.

---

[18] Ernst Bloch, *Natural Law and Human Dignity,* Dennis Schmidt, (trans.) (Cambridge Mass., MIT Press, 1988), Chapter 13.
[19] Hanna Arendt, *On Revolution* (London, Penguin, 2006), 30.
[20] Lewis Beck, 'Kant and the Right to Revolution', *Journal of the History of Ideas,* 32 (1971), 411.

This prohibition is *absolute*.[21] It would be an 'obvious contradiction if the constitution included a law ... entitling the people to overthrow the existing constitution, from which all particular laws are derived.'[22] Respect should be extended to constitutions 'affected by injustice ... For any legal constitution, even if it is only in small measure lawful, is better than none at all'.[23] Even evil constitutions create a duty of obedience and those who rebel against them would 'rightly be subjected to the penalties of rebellion during the revolution itself'.[24]

The right to revolution is an affront to legal positivism and formalism. The law is the highest expression of the 'general will'; no higher source exists to authorise its overthrow. 'The reason why it is a duty of the people to tolerate even what is apparently the most intolerable misuse of supreme power is that it is impossible to conceive of their resistance to the supreme legislation as being anything other than unlawful and liable to nullify the entire legal constitution.'[25] A right to revolution would imply that the head of state is not the supreme power; people could appeal to a higher authority. In such a case, a second sovereign exists and, absurdly, a third to decide conflicts between the first two. Furthermore, law's formalism cannot allow revolutionary lawlessness to destroy the 'sacred' constitution and revert to the state of nature. 'Revolution under an already existing constitution means the destruction of all relationships governed by civil right, and thus of right altogether. And this is not a change but a dissolution of the civil constitution; and a *palingenesis* [new birth], for it would require a new social contract on which the previous one (which is now dissolved) could have no influence.' As Illan Rua Wall puts it, 'there is no "the people" in the state of nature. For the people to oppose the general will, it must be constituted through the general will ... It cannot be right to revolt because there is no people who can embody such a right.'[26] The final argument addresses the necessary publicity and generality of law. The maxim authorising revolution cannot be advertised in advance as revolution is a crime.[27] A rebellion is therefore unjust because 'if the maxim upon which it would act were publicly

---

[21] Immanuel Kant, 'On the Relationship of Theory and Practice in Political Right', in *Political Writings*, H.S. Reiss, (ed.) (Cambridge University Press, 1991), 81, emphasis in the original.

[22] Ibid., 84.

[23] Immanuel Kant, 'Perpetual Peace: A Philosophical Sketch', in *Political Writings*, H. S. Reiss, (ed.) (Cambridge University Press, 1991), 118 n..

[24] Ibid., 118

[25] Immanuel Kant, 'The Metaphysics of Morals', in *Political Writings*, H. S. Reiss, (ed.) (Cambridge University Press, 1991), 145.

[26] Wall, *Human Rights*, 54, 55.

[27] Beck, 'Kant and the Right to Revolution', 412–414.

acknowledged, it would defeat its own purpose. This maxim would therefore have to remain secret.'[28]

For Kant, the revolution is both impossible and barred by legal and political arrangements. Law's job is precisely to foreclose, ban and prevent revolution. But while the right is rejected, revolution has a crucial role in Kant's philosophy of history. The essays on cosmopolitanism, perpetual peace and the contest of faculties written at the time of the French revolution accepted the inevitability and significance of revolution. Kant's philosophy of history is teleological: the purpose of history is the universal emancipation of mankind.[29] 'The history of the human race can be regarded as the realization of a hidden plan of nature's to bring about ... a perfect political constitution.'[30] Kant adopted from Augustine the idea of *pax aeterna* and turned it into secular perpetual peace, the aim of history. He substituted reason for providence and detected an inexorable forward movement behind random historical events. Humanity is progressing towards perpetual peace and cosmopolitan union exploiting its inherent 'unsocial sociability'. The 'unsocial' part refers to man's egotistical drives, motivated by the pursuit of gain, the fear of others and conflict. While 'man' wills 'concord, contentment and affection', nature, the Kantian providence, instils 'vainglory, lust for power and avarice' for possessions and rule. This 'natural' propensity to conflict drives humanity to develop its talents, taste and culture.[31] Competition results from man's unsocial nature and becomes co-ordinated at a higher unplanned level. The market, for example, makes unsocial behaviour serve a secret plan and reveals a deeper sociability.

Nature's plan to bring forth a perfect civil union of humanity unravels in history. This orientation of 'Nature – or, better of Providence' makes the philosopher adopt the standpoint of 'world history', a universal history of humanity that inexorably leads to cosmopolitanism.[32] While conflicts, wars and revolutions are full of criminal and evil acts they are also 'the means nature uses in realizing her "secret plan" for mankind'.[33] The French revolution is a clear example of this historical teleology. Revolutionaries may have committed terrible acts. But they contributed to the realisation of history's purpose and offered evidence to the moral progress of mankind. The revolution is a historical sign, which reminds,

---

[28] Kant, 'Perpetual Peace', 127.

[29] Costas Douzinas, 'The Metaphysics of Cosmopolitanism', in Rosi Braidotti, Patrick Hanafin and Bolette Blaagaard, (eds.), *After Cosmopolitanism* (Abingdon, Routledge, 2012), 57–76.

[30] Immanuel Kant, 'Idea for a Universal History with a Cosmopolitan Purpose', in *Political Writings*, H. S. Reiss, (ed.) (Cambridge University Press, 1991), 50.

[31] Ibid.,Theses 4 and 5, 45–6.   [32] Ibid.,Thesis 9, 51–3.   [33] Ibid.,Thesis 4, 45.

declares and forecasts that humanity has a tendency to moral progress.[34] The moral aspect of the revolution was evident in the enthusiasm it created around the world. The neutral observers who welcomed the revolution proved that it 'is not to be forgotten, for it revealed a tendency and faculty in human nature for improvement' which brings nature and freedom together in conformity with the 'inner principles of right'.[35] For Kant, therefore, despite his aversion to revolutionaries, 'the revolution finds in the hearts of all the spectators (who are not themselves implicated in the play) a sympathy of aspirations that border on an enthusiasm and the expression of which is itself a danger; consequently this sympathy cannot have any other cause than a moral disposition of the human race'. The revolution as a 'spectacle, and not a gesture' reveals the primordial moral disposition of humanity, its contemporary moral commitment and its future realisation.[36]

Kant's response to the revolution appears complex and paradoxical. His belief in historical teleology helps explain the contradiction between the enthusiasm for the revolution and his attacks on the right to revolution. If a cosmopolitan future is the destiny of humanity, *sub specie historiae* (history or *saeculum* replacing *aeternitas*) the illegal revolution is a key moment in the promotion of Nature's plan. But Kant's ambivalence goes further as he does not always condemn the dreaded right to revolution. In unpublished notes, Kant argued that resistance could be justified if a constitutional norm had been violated and a clear legal determination to this effect could be made.[37] This incidental note helps us unravel the paradox: the historical incarnation of the (moral) law is humanity's *telos*. If a basic legal norm has been violated, revolution could be justified. For the mature Kant, however, this hypothetical case is impossible: the state introduces general laws; law's form makes it morally legitimate, disallowing disobedience. The subject has a duty to obey the law even when the law commits an 'unbearable abuse of political authority' or the ruler 'exercises the oppressive powers of a tyrant'.[38]

Yet Kant is partially rescued by his philosophy of history. Resistance and revolution violate current law and right but contribute to their eventual victory. In this sense, history and jurisprudence are both enemies and allies. As Lewis Beck puts it, 'the moral aspirations of mankind are not satisfied by punctilious obedience to the powers that

---

[34] Immanuel Kant, 'The Contest of Faculties, in *Political Writings*, H. S. Reiss, (ed.) (Cambridge University Press, 1991), 181.

[35] Ibid., 182.   [36] Ibid.

[37] Beck, 'Kant and the Right to Revolution', 412.

[38] Sven Arntzen, 'Kant on Duty to Oneself and Resistance to Political Authority', *Journal of the History of Philosophy*, 34(3) (1996), 410.

be; they demand that the powers that be should earn our respectful obedience, and they sometimes justify disobedience to the positive law out of obedience to a "higher law"'.[39] Even for Kant a spectral logic, a law beyond state law, authorises the event of revolution and contributes to moral law's eventual triumph. For Illan Rua Wall, Kant 'in a rather complex manner asserts that the very "will to revolution" is the sign of progress'.[40] This will to revolution is a second source of right, separate from the will that legal rights enforce.

Hegel's radical right

Hegel too rejects the legal right to disobedience and resistance on similar grounds. A legal right is justified and enforceable will. It can be asserted and enjoyed without risk. Disobedience and rebellion, on the other hand, are risky enterprises. The virtual force of the rebel is posited against the overwhelming force of the state, which obliterates its opponents. This does not mean, however, that resistance and revolution are illegitimate in every case. In the Hegelian philosophy of history, revolution does not result exclusively from subjective activity. Its necessity emerges in reality. The opposition between subject and substance or between will and the world, assisted by contradictions in the social order, prepares radical change. The operation of the dialectic brings the old system to the edge of the precipice. Human will gives the final push. In the French revolution, for example, the negative drive of the Enlightenment against feudal social structure and monarchical principle destroyed a socio-political system, which had already reached the edge of the precipice. The *ancien régime* had lost all reason for existence and had become obsolete before the revolution, which simply completed the task.

Hegel explores in several places the circumstances leading to a separation between legal right and historical necessity. In the ethical state (*Sittlichkeit*), the highest stage of human development, morality is aligned with moral conscience and its principles are incorporated in institutions, law and customs. In other periods, however, moral subjectivity and institutional ethics diverge. When this happens, the self-reflecting moral individual finds that 'what is recognized as right and good in contemporary manners cannot satisfy the better will. When the existing world of freedom has become faithless to the will of better men, that will fails to find itself in the duties there recognized and must try to find in the ideal world of the inner life alone the harmony which the actuality has

[39] Beck, 'Kant and the Right to Revolution', 420.
[40] Wall, *Human Rights*, 57.

lost.'[41] The moral (today the ethico-political subject) finds herself in deep conflict with the state of the world (the 'actuality'). At these points, ethics turns into its opposite, an 'alien essence' and invites its overthrow. The dissident moral subjectivity may either withdraw into the aloofness of the beautiful soul or 'end up acting, directly or objectively, in a "Revolutionary" direction'.[42]

For Hegel, therefore, the right to resistance is part of the concrete historical process but not a legal right. Hegel's world spirit unravels in human history and stands higher than state law. As Domenico Losurdo puts it, 'a right to resistance can be found not in the legal order, but only in the "World Spirit," in history'.[43] History dictates the necessity of the revolution that explodes illegally and becomes legitimate *post factum*. In this sense, history has a quasi-natural character that justifies what the law prohibits. The legitimacy of the rebel derives not from a legal norm but from concrete historical and social conditions. Such rebels are world historical individuals; their crimes against public morality and law become catalysts for moral progress. The world spirit and the cunning of reason give rise to men who 'pull the chest nuts out of the fire for the world spirit' and are judged immoral by schoolmasters and valets, 'those exquisite discerners of spirits'. Their righteousness and effectiveness will be judged *post factum*.

The rejection of the legal right to resistance does not deter history's right to overthrow the whole legal order. Hegel celebrated every revolution including the English, American, Dutch and French. Slave rebellions represented the slaves' desire to become free and offered Hegel a model for the famous 'master and slave' dialectic in the *Phenomenology* which eventually leads to the slaves' emancipation and modernity. Hegel knew about the Haitian revolution and offered an 'astonishingly progressive and sympathetic analysis' of its success.[44] As Nick Nesbitt puts it, for Hegel 'freedom as a concrete and actual universal Idea is only to be attained through the institution of a (potentially universal) state, that is to say, through the total overthrow and destruction of the social system (colonialism) that instituted the slave's debasement to a mere natural, animalistic being'.[45] The established social order holds no attraction for Hegel if it has outlived its purpose; it will be swept aside in a combination

---

[41] *Hegel's Philosophy of Right*, T. M. Knox, (trans.) (Oxford University Press, 1967), 92, para. 138 [A].

[42] Losurdo, *Hegel*, 243.

[43] Ibid., 84.

[44] Nick Nesbitt, 'Troping Toussaint, Reading Revolution', *Research in African Literature*, 35(2) (2004), 18. Susan Bucks-Morss, *Hegel, Haiti and Universal History* (University of Pittsburg Press, 2009).   [45] Ibid,. 27.

of historical necessity and voluntary action. Such was the state of the Roman Empire before the advent of Christianity, of the French *ancien régime* before the revolution and of Czarist Russia before the Bolshevik revolution we could add. This is the state of the world today as people rise up against the injustice of neo-liberal capitalism.

The Hegelian position is even more complex. Hegel considers the right to property as the important first step in the struggle for recognition which leads to the emergence of identity of the autonomous person. But he rejects an absolute right, subordinating property to the political community. Locke had privileged property over life and considered theft and damage to property the vilest of crimes. The property-owner has the right to kill the burglar. Hegel argues exactly the opposite. Limited freedoms, such as property, can be violated to prevent the total loss of rights. Life is a higher value than property and takes precedence during war as well as in cases of extreme need. A starving man has the right to steal in order to survive; theft is unlawful but not wrong. While the abstract thought of Kantianism condemns all violations of the law, a starving man who steals does not violate the concept of right (something sacrosanct for Hegel) but its particular instantiation. Theft for survival affirms the superiority of (the right to) life over property. Hegel's radicalism is highlighted by Anatole France; as he sarcastically put it, the law punishes equally the rich and the poor for stealing bread and sleeping under bridges. Hegel had said so a century earlier.

The discussion of starvation and theft is carried out in the context of the concept of *Notrecht*, the right of distress or extreme need. *Notrecht*, a German legal concept, is the exceptional power to suspend legal rights in order to save lives. Hegel argued, against the dominant view at the time, that *Notrecht* does not apply only in cases of emergency such as an earthquake or flood. It extends to the right of the starving to survive and, by analogy, to the poor to have an acceptable level of material life. The explanation brings together historical necessity and moral disposition. The poor have a formal right to property. They are conscious of themselves as free beings and demand that their material existence matches this consciousness. But their lack of the basics both destroys their chances of a dignified life and their (self-) respect. It splits their identity between the abstract dignity of right and the concrete degradation of a life of dependency.[46] An 'inner rebellion' develops when the poor feel excluded and mocked, but this does not turn them into revolutionaries. The various palliatives offered by society (charity, harsh policing, removal

---

[46] Costas Douzinas, 'Identity, Recognition, Rights: What Can Hegel Teach us about Human Rights?', *Journal of Law and Society*, 29 (2002), 379–405.

to the colonies) stop the inner determination from becoming political action. These mitigating measures are not available to the starving man; he has an absolute right therefore to steal and violate another's property, in order to survive. 'When motivated by hunger, by the necessity to preserve life, the violation of the right to property does not stand for arbitrariness and violence but for the affirmation of a superior right.'[47] In this context, Hegel goes close to accepting the right to revolution. 'This feeling, this rebellion, is inherent in extreme need. This right must be attributed to man in the rebellion caused by extreme need.'[48] There is more: crime, the negation of law, causes the law to move forward from its formal and abstract state of full protection of property to its more nuanced and concrete stage of political and economic rights. Revolution and crime are the motors of history and law.

One of Hegel's provocations was to uncover an ethical aspect in warfare. It shakes men up, removes them from their routine insignificant life and introduces them to the universality of death, their 'master'.[49] The same argument applies by analogy to resistance and revolution. The arbitrariness and contingency confronting the poor deprive them of self-respect and freedom. People who do not enjoy the basic recognition of rights have a right to rebel. The 'rabble' is precisely the people excluded from a society of alleged freedom and equality; they are therefore the representatives of the universal. As Slavoj Žižek puts it, 'if a class of people is systematically deprived of their rights, of their very dignity as persons, they are *eo ipso* also released from their duties towards the social order, because this order is no longer their ethical substance'.[50]

For Hegel, history's arrow can only be understood retrospectively, with the 'flight of Athena's owl at dusk' once a historical epoch has run its course. History itself becomes the tribunal of the world. For Kant, nature was the backroom artiste or puppeteer manipulating the strings of history's puppet; Hegel's 'cunning of reason' does the same job. It brings together individual action, historical pattern and divine plan working behind the actions of passionate men as their invisible agent.

Only for Marx was revolution the way for overcoming the limitations of capitalism and of the rights of man. Commenting on the 1848 Revolution, he spoke of a different right: 'The right to work is, in the bourgeois sense, nonsense, a wretched, pious wish. But behind the right to work

---

[47] Losurdo, *Hegel*, 155. [48] Hegel quoted in Losurdo, *Hegel*, 164.

[49] Tarik Kochi, *The Other's War: Recognition and the Violence of Ethics* (Abingdon, Birkbeck Law Press, 2009).

[50] Slavoj Žižek, *Less than Nothing: Hegel and the Shadow of Dialectical Materialism* (London, Verso, 2012), 433.

stands power over capital: the appropriation of the means of production, their subjection to the associated working class. That is the abolition of wage labour, capital and the mutual relationship.' The communist revolution will realise the universal promise of rights by negating moralistic form and idealist content. Freedom will stop being negative and defensive and will become a positive power of each in union with others. Equality will no longer mean the abstract comparison of unequal individuals but catholic and full participation in a strong community. Property will cease being the limitation of each to a portion of wealth to the exclusion of all others and will become common. Real freedom and equality look to the concrete person in community, abandon the formal definitions of social distribution and inscribe on their banners the principle 'from each according to his ability, to each according to his needs'.[51] As revolution is the only way to radical change, Marx defends the right to revolution, the defamed and abandoned part of the Declaration, against its hasty philosophical and legal dismissal and its repeated and brutal political suppression.

Is there a right to revolution?

At the end of this tour of philosophical equivocation can we say that a right to resistance and revolution exists? Let us go back for a last time to the tension between the philosophy of law and history. Kant's jurisprudence rejects revolution. But he welcomes and celebrates the French and other revolutions as indications of humanity's moral progress. The obvious contradiction is partly resolved by the argument that while legal and moral philosophy prohibits rebellion, a non-participant observer judges its wider effects *sub specie aeternitatis*. Can these positions be reconciled? An obvious answer is that the philosopher prescribes while the observer describes. The legal position is clear. Once the revolution has overthrown the *ancien régime* and instituted its own the new constitution deserves the same obedience and protection as the order it defeated. 'If the people were to rebel successfully, the head of state would revert to the position of a subject; but he would not be justified in starting a new rebellion to restore his former position.'[52] Even if the new constitution has been attained by 'unlawful means, i.e. by violent revolution, resulting from a previous bad constitution, it would then no longer be permissible to lead the people back to the original one'.

---

[51] Karl Marx, 'The Class Struggle in France: 1848–1850' in *Selected Writings*, David McLella, (ed.) (Oxford University Press, 1977), 569.
[52] Kant, 'On the Relationship of Theory and Practice', 127.

Kant goes further. The leaders of the great revolutions 'have done the greatest degree of wrong in seeking their rights [by means of rebellion]'.[53] But once the new regime and its law become binding, the legal position and moral standing of the rebels changes dramatically. 'If the revolutions whereby Switzerland, the United Netherlands or even Great Britain won their much admired constitutions had failed, the readers of their history would regard the execution of their celebrated founders as no more than the deserved punishment of great political criminals. For the result usually affects our judgement of the rightfulness of an action.'[54] Success, a question of fact, changes the legal position retrospectively. Whether one is a great criminal or a hero is decided by the outcome of the rebellion. The *is* reverses the *ought*. The rebels are heroes not only after victory; they have been heroes all along, even when they were treated as criminals. The criminality at the time of the revolution is expunged and its effects are deleted.

The terrorist/freedom fighter conundrum depends therefore on the state of two relationships: between present and past and between law and fact. For positivist jurisprudence, norms precede temporally the facts they are called to regulate; facts on the other hand have (or ought to have) ontological solidity which, correctly interpreted through evidentiary rules, allows their subsumption to the relevant norm. But the presumed temporal primacy and ontological consistency do not go unchallenged. An obvious 'anomaly' appears in the legal distinction between void and voidable legal acts. A contract is void if it is null from the beginning and cannot be enforced. A voidable contract, on the other hand, suffers from a smaller defect and can be avoided through the legal action of the injured party. A marriage is void if one spouse is already married; it may be voidable if the spouse has misrepresented an important characteristic, for example, the fact that she is a transsexual. Contracts with an illegal object (to kill someone, or to sell drugs) are void; they are voidable if they have been obtained by fraud. The legal defect flows from the classification of the act. Once the nullity of the contract has been declared, it is as if it never entered the legal universe, as if it never happened. Legal effects are retrospectively eliminated even though reality may have changed: the assassination has taken place, the drugs have been snorted. The contract is a performative act that changes the world; the declaration of nullity is a world-unmaking legal fiction. Like a time machine it goes back and deletes what legally happened. The law deletes the origins of the legal performance acting like a 'negative performative' act.

[53] Ibid., 82.   [54] Ibid.

A successful revolution is the mirror image of the same operation. For Kant and Hegel, success makes the rebellion a necessary station of historical progress. At the same time, the revolution deletes the legal record, changing criminality into lawfulness, crime into right, the criminal into hero. When an act is void, the law negates what happened in actuality; in the revolution, actuality negates what the law has ordained. The revolution does not redress the effects of the law as is the case with mercy or amnesty which forgive committed crimes; the revolution negates and reverses the law itself. We can call this amazing effect, the 'normative force of the real': it retrospectively obliterates the earlier legal position as well as the conditions that led to it. The force of law is negated *ab initio*, linear temporality is unravelled and reversed. Legal synchrony takes over and sets aside historical diachrony. Because the law wishes to be complete, coherent and closed, because it must appear a 'seamless web' in Dworkin's terms, what happened at a later time is presented as being always and already there. Past evil becomes honourable from the start, crime the exercise of a right that determined later events. The right to revolution will have been a foundational right even when it was rejected. Indeed the idea of creating *ex nihilo*, legalising the illegal, unravelling time and legitimising the criminal was always an operation of law, initially held by the Pope and then passed on to Emperor, King and law. The Pope is 'someone who makes something out of nothing' states a Papal decretal of 1220. The Pope could give dispensation against the law, thus turning justice to injustice: '[The pope can make an illegitimate legitimate, and can make a monk a canon', states a typical gloss. The mark of law is the ability to unsettle temporality and turn fact into law and the opposite. It is the sovereign and his representatives that decide time. But they are vulnerable and can be unseated by the timeliness of the revolutionary *kairos*.

At the moment of the revolution two alternatives exist: success or failure. The failure of rebellion confirms the existent; actuality endures and confirms itself. The possibility of success, on the other hand, is pure potentiality: both negation and an alternative to the existent. Two possibilities therefore appear when revolution breaks out: the first continues actuality; a second virtual possibility radically challenges it. If the revolution succeeds, the virtual replaces the actual and the potential becomes real. The new regime will have been both normatively authorised and historically necessary right from the start. The rebel operates at both levels: he acts now as if the new law he wants to inaugurate were already applicable, his actions at the service of history's plan. He exercises his right to rebel, as if the rebellion has been already successful and has changed what appears as crime and sedition into right and duty. The rebel's time is therefore the future perfect; the revolution will have been an exercise of legal entitlement even when resistance was a crime. The contingent beginnings will have turned into historical inevitability. The revolution does not just delete the past. It retrospectively creates the conditions of its own success. Revolutionary victory is not the felicitous outcome of political action but the inevitable end point of historical necessity.

This unravelling of temporality and ontology is perfectly described by philosopher Jean-Pierre Dupuy: 'An object possesses a property x until the time t; after t, it is not only that the object no longer has property x; it is that it is not true that it possessed x at any time. The truth value of the proposition "the object o has the property x at the moment t" therefore depends on the moment when the proposition is enunciated.'[55] In law, it becomes more striking: 'Act c is a crime until time t. At time $t + n$, act c is no longer a crime but the exercise of a right. Moreover c was a right and not a crime at all times. The statement "act c is a crime" becomes "act c is a right" at time t.' Fact and law, revolution and right are closely intertwined; the time arrow reversed. It is not that the past teaches lessons to the present but that the past is the continuation of the present. In this sense, every rebellion is (and will have been) the exercise of the right to revolution. Right and revolution, instead of being opposed, are coeval, supporting each other.

Hegel's cases of rightful resistance were instances of creation of new subjects. When the universal is incarnated in someone who rebels against the particularity of a world that has become obsolete, he becomes a world hero such as Robespierre, Lenin, or Mao. The second type of resistance creates 'ordinary' resisting subjects. The universal will of formal and abstract law stands against and thwarts the particular will. An 'inner rebellion' follows and unsettles people who are promised but do not enjoy the recognition of rights. For Hegel this was the 'rabble': people excluded from a society of alleged freedom and equality. The crimes they commit help the law move forward but they don't become political subjects.

The post-1989 order promised to transcend the split between universal will and individual particularity. Cosmopolitanism, globalisation and the ethics of communication allegedly turn us all into citizens at peace with the world. Neo-liberal economics, human rights and international organisations have combined into a normative and institutional realm, which transcends earlier conflicts and tensions. In Hegelian terms, cosmopolitan law reconciles abstract individuality and concrete subjectivity, neither the heteronomous ethics of the *polis* nor the inhuman generalisation

---

[55] Quoted in Slavoj Žižek, 'Legal Luck', *Unbound*, 4(1) (2008), 5.

of Kantian morality. As Jurgen Habermas keeps arguing with increasing desperation, cosmopolitan law is no longer an alien substance but our own creation, subject become substance. We are well on the way to the postmodern ethical state of perpetual peace.

The 'rebirth of history' in the rebelling squares and streets of the world negates these claims. The contradictions and conflicts Hegel diagnosed in the nineteenth century are still fully active in different forms. The structural contradiction between social being, a socio-economic system that creates huge inequalities, and social consciousness, a juridico-political order that promises equality and freedom, leads late capitalism to the edge. It is experienced as a gap between the promise of universal equality and freedom and the reality of unemployment, poverty, repression and exclusion. The old dialectic of subject and substance awakens and leads to the politics of rebellion. Finally, Hegel's 'rabble' becomes political subject.

Hegel's dialectic showed the necessity of 'a rebellion, which shakes the power edifice from its complacency, making it aware of both its dependence on popular support and of its a priori tendency to "alienate" itself from its roots'.[56] Or as Jefferson put it, 'a little rebellion now and then is a good thing, and as necessary in the political world as storms in the physical'.[57] History has proven both right.

The metaphysics of will

The apparent contradiction and deeper link between law and history or between jurisprudence and philosophy points perhaps to the existence of two different sources of right and will. German idealism resolved the tension by distinguishing right and revolution ontologically. Right belongs to law, revolution to the grand historical trajectory. The English approach was more modest but perhaps more perceptive. The conditions activating the right to revolution vary according to ideological and historical priorities. But such a right exists, law and politics are not divorced. Is it, however, a right in the strict sense of the term? A brief look at the history of right may help.

The peregrinations of right offer an insight into western metaphysics. The pre-moderns discover what is the right thing to do, in the cosmos, the natural order of things. The moderns invent individual rights and give them to select categories of people who become subjects, armed with

[56] Žižek, Less than Nothing, 450.
[57] Letter from Thomas Jefferson to James Madison, quoted in Howard Zinn, A People's History of the United States (New York, HarperCollins, 2001), 95.

rights. Finally, late-modern rights repeat, copy and legalise pre-existing desires, socially accepted demands, the claims of a proliferating collection of identity groups and lifestyle choices. Let me explain. In pre-modern ethics and law, the will (a concept non-thematised at the time) followed the *norma agendi*, a mandatory norm of action, prescribed variably by divine, natural or ecclesiastical law. A modern legal right, on the other hand, is a *facultas agendi*, a *possibilité d'agir* as Michel Villey put it in *Le Droit et les Droits de l'Homme*,[58] a recognised and effective capacity to will and act on the world. A right is a normatively justified and publicly enforced individual will. It is will raised to the level of general will or law, a will given objective existence. In this sense, rights belong to subjects and establish the subject as metaphysical ground. If modernity is the period of 'subjectivisation' of the world, rights are manifestations of man occupying the centre, individual will becoming sovereign. The law dresses the subjective will with value and validity and enforces its object.

Pre-modern law prescribed duties and authorised a limited number of acts, modern law prescribes rights and allows limited constraints on action. For this to happen, the law had to abandon the teleology of reason and the eschatology of redemption; it had to discard the moral temptation and make practical reason morally celibate. This raising of subjective will into law freed the moderns from ethics, the morality of duty and the pathos of tragic conflicts. The strict distinction between private good and public right allows the subject to rule over his property, his body and his private life. Historically, the first claim to right was that of the property-owner, specifically of the creditor against the debtor. Rights were formed in a long legal process to protect the creditor and enshrine property into law. It was this model of right that migrated from private to public law in the eighteenth century and from debates about dominium, apostolic poverty and credit protection to the relationship between citizen and state.[59] Property right was the first right and the rights of man, civil and political rights, were modelled on the right to property.

Legal right, whether private or public, the right to property or to vote, appears as one, in-dividual, un-divided and in-divisible. It claims a single source, the subject's will, a single justification, law's recognition, a single effect, the will's ability to act and shape the world. The modelling of political rights on property, however, contaminated their operation. A yawning gap separates the will from its effects, the ideal from the actual, the normative weight from empirical operation. Formal right, the legal subject's capacity to will, is theoretically limitless. But real

---

[58] Michel Villey, *Le Droit et les Droits de l'Homme* (Paris, PUF, 1981).
[59] John Milbank, 'Against Human Rights', Chapter 3 in this volume.

people are embedded in the world, class, gender or colour inequalities
that condition them, preventing formal rights from becoming effective.
We are all legally free and nominally equal, unless of course we are
improper men, in other words men of no property, women, colonials,
of the wrong colour, religion or belonging.

This was partly the reason why will, the first source of right, soon
diversified into a second, adopted by the dominated and the oppressed.
For the wretched of the earth, right is not about law and judges, a game
they can scarcely play. It is a battle-cry, the subjective factor in a struggle,
which asks to be raised to the level of the universal. Right is the demand
not to be treated as an object or as nobody. It is the claim of the dissident
against the abuses of power or the revolutionary against the existing
order. As Ernst Bloch, the messianic Marxist, argued, individual rights
were initially created for the protection of the creditor and 'adopted in a
quite different way by the exploited and oppressed, the humiliated and
degraded. It is precisely this that appears in its incomparable second
sense as the subjective catchword of the revolutionary struggle and
actively as the subjective factor in the struggle.'[60] The legally created
rights call for obedience, the right to insubordination, as Maurice
Blanchot put it, expresses the exercise of freedom. 'Where there is a
duty, we merely have to close the eyes and blindly accomplish it; then
everything is simple. A right, on the contrary refers only to itself and to
the exercise of freedom of which it is the expression; a right is a free
power for which everyone is responsible, by himself, in relation to himself, and which completely and freely engages him: nothing is stronger,
nothing is more serious.'[61] This second right is the exercise of free will, a
justified free power that draws its force from morality instead of legality.

Right has therefore two metaphysical sources. As a claim accepted or
seeking admission to the law, right is a publicly recognised will, which
finds itself at peace with the world, a world made in its image and for its
service. But secondly, right is a will that wills what does not exist, a will
that finds its force in itself and its effect in a world not yet determined all
the way to the end. This second right is founded *contra fatum*, in the
perspective of an open cosmos, and the belief that it cannot be fully
determined by (financial, political or military) might. It eventually
confronts domination and oppression, including those instituted and
tolerated by the first legalized will. 'The *second origin* of the *facultas agendi*

---

[60] Bloch, *Natural Law*, 217.
[61] Maurice Blanchot, 'Declaration of the Right to Insubordination in the Algerian War
(Manifesto of the 121)', in Maurice Blanchot, *Political Writings*, Zakir Paul (trans.) (New
York, Fordham University Press, 2010), 33–34.

enters here in a thoroughly decisive way, as an origin conforming more than ever before to the hegemony in men (according to a Stoic expression) that lets men walk with their head held high.'[62]

Two conceptions of right or the universal are in conflict. On one side, an acceptance of the order of things raised to the dignity of general will. It dresses the dominant particular with the mantle of the universal. The second universality is founded on a will created by a diagonal division of the social world that separates rulers from the ruled and the excluded. This dimension of truth does not rest on the existing order but on its negation. It forms an agonistic universality; it does not emerge from neo-Kantian philosophical texts but from the struggle of the excluded from social distribution and political representation. The excluded, the contemporary 'rabble', are the only universal today in a legal and social system that proclaims incessantly its egalitarian credentials.

Legal right enforces individual will. The second type of will starts as individual disobedience and matures into collective resistance and perhaps revolution. It confronts the formalism of law and has motivated the struggles for group, economic and social rights. The will to change the world and create a society of equality, freedom and justice has taken various historical forms. It appeared as the republican idea in the great eighteenth-century revolutions, as the socialist idea in the nineteenth century, it became linked with the communist party and state in the twentieth and suffered as a result of the betrayal of the revolution. Today this will brings together the ideas of radical equality, resistance and democracy. Democracy not just as a system of parliamentary representation and elections but as a form of life that extends into all aspects of the social fabric, from home to work to social and cultural life. The resistances, insurrections and revolts of the last few years resulted precisely from the combination of popular will with ideas of social justice and democracy, which initiated autonomous collective political action and direct, unmediated democratic forms.

Radical change results from the dialectical relationship between ideal and necessity accelerated by will. Will and idea come together in a dialectical voluntarism, as Peter Halward puts it.[63] When this happens, will no longer gives passive consent to power; it becomes an active force that changes the world. History is full of such confrontations, eternally condemned and eternally returning. Disobedience is the first step. It manifests a rift between the normatively guided will and the existing

---

[62] Bloch, *Natural Law*, 219.

[63] Peter Halward, 'Communism of the Intellect, Communism of the Will', in Costas Douzinas and Slavoj Žižek, *The Idea of Communism* (London, Verso, 2010), 117.

political and legal reality. Dissident will does not disobey the law. Let me repeat that the obligation to obey the law is absolute only when accompanied by the judgement that the law is morally just and democratically legitimate. Disobedience is the beginning. Protests mostly challenge law's conserving violence, breaking public order regulations in order to highlight greater injustices.[64] As long as the protesters ask for this or that reform, this or that concession, the state can accommodate them. When will no longer recognises itself in existing social relations and their legal codification, disobedience becomes a collective emancipatory will. What the state fears is the fundamental challenge by a force that can transform the relations of power and present itself as having a 'right to law'.

Despite the reservations of the liberal philosophers, revolution has become a normative principle, the modern expression of free action when the order of the world decays and suffocates.[65] 'The *ultimate subjective right* would be the license to *produce according to one's capabilities, to consume according to one's needs*; this license is guaranteed by means of the *ultimate norm of subjective right: solidarity*.'[66] The normative weight of this right is felt every time a Bastille is taken, a Tahrir, Syntagma or Taksim Square filled. In the same way that the psychoanalytical real, a void in human existence, is both impossible and banned but sustains subjectivity, the right to revolution is the void that sustains the legal system. Without it, the law becomes sclerotic, moribund. Paraphrasing Alain Badiou, we can say that rights are about recognition and distribution among individuals and communities; except that additionally there is an indelible right to resistance.

---

[64] Walter Benjamin, 'Critique of Violence', in *Reflections*, Edmund Jephcott, (trans.) (New York, Schocken Books, 1978), 277–300.

[65] Costas Douzinas, '*Adikia*: On Communism and Rights', in Douzinas and Žižek, *The Idea of Communism*, 81–100.

[66] Bloch, *Natural Law*, 221, italics in the original.

6   On a radical politics for human rights

*Illan Rua Wall**

There is a perpetual debate in human rights law surrounding the question of whether to create new human rights. On one side many bemoan the incessant generation of rights. They insist that such 'new' rights may be adequately accommodated within existing frameworks, and that multiplication of international instruments and obligations merely waters down the 'core' set of demands.[1] On the other side are those who insist on the necessity of a supple and fluid usage of the discourse that is responsive to events. The debate around 'new' human rights has focused upon making 'second-generation' rights like water and sanitation substantive;[2] and generating 'third-generation' rights[3] like development, peace or truth.[4]

---

* I would like to thank Costas Douzinas and the other organisers of the Leverhulme *Between Cosmopolitanism and Empire* Network for inviting me to present an early draft of this chapter at PUC, Rio de Janeiro, in 2012. I am also deeply grateful to Sam Adelman and Brid Spillane, who both read and commented on early drafts of the chapter.

[1] For instance in its response to the UN Human Rights Council's resolution on the human right to safe drinking water and sanitation, the UK government observes: 'While the intent behind recognizing new rights may be noble, doing so without proper consideration undermines the UN's human rights project and could ultimately devalue the notion of human rights as a whole.' (Explanation of Position on Human Rights Council Resolution 15/414 of 30 September 2010, available at www.gov.uk/government/uploads/system/uploads/attachment_data/file/35453/explanation-of-position-hrr15.pdf).

[2] For an institutional discussion see: 'Human Right to Water and Sanitation', available at www.un.org/waterforlifedecade/human_right_to_water.shtml (accessed on 21 February 2013).

[3] Sometimes called 'solidarity' rights in the narrow sense that they are about political being-together, see T. Landman, *Studying Human Rights* (Abingdon: Routledge, 2006), 8.

[4] The academic discussion is voluminous; however, see B. Morvaridi, *Social Justice and Development* (Houndmills: PalgraveMacmillan, 2008); A. Sengupta, A. Negri and M. Basu, *Reflections on the Right to Development* (London: Sage, 2005); D. Aguirre, *The Human Right to Development* (Aldershot: Ashgate, 2008); I. Bunn, *The Right to Development and International Economic Law* (Oxford: Hart, 2012). For the right to peace, see for instance, T. Hideko, 'Rethinking Rights in the Twenty-First Century: The Right to Life and the Right to Peace from a Buddhist Perspective', *The International Journal of Human Rights*, 11(4) (2007) 381. For the right to trust see, D. Groome, 'The Right to Truth in the Fight Against Impunity', *Berkeley Journal of International Law*, 29(1) (2011) 175; W. Schabas, *Unimaginable Atrocities: Justice, Politics and Rights at the War Crimes Tribunals* (Oxford University Press, 2012).

Ultimately this debate represents what Upendra Baxi calls the politics *of* human rights – i.e. the manner in which they should be deployed in the management of the current distribution of power.[5] He distinguishes this from a politics *for* human rights, which would name an alternative, ruptural view of the discourse. The debate over new rights – to which I shall return at the end of this chapter – presents itself as a mortal battle. But ultimately neither side challenges the underlying presumptions of rights, and both sides agree on a basic strategy of turning to rights-talk. This chapter seeks to displace the many presumptions of this argument by shifting the grounds of the debate and focusing upon a politics *for* human rights. That is, the question posed by 'new rights' is displaced entirely from one of conserving the established and legitimate discourse, to a strategic question of engagement with and against law.

Right-ing and critical legal strategy

There is a difference or incommensurability at the heart of human rights between their traditional rendering in law and their many varied radical instantiations. The position of rights within the (neo-)liberal state allows the individual to restrain the state through the juridical apparatus. But as many in this volume have explained, alongside this restraint rights have also become a discourse that buttresses regimes: the language of liberation but also of state authority. In terms of globalisation, human rights are supposed to be the moral and ethical refusal of sovereign power, yet they consistently re-inscribe sovereignty and find no place for the politics of anti-capitalism or anti-imperialism in their more expansive forms. Rancière insists that human rights are all too often 'part of the configuration of the given. What is given is not only a situation of inequality. It is also an inscription, a form of visibility of equality.'[6] Human rights remain part of the distribution of the sensible (*partage du sensible*). '[T]he distribution of the sensible sets the divisions between what is visible and invisible, sayable and unsayable, audible and inaudible.'[7] The everyday politics of this order is a process of counting, of managing who and what counts, and the manner in which they count.[8]

---

[5] U. Baxi, *The Future of Human Rights* (Oxford University Press, 2002), 40–41.

[6] J. Rancière, 'Who is the Subject of Rights of Man?', *South Atlantic Quarterly*, 103(2/3) (2004), 303.

[7] S. Sayers, 'Review of The Politics of Aesthetics, *Culture Machine* (2005), www.culturemachine.net/index.php/cm/article/view/190/171 (accessed on 19 February 2013).

[8] Rancière says: 'The distribution of the sensible reveals who can have a share in what is common to the community based on what they do and on the time and space in which this activity is performed ... it defines what is visible or not in a common space, endowed

In this sense, human rights render a relatively predictable and limited power to reshuffle positions within the given distribution.

However, they also have a second irruptive and radical character. 'The Rights of Man are the rights of the *demos*, conceived as the generic name of the political subjects who enact – in specific scenes of dissensus – the paradoxical qualification of this supplement.'[9] For Rancière, the *demos* is not the name of the totality of people under the state. Rather, it is the excess of the distribution of the sensible, those who find no place in the everyday consensus. These characters come forth in momentary displays of dissensus and manifest the wrong that they have suffered. Rancière insists: 'There is no man of the Rights of Man, but there is no need for such a man.'[10] Rather, there is the 'back-and-forth movement between' the subject of consensus and the actors who manifest dissensus. This double sense of human rights is crucial to critical responses to the discourse.

One of the most important renderings of this differential sense of rights can be found in *The End of Human Rights*. There, Douzinas posits the term 'right-ing' for the idea of a human rights that disturbs the given consensus. Right-ing would be the element of human rights that eschews (pre-given) right. He says: 'To coin a term, this would be a process of "righting" and not a series of rights and, like writing, it would open Being to the new and unknown as a condition of its humanity.'[11] Human right-ing would refuse to set a final metaphysical horizon. There would be no pre-given human essence, no freezing of the features of the human in a code or convention. Where human rights would ascribe a relation to the sovereign, right-ing would turn away from the authoritative sovereign power that might decide on the legitimacy of its claim. Instead, right-ing would consist of antagonistic right-claims without end. As Rancière insists, it is *not* a matter of communities ensuring and requesting their rights, but rather right-ing is the moment when a group exceeds the rights that are given to them in order to re-construct the social bond. In this way, right-ing is the unauthorisable call to exceed human rights (and the given order of things and people). Of course, as its excess, right-ing remains incommensurable with the traditional idea of rights.

---

with a common language, etc.', J. Rancière, *The Politics of Aesthetics: The Distribution of the Sensible* (London: Continuum, 2004), 12–13.

[9] Rancière, 'Who is the Subject of the Rights of Man?', 305.

[10] Ibid.

[11] C. Douzinas, *The End of Human Rights* (Oxford: Hart, 2000), 215–216.

As Fitzpatrick suggests, law (and rights in particular) is both determinative and responsive to that which is beyond it.[12] Human rights
have 'the incessant capacity to be something other than what they
determinately are' but in this, they become vacuous.[13] This vacuity is
not a critique for Fitzpatrick, rather it means that they 'are susceptible to
occupation by effective powers – by nation and nations, by empire and
"the market", and so on', but also 'this very vacuity shields human rights
from definitive subjection to any power, from enduring containment by
any power'. They 'remain ever capable of extending beyond, of surprising and countering, the determinacy of any power'.[14] In these days of
capitalist and neo-liberal global hegemony, such a excess means that
human rights do not *only* lead to the establishment of some pacified
neutered analysis of the global order that would facilitate further market-
isation and neo-colonisation. They also mark a dissensus, rupturing
and tearing through the pacifying tedium of everyday relations, with
the demand that things should and could be otherwise. However, as
Christodoulidis cautions, we must be careful not to fall into an over-
optimistic insistence upon the excess of law and rights which would miss
the manner in which such an excess is pacified. While focusing upon
right-ing as the excess of human rights may help us think about the
manner in which the everyday is ruptured, it tells us little more
than that. Ultimately, while 'law is an unstable order… it thrives on
disturbance that it domesticates as opportunity both to reconfigure
expectations… *and* re-trench them, re-embedding its structures.'[15]
Simply 'stating the concern [with the excess of law or human rights] is
not in itself an answer to law's crushing force of homology, its mechanisms of deadlock, or to its extraordinary power of co-option, and thus
hardly emancipatory per se'.[16] Law is more likely to crush the attempt
to open the existing order, than to remain responsive to it. Thus, the
identification of an excess is only the beginning of this analysis.

---

[12] See P. Fitzpatrick, *Modernism and the Grounds of Law* (Cambridge University Press,
2001) and P. Fitzpatrick, *Law as Resistance: Modernism, Imperialism, Legalism* (Aldershot:
Ashgate, 2008).

[13] P. Fitzpatrick, 'Is Humanity Enough? The Secular Theology of Human Rights', *Law,
Social Justice and Global Development*, 1 (2007) 10.

[14] Ibid.

[15] E. Christodoulidis, 'Strategies of Rupture', *Law and Critique*, 20(1) (2009), 21. For a
discussion of this, see R. Bailey, 'Strategy, Rupture, Rights: Reflections on Law and
Resistance in Immigration Detention', *Australian Feminist Law Journal*, 31 (2009), 40,
and B. Bhandar, 'Strategies of Rupture: The Politics of Judgment', *Windsor Yearbook of
Access to Justice*, 30 (2012), 59.

[16] Christodoulidis, 'Strategies of Rupture', 20.

Instead of simply theorising excess, Christodoulidis suggests focusing upon the moment when the excess is reinserted into law. Thus, he turns to the question of critical legal strategies, suggesting three 'points along a spectrum': (1) Internal critique is useful where a deadlock might be redressed. It is the process of playing the system to gain advantage for those ordinarily excluded and dismissed by power. (2) Immanent critique would involve utilising legal forms and norms in order to confront the state with the difference between its stated high principles and its base and vicious action: 'The tapping of contradiction aims to hold up the system to its own claims, force it to face up to its stated principles, to equality, to procedural fairness, etc., where this measuring up forces it beyond what it can possibly "contain" within its economy of representation.'[17] (3) Finally, he suggests 'meta-level struggles' which would involve a direct confrontation and refusal of legal norms.

Where human rights usually conceive of strategy through the prism of internal critique, it becomes more difficult to think about right-ing in these strategic terms precisely because of its excessive nature. At what point, and in what manner could the excess of human rights (*qua* law) articulate with the given forms of the legal system? In Christodoulidis' spectrum of strategy, it would presumably have to play between immanent critique and meta-level struggle. However, in a way such a framing remains far too traditional. Each of these strategies involves engagement with law in a critical sense, but they ultimately imply a classical leftist (party) struggle in which all actions are considered in relation to a transcendent political project. In other words, were this the full extent of Christodoulidis' strategy it would simply be a matter of framing one sovereign project against another. However, there is something more complex going on. Firstly, Christodoulidis turns to Jameson to underline the negative utopian conception at play in these strategic encounters with law. Its 'function is not in helping us to imagine a better future but rather in demonstrating our utter incapacity to imagine such a future – our imprisonment in a non-utopian present without history or futurity – so as to reveal the ideological closure of the system … in which we are confined'.[18] This absence of utopian end withdraws the telos toward which the strategy would be oriented. There is no programmatic struggle that transcends the strategic

---

[17] Ibid., 5.

[18] F. Jameson, 'The Politics of Utopia', *New Left Review*, 25 (2004), 46; F. Jameson, *Archaeologies of the Future* (London: Verso, 2005), 203–210.

engagement with law.[19] Instead this strategic engagement focuses upon rupture, circling around the question of how to generate a tear in the political fabric. It does this, as Daniel Bensaïd suggests, without a model of the world, but instead with a strategic hypothesis which operates as a 'guide to action that starts from past experience but is open and can be modified in the light of new experience or unexpected circumstances'.[20] Without a substantive positive utopian end (*telos*) or model of a future society, a strategic engagement becomes a 'means without end'.[21]

Even still, within this, Christodoulidis' strategies seem to remain quite a traditional critical take on law. They would, for instance, be familiar to the early wave of American critical legal scholars[22] who insisted that law stood for mystified power structures where political possibilities were limited by law's formalistic abstraction. For the early critical legal scholars, politics was open and contingent, and so they framed their loose movement through the catch-phrase 'All Law Is Politics'. This was meant to signify that law itself was not necessary or natural, but that its openness was mystified and secured in the name of a conservative politics. The problem with this early mantra was that the Crits tended to have a relatively banal conception of politics that lead them back to law (albeit in a newly 'trashed' manner) as the solution.[23] Thrashing of legal norms, seeking out the 'fundamental contradiction' and all of their other critical legal strategies, ultimately moved too quickly from law to politics and back to law. In this, they risked the crucial role of the political.

Christodoulidis is alive to this danger, and so insists upon the differencing of politics from the political. The political requires a deeper thinking about politics, and withholds any simple programmatic answer to the problems of law. To explain, Christodoulidis quotes Lefort:

The political is revealed not in what we call political activity, but in the double movement whereby the institution of society appears and is obscured. It appears

---

[19] There is no given substantive struggle that would allow for sublation of current activity in a community yet to come. See Nancy's critique of the classical sublation of death in communist struggles, J.-L. Nancy, *The Inoperative Community* (Minneapolis, Minn.: University of Minnesota Press, 1991), 13.

[20] D. Bensaïd, 'The Return of Strategy', *International Socialism*, 113 (2007), available at www.isj.org.uk/?id=287 (accessed on 11 July 2013).

[21] G. Agamben, *Means without End: Notes on Politics* (Minneapolis, Minn.: University of Minnesota Press, 2000); I. R. Wall, *Human Rights and Constituent Power* (Abingdon: Routledge, 2011).

[22] For a loose periodisation of these waves of critique, see C. Douzinas, M. Stone and I. R. Wall, *New Critical Legal Thinking* (Abingdon: Birkbeck Law Press, 2012).

[23] See P. Goodrich, 'Sleeping with the Enemy', in P. Goodrich, *Law in the Courts of Love* (London: Routledge, 1996).

in the sense that the process whereby society is ordered and unified across its divisions becomes visible. It is obscured in the sense that the locus of politics (the locus in which parties compete [,etc.]. . .) becomes defined as particular, while the principle that generates the overall configuration is concealed.[24]

The political is the appearing and obscuring of an ordering of society as such. However, as Nancy and Lacoue-Labarthe note, the political, which they suggest is that which is *most political* in politics, increasingly withdraws from politics itself.[25] Politics is understood simply as the institutional setting of government (*qua* the management of population). Within this everyday sense of politics the radical possibilities of our being-together are domesticated and pacified. The insistence upon the difference between politics and the political facilitates a thinking of the potentiality of politics rather than falling foul of the hopelessness of the current configuration of power. Thus, the purpose of Christodoulidis' strategies of rupture is to pose the question of the 'institution of society' that is constantly appearing and withdrawing from law and politics.

Ultimately, by posing the question of the political, Christodoulidis returns us to right-ing as the excess of human rights. Human rights tends to suggest an internal critique which would shuffle the positions in the distribution of the sensible. Such a shuffling, even when it leads to a redistribution of people and things, ultimately maintains the withdrawal of the political. In fact many would argue that such a strategy is the very epitome of the withdrawal of the political, by providing right answers to political questions through a pre-given law.[26] In this, the 'institution of society' or indeed the essence of the political, remains un-thought. Right-ing as a strategy may engage through immanent critique or meta-level struggle, but the political remains theoretically prior to such a determination. Put otherwise, law as the end (telos) of right-ing is displaced.

A vocabulary of right-ing

It remains difficult to retain a constant focus upon right-ing (*qua* 'the institution of society') without falling back upon thoughts of traditional

---

[24] E. Christodoulidis, 'Against Substitution', in M. Loughlin and N. Walker, *The Paradox of Constitutionalism* (Oxford University Press, 2008), 193, quoting C. Lefort, *Democracy and Political Theory* (Cambridge: Polity, 1988), 11, emphasis in the original.

[25] J.-L. Nancy and P. Lacoue-Labarthe, *Retreating the Political* (Abingdon: Routledge, 1997).

[26] J.-L. Nancy, *Being Singular Plural* (Minneapolis, Minn.: University of Minnesota Press, 2000), 47. See also I. R. Wall, 'Politics and the Political: Notes on the Thought of Jean-Luc Nancy', *Critical Legal Thinking*, available at http://criticallegalthinking.com/2013/02/20/politics-and-the-political-notes-on-the-thought-of-jean-luc-nancy/ (accessed on 20 March 2013).

human rights. Yet the traditional international human rights law frame-works, by their nature, miss the fact that historically rights were often the tools of sedition. The challenge therefore is to try to draw out a vocabulary of right-ing (*qua* sedition). I suggest that recent discussions of constituent power, that is the disputation of 'public right' and sovereign authority, are particularly useful. In a sense, right-ing *is* a type of constituent power. Constituent power is: the democratic power of a collectivity to determine the nature of its being-together; it is the power of world-making, exercised collectively by a multitude, a people, a proletariat, etc.; it is a radical democratic power to generate new modes of political being-together. That said, when it falls into the hands of legal theorists, it tends to be limited and pre-determined. Over and again constitutionalists seek to inscribe and encase constituent power in a lead-lined tomb where its contagion can be confined and guarded against. Thus, let me mark a difference between a radical conception of constituent power and the version perpetuated in western constitutionalism.

Western constitutionalist thought tends to link constituent power with the constitution. It tends to do this in a base dialectical fashion. The effect of this base dialectic is that constituent power becomes determined and defined by the constituted order that comes afterwards.[27] We can trace this in any variety of theorists from Sieyès and Schmitt to Kant and Kelsen. As a recent example of this dialectic, however, let me focus upon the attempt by Martin Loughlin to reconceive a 'pure' public law. Loughlin proposes that constituent power should be understood as that which constitutes the law's authority. It helps us, he says, to 'locate the source of modern political authority, and ... identify the base upon which the structure of the legal authority rests'.[28] For Loughlin, constitu-ent power is other to the constituted order, it 'cannot be absorbed into some basic norm'.[29] Instead its alterity generates the 'open, provisional, and dynamic qualities' of constitutions. He demands that there is a dialectical relation at work between the people as a constituent power and the constituted power performed by the 'office of government'.[30] This dialectic draws a people 'together ... in ties of allegiance to a particular constitution of the state'.[31]

This understanding of constituent power becomes deeply problematic when we begin to think about the constituent moment itself. Essentially,

---

[27] This is similar to the way that human rights domesticate their excess of right-ing.
[28] M. Loughlin, *The Idea of Public Law* (Oxford University Press, 2004), 99.
[29] Ibid., 113
[30] M. Loughlin, *Foundations of Public Law* (Oxford University Press, 2010), 228.
[31] Ibid., 229.

Loughlin falls into the trap described by Agamben. The constituent moment is defined by way of its *telos* in the new constitutional order. Or as Agamben would say, the constituent moment is included in the constitution by way of its exclusion. As such, it becomes a part of sovereign power. Loughlin's version of constituent power, which is shared by many others, ultimately misunderstands the constituent moment by framing it through the lens of the state that ensues from it. However, as Negri explains, constituent power is an open power, in the sense that it does not simply institute a new order. To focus upon the 'end' of the constituent moment allows easy periodisation, but fails to see how the constituent disruption continues under the surface. In this sense, if there is a dialectic at play it is a much more complex one than a simple Lockean tyranny–revolt–constitution. We might think of this as a broken dialectic, where the negation of the negation never manages to reach completion. Thus on one level there may be tyranny–revolt–constitution but there is also unrest–organisation–resistance running contemporaneously.

Negri argues that constituent power is 'the ungrounded and intrinsically disruptive strength of institutionally unmediated collective action'.[32] It is not difficult to see the tension between this sense of constituent power (as disruptive, institutionally unmediated and collective) and traditional conceptions of human rights. Yet in a curious sense each of these aspects of constituent power sound close to the language of the early human rights devotees of the 1970s and 1980s: they were seen to be resistant to state power, unmediated by states and gathering a band of supporters to change the international realm. However, the differences are all too clear. While human rights are often disruptive in the sense that they are the term used for political 'conflicts of interest' between individuals and the state, any suggestion of a deeper dissensus tends to be closed off in advance through the juridical apparatus. In terms of institutional mediation, by reaching to a different order of right – other than the state's conception of public right – human rights displace the state as the site of the mediation of law. Yet they do this by generating their own mediation in the sphere of international law. Crucially this is then designed to loop back into state practice, allowing human rights to become the institutional mechanism of public right. In this sense, they become the acme of the legitimation of

---

[32] A. Negri, quoted in J. Frank, 'The Abyss of Democracy: Antonio Negri's Democratic Theory', *Theory & Event*, 4(1) (2000), emphasis in the original. It is important to note that this is by no means a universally accepted definition, the debates around constituent power are intense. For further discussion, see I. R. Wall, 'Notes on an "Open" Constituent Power', *Law, Culture and the Humanities* (forthcoming, 2014).

state practice. Finally, as Wendy Brown insists, 'rights sought by a politically defined *group* are conferred upon depoliticized *individuals*; at
the moment a particular "we" succeeds in obtaining rights, it loses its
"we-ness" and dissolves into individuals'.[33] As Brown sees with perspica-
city, the tedious debate on whether we could/should recognise collective
rights ultimately misses the point that in popular struggle, rights gather
together the many to demand recognition. However, as an established
discourse they remain alienating and individualising. On the face of it,
then, human rights and constituent power remain distinct and in tension.

Yet already, with Wendy Brown's comments, we can begin to see the
shadow of constituent power cast by human rights. Human rights are
often collective before they are individual. In fact we know they are often
collective even after they have been established. The 2011–2012 'Chilean
Winter' of student protests demonstrates this. There, massive student
demonstrations were joined by trade unions and other left-wing organisations to fight for the re-establishment of public institutions that would
be run on a not-for-profit basis. They argued against the private universities and secondary schools that rendered education as a commodity,
but they did this in the context of the 'right to education'. Similarly, in
Colombia in 2011, student protests managed to overturn the complex
and confusing *Law 30*, which would have privatised the remaining public
universities and increased non-state control of academics under the guise
of increasing funding. In both instances students organised around the
right to education. Traditional human rights techniques were eschewed:
there was no neutral observation of violation with report-writing for
international juridical, economic or political bodies. Instead human
rights became a direct and popular politics. They were used to generate
an antagonism within the right to education. The state claimed to want
more students to go to third-level education, it claimed to be protecting
the right to education. Yet it proposed to do this by placing education in
the private sphere where it would be subject to the vast expanses of
accumulated economic power and the vagaries of the market. In this
sphere education would become further commoditised, with increasing
naturalisation of the power of wealth, and further exclusion of the poor.
Crucially, however, the narrow political goal (of preventing or rowing
back privatisation of education) also opened on to a radical societal
reconfiguration. This combined both a thinking of the political (the role
of the 'private' in neo-liberalism) with the strategic (the use of human
rights in a non-juridical and collective way) and the negative utopian.

---

[33] W. Brown, *States of Injury: Power and Freedom in Late Modernity* (Princeton University
Press, 1995), 98.

The problem with such uses of human rights is that they remain somehow improper. International human rights law is fixated upon the *proper*.[34] The phases of the development of this body of law, from enumeration and standard-setting through to enforcement and most recently to the responsibility to protect, emphasise (or bemoan the absence of) a central authority capable of rendering a settled meaning to a particular text. International human rights law insists that its texts are authoritative regarding what human rights actually are. To know ones' rights, we are told, one needs simply to study the Universal Declaration. There we can find the proper terms of the discourse. The juridical form of human rights lies at the heart of this question, but the structure of authenticity and properness is problematic. On a political level, the danger of this idea of an authentic or proper human rights is that it generates a static image of human rights whereby their shifting functions and apparatuses are generated to meet the techno-economic needs of liberal-capitalism or the well-meaning but empty ethico-political visions of left-liberals.[35] The proper generates a field in which it is possible for the judge or philosopher to know what is right in rights.[36] It establishes a hierarchy whereby certain rights-claims can be dismissed as improper. This then is the classic sovereign logic – it becomes the discourse that allows the sovereign to decide on inclusion and exclusion.

What is crucial about this deep sovereign logic of rights is the manner in which it is closely tied to an understanding of human *being*. We are told that human rights originate in an understanding of what is proper to

---

[34] The proper or authentic is a mode of thinking which seeks to understand the essence of its subject in order to align the essence with an action, to be able to say whether the action is authentic. Perhaps most famously in philosophy, Heidegger argued in *Being and Time* (J. Mcquarrie and E. Robinson, (trans.), Oxford: Blackwell, 1978) for a way of being that remained authentic to the question of Being itself. Among many others, Derrida critiqued the authentic or the proper in Heidegger, as being crucial to his turn to Fascism. For further discussion of authenticity in Heidegger, see M. de Beistegui, *Heidegger and the Political* (London: Routledge, 1997); R. Beardsworth, *Derrida and the Political* (London: Routledge, 1996) and Wall, *Human Rights and Constituent Power*.

[35] What is more surprising is that the proper also lies at the heart of many of the old critiques of human rights. The classic Marxist position, for instance, points to Locke's famous reification of rights. Locke tells us that 'each Man has property in his own person'. The role of government is to protect each person's 'life, liberty and estates'. Thus, Marx can diagnose the possessive individual as the subject of rights. Of course, such a rendering forces the elision of any proletarian historical subjectivity from the discourse. Marx and classical Marxists can therefore reject rights-talk, because it must always already presuppose an ejection of radical potential. This easy rejection of human rights discourse re-inscribes the proper, insisting once more on an authentic or proper human rights that are the bourgeois artefacts.

[36] See, for instance, Foucault's critique of Kant in M. Foucault, *Society Must be Defended* (New York: Picador, 1997).

the human.[37] Because the human eats, speaks, possesses and associates, she must have rights. Thus, rights belong to the human by way of her human-ness, her dignity or her nature. In one of the first of Philippe Lacoue-Labarthe's papers translated into English, he glosses Heidegger's famous critique of humanism, suggesting that: 'The access to being ... depropriates man absolutely.'[38] Throughout the piece, Lacoue-Labarthe plays with the question of the proper and the improper, the authentic and inauthentic, or the familiar and the uncanny. To de-propriate is to displace and turn away from the sovereign logic of the proper and improper. For Lacoue-Labarthe the human is she who is never complete, but always un-working or de-propriating herself. I want to suggest that if the human is the one who reaches for a de-propriation, the focus in human rights on the proper is paradoxically entirely improper. The flipside of this paradox is that if human rights are to remain proper to the human, they must turn away from the juridical logics of the proper. However, what would it be to think about human rights as a practice of de-propriation?[39]

Conclusion

At this point, it would be a good idea to return to my original question. The generation of new rights is problematic when understood from within the canon of human rights (represented by the established orders of the various UN conventions, regional bodies and domestic constitutional systems). However, what this debate misses is that the disruptive creativity of rights cannot be simply tied to the international sphere. My argument ultimately is that if we shift away from human rights as a totalising system designed to generate some sort of perpetual peace,[40] and instead focus upon right-ing in strategies of rupture we come to a much more interesting problem than the simple debate which surrounds 'new rights'. From the perspective of right-ing, it is *always* a matter of thinking creatively with the given human rights framework. This may involve generating new rights (of which more below) or using old rights to re-frame the question. The point is not to think about conserving the

---

[37] J. Donnelly, *The Concept of Human Rights* (London: Croom Helm, 1985).

[38] P. Lacoue-Labarthe, 'In the Name of ...', in J.-L. Nancy and P. Lacoue-Labarthe, *Retreating the Political* (London: Routledge, 1997), 66.

[39] It is useful to think about Christodoulidis' strategies of rupture alongside Costas Douzinas' critique of critique ('Oubliez Critique', *Law and Critique*, 16 (2005), 47). Critique as *strategy* de-propriates critique from the legal habit that Douzinas identifies.

[40] For a critical interrogation of this, see C. Douzinas, *Human Rights and Empire* (Abingdon: Routledge, 2007).

existent constituted discourse, but rather to radically open a particular situation to being-otherwise.

I have already talked about the Chilean and Colombian use of existent rights (the right to education) in the context of 'meta-level struggles', so let me suggest a different 'new right' which would be strategically distinct: the 'right of autogestion'. Autogestion has been making something of a come-back in the last ten years. In its simplest sense, autogestion means self-production or self-constitution. It was a tactic floated by the Eurocommunists, and various groups across Latin America in the 1960s and 1970s, as a way in which factories could be run spontaneously by the workers. However, over the last ten years it has become crucial, linking the Brazilian landless workers' movements with Argentinian worker-recuperated enterprises (*empresas recuperadas por sus trabajadores*),[41] and more recently with attempts to develop similar ideas in Greece and Spain following the closure of companies and factories.

For the purposes of space, I will focus upon Henri Lefebvre's conceptualisation of the idea as a way of drawing out the matter. At his most radical, Lefebvre insists that '*autogestion* must be studied in two different ways: as a means of struggle, which clears the way; and as a means for the reorganisation of society, which transforms it from bottom to top, from everyday life to the State'.[42] On the first level it is one (among many) of the ways of organising in order to 'change life'. By taking over individual workplaces, it becomes a strategy of changing society in a capillary fashion. However, by so doing, the workplace itself becomes a paradigm of a re-imagined society. Were it to remain on the level of individual workplaces, Lefebvre felt that it would remain a thoroughly precarious practice. Crucially, he argued that it also 'carries within itself the *possibility* of its generalization and radicalization ... at the same time it reveals and crystallizes the contradictions of society before it'.[43] In other words, autogestion holds within itself a much deeper potentiality – the possibility of generalisation.[44]

---

[41] See for instance, M. Sitrin, *Everyday Revolutions* (London: Zed Books, 2013).

[42] H. Lefebvre, *State, Space, World: Selected Essays* (Minneapolis, Minn.: University of Minnesota Press, 2009), 149.

[43] Ibid., 147, emphasis in the original.

[44] Of course, it is always subject to appropriation. Lefebvre rails against practices of co-gestion, which were beginning to emerge when he was writing in the 1970s but which are now all around us. Co-gestion or co-management is the practice of granting workers shares in the enterprise in order to engender a sense of shared ownership. For Lefebvre, this was the destruction of autogestion. But that is not all. Autogestion itself may become co-opted or subjugated to a different purpose, as in Toyota-ism (practices which give labourers powers to innovate within their job in order to improve productivity and job satisfaction).

Crucially, autogestion is improper when looked at from the perspective of property rights. Those with property rights in the land and the machinery upon which the enterprise relies will resist. This is particularly the case with the banks and other creditors who will hold mortgages and securities over the companies in liquidation. They will seek to set the force of law loose on these practices, with injunctions, possession orders and bailiffs. This is where Lefebvre's suggestion of the 'right to autogestion' is particularly important. It seeks to order the radical political practice of autogestion, by way of a strategy of rupture. In economies wracked by mass default and the collapse of production, it may be possible to exhaust this force of law. However, the 'right to autogestion' is not simply a question of exhausting law, it also works to generate a different approach to legality without a unified sovereign. It is not a right that might be claimed from the state, nor does it accord to a determined and determinative human essence. Rather it operates as both 'the site and stake of struggle'.[45] This formulation is crucial as it returns us to the question of a 'means without end'. There is no end (*telos*) of autogestion that is not already part of the means of achieving the right. In this, the 'right' itself is consumed in its own practice. The right of autogestion entails an initial withdrawal from legal form, in an attempt to re-imagine what is thinkable within the rights framework. It generates an excess that is lived-life. However, it also reinserts this excess back into law. The experiments with autogestion will be subject to juridical and police apparatuses. They will be litigated and policed. However, they are not *determined by* law. The autogestion consumes the right, rather than the other way around. It generates an excess of law, while simultaneously engaging with law in order to produce a barb of contradiction within the given political order.

The point is that this 'new' right is not aimed at international recognition and convention-based norm-building. Rather it seeks to exploit contradictions between economic and political rationalities. This is not the innocent (post-)Marxist or critical legal belief that if we can just reveal the (fundamental) contradictions the society around us will crumble. Rather, radical rights-claims like autogestion attempt to generate practices that would bring a new world to presence. Right-ing, more generally, is the excess of human rights. It is the point where they begin again to generate new radical political practices which de-propriate the discourse, thereby (paradoxically) setting lose the world-creation that is proper to them. However, it is not enough to think philosophically about

---

[45] S. Elden, *Understanding Lefebvre* (New York: Continuum, 2004), 227.

such a possibility. I have suggested that through a strategic engagement with law, and the discourse of constituent power, we can begin to understand a different vocabulary of right-ing: It is ruptural, collective and lacks institutional mediation. It is creative and generates new rights, not to ensure their protection by a state, but to begin to fashion a new life. However, ultimately, this right-ing praxis is only useful if it can attach to a point of torsion. Our task is to begin to identify such points, and draw out the significance of rights and right-ing in those contexts.

7   Fanon today

Drucilla Cornell

In this chapter, I will argue that we need to return to African and Afro-Caribbean revolutionary thought if we are to reconsider the meaning of the human beyond what Sylvia Wynter has called the "episteme of man" that inevitably liminalizes the damned as beyond the reach of the hegemonic conception of the human. Even once we have made this return to African and Afro-Caribbean revolutionary thought, we still need to separate out its struggle for a radical mutation of the human from the dominant recent view of human rights which, as a number of thinkers have argued, is actually a rejection of this revolutionary intellectual heritage.[1]

Frantz Fanon's work is so significant to us today because it continues to give us an entirely different philosophical perspective on the ethical and political significance of a new way of being human together. Fanon both rejects traditional European narratives of why humans are unique and deserving of dignity and those anti- or post-humanists who argue that we are already beyond the human, either through evolution or in a political and ethical sense. To put it simply: the colonial situation is one of systematic dehumanization. The human, however, is not a set of attributes, whether real or ideal. Instead, what it means to be human together in a world beyond the terrifying brutalities of colonialism is only to be found in the revolutionary struggle itself.

For Fanon, the colonial situation generates what he calls a "phobogenic" world in which black subjectivity is denied its existence by the colonial other. Thus, for Fanon, mental illnesses among colonial subjects are rooted in a social world that militantly seeks to repress any individual self-assertion on the part of human beings identified as black by the colonial authorities. For Fanon, psychoanalysis goes wrong when it attempts to root neuroses and psychoses exclusively in individual family relations. Instead, we must understand them as reactive formations that are inseparable from the

---

[1] See Samuel Moyn, *The Last Utopia: Human Rights in History* (Cambridge, Mass.: Belknap, 2010), particularly Chapter 3: "Why Anticolonialism Wasn't a Human Rights Movement."

racism that renders black humanity a contradiction in terms. Therefore, there can be no individual solutions to break out of the colonial world. Yet in Fanon's "untidy dialectic," there must be a moment of assertion that a black person is indeed an "I," even though this cannot be done without both an aesthetic and ethical rebellion against the disidentification of blackness with all that is *considered* human. We can understand movements like *négritude*, then, for Fanon, as being a necessary part of this untidy dialectic, precisely in their assertion that black, African/Arab, and the human can be brought together without any connection to white definitions of what it means to be black. Fanon writes:

The concept of *négritude* . . . was the affective if not logical antithesis of that insult which the white man had leveled at the rest of humanity. This *négritude*, hurled against the contempt of the white man, has alone proved capable in some sectors of lifting taboos and maledictions.[2]

Many critics of identity politics, as well as some of those who seek to define identity politics as recognition, fail to understand the originality of Fanon on this point. The assertion that "I am black and I am I," in Fanon's interpretation of Hegel, does not take place in the famous master–slave dialectic, but comes before the opening up of the dialectic of desire in that famous part of the *Phenomenology*, as Nigel Gibson has underscored as well. To quote Hegel:

As self-consciousness, it [self-consciousness] is movement, but since self-consciousness *merely* distinguishes *itself* from itself *as itself*, that distinction as an otherness is in its eyes *immediately sublated*. There simply *is* no distinction, and *self-consciousness* is merely the motionless tautology of "I am I." (par. 167)

Simply put, the European is denied the status of an originating self-consciousness, and assertions of movements like *négritude* in a profound sense turn the world into a place where blacks can be self-defining as to the meaning of blackness without any appeal to whites in a call for recognition. Movements like *négritude*, for Fanon, are a necessary part of the untidy dialectic, because it is in this preliminary assertion that a consciousness that is not for the white man is initially developed, and therefore, the "I" makes the seemingly impossible gesture that he or she is already living beyond the "phobogenic" world. The crucial point here, in answer to recent debates about identity politics, is that this assertion of a black "I" refuses to recognize the white other as a source of recognition. In a profound existential sense, it is "creating" an "I" out of the

---

[2] Frantz Fanon, *The Wretched of the Earth*, (trans.) Richard Philcox (New York: Grove, 2004), 150.

nothingness imposed upon blacks under the brutal realities of colonial life. Of course, this is not enough for Fanon, as it was not enough for Hegel either, since Hegel understands this is a tautology that must break down through a confrontation with the other and otherness. It is a relation that denies relation, and *has* to, because, paradoxically, under colonialism there *is* no relationship between whites and blacks that can be considered anything like an ethical connection between human beings.[3] I want to underscore this point, that colonialism, for Fanon, is not a relationship between human beings, but the violent exclusion of the colonized from the register of the human:

Colonialism is not a type of individual relations but the conquest of a national territory and the oppression of a people: that is all. It is not a certain type of human behavior or a pattern of relations between individuals. Every Frenchman in Algeria is at the present time an enemy soldier. So long as Algeria is not independent, this logical consequence must be accepted.[4]

We will return shortly to the inevitability of violence in the struggle for national liberation, which in Fanon is always inseparable from the struggle for a new way of being human together, which must involve the battle, not only of anti-black racism, but also for socialism. Indeed, this is a struggle to bring about the radical mutation towards the human. For now, I want to emphasize that without this originary assertiveness, there cannot be a full grasp of the depths of oppression, because it is when one asserts that "I am black and I am human" that the horror of the denial of one's humanity hits home in full force. This assertion of the black "I," then, is always a necessary moment in what Fanon calls the untidy dialectic of revolutionary struggle. There has to be an "I" that asserts its own existence against the other for the full impact of the lack of the ethical relationship to be experienced by the masses of the oppressed under colonial domination. And hence we come, of course, to Fanon's most controversial writing on violence.

---

[3] "The search for recognition that emerges in Fanon's penultimate chapter fails, then, because the necessary conditions for self–Other relations also fail: neither the Hegelian master nor the structural White Man wants recognition from blacks; each wants *work*, and bodies without points of view. Here we see why the demands of classical liberalism and Kantian humanism fail: they depend upon symmetry. White–black relations are such that blacks struggle to achieve Otherness; it is a struggle to be in a position *for the ethical to emerge*. Thus, the circumstance is peculiarly wrought with realization of the *political*. Fanon's book ends, then, politically and existentially. Politically, like the author's romanticized African American, the call is to fight, to struggle against the system of his oppression. But in that struggle, Fanon calls for a pedagogy to build (*édifier*, "to edify," "to build") a questioning humanity." Lewis Gordon, *Existentia Africana: Understanding Africana Existential Thought* (New York: Routledge, 2000), 35, emphasis in the original.

[4] Frantz Fanon, *Toward the African Revolution*, (trans.) Haakon Chevalier (New York: Grove, 1967), 81.

Some critics of Fanon, like Hannah Arendt – even though she recognizes some of his subtleties as a thinker – have argued that violence and the "brotherhood" that ensues in the revolutionary struggle are rooted in death and the willingness to face it in the name of freedom. To a certain extent, Arendt is – consciously or not – echoing Hegel in Hegel's own rendition of the purportedly "pre-social" situation in which human beings can only encounter one another as a destructive oppositional force. I want to emphasize here that the opening moves of the famous master–slave dialectic, in which two self-consciousnesses can only meet in opposition and violence, is not the beginning of relationality: it is a rendition, or Hegel's own fable of the pre-social condition. The social only arises in the slave's relationship to the significance of her own labor, which opens up a self-consciousness that understands relationships to be fundamental and triggers the dialectics of the rest of the *Phenomenology*, in which the self-consciously social self has to struggle with all the anguish of the denial of the possibility to actualize freedom in a shared world. Thus in Hegel, opposition is never ontologized: it is part of the pre-social world, and thus on this reading, Hegelians need not end with a pessimistic casting of some kind of core of our human being-together which can never completely forego violence. Ultimately, as we will see, Fanon also refuses the pessimism of an ontologized violent moment as part of social individuality.

In Hegel, the only way out of the pre-social oppositional encounter to self-consciousness is for one to subject himself to the other. For Fanon, unlike Hegel, it is not labor that first opens up the slave's creative activity in the world, and thus the beginning of a self-consciousness of a transindividual social self connected to both things and other subjects. It is, instead, the national liberation struggle. So what exactly am I trying to say here? For Fanon, colonialism is in fact a violent world of a pre-social universe that cannot be ethical and, therefore, anything like reciprocity between human beings can only begin in the course of the revolutionary struggle, in which a truly social world arises in all its richness and complexity. Lewis Gordon has powerfully argued that there is no ethical relationship in colonialism, because black people are not recognized as an embodied self-consciousness that is there in the world. What I am adding here is that it is not only the ethical that is obliterated: it is also the social, and therefore, the only way out of the phobogenic universe that obliterates the social is through a rejection of the originary self-consciousness of the European "I." There is no shared world in this Manichean universe, and therefore there can be no discussion of values between the colonizer and the colonized, as long as the situation of colonialism exists. For Fanon, colonialism is violence, and is inseparable from the anti-black racism that denies humanness and subjectivity to the black majority. Dehumanization, then, is integrally part of racism.[5] Racism is inseparable from violence and exploitation. It is thus a necessary consequence of enslavement and unfree black labor. Fanon writes:

In reality the nations that undertake a colonial war have no concern for the confrontation of cultures. War is a gigantic business and every approach must be governed by this datum. The enslavement, in the strictest sense, of the native population is the prime necessity.[6]

So why, then, if the purpose of colonialism is explicitly super-exploitation, does the colonizer have to engage in another kind of war, a war to "petrify" and thus demean the cultural productions of the colonized? The answer for Fanon is simple. If the colonized are recognized as human, then they of course have their own culture, their own intellectual traditions, their own values, because human beings never live outside not only language but the "symbolic forms" in which they are constituted.[7] But if one is thrown off the register of the human, then such creatures, by definition, do not have a culture worth taking into account. This gives another dimension, for Fanon, of struggles such as *négritude*, which is not only the assertion of the "I" that is black but, also, the insistence that this "I" is part of a people who can claim their humanness as makers of culture:

Let us delve deeper; perhaps this passion and this rage are nurtured or at least guided by the secret hope of discovering beyond the present wretchedness, beyond this self-hatred, this abdication and denial, some magnificent and shining era that redeems us in our own eyes and those of others. I say that I have decided to delve deeper. Since perhaps in their unconscious the colonized intellectuals have been unable to come to loving terms with the present history of their oppressed people, since there is little to marvel at in its current state of

---

[5] "Racism, it is said, emerges through an anxiety over the Other. The Other is supposedly a mark of inferior difference. The problem with this view is that it fails to deal with the meaning of the *Other*. Implicit in *Other* is a shared category. If one is a human being, then the Other is also a human being: here I am and there is *another human being*. Dehumanization takes a different form: there one finds the self, another self, and those who are not-self and not-Other. In effect, as Fanon points out in the seventh chapter of *Black Skin, White Masks*, there is a schema in which self–Other relations might exist between whites and between blacks, but white-black interaction does not signify a self–Other relation. Rather, it is self–below–Other relation. A black–white interaction, on the other hand, signifies a self–Other relation. For the black, in other words, the white is another human being, but the structure of antiblack racism is such that for the antiblack racist, the black is not another human being. The struggle against antiblack racism is such, then, that it involves an effort to achieve Otherness. It is a struggle to enter the realm, in other words, in which ethical relations are forged." Gordon, *Existentia Africana*, 85, emphasis in the original.

[6] Fanon, *Toward the African Revolution*, 33.

[7] See Drucilla Cornell and Kenneth Michael Panfilio, *Symbolic Forms for a New Humanity: Cultural and Racial Reconfigurations of Critical Theory* (New York: Fordham University Press, 2010).

barbarity, they have decided to go further, to delve deeper, and they must have been overjoyed to discover that the past was not branded with shame, but dignity, glory, and sobriety. Reclaiming the past does not only rehabilitate or justify the promise of a national culture. It triggers a change of fundamental importance in the colonized's psycho-affective equilibrium. Perhaps it has not been sufficiently demonstrated that colonialism is not content merely to impose its law on the colonized country's present and future. Colonialism is not satisfied with snaring the people in its net or of draining the colonized brain of any form or substance. With a kind of perverted logic, it turns its attention to the past of the colonized people and distorts it, disfigures it, and destroys it. This effort to demean history prior to colonization today takes on a dialectical significance.[8]

Thus, there is a dialectical significance to violence in Fanon, which has led him to make some of his most infamous pronouncements on violence, particularly the killing of a white person, in which the white person's self-consciousness is in a deep sense denied, and is literally deflated as a source of meaning of the entire world and of culture. In the Manichean universe, the master's self-consciousness only arises out of fear, the fear that necessarily arises when, for the first time, what had become a thing arises in all the ferocity of their assertion of an "I" that is human, and therefore can shoot back. This, of course, differentiates the struggle of the colonized from the master–slave dialectic in Hegel, where the slave can realize through labor that there is an integral relation to otherness that cannot simply be disavowed, but must be worked through and engaged in the struggle to actualize freedom. Thus, the assertion of a certain form of subjectivity is integrally tied, in Fanon, to the movements that bring to life the cultural and intellectual traditions of the colonized, the spontaneous violence and rage that result from the claim that one is human, and can fight back. But ultimately, the violent struggle must self-consciously grasp itself as part of the creation of a new national culture, which is inseparable from the becoming of a people out of their own self-mobilization. This becoming a people out of mobilization is the basis for what Fanon calls "national culture." Violence, then, is never justified in and for itself. It is necessary, if there is to be an ethical, social, or human world at all, because such a world is simply impossible in the colonized situation. Thus, for Fanon, there is literally a new "species" of men and women who arise in the process of destroying the colonized situation:

National liberation, national reawakening, restoration of the nation to the people or Commonwealth, whatever the name used, whatever the latest expression, decolonization is always a violent event ... What is singularly important is that it starts from the very first day with the basic claims of the colonized. In actual

---

[8] Fanon, *The Wretched of the Earth*, 147–149.

fact, proof of success lies in a social fabric that has been changed inside out. This change is extraordinarily important because it is desired, clamored for, and demanded. The need for this change exists in a raw, repressed, and reckless state in the lives and consciousness of colonized men and women.[9]

It is important to note, however, that for Fanon what the revolutionary struggle brings about is a radical mutation in how human beings come to be together. This radical mutation is what allows new meanings to be given to the human in what is now a social relation that is in turn inseparable from revolution. It is not, then, just that revolution is inevitably a social process: it is that revolution brings the social into existence. And why does this need to be done through armed struggle? As I have already noted, it is part of a radical moment of self-assertion. But it is also a necessary movement to overthrow colonial domination, since this form of domination turns on the complete dehumanization of "blackness" and "Africanness." There is, therefore, no way for an ethical movement to succeed in a world that has destroyed the ethical. The revolutionary struggle must, then, involve the complete overthrow of the conditions that have obliterated the social in the first place. Since according to Fanon, what whites want in conditions of colonial domination is not recognition but unfree black labor, there is no way to open up the dialectic of recognition *within* colonialism.

Does that mean that Fanon completely rejected Hegel, and that in a certain sense, as Arendt argues, it is the violent confrontation with death that creates the "brotherhood," which according to Arendt's critique would inevitably lead to a "dead end"? The answer, as I have already suggested, is that freedom involves violent struggle because it is the only way to bring to life a truly social world in which the dialectic of recognition and reciprocity would be something other than empty hypocritical phrases mouthed by whites who want to keep blacks in their place. But is there some abstract definition of freedom, or of what it means to be fully human in Fanon? Yes, there is certainly the emphasis on the centrality of freedom, but what it means to be free and what it means to be human is itself a process.

I have already suggested that for Fanon national liberation is inseparable from the creation of a new species of the human, beyond the imposed living death on the colonized within colonialism. But the nation, here, is the coming together of the people to declare their independence through the destruction of colonialism and through the mobilization of new forms of participatory democracy which include, and must include

---

[9] Fanon, *The Wretched of the Earth*, 1.

for Fanon, the complete end of economic and social conditions of exploitation. Therefore, there can be no coming together of the people simply as a political movement, without a challenge to economic oppression, and this is where Fanon profoundly disagreed with some of the African leaders in the 1960s, like Léopold Senghor, who insisted that the political comes first, and that economic transformation could wait until another day. The people coming together, then, must not only create participatory modes of democratic mobilization, which demands a changed subjectivity for those who had been brutally robbed of their land. The people coming together must also demand the return of land, not simply because it has been stolen, but because without land, human beings are unable to live and control their conditions of production in common. As Fanon writes:

> For a colonized people, the most essential value, because it is the most meaningful, is first and foremost the land: the land, which must provide bread and, naturally, dignity. But this dignity has nothing to do with "human" dignity. The colonized subject has never heard of such an ideal.[10]

Why does Fanon put "human" in quotation marks? It should be clear by now that, for Fanon, the question of man, or the human, is absolutely inseparable from the question of revolutionary nationalism, but in the specific sense I have described above. The mutated new "species," the new human world in which we might live together, does not grow out of a set of metaphysical commitments. It is, instead, rooted in revolution, and therefore, it is a completely different form of humanism than those that are rooted in the "armored cosmopolitanism," to use Paul Gilroy's telling phrase, that is integral to current human rights discourse. But Fanon always considered this "nationalism" a mobilizing of the people as part of a pan-Africanist, transnational struggle.

Philosopher Étienne Balibar has argued that the inextricably linked notions of "man" and the subject are inseparable from the history of revolution, and particularly, a human subject that asserts "equaliberty" as the basis for belonging together as citizens. Balibar credits Kant for the idea that the question of man can only be given an answer within the practical horizon of cosmopolitical belonging of a particular view of the world citizen:

> To ask "What is Man?" for Kant is to ask a concrete question, a question which is therefore more fundamental than any other, because it immediately concerns the experience, knowledge and practical ends of Man as a *citizen of the world*. Indeed the Kantian *question* already involves and predetermines a formal *answer*. "Man"

---

[10] Fanon, *The Wretched of the Earth*, 9.

is a (the) citizen of the world; his "essence" is nothing other than the horizon within which all the determinations of that universal "citizenship" must fall. The only thing that remains to do, then, is to elaborate and clarify the meaning of all this.[11]

Balibar's originality is to connect this philosophical question directly with the question of revolution, equaliberty, and the citizen-subject. But many have rightfully critiqued – and Balibar would be one of them – the Kantian horizon of the cosmopolitical world, because it naively runs up against the brutal imperialism of what Balibar calls "real universality." It is important to add here that Balibar's re-interpretation of the politics of the rights of man and the citizen-subject should not be confused with a defense of human rights as such defenses have recently come to be understood, from the 1970s forward, namely as a set of moral claims, "as entitlements that might contradict the sovereign nation-state from above and outside rather than serve as its foundation."[12] Even in Kant, the cosmopolitical horizon was one of perpetual peace between republics. It was not a moral discourse that was meant to replace the struggle to achieve a republic in the first place. Thus, it is a serious misinterpretation of Balibar to consider him a defender of human rights in the current sense of the term. Instead, Balibar is a defender of the meaning of "man" as a practical philosophical question, inseparable from revolutionary conceptions of the citizen-subject. Even if we reject the content of Kant's cosmopolitical horizon, then, perhaps we need not and should not reject the fundamental insight of Balibar, but recast it in relation to Fanon's own understanding of why the national revolution in Africa can never simply be national, nor even pan-Africanist – although it must be that as well – but always implies the ethical and political horizon of a radically mutated humanity that grows out of revolutionary struggle.

Sylvia Wynter, in her own writing on Fanon,[13] has argued that what she has called "the episteme of man" that developed out of the Renaissance in Europe necessarily "liminalizes" the damned of the earth, by

---

[11] Étienne Balibar, "Subjection and Subjectivication," in *Supposing the Subject*, (ed.) Joan Copjec (London: Verso, 1994), 1–16, 7, emphasis in the original.

[12] Moyn, *The Last Utopia*, 13.

[13] Sylvia Wynter, "Unsettling the Coloniality of Being/Power/Truth/Freedom: Towards the Human, After Man, Its Overrepresentation – An Argument," *The New Centennial Review*, 3(3) (2003), 257–337; Sylvia Wynter, "Towards the Sociogenic Principle: Fanon, The Puzzle of Conscious Experience, of 'Identity' and What It's Like to be 'Black'," in *National Identity and Sociopolitical Change: Latin America Between Marginalization and Integration*, (ed.) Mercedes Durán-Cogan and Antonio Gómez-Moriana (Minneapolis, Minn.: University of Minnesota Press, 1999); Antony Boques, *Caribbean Reasonings: After Man Towards the Human – Critical Essays on Sylvia Wynter* (Kingston: Ian Randle Publishers, 2005).

which she means not only the rendering of the other as black but as blackness itself as a category of the chaotic and the irrational. A full discussion of Wynter is unfortunately beyond the parameters of this short chapter. However, the significance of what she calls the "afterman" involves a powerful critique, not only of Nietzsche's *Übermensch* or other powerful critiques of the episteme of man, such as that of Michel Foucault, in the name of a new socio-poesis, or in Fanon's words, radical mutation of the human. For Wynter – and this is her interpretation of Fanon – we have yet to begin the history of the human, because it has been completely captured by the episteme of man, and therefore we do not need to reject humanism, but rethink it within the context of revolutionary struggle.

As Fanon writes:

Among colonized peoples there seems to exist a kind of illuminating and sacred communication as a result of which each liberated territory is for a certain time promoted to the rank of "guide territory." The independence of a new territory, the liberation of the new peoples are felt by the other oppressed countries as an invitation, an encouragement, and a promise. Every setback of colonial domination in America or in Asia strengthens the national will of the African peoples. It is in the national struggle against the oppressor that colonized peoples have discovered, concretely, the solidarity of the colonialist bloc and the necessary interdependence of the liberation movements.[14]

But this is a very different vision of internationalism or transnationalism than the one evoked by current human rights discourse, as Samuel Moyn has argued in his history of human rights. As Moyn points out, thinkers as diverse as Fanon, Du Bois, and Malcolm X only use the phrase "human rights" as part of the struggle of anti-black racism and against all forms of colonialism. Fanon's pan-Africanism, which points to a new humanism that grows out of revolutionary struggle, is a horizon in which the question of what it means to be human can be raised, but only in the dynamism of revolution, and therefore there is no being in the human without revolutionary struggle. We are far away from current conceptions of human rights, and indeed are returned to what Paul Gilroy has called the right to be human, a "right" which for Gilroy is inseparable from the struggle against anti-black racism, and for a different transnational and transmodern vision of pan-Africanism. To quote Gilroy:

The antiracism that inherited a worldly vision from pan-Africanism and passed it on to the anti-colonial movements did not descend to the present through the temperate landscape of liberal pieties. It came via disreputable abolitionism and

---

[14] Fanon, *Towards the African Revolution*, 145.

translocal, multicultural, and anti-imperial activism that was allied with the insurrectionary practice of those who, though legally held in bondage, were subject to the larger immoralities of a race-friendly system of domination.[15]

If the right to be human can only configure itself within the revolutionary struggle, then what must it entail? We have already seen that, for Fanon, national liberation is inseparable from the re-appropriation of the land. The great South African philosopher, Mabogo Percy More, has underscored the point that the right to claim land is inseparable from the right to be human, and to the connected right to life. More argues:

If, as I have indicated, land gives life to human beings, then there is an inextricable organic connection between land and life. If colonialism, as Fanon counsels us, is indeed "the conquest of *national territory* and the oppression of a people" . . ., and if conquest in colonial situations occurs through violence, then the forcible expropriation of land from and the consequent denial of reasonable access to land to the rightful owner is equivalent to a denial and refusal to recognize the right to life of the dispossessed. But if one's right to life is threatened, then morality, politics, and law all agree about Fanon's appeal to violence as a form of justifiable self-defense.[16]

But these rights, as we have seen, are not conceived at all as rights rooted in individual entitlement, based on some notion of shared attributes that mark out our humanity against other creatures. Nor are they the empty rights of the victims of the many brutal wars and states of impoverishment brought about by neo-liberal global capitalism. Famously, Hannah Arendt argued that human rights were hopelessly caught in a paradox. Either they were the rights of those who had no rights, such as the refugees who had no nation-state in which they could claim national belonging and thus citizenship. Or human rights were simply another name for the rights of citizens of a nation-state. Either way, an appeal to human rights was caught up in this paradox, so that such rights were either an impossible claim made on the part of those who had no rights or a redundant claim made on the part by those who already had them as citizens.[17]

The philosopher Jacques Rancière has profoundly challenged Arendt's paradox or tautology and argued that there is a whole different way of thinking about the rights of man, as the politics of the rights of man can inform our current thinking about the possibility intended in human rights. It is important to note, before proceeding with Rancière's rethinking of

[15] Paul Gilroy, *After Empire* (Abingdon: Routledge, 2004), 62.
[16] Mabogo Percy More, "Fanon and the Land Question in (Post)Apartheid South Africa," in *Living Fanon*, (ed.) Nigel C. Gibson (New York: PalgraveMacmillan, 2011), 173–186, 181, emphasis in the original.
[17] Hannah Arendt, *The Origins of Totalitarianism* (New York: Harcourt, 1976), 290–302.

human rights, that Rancière completely rejects the idea of *homo sacer*, in that, for him, no human being is ever completely reduced to bare life, and that to portray such a human being in that light is, sadly, to reduce the subaltern to the silent images of hapless victims that we see night after night on television.[18] We have already seen that the black struggle for the right to be human in no way can be understood as the right of victims who have no rights. I want to argue here that the black revolutionary understanding of human rights, which has been the specter of the liberal humanitarian rights discourse, can best be understood through Rancière's unique defense of the politics of human rights or the rights of man. Rancière argues that "the Rights of Man are the rights of those who have not the rights that they have and have the rights that they have not."[19] Rancière uses Olympe de Gouges, a revolutionary woman during the French Revolution, to underscore his basic assumption about the politics of the rights of man or human rights. Women did not have equal rights under the declaration of the rights of man, but Olympe de Gouges not only argued that they *should* have them: according to de Gouges, women *did* have those rights, because if they had the "right" to be killed at the guillotine, they had the right to equal citizenship.[20] In Rancière's language, the rights of man leave behind an egalitarian trait, an inscription of a community as free and equal. When those who do not have rights, such as blacks under the colonial situation, demand that that description be true, they are not, in Rancière's language, appealing to rights they do not have: they are contesting the reality that denies them those rights by acting now as if they had them. By acting now as if they had human rights, they actually create conditions of verification that they are fully equal human beings, and that anyone who denies that they actually have those rights are forced to run up against their political enactment. This is exactly the politics of the rights of man that we see throughout the movements against anti-black racism. As Rancière writes:

Not only is there no man of the Rights of Man, there is no need for one. The strength of those rights lies in the back-and-forth movement between the initial inscription of the right and the dissensual stage on which it is put to the test. This is why the subjects of the Soviet constitution were able to make reference to the Rights of Man in opposition to the laws that denied their effectiveness.

---

[18] Cf. Giorgio Agamben, *Homo Sacer: Sovereign Power and Bare Life* (Stanford University Press, 1998). See also Jean Comaroff and John L. Comaroff, "Beyond Bare Life: AIDS, (Bio)Politics, and the New World Order," in *Theory from the South, or, How Euro-America is Evolving Towards Africa* (Boulder, Col.: Paradigm, 2012), 173–190.

[19] Jacques Rancière, "Who is the Subject of the Rights of Man?," in *Dissensus: On Politics and Aesthetics*, (ed. and trans.) Steven Corcoran (New York, Continuum, 2010), 62–75, 69, emphasis in the original.

[20] Rancière, "Who is the Subject of the Rights of Man?," 68.

This is also why they can be invoked by the citizens of states ruled by religious law or governmental fiat, the populations in refugee camps. When such groups can – and there are always individuals among them that do – make something of these rights to construct a dissensus against the denial of rights they suffer, they really have these rights.[21]

It is important, then, to underscore what dissensus might mean here. Rancière defines dissensus as a dispute over what is given, and a challenge to the very frame through which we see and hear a world as simply given to us. When subjects who do not have rights enact them in the case of anti-colonial struggles by, for example, seizing the land in the name of the right to land, they create what Rancière calls a dissensus. They are not rightless victims, which is how they are identified by Arendt and later by Agamben. To quote Rancière, who is speaking again of women in this case, but I believe it is equally applicable to the black enactment of the right to be human:

Women, as political subjects, set out to make a twofold statement. They demonstrated that they were deprived of the rights that they had thanks to the Declaration of Rights and that through their public action that they *had* the rights denied to them by the constitution, that they could *enact* those rights. They acted as subjects of the Rights of Man in the precise sense that I have mentioned. They acted as subjects that did not have the rights that they had and that had the rights that they had not. This is what I call a dissensus: the putting of two worlds in one and the same world. The question of the political subject is not caught between the void term of Man and the plenitude of the citizen with its actual rights. A political subject is a capacity for staging scenes of dissensus.[22]

Often Rancière's expression, "the part of no part," is taken to designate the radically excluded who, as Rancière puts it, have no "signs of politicity."[23] For Rancière, to deny someone that they are the bearer of what he calls "politicity" is to deny that they are a human being. The point of the struggle against anti-black racism is precisely that they are bearers of the signs of politicity in the enactment of radical politics, including their right to be human. Thus, again it needs to be underscored here that the last thing that these struggles do in their enactment of the right to be human is underwrite themselves as victims.

As I have written earlier in this chapter, Moyn rightfully understands the African and/or black politics of human rights to be completely different than that of contemporary humanitarian rights discourse. But what

---

[21] Rancière, "Who is the Subject of the Rights of Man?," 71.
[22] Rancière, "Who is the Subject of the Rights of Man?," 69, emphasis in the original.
[23] Rancière, "Ten Theses on Politics," in *Dissensus: On Politics and Aesthetics*, (ed. and trans.) Steven Corcoran (New York: Continuum, 2010), 38.

Rancière underscores is that the humanitarian interpretation of human rights is inseparable from a series of moves made in political philosophy that either reduce the other to radical heterogeneity, and therefore take that other out of politics, or turns us all into bare life, as we live in the state of exception of the nation-state now understood as a camp (Agamben). Thus, in a profound sense, how we think about the politics of the rights of man is crucial for thinking through politics at all, and this insight, I want to suggest, has long been understood by the struggles against anti-black racism and colonialism in Africa. Rancière writes:

Just as we saw with Agamben, this means infinitizing wrong and replacing its political processing with a sort of ontological destiny that permits only of "resistance." Such resistance is no manifestation of freedom, however. Resistance here means faithfulness to the law of Otherness, thereby ruling out any dreams of "human emancipation." This is the philosophical understanding of the rights of the Other. But they can also be understood in a less sophisticated and more trivial sense as follows: if those who suffer inhuman repression cannot exercise the Human Rights that are their last recourse, then it is up to others to inherit these rights and exercise them in their place. The name for this is the "right to humanitarian interference" – a right that some nations have arrogated because they claim, very often against the views of humanitarian organizations themselves, that it will help the victimized populations. The "right to humanitarian interference," then, is like the return of the disused rights sent to the rightless back to their senders.[24]

The danger, then, of "disuse" is precisely that it underscores the neo-liberal interpretation of human rights that has, paradoxically, justified the worst kind of violence. Costas Douzinas has profoundly disagreed with Rancière's reformulation of the tautology of human rights critiqued by Hannah Arendt. He argues that there cannot be any radical potential of human rights, because they are part of what Rancière calls the politics of consensus, and that they provide a dangerous frame for what is possible in the realm of revolutionary challenge to the existing world order. For Douzinas, any modern legal system is inevitably the gatekeeper of who comes in and who comes out, and therefore promotes a radically excluded other at the same time that it defines conditions of belonging, and with these conditions, the rights of citizenship. Thus, he argues:

In the new world order, the excluded have no access to rights and none is possible. They are outside Rancière's regime of visibility and access is foreclosed by political, legal and military means. Economic migrants, refugees, prisoners in the war on terror, torture victims, inhabitants of African camps, these "one use humans" attest to total and irreversible exclusion. These people cannot be a part within or outside the political space nor can they represent the universal in whose

---

[24] Rancière, "Who is the Subject of the Rights of Man?," 74.

name inclusion can be asserted. They are just no part; they are the indispensable precondition of human rights but at the same time the living, dying rather, proof of their impossibility. The law not only cannot understand the surplus subject, its very operation prevents the emergence of such subjects. On the way to the new world order, human rights as the ideology at the "end of history" plugs the interval between man and citizen, universal and particular, law and fact, appearance and reality, the spaces that generated exclusions and created the hope of their transcendence. This type of human rights politics leads to the acceptance of the given distribution of power and fuller and more committed participation in it.[25]

There are two points I want to oppose to Douzinas' reading of Rancière. The first is that he identifies the "part of no part" with those who are radically excluded. Rancière carefully avoids this designation. Instead, Rancière argues that the "part of no part" is meant to signify those who are to rule without qualification, and therefore it is about a definition of the *demos*, not a designation of a particular group. But there is also another point that Rancière seeks to underscore: there is no radically excluded other that has completely lost its "politicity." In other words, we are never reduced to just bare life. My point is that the massive upheavals of anti-colonial struggles in Africa and the continuing struggles against anti-black racism point precisely to the dissensus inherent in the demand that "I am black, I am human, and I am your equal." That declaration lies at the heart of Fanonian politics. But do we reject Douzinas' critique? Not at all. It should be read as a powerful critique of exactly the humanitarian reduction of human rights which, as Rancière points out, is inseparable from their "disuse" by the radical left within the terms of the Fanonian framework I have defended here.

Douzinas has also argued that revolutionary equality, which for Fanon is always asserted in the national liberation struggle within the horizon of a pan-Africanism that declares a new humanity, is both the rejection and the sublation of a certain human rights culture, or of a rights culture more generally.[26] I want to insist on the caveat that it should be read as a rejection of a specific human rights culture, one that would not lead us to turn away from Rancière's radical re-reading of human rights, particularly once that re-reading is put in the context of Fanonian revolutionary humanism. Indeed, Douzinas' sublimation turns us to a new conception of being in the right, or "right-ing being," towards the famous communist idea, from each according to her ability to each according to her need. We have seen that in the colonial situation, for Fanon, what the colonized

---

[25] Costas Douzinas, *Human Rights and Empire: The Political Philosophy of Cosmopolitanism* (New York: Routledge, 2007), 107–108.

[26] Costas Douzinas, "*Adikia*: On Communism and Rights," in *The Idea of Communism*, (ed.) Costas Douzinas and Slavoj Žižek (London: Verso, 2010).

are denied is exactly their right to be at all, at least if we understand "being" as the right to overcome the social death of colonial oppression. For Fanon, as we have seen, there can be no right to be without not only the overthrow of the colonial situation and the assertion of national independence, but also the end of economic exploitation. Yet Fanon gives us a graphic description of how the right to be, even in the most day-to-day activities, is taken away from the colonized, and left to him or her only to dream of being a subject who can freely move and assert themselves in the world. To quote Fanon:

The colonial subject is a man penned in; apartheid is but one method of compartmentalizing the colonial world. The first thing the colonial subject learns is to remain in his place and not overstep its limits. Hence the dreams of the colonial subject are muscular dreams, dreams of action, dreams of aggressive vitality. I dream I am jumping, swimming, running, and climbing. I dream I burst out laughing, I am leaping across a river and chased by a pack of cars that never catches up with me. During colonization the colonized subject frees himself night after night between nine in the evening and six in the morning.[27]

For Fanon, the revolutionary struggle is one in which the power of the mobilizations opens the pen and, through the insistence on the right to be in the human, what was a dream becomes part of the struggle to actualize freedom.

Some might argue that this intellectual heritage in revolutionary humanism has lost its power and is now outdated. I strongly disagree with this position without, of course, thinking that anything like a simple revival is possible. Further, this intellectual heritage continues to influence the movements breaking out throughout the world – and, yes, in the African Spring – against empire, for socialism, and for what the Shantydwellers movements in South Africa call "living communism."If Moyn is right – and I believe he is – that current human rights discourse grew out of both the loss of faith in African revolutionary humanism and the very idea of revolution with which it is inextricably connected, we cannot begin to rethink humanism and move beyond a certain humanitarian discourse without a profound rethinking of the significance of the "Aftermath" in African and Afro-Caribbean philosophy. And is this not our biggest challenge today, to rethink revolutionary possibility against the sorrowful, often self-righteous worldview of a certain human rights discourse?

---

[27] Fanon, *The Wretched of the Earth*, 15.

8   Race and the value of the human

Paul Gilroy

Atheism, being the supersession of God, is the advent of theoretical humanism, and communism, as the supersession of private property, is the vindication of real human life as man's possession and thus the advent of practical humanism. Atheism is humanism mediated with itself through the supersession of religion, while communism is humanism mediated with itself through the supersession of private property. Only through the supersession of this mediation – which is itself, however, a necessary premise – does positively self-deriving humanism, *positive* humanism, come into being.

Marx

Fanon's advocacy of revolutionary change was distinguished by his preparedness to speak in humanity's name, yet the commitment to a *new* humanism that runs through his writing has proved to be a tricky subject for contemporary commentators. As a result, his humanism is rarely discussed. However, the claims to novelty and distinctiveness that frame it are ripe for re-assessment today. He makes a series of arguments that move towards what, following the South African psychologist and TRC commissioner, Pumla Gobodo-Madikizela, we can call a "reparative" humanism.[1] This tantalizing prospect can help to clarify a number of problems that characterize the *postcolonial* world.

The reparation involved in this new humanism is neither straightforwardly financial nor moral. Fanon had an ontological reparation in mind and it was rooted in the specific task of undoing the damage that had resulted from the violent institutionalization of racial orders. Those repairs raised a second important possibility: we may need to begin to

---

[1] Pumla Gobodo-Madikizela, "Alternatives to Revenge: Building a Vocabulary of Reconciliation Through Political Pardon," in Charles Villa-Vicencio and Eric Doxtader, (eds.), *The Provocations of Amnesty: Memory, Justice and Impunity* (Trenton, NY, New World Press, 2003), 51–60.

become human outside of (as well as in opposition to) racial–corporeal schemas and the epidermalized worlds that they generate.

Fanon's humanism was configured by a larger anti-colonial project: the *revolutionary* overcoming of the racial orders created by colonial rule as well as those that gave rise to it. The pressing need for a new humanism emerged in tandem with active pursuit of national liberation, a goal that Fanon qualified by introducing an equally novel and emphatically post-colonial world consciousness that exceeded the formalities of abstract internationalism. These universal hopes had been formed by the Second World War and the wars of decolonization that followed as well as by his conviction that an authentic existence, celebrated in human desire, could remain uncorrupted by the intrusion of raciality. Additionally, a distinctive cosmopolitanism was signaled by Fanon's insistence that Europe's colonial crimes and errors should not be repeated by newly independent, postcolonial states – a historic determination that resonated loudly with his choice of a cosmic rhetoric that is wrongly written off as mere juvenilia. As Ato Sekyi-Otu has suggested,[2] an affirmative rather than a negative conception of the human was introduced by formulations such as: "the human being is a yes that vibrates to cosmic harmonies." It bears repetition that Fanon's idiosyncratic response can be seen to have been shaped by the need to respond to the exclusionary power of racism which specifies blacks as infrahuman.

Gobodo-Madikizela adds to Fanon's unfashionable commitment to a new humanism by making an unlikely argument about the transformative power of empathy. Her suggestion is similarly unsettling to the closed system of contemporary scholastic theory. She presents the restoration of amputated and alienated humanity as a central component in a shared process whereby the victims of Apartheid – and, by extension, of colonial terror in general – might acquire the dignity that racism denies them. Simultaneously, and more controversially, criminal perpetrators of white supremacist brutality may gain access to the humanity they have neglected, if they are prepared to open themselves to the difficult, healing potency of telling the truth. The significance of that possibility increases when it is undertaken in the shadow of palingenetic, non-racial justice.

Taken together, these aspirations contribute to a distinctive figure of the human. Their confluence illuminates some of the difficult issues pending in the crisis of Europe's postcolonial multicultures and the ongoing battle against racial ordering of the world that has recently been recast in civilisationist language.

---

[2] Ato Sekyi-Otu, *Frantz Fanon's Dialectic of Experience* (Cambridge, Mass., Harvard University Press, 1996).

A distinctive political agenda emerged from the pursuit of a habitable multiculturalism in Europe's postcolonial countries and the resulting need to appreciate exposure to alterity as something beyond mere plurality and something apart from loss, anxiety and risk.[3] Those struggles have helped to shape responses to the belligerence that has lately come to define Europe's geopolitical predicament while cementing the conviction that cultural diversity cannot co-exist with either democratic fraternity or social solidarity.

History

Understanding of Fanon's approach to the human is only enriched by familiarity with the French intellectual and political scene in which his intervention first took shape. However, the enduring currency of *The Wretched of The Earth* shows that the significance of the issues he raised extends far beyond that original setting.[4] I cannot reconstruct those debates in their entirety here, but we should note that they involved a mixture of political and philosophical argument. His contribution to debates over phenomenology, corporeality, subjectivity, and temporality were conditioned by the aftermath of the war against the Nazis that had left the French polity deeply fractured. It is harder, but no less important, to appreciate that those discussions were also addressed to the new context emerging from war against the Vietminh. The conflict over decolonization was reignited in 1945, just after French forces moved into Sétif, Guelma, Kherrata, and other Algerian towns to extinguish the pro-independence sentiment evident among soldiers returning from Europe's battlefields. In that context, Fanon was not just indicting previous humanisms for being too readily reconciled to racial hierarchy. He was also taking aim at the complacent brand of anti-humanism that had been catalyzed by those wars. Indeed, the need to establish a connection between the ethics and politics of anti-Nazi resistance and the moral momentum of anti-colonial struggles provided the trigger for his reflections on the pitfalls that resulted from racializing humanity. His thoughts were framed by an anti-racist disposition that could not have been more broadly defined. The social habits required by humanity's epidermalization presented Fanon with a particular target and he placed his analysis of them in a world-historic setting:

[3] Charles Taylor, *Multiculturalism and "The Politics of Recognition"* (Princeton University Press, 1992); Stuart Hall "The Multicultural Question," in B. Hesse, (ed.), *Un/settled Multiculturalisms* (London, Zed, 2000).

[4] James D. Le Sueur, *Uncivil War: Intellectuals and Identity Politics During the Decolonisation of Algeria* (University Park, Pa., Penn State University Press, 2001).

In reality, the national flow, the emergence of new states, prepare and precipitate the inevitable ebb of the international colonialist cohort. The advent of peoples, unknown only yesterday, onto the stage of history, their determination to participate in the building of a civilization that has its place in the world of today give to the contemporary period a decisive importance in the world process of humanization.[5]

Other aspects of Fanon's call for a new humanism prove equally perplexing to a contemporary readership. The first is his non-immanent critique of race. The idea of race is presented and then dismissed as a symptomatic feature of modern, political ontology that had been marked indelibly by Europe's colonial contacts and conflicts. This distinctive stance amplified Fanon's vociferous attachment to the idea that the variety of humanism he proposed was entirely novel. His determination that implacable opposition to raciality made this different from other humanisms resonates with his earlier identification of what he had termed "the real dialectic between my body and the world."[6]

The original formulation of that rare, dialectical possibility arose in a difficult passage from *Black Skin, White Masks* in which Fanon was at his closest to both Merleau-Ponty and Césaire. It still repays careful study.[7] A racialized – and therefore, in his terms, an alienated – modality of being in the world: "the corporeal–racial schema" is contrasted negatively with the altogether different kind of existence evident in the ordinary operations of bodily schema outside of, or more accurately, both prior to and after, the socio-genesis of a racialized world born from bloody conquest and reproduced by brutal colonial administration. This race-producing aberration from the normal mechanisms that assemble human subjects provides an additional stimulus for the embodied curiosity which Fanon invested with revolutionary force towards the end of his first book. His perspective involved a view of selfhood being composed slowly as different human bodies move – with varying degrees of difficulty – through time and space.

In conjunction with colonial domination, Manichaeism both creates and supports racial orders – mutually reinforcing ensembles that are essentially unstable. The tropical para-politics formalized in governmental instruments like the British dual mandate[8] constitute what we can call

---

[5] Frantz Fanon, *Toward The African Revolution* (hereafter, *TTAR*), (trans.) H. Chevalier (New York, Monthly Review Press, 1967), 146.

[6] Frantz Fanon, *Black Skin, White Masks* (1952), (trans.) Charles Lam Markmann (London, Pluto Press, 1967).

[7] Sekyi-Otu, *Frantz Fanon's Dialectic of Experience*, 95.

[8] Frederick John Dealtry Lugard, *The Dual Mandate in British Tropical Africa* (London, W. Blackwood & Sons, 1922).

unfinished or pseudo-polities – formations that disrupt natural and social processes among the conquered and colonized. The damage that results from them is manifest in a deep estrangement from the human that is always transacted under the ontological architecture of race. Here, we are obliged to acknowledge that Fanon's approach to alienation differs substantially from Hegelian and Marxist understanding of that concept. In an example of what it meant practically to stretch Marxian analysis until it became adequate to colonial settings, his emphasis falls, not, as is usual, upon the interrelated dynamics of domination, mystification and recognition but on two adjacent problems. First, the issue of systematic misrecognition and, second, the need for a sharpened sense of mutual relation which will, we are told, pave the way to "the reciprocal relativism of different cultures, once the colonial status is irreversibly excluded."[9]

Fanon's presentation of a profound, deeply racialised variety of alienation shares something with the disturbing work undertaken on the same topic by one of his key African-American influences: Richard Wright. The novelist had steered similar paths through the analytical problems presented by interwar Marxism and the relationship between racism and fascism. Wright had tried to theorize these problems during the 1940s while still fighting his way out of Communist orthodoxy.[10] Both thinkers acknowledged the metaphysics of race that was inscribed in a sequence which involved several stages. Initially, one sees oneself being misrecognized. Then, one experiences the effect of being coerced into becoming reconciled with the dismal, infrahuman object with which one has become confused: the Negro, nigger or negre. Lastly, the habitual, social character of the whole destructive process becomes apparent through appreciation of its ubiquity:

The word "Negro", the term by which ... we black folk in the United States are usually designated, is not really a name at all nor a description, but a psychological island whose objective form is the most unanimous fiat in all American history; a fiat buttressed by popular and national tradition ... which artificially and arbitrarily defines, regulates, and limits in scope and meaning the vital contours of our lives, and the lives of our children and our children's children.

This island, within whose confines we live, is anchored in the feelings of millions of people, and is situated in the midst of the sea of White faces we

---

[9] Frantz Fanon, "Racism and Culture," *TTAR*, 50.

[10] Fanon, "Racism And Culture," 41. Exploitation, tortures, raids, racism, collective liquidations, and rational oppression take turns at different levels in order literally to make of the native an object in the hands of the occupying nation.

This object man, without means of existing, without a *raison d'être*, is broken in the very depth of his substance. The desire to live, to continue, becomes more and more indecisive, more and more phantom-like. It is at this stage that the well-known guilt complex appears. In his first novels, Richard Wright gives a very detailed description of it.

meet each day; and, by and large, as three hundred years of time has borne our nation into the twentieth century, its rocky boundaries have remained unyielding to the waves of our hope that dash against it.[11]

Whether or not they are specifically colonial, all racial orders reveal how the damage to humanity accumulates. Wherever they are, eventually, those formations initiate something like a habitual culture of their own. For Fanon, their undoing can only commence once the liberating refusal to "accept the present as definitive" becomes shared and the door of every consciousness is opened by "the real leap" that introduces "invention into existence."[12] That huge transformation involves decisionistic acts of freedom-seeking which confidently refuse the diminished, in Fanon's terms, the "amputated" or "mutilated" humanity offered by alienated Europe's "constant denial of man" and its symptomatic accompaniment: an "avalanche of murders."[13] *The Wretched of the Earth* sets out what these transformative aspirations involved in the context of national liberation.

Postcolonial Europe

The postcolonial settlers who, like Fanon, made their way to Europe as its empires were painfully being renounced have now created a substantial archive in many languages that extends his projects and shows their significance at both ends of the no-longer-imperial chain. Today, European readers can turn to the fruits of a multilingual, anti-racist tradition which, like Sven Lindqvist's paradigmatic *The Skull Measurer's Mistake*[14] explores how the perennially unfashionable commitment to a world without racism might specify a division of labor for transformative endeavors even when they are conducted inside the fortifications of post-imperial and neo-colonial countries.

The ongoing debate over Anders Breivik's murderous, civilizationist assault on multiculturalism in Norway and on Islam in Europe is likely to bring renewed urgency to this task. It is impossible to understand his Islamophobic actions or the xenophobic justification he has provided for them without paying attention to the histories of European raciology. The analysis of his crimes conducted so far has not only generated a

---

[11] Richard Wright and Edwin Roskam, *12 Million Black Voices: A Folk History of the Negro in The United States* (1941) (London, Lindsay Drummond, 1947), 30

[12] Fanon, *Black Skin, White Masks*, 218.

[13] Frantz Fanon, *The Wretched of The Earth* (1963), (trans.) Richard Philcox (New York, Grove Books, 2004), 236.

[14] Sven Lindqvist, *The Skull Measurer's Mistake* (New York: The New Press, 1997).

particular political geography which encompasses the virtual world but also shows how successive layers of respectable racism and ultranationalism have organized the relationship between fringe and mainstream strands of political opinion.[15] The complexities of the trans-local formation that sustained his murderous ideology are still evolving but they exhibit the general features of the racism that endorses it. Its hatred, like its noisily announced libertarian credentials, is framed by appeals to racial rationality.[16]

Lest the immediate significance of Fanon's stubborn humanism is made to appear too self-evident in that setting, we should also note that the warm and cold currents of structuralist and post-structuralist thought converged around the idea that humanism was, at best, an anachronism. In different ways, Fanon's earnest and, today, firmly disreputable commitment to an *anti-racist* humanism, fell foul of the founding presuppositions of twentieth-century critical theory. Following the viral circulation of the UN Declaration of Human Rights and its various vernacular recodings by anti-racist and anti-colonial struggles, the Cold War-era politics of humanism developed in antinomic patterns that still haunt our own situation. As a result, the pressure to reformulate the human in both human rights and humanitarian intervention has initiated deeper conflicts than Fanon was able to anticipate.

I do not want my return to Fanon's humanism to be misunderstood. This is not a moment in which to indulge the facile idea that interpretation of the postcolonial world can or should proceed easily from the proposition that there is a human essence – as simple as it is universal – which gets somehow lodged in every individual subject. However, it is unrealistic to imagine that the power of that proposition can be answered simply by pretending that we can easily dispose of it and its extensive institutional consequences. What can be termed the tactical use of that idea has been made repeatedly. It has appeared in the political claims made by movements for democracy, national liberation and emancipation from the effects of racial hierarchy. It has recurred in the pursuit of civil and political rights which have long been intertwined with the thwarted aspiration to win recognition as fully human – an enterprise that now stains the post- and neo-colonial world just as it once marked the colonial era.

---

15 Niall Ferguson, "We Must Understand Why Racist Belief Systems Persist," *Guardian*, 11 July 2006, www.guardian.co.uk/commentisfree/2006/jul/11/comment.race?INTCMP=SRCH.

16 Sindre Bangstad, "Norway: Terror and Islamophobia in the Mirror," www. opendemocracy.net/sindre-bangstad/norway-terror-and-islamophobia-in-mirror.

The argument below follows Fanon in making a much more specific demand: the damage done by racism, raciology, raciality, and racial hierarchy requires particular forms of acknowledgement. They must involve not only political and juridical gestures but also philosophical ones. They must amount to significantly more than a vague admission that people are doomed always to do bad, hurtful things to each other – perhaps because their self-hatreds and resentments consistently interact with, and usually corrupt, their relationship to alterity. Several historical and conceptual problems become evident here.[17] Addressing them demands a much larger inventory of the toll that race-thinking has taken from the age of European universalism than is currently conventional, even from the left. The political ontology of races necessitates a revision of modernity understood as epistemology, *techne* and aesthetics as well as the historic union of capitalism with democracy. In an insightful and provocative piece on racism, Cornelius Castoriadis linked the vitality and ubiquity of misoxeny and racial hatred to the "natural inclinations" that underpin human sociality as well as the self-creation and self-loathing that distinguish modern society and ipseity. We do not have to travel the full distance with him in order to see that the unsettling path he has identified may lead us away from the idea that confronting racism is an important task of political struggle.

The Jamaican-American philosopher, Sylvia Wynter, has suggested that the pursuit of these aims can be strengthened if it is articulated together with Fanon's view of racism's socio-genesis and his plan for the destruction of its psycho-existential complexes.[18] In the longer term, those battles may be able to contribute to what she describes as humanism's "re-enchantment," a creative and joyful process that, in Jamaica, had been dominated by the subversive Ethiopianist re-workings of UNESCO's blank poetics by insubordinate roots reggae artists like The Abyssinians, The Heptones and Burning Spear, all of whom authored anthems on the theme of humanity and human rights which have endured while the vindicationism, Pan-Africanism and Garveyism, from which they grew, have ebbed away.

---

[17] Cornelius Castoriadis, "Reflections On Racism," *Thesis 11*, 32 (1992), 4, "The idea that to me seems central is that racism participates in something much more universal than one usually wants in fact to admit. Racism is an offspring, or a particularly acute and exacerbated avatar – I would even be tempted to say: a monstrous specification – of what, empirically, is an almost universal trait of human societies. What is at issue is the apparent incapacity to constitute oneself as oneself without excluding the other, coupled with the apparent inability to exclude the other without devaluing and, ultimately, hating them."

[18] Antony Boques, *Caribbean Reasonings: After Man Towards the Human – Critical Essays on Sylvia Wynter* (Kingston: Ian Randle Publishers, 2005).

The costs of anti-humanism

The twentieth-century anti-humanists who first authored the dubious positions that still warrant today's campus commonsense have enabled unsympathetic interpretations of Fanon that masquerade as critiques of his perspective delivered from the left. His daring hopes are represented as naive or incompletely thought-through responses that – their supposedly enthusiastic view of violence aside – spill over into empty, compromised humanism of the Liberal and UNESCO varieties. From this angle, Fanon is judged to have remained too fixated on Europe's oblique redemption rather than its systematic provincialization. So far, that absurd verdict – which involves a grave misreading of his arguments about the necessity of *and* the costs involved in colonialism's violent overthrowing – has not been tested.

During the phase of decolonization, it was not only dissenting fragments of the colonial elite who observed that discussion of the integrity (and the boundaries) of the human was being conditioned by the aftermath of the struggle against Hitlerism. Then, as now, it was neither respectable nor polite to focus on the constitutive power of racism as populism or to analyze Nazi statecraft as the governmental implementation of a racial hygiene directly connected to the genocidal history of colonial rule conducted both inside and beyond Europe. Old, twentieth-century rules still prevail in the rarified world of scholastic, anti-humanism. The vestigial disciplinary force mustered by fascism's philosophical apologists does not sanction any uncomfortable considerations of their own relationship to the political ontology of race that was celebrated and affirmed by the likes of Heidegger, Schmitt and the other Nazi colossi of contemporary theory. However, the influence of those figures helps to make Fanon's reparative, anti-racist humanism, like his politics of national liberation, appear facile. If Nazism was, after all, not radical evil but rather a catastrophic trace of metaphysical humanism that reveals the problems with all forms of humanism, few brave souls will be prepared to subscribe to the grand folly of humanism's reconstruction.

The Marxian philosophical anthropology with which Fanon's project had been enmeshed moved in different directions under the impact of Foucault's work. At the same time, a variety of feminist pronouncements raised questions about the relationship of gendered categories to humanity and citizenship as well as to the prospects of trans- and post-humanity after the end of our species' natural evolution. Donna Haraway's classic pronouncements on this theme resolved it by collapsing the agency of the military cyborg into the post-human affinities of California's women of color. In her later work, Haraway's disaggregation of the human seems to have required her to displace the challenges of alterity and interdependency on to inter- rather than intra-species relations. The distinctive US conditions in which she operates specify that racialized interactions should continue as long as they are purged of hierarchy as far as practicable. She transmits a sense of her priorities in this passage:

The discursive tie between the colonized, the enslaved, the noncitizen, and the animal – all reduced to type, all Others to rational man, and all essential to his bright constitution – is at the heart of racism and flourishes, lethally, in the entrails of humanism.[19]

Rather than making humanism responsible for the development of racism Fanon, who has no interest in reifying racial identity, approaches racism as a cause of the corruption of humanism that is evident in the history of colonial rule. In other words, he sees humanism as a factor in undoing Haraway's "discursive tie." Additionally, he provides us with an incentive to imagine a new humanism that has been contoured specifically by the de-naturing of race and the repudiation of racial orders.

Before we can proceed further, we must reckon with the fact that in the name of science, the proper name "humanist" has lately been hijacked and monopolized by the zealous secularism of Richard Dawkins and his ilk. They represent a proud formation that is studiously indifferent to the postcolonial re-configuration of the world and significantly refuses to make even the smallest gesture that might compromise its view of Islam as what the great scientist has recently termed "an unmitigated evil."[20] How debates over the human and its limits became linked to the political ontology of races and the resulting struggle against racial hierarchy is scarcely of interest to their belligerent, scientistic civilizationism. Whatever Defoe and Diderot, Montesquieu, and Mary Shelley had to say on the subject of human selves and human others, their subtleties do not detain today's ethnocentric caricatures of Enlightenment.

To follow Fanon's lead, we must accomplish what brittle, formulaic humanisms refuse to do and re-orient ourselves precisely by developing an intimate familiarity with Europe's continuing colonial crimes and the raciology and xenology that sanction them. Then, we may start to ask how a refiguration of humanism inspired by, but moving beyond, Fanon's own, might contribute to Europe's ability to acknowledge its postcolonial predicament.

[19] Donna Haraway, *When Species Meet* (Minneapolis, Minn., University of Minnesota Press, 2008), 18.
[20] http://richarddawkins.net/discussions/624093-support-christian-missions-in-africa-no-but (accessed 27 March 2012).

We must address the question of how to remake and improve Europe's relationships with its unwanted settler-migrants, refugees, denizens and illegals: all those racial and civilizational inferiors judged infrahuman, whose lives are accorded a diminished value even when they fall inside the elastic bounds of the law. That overdue adjustment is now an urgent matter. The problems associated with it have only been augmented by the way that the imperative of security saturates fading political institutions that are inadequately sustained by their supposed humanitarian commitments.

While new humanitarian military interventions are being planned in the name of our civilization, we cannot turn away from the full impact of this unfortunate alignment of forces. And yet, neither can we deny that debates over the particularity of our species life have a long, important and, I would submit, an unfinished history. Edward Said pointed to some of the relevant ground in his book *Beginnings* where, as part of a bigger argument over the implications of a recurrent pattern in which "humanism engenders its opposite,"[21] for a tantalizing moment he dared to place the legacies of Vico and Fanon in a provocative counterpoint:

When Vico speaks of a mental language common to all nations, he is, therefore, asserting the verbal community binding men together at the expense of their immediate existential presence to one another. Such common language – which in modern writing has appeared as Freud's unconscious, as Orwell's newspeak, as Lévi Strauss' savage mind, as Foucault's épisteme, as Fanon's doctrine of imperialism – defers the human center or *cogito* in the (sometimes tyrannical) interest of universal, systematic relationships. Participation in these relationships is scarcely voluntary, only intermittently perceptible as participation in any egalitarian sense, and hardly amenable to human scrutiny.

The formulations that Said lists emerge from what could be identified as a succession of "strategic" universalisms. Typically, their architects have attempted to liberate the human and, indeed, humanism, from the strictly bounded Cartesian space enclosed neatly on one side by a relationship with animal nature and on the other by an evolving account of ourselves defined by the most advanced or prosthetic technologies. Digitalia is a long way from clockwork but Said is right to identify this difficult, challenging agenda as a spine supporting the weight of Fanon's emancipatory, anti-colonial projects. In other words, he was right to place Fanon's scheme in that company.

If the challenge to humanism implied here is to endure into the era of genomics and biometrics, molecularization and humanitarianization,

---

[21] Edward Said, *Beginnings* (New York, Basic Books, 1975), 373.

depoliticization and neo-liberalization, it will have to be updated. We will be required to relocate the desire to re-assemble humanism so that it can appear in conjunction with an analysis of the alienated modes of social interaction that still derive from the racialization of the world and the Manichaean specifications which underpin it.

Fanon's demand for a new humanism is, as I have said, a key aspect of his non-immanent critique of racialized modalities of being-in-the-world. His historical ontology and his humanism should therefore be approached as vehicles for the reconstruction of social orders which manifest their enduring pathology via the attachment to race and the characteristic forms of alienation that raciology transmits and amplifies. Fanon's humanism is neither a residue of, nor a throwback to debates over philosophical anthropology that preceded the emergence of a scientific anatomization of capitalist domination and its human cost. That essential but also limited agenda was surpassed when he dared to place racial hierarchy, racial epistemology, and the political ontology of races at the center of a self-consciously anti-colonial yet firmly cosmopolitan analysis. At this point, we can begin to appreciate that humanism, as Fanon imagines it, is asking us to consider problems that previous humanisms have been reluctant to entertain.

The twentieth century saw the racial *nomos* that had been established in the process of European imperial expansion steadily being overthrown. The persistence of racism in postcolonial and multicultural societies renews the obligation to re-engage with and hopefully to re-enchant humanism. The anti-racist and hopefully reparative humanism that results, is, in effect, warranted by its detailed, critical grasp of the damage done to ethics, to truth and to democracy by racial discourses that would not be undone even by the therapeutic grotesqueries of "identity politics" that Fanon dismissed elsewhere as "the fraud of a black world."[22]

---

[22] Fanon, *Black Skin, White Masks*, 18:
    One duty alone: That of not renouncing my freedom through my choices.
    I have no wish to be the victim of the Fraud of a black world.
    My life should not be devoted to drawing up the balance sheet of Negro values.
    There is no white world, there is no white ethic, any more than there is a white intelligence.
    There are in every part of the world men who search.
    I am not a prisoner of history. I should not seek there for the meaning of my destiny.
    I should constantly remind myself that the real leap consists in introducing invention into existence.
    In the world through which I travel, I am endlessly creating myself.
    I am a part of Being to the degree that I go beyond it.

The human terrain: war, humanitarianism and human rights

The decolonization process is still incomplete. However, the terms of its legitimation have been redefined by the dominance of human rights discourse, by the new-found power of humanitarian political rhetoric that has been employed to justify a sequence of neo-imperial conflicts over scarce resources: energy, water, minerals, etc. and, in particular, by changes in communications technology. The way that racism can be articulated has also been altered, initially by a shift away from biology and hierarchy and towards cultural difference and plurality, and then by a further change which saw race projected and enacted on the molecular scale. Thus reconfigured, biology and political anatomy have returned with a vengeance in the "neuro" and the "nano."

Despite their postcolonial and neo-liberal framings endowed in them by the corporate multiculturalism of an emergent global elite, these developments support the tacit racialization of the world that is being pronounced so emphatically in culturalist and civilizationist terms. The old fantasy of linear progress is retained but can be offered in two new flavours: secular enlightened and post-secular Christian. They share a common foundation from which monolithic, medieval and despotic Islam can be repeatedly counterposed to attractive images of Europe and the west. The racialization process is cemented by the invocation of an absolute ethnicity that is signaled in religious terms: a pattern which circulates through the conflicts it feeds, consolidating and monopolizing the human in heavily culture-coded forms where issues of gender and generation are primary.[23]

The durability of this system can be explained both by its Manichean character and by the fact that postcolonial relations, including global counterinsurgency struggles and civilizationist wars, are no longer confined exclusively to obviously post-imperial states.[24] NATO's expansive role, like that of the ISAF war in Afghanistan, makes all the participating military forces into postcolonial actors whether or not they see themselves as having previously been beneficiaries of colonialism. More than that, there is a high degree of historical and geographical continuity between the wars of imperial decolonization and the global campaign that is currently underway.

---

[23] Vron Ware, "Infowar and the Politics of Feminist Curiosity," *Cultural Studies*, 20(6) (2006), 526–551.

[24] See Mattias Gardell on the meaning of Anders Breivik's crimes: "The roots of Breivik's ideology: where does the romantic male warrior ideal come from today?," www.opendemocracy.net/mattias-gardell/roots-of-breiviks-ideology-where-does-romantic-male-warrior-ideal-come-from-today.

These apparently interminable conflicts, which have developed far beyond the contested airwaves that had attracted Fanon's keen and curious ears, now feature the full repertoire of "smart power." The informational aspects of the war encompass all the digital mechanisms which Bob Zoeťick, then president of the World Bank, termed "facebook diplomacy" in 2008. Before he helped to find that proper name for them, something like that idea had already been taken up, instrumentalized and refined as a strategic instrument by a number of key thinkers in the US state department, the US military and their various corporate counterparts. This was long before 2011's "Arab Spring" brought infowars and social media tools into mainstream geopolitical view.

The most vocal and prominent of these governmental figures was Jared Cohen, who had served under both Bush and Obama administrations as a member of the Secretary of State's Policy Planning Staff charged with the development of twenty-first-century statecraft. Cohen, who left US government employment to become the director of Google Ideas, had been centrally involved with the task of diverting young Muslims from the "radicalization track." His wide-ranging analysis presented social media, youth and consumer cultures as key resources for organizing US interests in the Middle East. Drawing inspiration from events in the Philippines and Latin America, Cohen viewed the distinctive demography of the Middle East as an additional inducement to address the experience of the disenchanted young and to turn their frustrations into a novel political movement from which they might emerge, *de facto*, as vanguard parties of opposition to despotic regimes:

In Colombia, young people used Facebook to put 12 million people into the streets against the FARC, a 40-year old terrorist organization. As a result of what new technology offers, the current generation of youth can act one way at home and in their community, while having the option of taking greater risks online. More prescriptively, they have unprecedented tools for empowerment at their disposal.[25]

Waging an effective infowar requires exercising control over social media and cultural habits. The young are therefore to be influenced or steered remotely through the autopoietic, technological infrastructure of their own ludic, personal "empowerment." Cultural and indeed military diplomacy aspire to employ all the techniques of propaganda and public relations in conjunction with new digital tools in order to engineer the imagination. We must therefore concede the growing inadequacy of critical approaches based upon a too simple view of digital communications technologies as neutral or transparent.

---

[25] www.huffingtonpost.com/jared-cohen/digital-age-has-ushered-i_b_151698.html.

The trajectory of Jared Cohen's career supplies an indication that the relationship between private and governmental actors in this emergent field of power and statecraft has not yet solidified. Further clues as to the impact of that blurring can be deduced from the fact that the work of global securitocracy has been partially outsourced and contracted to secret and shady entities like XE Corp and is often conducted from an invulnerable distance by remote devices like drones.[26]

The latest sequence of doomed military adventures that is novel only in being warranted by the liberal goal of enforcing gender equality introduced what was called the "Human-Terrain System."[27] It ensured that anthropologists were embedded alongside kinetic and infowarriors in a total military effort that could engage directly with the problems of cultural difference, relation, and translation.

These schemes presented the human as a contested object on an enlarged battlefield. They dovetailed with an expanded definition of humanitarian intervention, a term which specifies that uniquely vulnerable groups – LBGT, women, children – must be protected from the cavalcade of medieval barbarity that is Islam. This will be done surgically through all the advanced killing equipment of a uniquely clean war: UAV drones, cluster bombs, depleted uranium shells. Kinetic warfare must be supplemented by softer and subtler technologies. In Afghanistan, for example, there will be an innovative system of corruption-reducing, capacity-building, banking based on mobile phones that will conveniently also double as cameras and screens for photographing oneself and loved ones rather than circulating unhelpful video clips of the latest war crimes and collateral damage.[28]

The same digital technology has other battlefield applications which not only help to identify exactly where the porous boundaries around vulnerable humanity are going to fall but also help to demonstrate how particular technologies assemble and project the human. The US military has recently invested in a new set of biometric devices which will, no doubt, eventually find broader applications in the fields of security and law enforcement at home and abroad. These methods were pioneered in the battle of Fallujah.[29] A dispatch from the Afghan frontline captured

[26] www.washingtonpost.com/wp-dyn/content/article/2010/06/03/AR2010060304965_pf. html.

[27] http://humanterrainsystem.army.mil/.

[28] www.telegraph.co.uk/technology/mobile-phones/8002755/Afghanistan-shows-the-UK-how-mobile-banking-should-be-done.html.   www.bloomberg.com/news/2011-04-13/ afghan-police-now-paid-by-phone-to-cut-graft-in-anti-taliban-war.html.

[29] www.wired.com/dangerroom/2007/08/fallujah-pics/.

their place in the unfolding of what one theorist of global counterinsurgency has called "armed social work":[30]

Things reached a chaotic peak when soldiers spotted a young man with a neatly trimmed goatee, apparently snapping photos with a cellphone camera. They stopped him, made sure the pictures were deleted from his phone and digitally scanned his irises and fingerprints with a BATS (Biometric Automated Tool Set) scanner. The young man was not detained, but now he was in the system.[31]

Man as usual: between animality and technology

These proliferations of biometric technology require that we acknowledge the emergence of a biometric humanity as something of a successor to the withered contours of "epidermalized man."

Even when it operates in the service of securitocracy and civilizationist warfare, biometric control specifies a degree of "somatic individualism"[32] and therefore points in a different direction from approaches to security that can be straightforwardly premised upon the logics of racial type and group profile.

If the boundary with technology has supplied one traditional axis of inductive investigations into human finitude, the other principal frame for those operations has been provided by imagined relationships with animal nature. The history of racism directs the latter interface to the problem of pain and its varieties that preoccupied so many early explorers of political anatomy.[33] Today, the themes of human dignity and rights cannot be disassociated from debating cruelty and torture and their recurrent utility in fighting the desperate kinds of conflict that re-specify legality and statecraft in the antique cultures of impunity that thrive when emergency becomes the rule.[34] The torturer may be targeted as "hostis humani generis" but torture is simultaneously rebranded and routinized, spun and banalized in the networked patterns of a military diplomacy that we cannot escape. This development should also be linked to the growing role of privately commissioned Special Forces

---

[30] David Kilcullen, "Twenty-Eight Articles Fundamentals of Company-Level Counterinsurgency" (May 2006), www.au.af.mil/info-ops/iosphere/iosphere_summer06_kilcullen.pdf.

[31] www.wired.com/dangerroom/2009/08/danger-room-in-afghanistan-the-perils-of-armed-social-work/.

[32] I am thinking here of the work of Nikolas Rose. See his *The Politics of Life Itself* (Princeton University Press, 2007).

[33] Immanuel Kant, "On The Different Races of Man," (trans.) Katherine Faul, in Emmanuel Eze, (ed.), *Race and The Enlightenment* (Oxford, Blackwell, 1997), 38–48.

[34] Gareth Pierce, *Dispatches From The Dark Side: On Torture and The Death of Justice* (London, Verso, 2010).

and remotely operated weaponry in prosecuting what we are told is a new paradigm of global warcraft.

The "Arab Spring" of 2011 highlighted how the old colonial double standards rooted in Victorian racial theory are still in evidence. The unsustainable repression in Libya and Syria was, for example, sharply distinguished from the bloody events simultaneously underway in Bahrain where US and British strategic interests summoned a different geopolitical ethics. The securitocracy of that Gulf state had been designed and implemented by a highly decorated, British police officer, Ian Henderson, who has been repeatedly and consistently accused of being a brutal torturer both during the Kenyan emergency where he won his security policeman's spurs as well as in Bahrain where he acquired the nickname "The Butcher of Bahrain" for the steel and energy with which he organized the government's response to the 1990s revolt.[35]

The serious crimes of which Henderson has been accused are played down, justified and garlanded with flowers in a self-serving memoir he penned in 1958 with the assistance of the Conservative politician, Philip Goodhart. What Henderson's career as a hammer of subversion and national liberation in Africa and the Gulf tells us now about the political geography of Europe's postcolonial statecraft cannot be adjudicated here. However, his text has other uses, not least of which is its figuration of the ambiguities intrinsic to the relationship between races and species. Henderson describes what he takes to be the characteristic feature of his many encounters with Mau Mau prisoners captured during Kenya's emergency while hunting for the Kikuyu leader Dedan Kimathi. Kimathi, like Fanon, had served in a European army fighting against the axis powers until 1945. Here is Henderson:

I often saw terrorists a few moments after their capture. Some would stand there wide-eyed, completely speechless, and shivering violently from shock and cold. They would think of the moment of death, and that moment seemed very near. Others would be past the stage of thinking at all. Mad with shock, they would shout and struggle or froth at the mouth and bite the earth.

Under these circumstances it was not easy to remember that they were fanatics who had enjoyed killing children and slitting open the stomachs of pregnant women. They were savage, vicious, unpredictable as a rabid dog, but because they were now cornered, muzzled, powerless, and terrified, one felt like giving them a reassuring pat.[36]

---

[35] www.guardian.co.uk/politics/2002/jun/30/uk.world; www.youtube.com/watch?v=ETMiHa8cdgg.
[36] Ian Henderson with Philip Goodhart, *Man Hunt In Kenya* (New York, Doubleday, 1958), 149.

There is much to say about this passage and the text from which it has been extracted. Its presentation of the captured, insurgent native as savage, primitive and effectively infrahuman belongs to the moral prescriptions associated with systems of racial classification in general. I have addressed those issues before.[37] Now, my attention is caught by Henderson's hint that the enemy's reduction to animal status creates a confusing range of different obligations and moral pressures in the mind of the capturer-cum-torturer.

Similar material can be found in the record of Africans and Caribbeans captured on European battlefields by the Nazis or shot down and incarcerated by them in POW camps where their fellow prisoners sometimes exceeded the guards in seeking the comforts of racial hierarchy and segregation as partial compensation for their loss of freedom.[38] For all the self-evident character of race as natural difference, the boundary lines between human and infrahuman, human and animal, human subject and object are not in the least bit obvious. Even, or perhaps especially, those who monopolize violence have to specify and determine that very boundary in a difficult psychological setting where torture, castration, and other highly sexual acts of brutality had to compete with "a reassuring pat" as the most appropriate outcome.

Though Henderson's impunity has been sanctioned repeatedly by several different sovereign powers, a complex and multi-sited sequence of litigation has arisen from the Kenyan case as a result of applying the contemporary legal standards defined indirectly by the language of human rights and the concept of crimes against humanity. That intervention continues to move slowly through the upper reaches of postcolonial Britain's judicial system. Apart from the effect that these cases have on the litigants and governmental actors involved, it is clear that they can also impact upon a nation's understanding of its colonial history and, deeper still, upon the idea that British people have of themselves as a political body imbued with civilized values. David Anderson, a professor of African politics who specializes in the Kenyan "emergency" recently told the BBC that a new batch of previously secret files about to be released by

---

[37] The distinct order of "racial" differentiation is marked by its unique label, by the peculiar slippage between "real relations" and "phenomenal forms" to which it always corresponds, and by a special (a)moral and (anti)political stance. It has involved not only confining "nonwhite" people to the status of animals or things, but also reducing European people to the intermediate status of that lowly order of being somewhere between human and animal that can be abused without the intrusion of bad conscience. Paul Gilroy, *Between Camps* (London, Penguin, 2000), 301.

[38] Cy Grant, *A Member of the RAF of Indeterminate Race: WW2 Experiences of a Former RAF Navigator and POW* (Bognor Regis, Woodfield Publishing, 2006).

the government as a result of the continuing court action would prove to be of "enormous significance." He continued:

These are a set of selected documents withheld for their sensitivity. We will learn things the British government of the time didn't want us to know. They are likely to change our view of some key places ... [their release] will clarify the last days of Empire in ways that will be shocking for some people in Britain.[39]

According to a damning internal review carried out by Anthony Cary for the Foreign Office, these documents were regarded by bureaucrats as a "guilty secret" and simply hidden.[40] How they came to be secret and how they acquired the capacity to shock people to this rare extent raises a number of questions that deserve detailed historical answers beyond those I offered in *After Empire*. Here too, part of what is really shocking is the way that disturbing instances of brutality can generate a painful acknowledgement of where the boundaries of the human should fall – the same lesson that is not being learned in managing refugees and others seeking entry to Europe.[41]

Following the classical contours of debate with regard to the boundaries of humanity, a further instance of how the human is being contested in post- and neo-colonial kinds of political and juridical conflict can be helpful. This final example relates to the future rather than the past. Fanon's sense of how colonial conflict discovers and exports new definitions and boundaries for the human can be applied to the emergent technological, legal, and moral environments involved in the deployment of robotic military systems.

Here, the pattern has not developed as Haraway might have predicted, that is by sublation of the human into a post- or transhuman cyborg figure. Automated and autonomous weapon systems will operate without immediate human control in changing circumstances deemed too complex and rapid to be amenable to human decisions – a change that does not remove us from the human, but returns us to it.[42] Peter Singer's book *Wired for War* provides an excellent introduction to this topic.[43]

---

[39] www.bbc.co.uk/news/uk-13317076; www.guardian.co.uk/commentisfree/2011/jul/25/ kenya-empire-mau-mau-britain?INTCMP=SRCH; www.guardian.co.uk/world/2011/ jul/21/mau-mau-torture-kenyans-compensation?INTCMP=SRCH; www.guardian.co.uk/ world/2011/apr/ 11/mau-mau-high-court-foreign-office-documents?INTCMP=SRCH.

[40] Ben MacIntyre, *The Times*, 6 May 2011, 20, www.historyworkshop.org.uk/britains-secret-colonial-files/.

[41] www.guardian.co.uk/world/2011/may/08/nato-ship-libyan-migrants.

[42] See also Peter W. Singer, "Robots at War: The New Battlefield," www.wilsonquarterly. com/printarticle.cfm?aid=1313

[43] Peter W. Singer, *Wired For War: The Robotics Revolution and Conflict in The 21st Century* (London, Penguin, 2009).

Britain's Ministry of Defence emphasizes that it "currently has no intention to develop systems that operate without human intervention in the weapon command and control chain."[44] Nonetheless, they chose recently to spell out relevant legal and ethical issues in an extensive briefing note, *The UK Approach to Unmanned Aircraft Systems*, that was prepared for senior officers in all branches of the services by the MoD's "thinktank," the Development, Concepts and Doctrine Centre (DCDC).[45] This needs to be quoted at length:

There is … an increasing body of discussion that suggests that the increasing speed, confusion and information overload of modern war may make human response inadequate and that the environment will be "*too complex for a human to direct*" [emphasis in the original].

The role of the human in the loop has, before now, been a legal requirement which we now see being eroded: what is the role of the human from a moral and ethical standpoint in automatic systems? Most work on this area focuses on the unique (at the moment) ability that a human being has to bring empathy and morality to complex decision-making. To a robotic system, a school bus and a tank are the same – merely algorithms in a program – and the engagement of a target is a singular action; the robot has no sense of ends, ways and means, no need to know why it is engaging a target. There is no recourse to human judgment in an engagement, no sense of a higher purpose on which to make decisions, and no ability to imagine (and therefore take responsibility for) repercussions of action taken. This raises a number of questions that will need to be addressed before fully autonomous armed systems are fielded. The other side of the autonomy argument is more positive. Robots cannot be emotive, cannot hate. A target is a series of ones and zeros, and once the decision is made, by whatever means, that the target is legitimate, then prosecution of that target is made mechanically. The robot does not care that the

---

[44] www.guardian.co.uk/world/2011/apr/17/terminators-drone-strikes-mod-ethics?INTCMP= SRCH. The US-manufactured General Atomics "Reaper" is currently the RAF's only armed unmanned aircraft. It can carry up to four Hellfire missiles, two 230 kg (500 lb) bombs, and 12 Paveway II guided bombs. It can fly for more than 18 hours, has a range of 3,600 miles, and can operate at up to 15,000 m (50,000 ft).

The Reaper is operated by RAF personnel based at Creech in Nevada. It is controlled via a satellite datalink. In 2012, David Cameron promised to increase the number of RAF Reapers in Afghanistan from four to nine, at an estimated cost of £135 million. The MoD is also funding the development by BAE Systems of a long-range unmanned aircraft, called Taranis, designed to fly at "jet speeds" between continents while controlled from anywhere in the world using satellite communications, Richard Norton-Taylor and Rob Evans, *Observer*, 17 April 2011.

[45] www.mod.uk/NR/rdonlyres/F9335CB2-73FC-4761-A428-DB7DF4BEC02C/0/ 20110505JDN_1_UAS_v2U.pdf.

target is human or inanimate, terrorist or freedom fighter, savage or barbarian. A robot cannot be driven by anger to carry out illegal actions such as those at My Lai.

This view of technology has been commonplace in the development of ever-more sophisticated means of killing.[46] It re-acquaints us with the fact that both of humanity's conventional boundaries, on one side with the animal and on the other with the machine, are being divined through events in the spaces of colonial statecraft. Seen historically, this observation necessitates a fundamental adjustment. Raciology may suggest otherwise, but the colonial space and the conflicts that arise there do not belong in the past. Encountering the native or colonized person is not, as commonsense dictates, a form of time travel. The challenge presented by exposure to alterity as something other than loss or jeopardy, is being able to dwell in the same present as the others whose difference we deploy in order to represent our past. That achievement alone provides access to the portal through which belated entry into a universal, disalienated history can obtained.

Achille Mbembe has approached these dilemmas through a meditation on what appears to be their animating political theology. He has assembled new forms of theologico-political criticism and turned to the ethico-juridical in order to answer the unsettling effects of a "radical uncertainty" prompted less by civilizational conflict and technological transformation than the steady re-ordering of the world that has been consequent upon its continuing decolonization:

We no longer have ready-made answers to such fundamental questions as: Who is my neighbour? What to do with my enemy? How to treat the stranger or the prisoner? Can I forgive the unforgivable? What is the relationship between truth, justice, and freedom? Is there anything that can be considered to be so priceless as to be immune from sacrifice?

It is difficult to see how the history of race as political ontology, aesthetics and *techne*, and of racism and its racial orders, can be made to count as part of how this crisis is to be answered. However, I am certain that Fanon can help us with that task. Indeed, his approach to the human and, in particular, his final alignment of self and humanity in the transcendence (though not the redemption) of Europe remain suggestive. Perhaps it is best to say that approaching the human outside of the alienated and alienating configurations demanded by Manichaeism delirium and the racial–corporeal schema can contribute both to Sylvia

---

[46] Sven Lindqvist, *A History of Bombing*, (trans.) Linda Haverty Rugg (New York, The New Press, 2001).

Wynter's proposed re-enchantment and to what might be called the elusive, reparative element in Fanon's thinking.

That proposal, which would be easy to dismiss as utopian has, in one form or another, been a goal common to every major political thinker of decolonization and racial democracy. All of them turned in that direction, seeking ways to enforce modes of human dignity and recognition that had been consistently denied and thwarted by the invocation of race. Fanon's is only the loudest, clearest voice in that unhappy congregation for precisely the reasons that irritate the unassailable conventions of "identity politics" and its sophist tribunes.

Part III

Rights, justice, politics

9   From "human rights" to "life rights"

Walter D. Mignolo

The limits of the "Declaration of Rights of Man and of the Citizen" and the "Universal Declaration of Human Rights"[1]

The 500 years of "rights" (from Rights of the People, to the Rights of Man and of the Citizen to the Universal Declaration of Human Rights) is a history entrenched in the imaginary of western modernity. It is, in other words, only half of the story. The other half is the history of coloniality, the darker side of modernity. I have made this argument elsewhere.[2] Here I will focus on the future more than on the past. The strong thesis is that the Universal Declaration of Human Rights was not only a Euro-American and North Atlantic invention, it was an invention to correct the errors and mistakes of a handful of Western European states and the United States. I quote:

On September 28, 1948, Eleanor Roosevelt, former First Lady and delegate of the United Nations, delivered a speech entitled, "The Struggle for Human Rights." This speech was delivered at the Sorbonne in Paris, to an audience of thousands of French citizens and delegates of the United Nations. "The Struggle for Human Rights" dealt with the struggle toward universal acceptance of human rights from those states that were considered, by the United Nations and Roosevelt, non-compliant. Those non-compliant states consisted of the USSR, Yugoslavia,

---

[1] I continue here the argument I started in "Who Speaks for the Human in Human Rights,", reprinted in José-Manuel Barreto (ed.), *Human Rights from a Third-World Perspective: Critique, History and International Law* (Newcastle: Cambridge Scholars Publishing, 2013), and followed up in "Racism and Human Rights," 2008, http://boliviachanges. blogspot.com/2008/06/racism-and-human-rights.html. See also Alana Lentin, "Racism and Human Rights. Toward a New Humanism?," 2005, www.voiceoftheturtle.org/ show_article.php?aid=426.

[2] "The Many Faces of Cosmo-polis: Border Thinking and Critical Cosmopolitanism," *Public Culture*, 2000 12(3): 721–748; "Cosmopolitanism and the De-Colonial Option," in Toril Strand (ed.), *Cosmopolitanism in the Making: Studies in Philosophy and Education 2009*, vol. 29(2); "Coloniality: The Darker Side of Western Modernity," in the catalog of the exhibit *Modernologies Contemporary Artists Researching Modernity and Modernism*, curated by Sabine Breitwieser (Barcelona: MACBA, 2010).

Ukraine, Byelorussia, and other member states who had refused to accept the Universal Declaration of Human Rights, thus denying every human being fundamental rights and freedoms. This declaration was written with the intent to unify all nations through common terms and principles surrounding the issues of human rights and freedoms. Roosevelt felt that she must persuade those non-compliant countries to come to an understanding of the fundamental principles agreed upon by the United Nations through the means of establishing unification with her democratic audience.[3]

Mine is a decolonial approach on the proclaimed universality of human rights. I will argue that a distinction between "thinking differently" and "thinking otherwise" is absolutely necessary. The first is a Euro-US critique; the second comes from the receiving end of human rights in the rest of the world. More than 80 percent of the world at the time of the Universal Declaration of Human Rights had nothing to do with the conflicts and crimes committed in the struggle for world domination that involved Western Europe and the United States, the USSR and the imperial dreams of Japan, the last of these, confident after her victory in the Sino-Japanese and the Russo-Japanese wars at the end of the nineteenth and beginning of the twentieth centuries. By underlining the limits of western framing of "universality," "humanity," and "rights" I point out that the defense of human rights engenders and hides its violation by the same actors and institutions that claim themselves as saviors. I will briefly bring to the fore both the double edge of human rights (modernity/coloniality) and current decolonial challenges, mainly through claims of the "right of nature" and "rights of life" that sustain the need to "think otherwise." What it amounts to is the "appropriation" of human rights by the victims to enact their own struggle for their own rights. When the victim became its own savior, the savior and defender of human rights is placed on the side of the perpetrator. Thus, the urgent need to "think otherwise."

Four spheres in the life-world prompt, today, new questions about the limits of "human rights". The first is the sphere of migrations to the core countries of the European Union and to the United States. The migrants come mainly from Asia and Africa and, secondly, from Latin America and the Caribbean. The second sphere is that of humanitarian intervention. Major western states invoke human rights to prevent authoritarian rulers from abusing their power against their own populations. The mining industry is the third sphere of activity that challenges ideas of

---

[3] Amanda Smith, "E. Roosevelt and The Struggle For Human Rights: A Neo-Aristotelian Analysis," U.T. Tyler speech communication, March 18, 2004, accessed November 4, 2013.

rights. Open pit mining, and mining in any form in order to extract "natural resources" leads to war and genocide (as is the case of the Congo). Finally, the commodification of food leads not only to market speculation and food shortages, but also to the use of chemical poisoning to accelerate and increase the production of food as a commodity and not as a life necessity.[4] These are obvious violations of "rights to life" that escape the classical paradigm of rights – the rights of people (*ius gentium* in the sixteenth century), the rights of man and of the citizen in the eighteenth century and human rights in the twentieth century.

The first two spheres belong to the traditional paradigm of "human rights." The third and fourth call for an urgent reconceptualization of human rights as far as they bring forward the limits of the traditional paradigm illustrated by the first two.[5] The emphasis on the legality of rights has put the "expert" and the lawyer above the "human" and has obscured the fact that the "expert" is as human as the rest of us. However, the "expert" is endowed with an authority that can legitimize racism: his or her "authority" is sufficient to classify which lives are valuable and which lives are disposable or dispensable. Racism is not a biological issue but an epistemic one: it is built on he who controls knowledge and has the authority to classify and rank people and regions. Classification and ranking are epistemic operations that create ontologies instead of ontologies which are "represented" by epistemic operations. Thus, when the Universal Declaration of Human Rights states that we are all born equal, it doesn't mention the fact that we stop being equal

---

[4] http://foodfreedom.wordpress.com/tag/andres-carrasco/; www.globalissues.org/news/2011/12/09/12171; Alejandra Paganelli, Victoria Gnazzo, Helena Acosta, Silvia L. López, and Andrés E. Carrasco, "Glyphosate-Based Herbicides Produce Teratogenic Effects on Vertebrates by Impairing Retinoic Acid Signaling,"Laboratorio de Embriología Molecular, CONICET-UBA, Facultad de Medicina, Universidad de Buenos Aires, Paraguay 2155, piso (1121), Ciudad Autónoma de Buenos Aires, Argentina, received May 20, 2010. The problems and consequences of open pit mining have already been covered, in Spanish and English, mainly through blogs and the web. Little as may be expected is found in mainstream media. Just one example, http://upsidedownworld.org/main/argentina-archives-32/2376-resisting-mining-brutal-repression-and-uprising-in-argentina. The health consequences are well documented, http://news.bbc.co.uk/2/hi/health/546685.stm. On the other hand, representatives of the state and corporations, promote the benefits of "development," www.mine-engineer.com/mining/open_pit.htm.
I am not advocating the stopping of mining but rather the need constantly to remind us that mining in a capitalist society sacralizes gold and other metals necessary for mobile phones and other gadgets. See www.youtube.com/watch?v=3OWj1ZGn4uM; www.youtube.com/watch?feature=endscreen&v=8YPldzhAKgk&NR=1.
[5] This call was forcefully made in the "Juicio Ético a las Transnacionales," in Buenos Aires in the first week of November 2011. See a video of "Lectura de la Sentencia" at http://juicioalastransnacionales.org/2011/11/sentencia-final-del-tribunal-del-juicio-ético-a-las-transnacionales/#more-536.

shortly after birth and that one of the reasons for losing our equality, in the modern/colonial world, is racism.[6] Racism is not a matter of skin color, but of the place people occupy in the ranking of "humanity."[7] The classification and ranking on the scale of "humanity" are man-made. The question of "rights" is always related to what kind of "human" the perpetrator and the victim are.

The pragmatic model of "human rights" has three types of agency: a perpetrator, a victim, and a savior. In this model, "human rights" are not just a set of principles established in the Universal Declaration. They materialize when a violation occurs so that a violation has already been inscribed in the Declaration. The interpretation of what constitutes a violation and who is the perpetrator is subjected to the control of legalities but also of a media that reports violations and their interpretation. Actors and institutions who detect human rights violations and act upon them are the "saviors"; they act in support of the "victim" to punish the "perpetrator." In the international arena human rights have been both a curse and a blessing: a blessing that, for example, allows us to do justice to the crimes of Augusto Pinochet but a curse when the hegemonic press accuses China of human rights violations and hides Guantánamo and the western invasion of Iraq and Libya to protect human rights violations. That is, the violation of human rights is enacted to prevent violations of human rights.

Consequently, the declaration of and action on behalf of human rights does not prevent future violations. At best, it ensures that the perpetrators are punished. At worst, it justifies imperial violations. What constitutes a human rights violation is an interpretation of the relevant principle, explicit or implicit, clear or ambiguous. A statement of rights is needed in order to interpret a given act as a "violation." Violations do not carry a tag saying: "beware, this is a violation of human rights." The construction of someone as perpetrator or victim depends on the overarching power structure of society and on the control of knowledge that authorizes interpretations. Similarly, the savior depends on the identity of victim and perpetrator. It is generally assumed that the perpetrator, the delinquent, and the victim suffer the consequences of the delinquent act and the savior – person

---

[6] Margaret Greer, Walter Mignolo and Maureen Quilligan, *Rereading the Black Legend. The Discourse of Race and Religion in the Renaissance Empires* (Chicago: Chicago University Press, 2008).

[7] "Racism and Human Rights," http://boliviachanges.blogspot.com/2008/06/racism-and-human-rights.html. The politics of human rights fall really short when violations are perpetrated by citizens of the country that champions human rights and assign itself the role of global human rights policeman, http://internacional.elpais.com/internacional/2012/03/12/actualidad/1331538127_294245.html.

and/or institution – keeps things in a just order. The problem is, as we will see, that human and life rights can be violated lawfully.

In the standard model, the victim is generally a person (journalist, academic, activist) who becomes the victim for criticizing, dissenting or confronting the perpetrator. The victim could be also an ethnic or ideological community. In the case of Hitler and Milosevich the victims were mainly ethnic communities. In Chile under Augusto Pinochet and in Argentina under Jorge Rafael Videla, the victims were ideological communities. In Syria, the victims of the state do not form a single ethnicity, ideology, or religion. The saviors could be NGOs with the support of democratic states. In international conflicts saviors are major states working with the United Nations. However, in some cases the state could be both perpetrator and savior. The government of Israel would violate the human rights of Palestinians but confront and join the international coalition to stop violations of human rights in Syria. The United States condemns the violence and human rights violations in Syria but remains silent regarding Israeli violations of the human rights of Palestinians. China is accused of violations of human rights by the United States while the Chinese have well-documented accusations about US violations. Keeping in mind the four spheres, this chapter concentrates on open pit mining and mega-extractivism as a legal violation of the rights of nature and humanity, a violation that demands a substantial revision of the classical concept of "human rights."

Rights to life: nature rights *are* human rights

The standard model of human rights is a top-down model. Adopting this model of human rights violation (the perpetrator, the victim, and the savior) and the four spheres where "rights" can be violated (migration, humanitarian intervention, open pit mining, and food commodification), it is evident that the standard model can be extended to spheres that are relevant from the "third world perspective." That is, what is needed is a bottom-up model of "rights" violation. What is at stake from the third world perspective is mainly "life rights." Immigration,[8]

---

[8] The logic of immigration control is extended to emerging economies. Now that the EU and the United States have a shortage of jobs, Brazil is facing an immigration problem. The logic is the same: qualified migrants have a much better chance to obtain visas than the poor and non-qualified, who are running away from the poverty of their own country. Conflict is between ethics and politics, between who is considered "human" (because valuable for the economy of the country) and who is considered "less human/*anthrōpos*" (and, therefore, lives that can be dispensed with). See "Sobre la nueva política económica de Brazil", http://alainet.org/active/53049.

humanitarian interventions, the exploitation of natural resources (open pit mining) at the cost of the life of nature and humanity, and the commodification of food (Monsanto's roundup) and water result from the same logic of capital accumulation and dispensability of life.

The classic "human rights" paradigm focuses on "bare lives": persons who one way or another are stripped of their citizen's rights, becoming legally "naked," persecuted, and/or killed. If they survive, they are humiliated human beings. The human rights paradigm was framed by political theory and the philosophy of law. Ethics was peripheral to it. The answer that is required is to the question "who speaks for the 'human' in "human rights?" Note that this is not "who is human?" a question that has no answer, but is rather "who has the privilege and the power to define and speak for the human?" In that respect, the Universal Declaration of Human Rights must be expanded to ethics, for it would bring racism to the foreground and by doing so lay bare the hierarchical ranking of "humanity." "Rights" is a legal question; "human" is an ethical question. Racism as a category classifies and ranks people, making them/us desirable or undesirable, and turning them into bare or dispensable lives. For that reason, the needed paradigmatic shift goes from "rights" to "life." This is a decolonial shift.

The "human rights" paradigm is limited by a Eurocentered vision of both "human" and "rights." The concept of the "human" and "humanity" is self-serving. It is used to classify and rank the others or "*anthropoi*," on a scale of lesser humans.[9] The lower the *anthrōpos* is in the ranking,

---

[9] "*Anthrōpos*" stands here for all that was needed, since the European renaissance, to affirm the idea and the image of "Humanitas" (Christianity, heteronormativty, whiteness). The "*anthrōopos*" is the rest, but it is not the ontological "other:" Humanitas and *anthrōpos* are two western concepts (like West and East and many others). This distinction was introduced as such by Japanese scholar Nishitani Osamu, "Anthrōpos and Humanitas: Two Western Concepts of "Human Beings,'" *Translation, Biopolitics, Colonial Difference*, (ed.) Naoki Sakai and Jon Solomon (Hong Kong: Hong Kong University Press, 2006). I have elaborated on this distinction in several places. See, for instance, "Who Speaks for the 'Human' in Human Rights?" Human Rights in Latin American and Iberian Cultures Hispanic Issues, online 5.1 (2009), reprinted in *Human Rights from a Third World Perspective*, (ed.) José-Manuel Barreto (London: Cambridge Scholars Publishing, 2013). Also "Epistemic Disobedience, Independent Thought and Decolonial Freedom," in *Theory, Culture & Society*, 26 (7–8), 1–23. See also Costas Douzinas "Seven Theses on Human Rights: The Idea of Humanity," *Critical Legal Thinking* (May 2013). Furthermore, the question of "what does it mean to be human" has an extensive elaboration, and dates back several decades among Afro-Caribbean intellectuals. See, for instance, Sylvia Wynter's canonical text on this issue, "Towards the Sociogenetic Principle: Fanon, the Puzzle of Conscious Experience and What does it mean to be Black," in *National Identity and Sociopolitical Change*, (ed.) Mercedes Durán-Cogan and Antonio Gómez-Moriana (Minneapolis, Minn.: University of Minnesota Press, 1999).

the closer "it" gets to nature. When "nature" is included in the paradigm of ethics and rights violations, the racialization of regions of the planet becomes apparent. Some regions are targeted because of their wealth in natural resources. Coincidentally, many regions rich in natural resources (the former third world) are inhabited by poor populations which tend to migrate to wealthy countries with fewer natural resources, but are wealthy industrially, economically and with high technological innovation and market concentration (the former first world).[10] As a result, a radical shift has emerged in the geopolitics of human rights: The "rights to life" unfold mainly in the sphere of the economy. The ethics of the corporations violate the rights of nature and humanity in the name of economic development: poisoning the land to increase agricultural production and poisoning waters to extract minerals from the mountains are two radical violations of life rights to increase wealth.[11] "Development" legitimates violations and legalizes illegalities. The victims are not "bare life," as is the case with refugees or victims of state genocide, but "dispensable" lives. The victims are not stripped of their rights, but deprived of their life.

Dispensable lives manifest themselves in two complementary ways. Persons have been treated as commodities since the sixteenth century and the Atlantic slave trade.[12] The slavery of women, children, and a market in human organs continues today. Not only continues but, as Rita Segato has convincingly argued, constitutes a "second state economy." The increasing growth of "social violence" is not a random manifestation of legal violation but rather constitutes signposts of a systemic unfolding parallel and interrelated to the "first state," the legal one. What we are facing then, with respect to human and life rights are not only the violations that occur in the "first state" but also the violations in the

---

[10] J.M. Barreto, 'Conquest, Independence and Decolonisation', in J.M. Barreto (ed.), *Human Rights from a Third-World Perspective: Critique, History and International Law* (Newcastle: Cambridge Scholars Publishing, 2012). See also Mako Mutua, *Human Rights: A Political and Cultural Critique* (Philadelphia, Pa.: University of Pennsylvania Press, 2002).

[11] Anna Grear, "Challenging Corporate 'Humanity': Legal Disembodiment, Embodiment and Human Rights," *Human Rights Law Review* 7(3) (2007), 1–33. See also Costas Douzinas, *Human Rights and Empire: The Political Philosophy of Cosmopolitanism* (Oxford and New York: Routledge–Cavendish, 2007).

[12] There was slavery before that point, but the slaves were not a commodity before capitalism. Commodification of human life is a constitutive part of the foundation of a capitalist economy in the sixteenth century. Commodification of life does not only mean that people are bought and sold. It means that, like any other commodity, people become a disposable object. See Eric Williams, *Slavery and Capitalism* [1944] (Chapel Hill, NC: The University of North Carolina Press, 1994).

sphere of the "second state," the sphere in which human and life rights does not apply.

The shift that is taking place towards "life rights" demands that we abandon the western distinction and separation between the natural and human order and also the interests of industrialized and developed countries in which the paradigm of human rights originated. From the former third world dissenting perspective (e.g. the formation of the global political society) the human body and nature are intertwined; violation of "the rights of nature" amounts to a violation of "human rights" and therefore of "life rights."

The Corporations' "Ethical Judgment" and the violation of "life rights"

The "Ethical Judgment to the Transnational Corporations" operating in South/Central America and the Caribbean was an important attempt in words and deeds to terminate the distinction between humanity and nature. This distinction, which is beneficial to transnational corporations, does not exist in the life and philosophy of Indigenous and peasant peoples.[13] For them life is at stake: ethics and politics come together to confront the discourse of corporations and states which celebrate development and economic growth as foundations of well being, and even of freedom.[14] Loosening the code of "human rights" and opening up the wider spectrum of "life rights" forms the foundation of the "Ethical Judgment." It opens up as follows:

After more than 500 years of colonization and recolonization of the subcontinent, this Tribunal affirms the difference between "to live out of nature" and "living with and in nature." The Ethical Judgment against transnational and national corporations in trial, all of them involved in mega-extractivism, had – for this Tribunal – a precise and profoundly human meaning: the protection of life and its reproduction, today and in the future and in all its dimensions and implications. The criteria for discerning an ethical scale from the most to the less ethical has no other reference than life itself: anti-ethical is everything that kills life or that can, at the short and long run, kill life.[15] Ethical is every attitude that moves for life, for the integrity of life,

---

[13] See the website of the tribunal at http://juicioalastransnacionales.org/.

[14] Amartya Sen, *Development as Freedom* (New York: Anchor, 2000). For a contrasting view, parallel to the one in Latin America, see "Modern India: an Interview with Arundhati Roy and Suddhata Deb," www.youtube.com/watch?v=xvII74O5tbY&feature=related.

[15] Nikolas Rose, *The Politics of Life Itself: Biomedicine, Power and Subjectivity in the 21st Century* (Princeton University Press, 2006) makes this statement either out of place or extremely timely. The vision of "life in itself" could be more far apart. The "Ethical Judgment" approaches the technological reproduction of life not only as a technical and

for all that Andean people [in the sense of person and community] name "Sumak Kawsay." The goal of this "Ethical Judgment" is to demand, from a basic Ethical attitude, that the juridical order be submitted and subsumed under the Ethical so that it demand of those at every level of political responsibility and every other responsibility – public or private – that interfere with the communal, that they act in an increasingly ethical foundation.[16]

Respect for "life rights" – both human and nature – will not be effective if the dominant ideology is that development is good, individual success is the destiny of life and wealth accumulation necessary for well being and happiness. "Life rights" are sacrificed because what is important is not life but development.[17] We need "to think differently," we need "a change of paradigm." The "Ethical Judgment" is already a way of "thinking otherwise." It has been made not just by Indigenous people or people of African descent who are learning to unlearn the European way of thinking and are relearning their own ways. South Americans of European descent, finally, are also learning to unlearn and relearn: to unlearn the legacies of European thought in order to relearn the Andean and Mesoamerican philosophy of ancient civilizations. Similarly, China and East Asia are learning to unlearn how the west devalued East Asian *traditions* while at the same time valuing western *traditions* like universalism. Human Rights, in all forms, belong to the regional and provincial western history. They were important, they were useful, they are now limited. The Universal Declaration of Human Rights is now under siege, not of course by the "violators" but by the "saviors." If human and life rights are to be taken seriously two principles have to be enforced: they cannot be the justification of imperial expansion and not be enforced when transnational corporations violate the right of nature and the right of the people who suffer the chemical consequences of economic growth and, secondly, there should be a geopolitical shift so that human and life rights are not controlled by former first world states.

political issue but as an ethical one. Who benefits from "the politics of life in itself" as argued by Rose?

[16] "Sentencia del Juicio Ético a las Transnacionales," Buenos Aires, November 2011, http://juicioalastransnacionales.org/2011/11/sentencia-final-del-tribunal-del-juicio-ético-a-las-transnacionales/#more-536.

[17] "On average, gold mining today produces 70 tons of waste for every ounce of gold, while also consuming and polluting massive amounts of water. An estimated 50 percent of these mining operations occur on native lands. For many Indigenous peoples, who often rely on their environment for food and necessities, mining threatens not only their livelihood, but also their spirituality and traditional way of life," *CorpWatch* (May 2007), www.corpwatch.org/article.php?id=14466.

The next section explores what I mean by a "geopolitical shift" and what it means "to think differently," to change the paradigm from human to life rights and, ultimately, what it means to "think and argue otherwise."

Thinking differently, changing paradigm, thinking otherwise

Professor Hans-Peter Durr, the 2006 Alternative Nobel Prize Winner, was asked by scientist friends to "update" the Einstein–Russell Manifesto. Durr's essay was entitled "Beyond the Einstein–Russell Manifesto of 1955: The Potsdam Denkschrift."[18] Referring to the 1955 Manifesto, Durr recalls that it was signed ten years after atomic bombs had destroyed Nagasaki and Hiroshima. The atomic bombs, Hitler's and Stalin's genocides and mass murders, were the disastrous consequence of western modernity that prompted the Universal Declaration of Human Rights. The Einstein–Russell Manifesto, drafted seven years after the Declaration, pointed to one of the major violations of human rights at the time: the atomic bombs dropped on Nagasaki and Hiroshima.

The conditions that led to the manifesto are of enduring concern. Honesty and good will are not what the ruling political, economic and military elite want to hear or know. Durr tells us that:

Justifiably worried that Hitler's Germany could get the upper hand in building an atomic bomb, the convinced pacifist Einstein wrote a letter to President Roosevelt shortly before the beginning of the Second World War adding his voice to what led the President to initiate America's Manhattan Project. The resulting fission bombs were used sixty years ago in 1945, soon after Germany's capitulation, against Japan. In great consternation, Einstein called for a fundamental political re-orientation to make wars impossible in the future. But without visible success. The development of fusion bombs (hydrogen bombs) increased the deadly potential of nuclear weapons of mass destruction to almost unlimited dimensions and, in the escalating confrontation between East and West, became a mortal danger for all of humanity.[19]

This may not have been the first, and will certainly not be the last, situation in which double standards obtain and set aside honest attempts to solve serious problems. The world has reached a stage

---

[18] www.mi2g.com/cgi/mi2g/frameset.php?pageid=http%3A//www.mi2g.com/cgi/mi2g/press/ 300806.php, accessed November 5, 2013.

[19] "Beyond the Russell–Einstein Manifesto of 1955," www.mi2g.com/cgi/mi2g/frameset. php?pageid=http%3A//www.mi2g.com/cgi/mi2g/press/300806.php, accessed November 5, 2013.

of no return. But the "rights" of life (both of nature and human) are either ignored or repressed. When the conditions are favorable to the interests of the rulers, humanitarian intervention is invoked to save human lives.

There is a memorable, and much-quoted, sentence in the Einstein–Russell Manifesto of 1955:

> We have to learn to think in a new way. We have to learn to ask ourselves, not what steps can be taken to give military victory to whatever group we prefer, for there no longer are such steps; the question we have to ask ourselves is: what steps can be taken to prevent a military contest of which the issue must be disastrous to all parties?[20]

These recommendations were made by European states addressing the disastrous conflicts and murders committed by western states and the Soviet Union implementing a post-European enlightenment. The rest of the world, perhaps 90 percent of it, had nothing to do with the Second World War, genocides and atomic bombs. The "Universal" Declaration of human rights was in fact a "Regional" declaration to solve "regional" problems.

Russell and Einstein's recommendations, made from the core of western civilization and addressed to western people, aimed at preventing further catastrophes. The rest of the world was neither a part nor were they asked, "to think in a different way." I am not among those asked to "think differently," simply because "we" all belong to the human species, but I know that I do not belong to the part of the human species making the call. Thus, the shift from "universal knowledge" to the "geopolitics of knowledge" is of the essence to end the scenario in which, like the IMF and the World Bank, the decisions are placed, first, in the hands of a European citizen and, second, a US citizen. However, I strongly support Russell and Einstein's call and even more so Durr's manifesto, and I hope it is not forgotten and buried. In that context conscientious westerners realized that the west needed to think differently.

It is imperative at this point that "we," the lesser humans or *anthropoi*, help unveil the double standards in the discourse of human rights. The three major events that prompted the Universal Declaration (Hitler's and Stalin's genocide and mass murder and the atomic bombs dropped in Hiroshima and Nagasaki) are the consequences of the rhetoric of modernity and the logic of coloniality. Genocide, mass murder and bombing were justified by the rhetoric of modernity: nationalism, communism, and war.

---

[20] www.pugwash.org/about/manifesto.htm.

The logic behind this rhetoric is that of coloniality: control of domestic authority through the state and control of global authority by asserting leadership by means of the atomic bomb. The theologian of liberation, Franz Hinkelammert, wrote the following about the humanitarian intervention in Kosovo:

The war in Kosovo made us aware of the ambivalence of human rights. An entire country was destroyed in the name of assuring the force of these rights. The war destroyed not only Kosovo, but also all of Serbia. It was a war without combatants of any kind; yet, it annihilated Kosovo and Serbia. The North Atlantic Treaty Organization (NATO) put in motion a great machine of death that brought about an action of annihilation. There were no possible defenses and NATO suffered no deaths; all of the casualties were Kosovars and Serbs, and the majority of them were civilians. The pilots acted as executioners that killed the guilty, who had no defenses. When they flew they said they had done a "good job." It was the good job of the executioner. NATO boasted of having minimal deaths. What was destroyed was the real base of life of the population. The economic infrastructure was destroyed, with all of its important factories, significant telecommunications, potable water and electricity infrastructure, schools and hospitals, and many houses. All of those are civilian targets that involve only collateral damage to military power. The attack was not directed so much against human lives as against the means of living of the entire country. This is precisely what Shakespeare meant when he said: "You take my life when you do take the means whereby I live."[21]

Shakespeare's quotation offers a useful transition from human rights to nature and life rights and from "thinking differently" (a postmodern critique of modernity) to "thinking otherwise" (a decolonial critique of modernity). The introduction of nature and life rights is already "thinking otherwise." It places ethics before politics and transforms the paradigm of rights by changing their subject. The claim for these rights came first and foremost from Indigenous people and peasants who see their life, the life of their community and their descendants endangered as it deteriorates with the "environment." Saving their life is about human dignity and the survival of their families. This challenge is not coming from scientists, western or non-western, following the western "scientific" paradigm.[22] "Thinking otherwise" has been incorporated into academic reasoning, but its origin

---

[21] Franz Hinkelammert, "The Hidden Logic of Modernity: Locke's Inversion of Human Rights," *Worlds and Knowledges Otherwise*, 1(1) (2004), 1–27.

[22] I write "scientific" because it is not universal but western and codified knowledge; it has been accepted around the world but at the same time it is already seriously questioned. See Walter Mignolo, "The Splendors and Miseries of 'Science': Coloniality, Geopolitics of Knowledge and Epistemic Pluriversality," in Boaventura de Sousa Santos (ed.), *Cognitive Justice in a Global World: Prudent Knowledges for a Decent Life* (Lanham, Md.: Lexington Books, 2007).

comes from ancestral Indigenous knowledge and from peasants knowing through experiences and experiences being inscribed in the body and in the memories of those inscriptions.

"Thinking otherwise" is a decolonial paradigm that coexists with Russell and Einstein's call to think in different ways. Scientists have disciplinary knowledge but their everyday knowledge and experience is limited. Aymaras, Quechuas, and Quichuas who forced the inclusion of the Rights of Nature in the Constitution of Ecuador[23] are not scientists but thinking human beings.[24]

Let us return to Durr's statement. He took seriously the Russell–Einstein challenge:

Taking this challenge seriously actually means setting off on a path of learning. The essential orientations are obvious: negative, calling for a turn back, and positive, encouraging different alignments. But thinking in a new way also means becoming familiar with other forms of thought than those of the problematical, still prevailing conventions; and even our use of language requires further development and supplementation . . .[25]

The modesty demanded by the new insights teaches us that, in a certain sense, the new natural scientific knowledge and its consequences can hardly be called "revolutionary," as it might appear to many modern people whose patterns of thought are oriented toward important partial aspects of the Enlightenment and the reductionist science based on it. We find this "new knowledge" confirmed in one way or another in the broad spectrum of cultural knowledge, in the diversity and forms of expression of human life in history, and in the broad variance of living and cultural realms. We can thus regard the "new" knowledge presented here as an additional scientific confirmation of the diverse ethical and moral value systems (if we, like many today, have thus far assumed an eternal validity of epistemic science). The necessary immaterial opening of the *Wirklichkeit* can be caught in a "mental" form that, in this description, however, goes beyond the human to include all life.[26]

Two interrelated points are of interest here. Scientific knowledge requires specific training and learning. On the other hand, there is knowledge in general, living knowledge interwoven with living labor.

---

[23] The *Guardian* reported in April 2011 that Bolivia was set to pass the world's first laws granting nature equal rights to humans. The Law of Mother Earth, now agreed by politicians and grassroots social groups, redefines the country's rich mineral deposits as "blessings" and is expected to lead to radical new conservation and social measures to reduce pollution and control industry, www.guardian.co.uk/environment/2011/apr/10/bolivia-enshrines-natural-worlds-rights.

[24] http://wpas.worldpeacefull.com/2011/04/un-treaty-mother-earth-has-a-right-to-life/.

[25] "Beyond the Russell–Einstein Manifesto," www.mi2g.com/cgi/mi2g/frameset.php?pageid=http%3A//www.mi2g.com/cgi/mi2g/press/300806.php.

[26] The Russell–Einstein Manifesto, 1955, www.mi2g.com/cgi/mi2g/frameset.php?pageid=http%3A//www.mi2g.com/cgi/mi2g/press/300806.php.

Since human beings have to work to live (before capitalism forced them to live in order to work), living labor and living knowledge cannot be supplanted, even less guided, by scientific knowledge. Our problem is that expert knowledge has supplanted living knowledge. The "universal declaration" of the rights of nature is an important call to return to common sense: the constituency that in 1948 launched the "universal declaration" of human rights had a limited experience and sense of what different people in the world need. The superiority of the expert and of the commission that wrote the "Universal Declaration" acted as an expert whose knowledge was not only valid for them but for the rest of the world. They put the cart in front of the horse: knowledge should be guided by experience, living labor and living local knowledge, rather than the other way around. From the former third world perspective, local experience (living labor and living local knowledges) does not square with the experience of the signatories of the Universal Declaration.

The statement of the "Ethical Judgment to the Corporations" introduced a significant variation – a shift in the geography of reasoning of the Einstein–Russell Manifesto and Durr's claim to go beyond it. Contrary to Durr, the decolonial perspective does not aim to go "beyond the beyond" but "to think otherwise," to delink from the western genealogy of thinking in a "different way." Decolonial "thinking otherwise" argues that there are many ways to "think in a different way" and that Durr's call, while necessary, is hardly sufficient. Life and nature rights pave the road to thinking otherwise next to thinking in different ways. The future is not one, and it is not laid out in a single, best option. Abstract universals have become out of place both in the sphere of the multipolar economic world as well as in light of the available epistemic, legal and ethical options. Life rights can neither be defined nor regulated according to the expertise of scientists and legal experts whose reasoning falls into the hegemonic coexisting options.

This "Ethical Judgment" shifts the geography of reasoning and introduces decolonial thinking. Why? First because it is an ethical and not a legal judgment and secondly because the investigation and the judgment has been carried on and enacted by "experts in living" and not experts in legal and ethical philosophy. The "Ethical Judgment" is *anthrōpic* reasoning for the life confronting the *humanitas* of the corporations caring for their wealth. It is not all humans who are destroying the planet but certain types of humans, those behind transnational corporations who commit daily ethical and legal violations, making human life dispensable. When we shift from the legality of rights to the ethics of human conviviality, "water" cannot be transformed into a commodity by poisoning it in order to wash with mercury and cyanide the rocks where the metals are incrusted. The poisoning of water by corporations and the deadly conditions for human beings thereby created is not only illegal but also un-human: it evinces the inhumanities of the *humanitas* and shows why there is need of a discourse that invents the *anthrōpos:* is the *anthrōpos* is the dispensable, the disposable economically speaking. This violation of life rights is justified and turned lawful in the name of economic growth and development. Former presidents have been taken to war crime tribunals. CEOs have been prosecuted for financial corruption. It is time to judge corporations when human rights are violated to secure profit at the cost of the wellbeing of entire communities and the environment.

The violation of rights to life that affect the quality of life of an entire population and its descendants is not solely a legal issue: it is above all an ethical one. The "human" component refers to handicapped bodies unable to become fully "human" because of birth defects, early deadly diseases, or lives subjected to the disease and death surrounding the community. When it comes to "dignity," life rights are no longer a legal but an ethical issue. "Dignity" cannot be solved legally or by public policy. The "Ethical Judgment to the Corporations" is first about life and dignity and then about rights. Without changing the horizon of life and shifting the geography of reasoning, the corporations will continue to legally violate the "rights to life" in the name of development and freedom, and of economic growth and happiness

At this point the model of "human rights watch" needs to be modified. The perpetrator is not a totalitarian but a "democratic" state that violates human rights in order to support transnational corporations in the name of development and economic growth. The victim is victimized for living in areas or regions where natural resources abound, be it the Amazon or the Andean regions. Lives are endangered, not because people are persecuted but because rivers and soil are polluted and carcinogenic conditions are created. The victims take their salvation in their own hands, transforming the model of human rights violations. The victims are at the same time the saviors, because they do not trust the states or the NGOs to fight for their dignity. "Dignity" is not something the state or an NGO can give; you have to "take it back" and you do not take it back legally but by engaging in ethical research, arguments, and advocacy.

Global crisis, life rights, and "thinking otherwise"

The "Ethical Judgment" forces us to ponder the ethical next to the legal dimension. The ethical dimension calls for dignity, the legal for rights. When your rights are violated you depend on the law to do justice, to protect yourself and to punish the perpetrator. Your dignity is being eroded. Diminishing the dignity of persons is the first step in preventing them from thinking and acting. The restitution of dignity demands changing the conditions that enable a person or corporation to erode the integrity of others. The sovereignty of inter-human relations should take priority over that of inter-state relations. Sovereignty of food is already an important step and a consequence of "thinking otherwise."[27]

The organizers of the "Ethical Judgment" defined it as a politico-pedagogical process guided by popular organizations, part of an "emerging global political society." This global political society is part of but goes beyond civil society. Civil society is normally divided between conservatives and dissenters with a gray area in between. Dissidents manifest their dissent in several ways, but do not usually take action around life, survival, and dignity, as is the case with the organizations leading the process of the "Ethical Judgment."[28] The latter involves several South and Central American organizations confronting the legal violation of life rights.

But why is a popular "Ethical Judgment" necessary? When the law defends private property and the patriarchal and racial order of society, placing care for people, communities, future generations and, above all, land and territories in second place, a basic ethical principle of human communal life is violated. The "Ethical Judgment" is necessary because existing law turns into criminals the people who, in defending life and dignity, rise up to denounce and stop the legal violations of life rights by the corporations. *Paradoxically, the victims in the human rights model become the violators of the rights of private property of transnational corporations.* When the victims become the violators, the victims themselves must become their own saviors. Since the law is in the hands of perpetrators of human, nature and life rights violations, the ethical is the only venue left to those who are seen, from the perspective of the law, as illegal disturbers of the social order hindering progress and development.

When Russell and Einstein asked the scientific community to "think differently," "thinking otherwise" was already taking place, but was not being heard. "Thinking otherwise" had its first institutional expression at

---

[27] www.youtube.com/watch?v=9fYGCHoP-HY.

[28] Many similar organizations exist. One is *La Via Campesina*, a global organization whose focus is sovereignty of food and dignity – "dignity" because the commodification of food creates problems for feeding animals and humans; also because it does not take into account the fact that the use of chemicals to increase food production damages life on the planet. Sovereignty of food is spreading all over the world. It requires decolonial thinking, "thinking otherwise," www.decolonialfoodforthought.com.

the Bandung Conference, in 1955. It was expressed in a very simple formula: neither capitalism, nor communism, but decolonization. Today we call it "decoloniality" since we have learned to differentiate colonization (specific historical moments in the past 500 years, and in particular imperial states) from coloniality (the logic of invasion – physical and psychological, industrial and financial). The "Ethical Judgment" is "thinking otherwise."

To discern ethical behaviors the basic criterion is life. The protection and healthy reproduction of life, the life of nature, is also the fundamental principle of Sumak Kawsay, the Quichua expression that can be translated as "to live in harmony and plenitude," and is commonly translated as "Buen Vivir." It is difficult to translate the expression "Buen Vivir" into English, for it could be easily understood as "to live well" or "good living," and so related to consumerism and to the increase of our income so as to "live better than our neighbors." "To live in harmony" is derived from Andean Indigenous philosophy as well as peasant philosophy, and not from some distinguished western thinkers. Interestingly enough, once you understand what Sumak Kawsay means you discover that it was the common philosophy of all existing civilizations on the planet before 1500: before the emergence of the Atlantic commercial circuit, the dispensability of human life introduced by the triangular slave trade, and the economy of accumulation (rather than storage and trade as existed all over the planet before 1500). The dispensability of human life, and of life in general after the Industrial Revolution (made on the basis of non-renewable energy), increased placing gains and economic growth first and life second. The cart was put in front of the horse, and "thinking otherwise" means to bring the horse back in front of the cart:

The real danger for the survival of the human species and, therefore, life on the planet (beyond of course living organisms walking upright and having their hands to work with), is market fundamentalism supported by military dictatorship and military forces, being used to legitimize the ideology of development and progress. An Indigenous intellectual in Panama has been quoted as saying: "This development is killing us."[29]

"Thinking otherwise" means a delinking from the illusion that capitalism is the only possible economic way, that the market and consumerism are the joys of life and that development is the final horizon of human life for the planet. This hegemonic principle may have a long life, but its content is

---

[29] See "Sentencia del Juicio Ético," http://juicioalastransnacionales.org/2011/11/sentencia-final-del-tribunal-del-juicio-ético-a-las-transnacionales/#more-536.

historical, it will not last forever. It would be wrong to conclude that thinking otherwise would be a "post-hegemonic" thinking within the same paradigm, a mere temporal "post." "Thinking otherwise" emphasizes the "de" over the "post." The "post" (like the "new" in "new ways of thinking") means changing the content but not the terms of the conversation. "Thinking otherwise" means to start from the fact that beyond, below and next to the hegemonic way, there is a wealth of life possibilities that are not simple "alternatives" but different. What was radical in the Bandung Conference was the shifting of the geography of reasoning: neither capitalism, nor communism. Both are hegemonic and western ideologies (in spite of Lenin and Mao Zedong) and they are effective because they do not let us see that there is another logic. Changing the horizon enables us to supersede the ways we have been thinking about rights (of people, of man and citizen, of the human race) and to start thinking about dignity first. Rights shall be at the service of dignity, and dignity will answer the question of who speaks for the "human" in human rights.

"Thinking otherwise" requires an other history, not the hegemony of universal histories taught by science (big bang, evolution), religion (creationism), secular philosophy (Hegel), or class struggle (Marx). Decolonial thinkers start from the fact that memory matters because modernity is a weapon to erase memory and to build forgetting. The Eurocentered Right and Left (in the ex-third world, the roots of the Left are Eurocentered) constantly erase the memories of coloniality. Decolonial histories began in 1500 AD, with the logic of coloniality and the rhetoric of modernity, of salvation, and the exceptionalism of western civilization. The "Ethical Judgment" brings together the memory of coloniality with the present of global coloniality:

After 500 years of colonization and recolonization of the continent, this Tribunal asserts that it is not the same to live "out of nature" as to "live with and in Nature." However, in defense of the insatiable assignments of the transnational corporations and the deepening of the capitalist logic and the widening of the frontiers for exploitation, the environment is destroyed and with it goes the extermination of entire towns of indigenous and peasant populations that today are considered as "the rest" of society.

"The rest of neo-liberalism" has been underlined toward the end of the twentieth century by the Zapatistas. This is nothing else but a reformulation of dispensability of human life (entire towns) as a consequence of killing nature, polluting the environment, and preventing the reproduction of life in favor of recycling the waste of mining extraction and the used commodities becoming quickly old in the psychology of an insatiable consumerist society.

Concluding remarks

The "Ethical Judgment to the Corporations" makes a powerful call about the need to enlarge the classical paradigm of human rights. This call comes from "thinking otherwise," from taking Indigenous philosophy seriously. The "new way of thinking" called for by Russell and Einstein and extended by Durr is an important complement to decolonial thinking coming from within the paradigm it critiques. Decolonial thinking and "thinking otherwise" depart from the paradigm that was expressed in the Bandung Conference as neither capitalism nor communism, life regulated neither by the economy nor by the state. The countries represented at the Bandung Conference accounted for half the population on the planet. They were united by their non-Christian religious beliefs and the experience of being racialized. Science is not universal but historical and local. It reached spectacular heights in the west. The achievements of science came with its splendors and miseries. The "new ways of thinking" demand an end to the misery caused by science. But the "splendors" cannot be maintained within the cosmology that brought both splendors and miseries, the visibility of modernity and the invisibility of coloniality. For science development is not a problem but an issue it supports and helps unfold. For the Tribunal, development is the philosophy that legalizes the violation of rights to life:

The Ético-Popular Tribunal is convinced that it is not possible to judge transnational corporations without condemning at the same time the so called "development model" and the capitalist system, which is patriarchal and racist, that generated such [a] model, maintain[s] and extend[s] it. The core subject of the system is the white male, bourgeois, owner, heterosexual, Westerner and Christian.

The shift in the geography of reasoning takes place when the victim becomes not only the savior, but also delinks in the process from the categories of knowledge that generated the history of "rights" from *ius gentium* to the rights of Man and Citizen to Human Rights. This is the genealogy of western thought; rights with their three stages were invented to solve the problems of western civilization. Since western civilization is one and is historical, it is not universal. Life rights emerged precisely in places and from people suffering the consequences of the miseries and splendors of western civilization. Those who speak for the "human" in human rights invented the *anthrōpos* (the lesser human) to be civilized. That cycle is closed. Now the *anthrōpos* is rising, becoming the savior of his/her self. By so doing s/he delinks, expands and decolonizes the narrow western paradigm of Human Rights.[30]

[30] See the manifesto "In Defensa de la Vida, del Agua y la Dignidad de los Pueblos" ("In Defense of Life, Water and Peoples' Dignity"), http://ecuarunari.org/portal/noticias/En-defensa-del-Agua-la-Vida-y-la-Dignidad-de-los-Pueblos. The manifesto is part of a general uprising in Ecuador on March 8, 2012: http://internacional.elpais.com/internacional/2012/03/08/actualidad/1331190707_452752.html.

10 Democracy, human rights and cosmopolitanism: an agonistic approach

Chantal Mouffe

How can we envisage the relation between democracy, human rights and cosmopolitanism from an agonistic perspective? To examine this question, I am going to bring together a series of reflections that I have developed in my previous work to show how the approach that I have been elaborating addresses some of the key issues in those debates. Since I cannot expect everybody to be familiar with my work, I will begin by delineating the basic tenets of my theoretical framework. It has first been elaborated in *Hegemony and Socialist Strategy*, co-written with Ernesto Laclau.[1] In this book, we argue that the two concepts necessary to grasp the nature of the political are 'antagonism' and 'hegemony'. Both notions point to the need to acknowledge the dimension of radical negativity that manifests itself in the ever-present possibility of antagonism which impedes the full totalization of society and which forecloses the possibility of a society beyond division and power. This, we claim, requires coming to terms with the lack of a final ground and the undecidability that pervades every order, visualizing society as the product of a series of practices whose aim is to establish order in a context of contingency. In our vocabulary, this means recognizing the hegemonic nature of every kind of social order. We call 'hegemonic practices' the practices of articulation through which a given order is created and the meaning of social institutions is fixed. Every order is the temporary and precarious articulation of contingent practices. Things could have been otherwise and every order is predicated on the exclusion of other possibilities, it is always the expression of a particular configuration of power relations. What is at a given moment accepted as the 'natural' order, jointly with the common sense that accompanies it, is the result of sedimented hegemonic practices; it is never the manifestation of a deeper objectivity that would be exterior to the practices that brought it into being. Every order is for that reason susceptible of being challenged by counter-hegemonic practices,

[1] Ernesto Laclau and Chantal Mouffe, *Hegemony and Socialist Strategy: Towards a Radical Democratic Politics* (London, Verso, 2001).

181

practices which attempt to disarticulate its particular power configuration in order to install another form of hegemony.

In later books: *The Return of the Political, The Democratic Paradox* and *On the Political*, I have developed my reflection on 'the political', understood as the antagonistic dimension that is inherent in all human societies.[2] I have proposed to distinguish between 'the political' and 'politics'; 'the political' refers to this dimension of antagonism which can take many forms and can emerge in diverse social relations, a dimension that can never be eradicated; 'politics', on the other side, refers to the ensemble of practices, discourses and institutions which seek to establish a certain order and to organize human co-existence in conditions which are always potentially conflicting because they are affected by the dimension of 'the political'.

The denial of 'the political' in its antagonistic dimension is, I contend, what impedes liberal theory from envisaging politics in an adequate way. Indeed the political in its antagonistic dimension cannot be made to disappear by simply denying it and wishing it away, which is the typical liberal gesture; such negation only leads to impotence, an impotence which characterizes liberal thought when confronted with the emergence of antagonisms and forms of violence that, according to its theory, belong to a bygone age when reason would not yet have managed to control the supposedly archaic passions.

An important part of my reflection has been dedicated to the elaboration of what I call an 'agonistic' model of democracy. My objective is to provide what Richard Rorty would call a 'metaphoric redescription' of liberal democratic institutions. A redescription which, I submit, is better able to grasp what is at stake in pluralist democratic politics than the two main models of democracy currently available: the aggregative and the deliberative ones.

In a nutshell, my argument goes as follows. Once we acknowledge the dimension of 'the political', we begin to realize that one of the main challenges for pluralist liberal democratic politics consists in trying to defuse the potential antagonism that exists in human relations, so as to make human co-existence possible. The fundamental question is not: how to arrive at a consensus reached without exclusion, because this would require the construction of an 'us' that would not have a corresponding 'them'. This is impossible because the very condition for the constitution of an 'us' is the demarcation of a 'them'. The crucial issue then is how to establish this us/them distinction that is constitutive of

---

[2] Chantal Mouffe, *The Return of the Political* (London, Verso, 2005); *The Democratic Paradox* (London, Verso, 2009); *On the Political* (Abingdon, Routledge, 2005).

politics in a way which is compatible with the recognition of pluralism. What is important is that conflict does not take the form of an 'antagonism' (struggle between enemies) but the form of an 'agonism' (struggle between adversaries). A well-functioning democracy calls for a confrontation of democratic political positions. If this is missing there is always the danger that this democratic confrontation will be replaced by a confrontation between non-negotiable moral values or essentialist forms of identifications.

It is on the basis of this theoretical reflection on the political that emphasizes the dimensions of antagonism that I have criticized the theorists who in a variety of ways are advocating the establishment of a cosmopolitan democracy. The problem, in my view, with the cosmopolitan approach is that, whatever its formulation, it postulates the availability of a world beyond hegemony and beyond sovereignty, therefore negating the dimension of the political. Moreover it is usually predicated on the universalization of the western model and therefore does not make room for a plurality of legitimate alternatives. All those who assert that the aim of politics – be it at the national or the international level – should be to establish consensus on one single model, end up foreclosing the possibility of legitimate dissent and creating the terrain for the emergence of violent forms of antagonisms.

My critique has been mainly directed to the model of cosmopolitan democracy put forward by theorists like David Held, Daniele Archibugi or Ulrich Beck, who claim that, in the present conditions of globalization and after the collapse of communism, the Kantian cosmopolitan project could finally become a reality.[3] But there are of course other kinds of cosmopolitanism, and a growing number of theorists have in fact been trying to reformulate the cosmopolitan project so as to take account of the critiques that have been directed at the traditional Kantian version. The American historian David Hollinger proposes, for instance, to distinguish between a full and an empty cosmopolitanism, between the traditional Kantian-inspired universalist cosmopolitanism of those who, like Martha Nussbaum, assert that our primary allegiance should be to the 'worldwide community of human beings' and the growing number of 'new cosmopolitans' who reject such a perspective and want to bring cosmopolitanism down to earth by loading the otherwise empty concept with history and the realities of power. This new cosmopolitanism comes in many versions, for instance the 'discrepant cosmopolitanism' of James Clifford, the

---

[3] David Held, *Democracy and the Global Order* (Cambridge, Polity, 1995); Daniele Archibugi (ed.), *Debating Cosmopolitics* (London, Verso, 2003); Ulrich Beck, *Cosmopolitan Vision* (Cambridge, Polity, 2006).

'vernacular cosmopolitanism' of Homi Bhabba and Paul Gilroy, the 'multi-situated cosmopolitanism' of Bruce Robbins, the 'critical cosmopolitanism' of Paul Rabinow, or the 'de-colonial cosmopolitanism' of Walter Mignolo. All those theorists try to reconcile cosmopolitanism, seen as an abstract standard of planetary justice, with a need for belonging and acting at levels smaller that the species as a whole. Their aim is to foster a sense of reciprocity and solidarity at the transnational level and they want to bring to the fore the negative consequences of the economic, political and cultural neo-liberal model. This new cosmopolitanism does not emphasize the values of rationality and universality and it criticizes the Eurocentrism that it sees at the core of the traditional cosmopolitanism, linked as it is to the Enlightenment and the European experience of modernity. The symbols of the cosmopolitan community, according to this perspective, are the diaspora, the refugees and the immigrants, presented as carriers of a radical critique of modernity. They are, says Bhabba, the representatives of a 'minoritarian modernity'.

I have of course sympathy for the critique of Eurocentrism that we find in the new cosmopolitanism. However I have serious reservations with their approach as far as politics is concerned. First, I do not really see the usefulness of trying to redefine the notion of cosmopolitanism, so as to make it signify almost the opposite of its usual meaning. It is no doubt important to stress the need for transnational solidarity and reciprocity, but this could be done by using a different notion, less tainted by the abstract universalism that they want to relinquish. Cosmopolitanism's basic idea of human unity and the possibility of a harmonious form of universal governance cannot easily be dissociated from the ideal of achieving a universal politics based on reason and detached from particular affiliations. Despite all the attempts of the new cosmopolitans to distance themselves from the abstract universalism of the traditional cosmopolitanism and to insist on the 'rooted' character of their vision, they cannot liberate themselves from its core objective, which aims at emphasizing the fact of common belonging beyond all differences and at diluting individual attachments to specific communities, and this is deeply problematic. The notion of a 'rooted' cosmopolitanism is, in my view, an oxymoron.

But, more importantly, my problem with the new cosmopolitanism is that I consider that, like the traditional cosmopolitanism, albeit in a different way, it also misses 'the political' in its antagonistic dimension. It is mainly concerned with the recognition of a plurality of allegiances and diverse forms of belonging and seems to believe that, once it is redefined according to their parameters, the cosmopolitan ideal could provide the ethical framework required by a democratic society. The abstract universalism of the Kantian model is rejected in favour of a new 'pluralist universalism', but what is absent from this approach is the recognition of the necessary conflictual character of pluralism. Their pluralism is a 'pluralism without antagonism' and this is why this new cosmopolitanism also conveys the illusion that there could one day exist a world without politics, a world beyond hegemony and beyond sovereignty.

I submit that for those who are keen to preserve the diversity of the world, while being open to different cultures and traditions, the cosmopolitan approach, even in its weak version, is not the most appropriate. One of the fundamental images evoked by cosmopolitanism pictures the world as a universe and this can bring about the desire for the advent of a single culture that could be shared by the whole world. Perhaps this would not constitute a serious problem if the new cosmopolitans limited themselves to proposing some guidelines for visualizing 'Ethics in a World of Strangers' to refer to the sub-title of the book on *Cosmopolitanism* by Anthony Appiah.[4] However, most of them have a higher ambition, since they aim at establishing the conditions for pursuing democratic politics in a globalized world. But such an objective requires a properly political approach that they are unable to provide.

In my view, to elaborate such a political approach, the challenge that we are facing is the following. First we have to acknowledge, contrary to the cosmopolitans, that every order is a hegemonic order and we need to abandon the very idea of a possible order 'beyond hegemony'. As a consequence the alternative to a unipolar world, organized around the hegemony of a single power can only be the pluralization of hegemonies and the development of a really polycentric world order. This is why I have argued that we should relinquish the illusory hope for a political unification of the world. Our objective, instead, should be to foster the establishment of a multipolar world organized around several big regional units with their different cultures and values. Such a world order would recognize a plurality of regional poles, organized according to different economic and political models without a central authority. I am aware of course that this would not bring the end of conflicts but I am convinced that those conflicts are less likely to take an antagonistic form than in a world where a single economic and political model is presented as the only legitimate one and is imposed to all parties in the name of its supposedly superior rationality and morality.

When it comes to envisaging the nature of a multipolar world, we can find important insights in the current discussion about the possibility of

---

[4] Anthony Appiah, *Cosmopolitanism: Ethics in a World of Strangers* (London, Allen Lane, 2006).

multiple modernities which has been articulated by a variety of theorists (Charles Taylor, S.N. Eisenstadt, David Martin and Peter Wagner, among others). One of the central ideas of this approach is that transitions that we might recognize as modernity took place in different civilizations and have produced different results. Modernity should therefore be conceived as an open-ended horizon with space for multiple interpretations. We have to accept that the path followed by the west is not the only possible and legitimate one. Non-western societies can follow different trajectories according to the specificity of their cultural traditions and of their religions. As far as democracy is concerned, this signifies acknowledging that the set of institutions constitutive of liberal democracy – with their vocabulary of human rights and their form of secularization – are the result of a contingent historical articulation in a specific cultural context. There is therefore no reason to see their adoption worldwide as the criteria of political modernity and as a necessary component of democracy.

This line of reflection brings to the fore the political role played by the dominant narrative propagated by the west about its exemplary and privileged path of development and the importance of challenging its central tenets. I agree with Dipesh Chakrabarty's claim that 'the recognition that Europe's acquisition of the adjective "modern" for itself is an integral part of the story of European imperialism'.[5] We should realize that to define the western form of democracy as 'modern' has been a powerful rhetorical weapon used by liberal democratic theorists to establish its superior form of rationality and its universal validity.

There is another debate that can provide interesting insights for criticizing the dominant narrative. It has been taking place among historians of political ideas around the very nature of the Enlightenment. This debate has highlighted the existence of rival enlightenments and the plurality of possible answers to the question 'What is Enlightenment?'. Ian Hunter, for instance, has argued that there was not one comprehensive German Enlightenment represented by the metaphysical approach of Kant and in his book *Rival Enlightenments: Civil and Metaphysical Philosophy in Early Modern Germany* he has reconstructed an alternative, non-transcendental 'civil' Enlightenment represented by Pufendorf and Thomasius who proposed a very different way of dealing with the relation between religion and politics and the sources of political obligation.[6] The metaphysical approach of Kant and Leibniz was able to gain hegemony

---

[5] Dipesh Chakrabarty, *Provincializing Europe* (Princeton University Press, 2000), 43

[6] Ian Hunter, *Rival Enlightenments: Civil and Metaphysical Philosophy in Early Modern Germany* (Cambridge University Press, 2001).

and it is their view that became the accepted one but in no way, says Hunter, should we see this as the expression of its superior rationality. As far as he is concerned, he sees the metaphysical tradition as being 'anti-political' and he finds in the civil tradition a more adequate conception of the world of politics.

Following the path opened by Hunter, James Tully has developed this approach by bringing into the picture other Enlightenment's traditions: the neo-Roman, the civic and the popular sovereignty. Tully argues that the nature of the Enlightenment which was formulated within the Kantian tradition as a transcendental question should be de-transcendentalized and respecified as a historical question.[7] He also suggests that this discussion should not be confined to the rival conceptions within Europe but should be extended to a broader dialogue with non-western enlightenments. By calling for an alternative to the Eurocentric approach, Tully's position dovetails with the approach which advocates the possibility of 'multiple modernities' and to its challenge of the universalist narrative propagated by the west about the exemplary character of its model.

What is a stake in those discussions is the elaboration of an adequate pluralist perspective that would envisage the world as a pluriverse. This is a view that has been forcefully defended by Carl Schmitt but we can also take our bearings from Claude Lévi-Strauss who has repeatedly argued that civilization implies the co-existence of cultures offering the maximum of diversity and maintaining their originality.[8] In his view, the crucial contribution of the different cultures reside in the multiple divergent variations ('écart differentiel') that exist among them and he insists on the necessity of preserving the diversity of cultures in a world threatened by homogeneity and uniformity. He urges us to acknowledge that no fraction of humanity possesses a formula valid for the whole world and that a humanity unified by a single mode of life is inconceivable because it would be completely ossified. This is what Lévi-Strauss expresses by the term 'écart différentiel' to stress that the identity of a culture is not to be found in a pre-given essence but in its divergence from others. To think in terms of divergences and not simply of differences is what the term 'écart différentiel' suggests. As François Jullien indicates in his book De l'universel, where he appropriates Lévi-Strauss' vocabulary, the importance of distinguishing between 'divergence' (écart) and 'difference' is that a divergence puts in tension what it separates, it shows how other possibilities can exist which cannot be reduced to mere variations of a common invariant. Instead of invariants

---

[7] James Tully, 'Diverse Enlightenments', *Economy and Society*, 32(3), (2003), 485–505.
[8] See for instance Claude Lévi-Strauss, *Race et Histoire* (Paris, Denoel, 1987).

and their cultural variations we should, according to him, look for 'equivalences' and search for the points of possible junctions among different cultures.[9]

This kind of reflection is also relevant for the discussion on the universality of human rights because it helps us to pose its key questions in a very different way. As many authors have pointed out, there is something very problematic about the idea of 'human rights' as it is usually envisaged, i.e. as a cultural invariant that should be accepted by all cultures. This is due to the fact that human rights are usually presented as being both universally valid and uniquely European in their origins. An important consequence of this formulation is that the universalization of human rights is generally seen as depending on the adoption by other societies of western types of institutions. Indeed most contemporary political theory – not to speak of western politics – asserts that western liberal democracy is the necessary framework for the implementation of human rights. Liberal democracy is presented as the 'good regime', the 'just regime', the only legitimate one. In fact a great deal of liberal democratic theory aims at proving that it is the kind of regime that would be chosen by rational individuals in idealized conditions like 'the veil of ignorance'(Rawls) or the 'ideal speech situation' (Habermas).

In several of my writings I have taken issue with such a view, challenging the idea that moral progress consists in the universalization of western liberal democracy, with its specific understanding of human rights. I advocate a pluralist conception allowing us to make room not only for the pluralism of cultures and ways of life but also of 'good', i.e legitimate, political regimes. In my view, liberal democratic institutions and the western language of human rights represent only one possible 'political language game' among others and it cannot claim to have a privileged relation to rationality. We should therefore accept the possibility of a plurality of legitimate answers to the question of the 'good regime'. I will come back to this issue later, but before that I would like to examine the possibility of pluralizing the notion of human rights.

An important source of inspiration can be found in the work of Raimundo Panikkar who, in an important article entitled 'Is the Notion of Human Rights a Western Concept?',[10] argues that in order to understand the meaning of human rights, it is necessary to scrutinize the function played by this notion in our culture. This allows us to examine

---

[9] François Jullien, *De l'universel, de l'uniforme, du commun et du dialogue entre les cultures* (Paris, Fayard, 2008), 135.

[10] Raimundo Panikkar, 'Is the Notion of Human Rights a Western Concept?', *Diogenes*, 120 (1982), 81–82.

later if this function is not fulfilled in different ways in other cultures. In other terms, Panikkar encourages us to enquire about the possibility of what he calls 'homeomorphic', i.e. functional equivalents of the notion of human rights. Looking at western culture, we ascertain that human rights are presented as providing the basic criteria for the recognition of human dignity and as being the necessary condition for a just social and political order. Therefore the question we need to ask is whether other cultures do not give different answers to the same question. Once it is acknowledged that what is at stake in human rights is the dignity of the person, the possibility of different manners of envisaging this question becomes evident, as well as the different ways in which it can be answered. Indeed, what western culture calls 'human rights' is a culturally specific form of asserting the dignity of the person and it would therefore be very presumptuous to declare that it is the only legitimate one.

Panikkar convincingly shows that the concept of human rights relies on a well-known set of presuppositions, all of which are distinctively western, namely: there is a universal human nature that can be known by rational means; human nature is essentially different from and higher than the rest of reality; the individual has an absolute and irreducible dignity that must be defended against society and the state; the autonomy of that individual requires that society be organized in a non-hierarchical way, as a sum of free individuals. All those presuppositions, says Panikkar, are definitively western and liberal and they are distinguishable from other conceptions of human dignity in other cultures. For instance, there is no necessary overlap between the idea of the 'person' and the idea of the 'individual'. The 'individual' is the specific way in which western liberal discourse formulates the concept of the self, however other cultures envisage the self in different ways. Thinking on similar lines Bikhu Parekh has shown how non-liberal societies rest on a theory of overlapping selves:

those bound together by familial, kinship, religious or other ties do not see themselves as independent and self-contained ontological units involved in specific kinds of relationships with 'others', but rather as bearers of overlapping selves whose identities are constituted by and incapable of being defined in isolation from these relationships. For them individual and self are distinct and their boundaries do not coincide, so that naturally distinct individuals may or may not share their selves in common. Each individual is deeply implicated in the lives of those related to him and their interests, lives and life plans are inextricably interlinked and incapable of individuation.[11]

[11] Bikhu Parekh, 'Decolonizing Liberalism', in Alexander Shtromas, (ed.), *The End of 'Isms'?* (Oxford, Blackwell, 1994), 89.

Many consequences stem from those considerations. One of the most important is that we should recognize that the idea of 'autonomy' which is so central in western liberal discourse and which is at the centre of our understanding of human rights cannot have such a priority in other cultures where decision-making is less individualistic and more co-operative than in western societies. This in no way signifies that those cultures are not concerned with the dignity of the person and the conditions for a just social order. What it means is that they deal with those questions in a different way. This is why the search for homeomorphic equivalents is an important one. We need to establish a cross-cultural dialogue based on the acceptance that the notion of human rights as formulated in western culture is one formulation among others of the idea of the dignity of the person. It is a very individualistic interpretation, specific to liberal culture and which cannot claim to be the only legitimate one.

Panikkar's approach chimes with Jullien's search for equivalents and his critique of invariants.[12] In both authors, although it is expressed differently, we find a critique of the Eurocentric view which postulates that moral progress takes place thanks to the development of a universal culture which advances through self-reflection. By putting the emphasis on equivalents, they lay the bases for a pluralist perspective which allows us to envisage the world as a pluriverse where no regional pole can claim to represent the highest point of development in terms of rationality or morality.

I would also like to stress the pertinence of this distinction between invariants and equivalents for the debate on 'alternative' or 'multiple' modernities. The two adjectives are often used indifferently but it has sometimes been argued that, by speaking of 'alternative' modernities, one is suggesting that there is a modernity of reference, the western one, which would be adapted to a variety of different contexts. Such a view is then rejected as being a 'Eurocentric critique of Eurocentrism'. There might perhaps exist some confusion among the theorists working under that umbrella, but it could be avoided by clarifying that when one speaks of multiple or alternative modernities, one is looking for equivalents of modernity in a variety of historical contexts and not for variations of an invariant western model considered to be the paradigmatic one.

When it comes to the issue of democracy, what I want to suggest is that a multipolar agonistic approach, which rejects the view that the western model of 'modern democracy' is superior in rationality and morality, should envisage the question in the following way. To begin with, we

---

[12] The critique of Panikkar by Jullien (*De l'universel*, 172) is in my view based on a misunderstanding.

have to abandon the view, which is predominant today, that democratization consists in the implementation of the western liberal democratic model. This will allow us to realize that democracy in a multipolar world could take a variety of forms, according to the different modes of inscription of the democratic ideal of 'rule by the people' in a variety of contexts. If we accept that, as I have argued in *The Democratic Paradox*,[13] liberal democracy is the articulation between two different traditions: liberalism, with its emphasis on individual liberty and universal rights and democracy, which privileges the idea of equality and 'rule by the people', i.e. popular sovereignty, then the contingent character of modern democracy becomes evident. Indeed such an articulation is not a necessary one but the product of a specific history. The liberal democratic model, with its particular conception of human rights, is the expression of a specific cultural and historical context, in which, as it has often been noted, the Judeo-Christian tradition has played a central role. Such a model of democracy is constitutive of our form of life and it is certainly worthy of our allegiance. This is not to deny of course the limitations in the current state of 'really existing liberal democratic societies' and the necessity of 'radicalizing' its institutions, but this is a different issue. My point here is that we should relinquish the claim that liberal democracy represents the only legitimate way of organizing human co-existence and to try to impose it on the rest of the world. The kind of individualism dominant in western societies is alien to many other cultures, whose traditions are informed by different values, and democracy understood as 'rule by the people' can therefore take other forms, in which for instance the value of community is more pregnant than the idea of individual liberty.

The pluralist perspective that I am advocating could be called 'agonistic' in the sense that it recognizes that divergences can be at the origin of conflict but that this conflict should not be perceived as a 'clash of civilizations'. Tensions will of course arise but they need not take the antagonistic form of a struggle between enemies but the agonistic form of a confrontation between adversaries. There is a term forged by Derrida which can help us. In his reflections on hospitality Derrida, following Benveniste, brings to the fore the deep ambivalence of the term 'hospitality', coming from two words with the same roots: 'hospis' (host) and 'hostis' (enemy).[14] To express this ambivalence and indicate the entanglement of hostility and hospitality, Derrida coined the term 'hostipitality'.

---

[13] Mouffe, *The Democratic Paradox*, Introduction.
[14] See Jacques Derrida, 'Hostipitality', in Jacques Derrida, *Acts of Religion* (London, Routledge, 2002), 356–420.

I think that an agonistic pluralist approach should envisage the pluriverse in terms of 'hostipitality' as the space where an agonistic encounter takes place between a diversity of poles that engage with each other without any one of them having the pretence of being the superior one. This agonistic encounter is a confrontation where the aim is neither the annihilation nor the assimilation of the other and where the tensions between the different approaches contribute to enhance the pluralism that characterizes a multipolar world.

11 Plural cosmopolitanisms and the origins of human rights

Samuel Moyn

In the course of 1948, the notion of human rights surged in western Europe, especially due to debates around the Universal Declaration, to be ratified by the United Nations in December of that year. While human rights did not rise so much as to define any live public option for politics in either the domestic or international spheres – notably, no movement in the service of human rights appeared — it is true that some people noticed.

One was the great German classicist Bruno Snell. When revising an essay for its inclusion in his still-renowned book *The Discovery of the Mind* as the debate proceeded, Snell added the following remarkable passage: "Euripides, in his *Medea*, is the first to portray a human being who excites pity by the mere fact of being a human being in torment," Snell declared. He continued: "[A]s a barbarian she has no rights, but as a human being she has. This same Medea is also the first person in literature whose thinking and feeling are described in purely human terms ... No sooner does man declare his independence of the gods, than he acclaims the authority of the free human spirit and the inviolability of human rights."[1] It is a remarkable set of assertions, and deserves to be placed in context. And it is helpful to define the conceptual task of writing the history of human rights even today, because it shows the need to depart from the model of the cosmopolitan discovery of humanity as a one-time breakthrough.

In 1947, Snell had published the essay on its own – without the above passage – as "The Discovery of *Humanitas*, and Our Relationship to the Greeks."[2] Actually, this English translation of the title – as rendered after the piece's inclusion in Snell's book-length sequence of articles — misstates the substance of the chapter, which dealt only in

---

[1] Bruno Snell, *The Discovery of the Mind: The Greek Origins of European Thought*, (trans.) T.G. Rosenmeyer (Cambridge, Mass., 1953), 250. The essay was added to the second German edition of the book, which is the basis for the English translation cited here.

[2] Bruno Snell, "Die Entdeckung der Menschlichkeit, und unsere Stellung zu den Griechen," *Geistige Welt*, 2(1) (1947), 1–9.

passing with the conundrum that it was not Greeks but Romans who invented the word "humanity." By then, this problem had become old and obsessive for German scholars who were so insistent on the Greek origins of everything valuable. Snell quickly acknowledged that the Greeks had no word for *humanitas*, while also citing learned evidence complicating prior discussions. In Snell's original German title for the piece, what was at stake was the discovery of *Menschlichkeit* – humanness, and humaneness, which did not necessarily coincide with the Latin term that his predecessors thought Greeks should have had even though they never coined it. The next year, it was from this *Menschlichkeit* that human rights turned out to derive.

Why did the origins of humanity matter to Snell, if not so much as a term then as a larger notion? One obvious reason was that the classical legacy had been abused by the National Socialists, not least by the classics profession itself. For this reason, in the mid-1940s it evidently seemed crucial to redeem both. Tellingly, Snell considered it perhaps most important to retrieve Greek *Menschlichkeit* and the human rights flowing from it without the "humanism" so bound up with the Greek legacy in modern times. "Humanism," Snell wrote in the first sentence of his piece, had "not always been of a congenial nature." In fact most of his essay engaged in polemic with a never identified Werner Jaeger, the great classicist who had argued for a "third humanism" before the Second World War and flirted for a few years with Nazi politics, before becoming a Harvard University professor. Given politicized claims of humanism it was imperative for Snell to insist on the recency and contingency of that notion ("created in 1808 by a Bavarian schoolteacher," Snell remarked derisively).[3]

The appeal to the classical past in "humanism," however, had to be replaced rather than given up altogether. Even as Snell criticized "humanism" as a novel and much-abused ideology, he insisted that the origins of "humanity" were different and older. Indeed, they were ancient and Greek, on condition of changing the problem from the superficial and distracting philological one of the coinage of the word to the difficult but

---

[3] Snell's bitter open critique of Jaeger's first instalment in *Paideia* had appeared immediately in *Göttingische Gelehrte Anzeigen*, 97 (1935), 329–353, rpt. *Gesammelte Schriften* (Göttingen, 1966). Jaeger, *Paideia: Die Formung des griechischen Menschen*, 3 vols. (Berlin, 1933–1947), in English as *Paideia: The Ideals of Greek Culture*, (trans.) Gilbert Highet (New York, 1939–1944). On Jaeger's "third humanism" and for larger context, see Suzanne Marchand, *Down from Olympus: Archeology and Philhellenism in Germany, 1750–1950* (Princeton, 1996), Chapter 9 and Anson Rabinbach, "Restoring the German Spirit: Humanism and Guilt in Post-War Germany," in Jan-Werner Müller, (ed.), *German Ideologies since 1945* (New York, 2003).

important one of the beginnings of the concept and cultural norm. If Snell rejected the ransacking of the past for Nazi purposes, in other words, he did not hesitate to orient himself for new reasons to history in general and the Greek legacy in particular. (Snell's famous book claims the "Greek origins of European thought," in the words of its English language subtitle, on a wide range of other issues too.)

Snell conceded that it was not obvious that the Greeks by definition had an implicit notion of "humanity" or "human dignity," though the same year Jaeger's colleague Herschel Baker published a now forgotten study based on exactly that premise.[4] "The truth is that [humanity] is neither Platonic nor even Greek in spirit," Snell wrote. "No Greek ever seriously spoke of the idea of man; the one time when Plato uses the expression . . ., he does so jokingly, and he follows it up with the ideas of hair, of dirt, and of filth."[5] By and large Plato was interested in "things divine," while Greek *paideia* – Jaeger's prized term – was meant to distinguish some humans from others along a scale of educational attainment. If the notion of humanity existed before the term, it usually involved belittlement or division rather than equalization and unification. Still, there were a few Greeks who saw things differently, Snell continued, viewing man as united with his fellows as all possible victims and therefore potential subjects of violated rights and objects of compassionate identification on the basis of this violation.

To say that the *Medea* is a parable about human rights is a rather remarkable assertion of course. Greek self-definition through tragedy – "inventing the barbarian," as Edith Hall calls it – seems much more a matter of drawing rather than erasing boundaries.[6] Yet the discovery of humanity as a fundamental notion mattered, according to Snell, because when decoupled from a regrettable arrogance and pedagogical elitism – one to which the Latin word *humanitas* itself long remained indentured! – Greek universalism became the lasting foundation for still relevant values. With Euripides, the breakthrough had been made though (Snell acknowledged) it took a while thereafter for the discriminatory connotations of being human to cede their place to the generalization in the western tradition of a more even-handed concern for the humanity of

---

[4] Herschel Baker, *The Dignity of Man: Studies in the Persistence of an Idea* (Cambridge, Mass., 1947), later rpt. and widely circulated as *The Image of Man: A Study of the Idea of Human Dignity in Classical Antiquity, the Middle Ages, and the Renaissance* (New York, 1961).

[5] Snell, *The Discovery of the Mind*, 247, citing Parmenides 130C.

[6] Edith Hall, *Inventing the Barbarian: Greek Self-Definition through Tragedy* (Oxford, 1989). See also Suzanne Saïd, "Greeks and Barbarians in Euripides' Tragedies: The End of Differences?," in Thomas Harrison, (ed.), *Greeks and Barbarians* (Edinburgh, 2002) or Jonathan M. Hall, *Hellenicity: Between Ethnicity and Culture* (Chicago, 2002).

each person regardless of rank. Nevertheless, Snell's rather sudden discovery that a Greek playwright two thousand years before the Universal Declaration had discovered its principles is the conclusion that counted for him. "No one who has been frightened by the barbaric forces which threaten all around us, will be able to disregard the cultivation of the spirit whose history starts with the Greeks," Snell concluded.[7]

I begin with Snell not to indict him personally, only to worry through his example about a general strategy of argument that remains surprisingly common today. For Snell's memory of the Nazis and his justifiable anger at Jaeger's abuses of the classical past do not really legitimate what remains a common trope in the new "history of human rights." In fact, the mixture of insight and incoherence in Snell's argument is a useful place to begin thinking about other ways to historicize "humanity" and therefore "human rights" of the 1940s and since. It might even suggest the need for an entirely different path.[8]

Snell was right simply to dismiss the backdrop of a pre-Second World War literature that wondered what to make of the fact that the Greeks had unfortunately failed to name humanity.[9] Except for certain unknowing heirs of this tradition, few today think the philological wordplay really matters. After all, the Greeks had the notion of and word for man (*anthrōpos*). And probably the Latin "humanity" came from translating and fusing the Greek terms *paideia* with its pedagogical associations and *philanthropia* with its compassionate ones, though debate continues about when (if ever) the truly universalist associations of "humanity" were achieved. None of this means that there is an easy move from Greek anthropology or Roman *humanitas* to modern visions of supranational human rights.

But if he was right to shift the debate away from philology, Snell was certainly wrong to conscript the Greeks into an invention of tradition. In his own essay on the subject, Paul Veyne, celebrated classical historian, observed that where his field had gone wrong was in its premise that "humanity" had been difficult to conceptualize in the first place. Since Snell's time, few have made anything of Euripides, perhaps because it

---

[7] Snell, *The Discovery of the Mind*, 262.

[8] This essay brings to the surface some implicit theoretical commitments and sources for my recent book *The Last Utopia: Human Rights in History* (Cambridge, Mass., 2010).

[9] Here is a small bibliography on this problem: Richard Reitzenstein, *Werden und Wesen der Humanität im Altertum: Rede zur Feier des Geburtstages Sr. Majestät des Kaisers am 26. Januar 1907* (Strasbourg, 1907); Rudolf Pfeiffer, *Humanitas erasmiana* (Berlin, 1931); Richard Harder, "Nachträgliches zu Humanitas," *Hermes*, 69 (1934): 64–74, rpt. in *Kleine Schriften*, (ed.) Walter Marg (Munich, 1960). Cf. Hannah Arendt, "The Crisis in Culture: Its Social and Political Significance," in Hannah Arendt, *Between Past and Future: Six Exercises in Political Thought* (New York, 1961), 297, n.17.

involves so strained an interpretation of his play. Instead, they have overwhelmingly credited later Stoic notions for the invention of humanity thanks to that philosophical movement's discovery of the cosmopolis. But what if "humanity" was, Veyne asked, actually an easy acquisition, and the problem – then and now – was living up to its implications? "The ancients knew that, in theory, humanity was one, but they did not want to know it," Veyne formulates the point. And the same, one might add, is true today.[10] Or more troublingly, one might contend that the appeal to universality tends most of all to provide a useful ideology of rule, with the cosmopolitanism masking what another Roman historian, Claude Nicolet, calls the "cosmocratic."[11]

Veyne, however, concluded from his insight into the easy availability of "humanity" that he should simply push the clock back on its discovery – and then investigate why no one who waxed eloquent about it ever actually believed in their high-minded rhetoric. "The discovery of the unity of humanity predated the Stoics by approximately four million years," Veyne wrote. "It dates from the first hominids, since all higher animals can recognize members of their own species."[12] It was not enough to disregard philology, like Snell, in order to move back from the Romans to the Greeks; the notion, as opposed to the word, may turn out to be coeval with humanity itself. That humanity was easy to discover, Veyne, a skeptic, concludes, mainly shows it has never meant very much, neither to the Romans nor to ourselves. Cosmocracy is simply the way of an evil world.

I agree with Veyne that humanity is a simple discovery rather than an epoch-making breakthrough. Any reader of Homer knows that, while various characters are children of gods and there were men in the age of heroes capable of things of which they were now incapable, they were men all the same. (The first chapter of Snell's book, an essay dating from 1939, was entitled: "Homer's View of Man.") Evidence from a series of other cultures confirms that the conception and even word for "man" are ubiquitous in history, even if Romans deserve credit for introducing "humanity" to its western career. But Veyne's conclusion that it is less

---

[10] Paul Veyne, "*Humanitas*: Romans and Non-Romans," in Andrea Giardina, (ed.), *The Romans*, (trans.) Lydia G. Cochrane (Chicago, 1993), 346.

[11] Ernest Badian, "Alexander the Great and the Unity of Mankind," *Historia: Zeitschrift für Alte Geschichte*, 7(4) (1958), 425–444; Claude Nicolet, *Space, Geography, and Politics in the Early Roman Empire* (Ann Arbor, 1991), esp. Chapter 2.

[12] Veyne, "*Humanitas*," 346. Richard Bulliet claims in a four-stage sequence of human-animal relations that the belief that humans were not animals (or different animals) is actually a different stage following primordial indistinction. See Richard Bulliet, *Hunters, Herders, and Hamburgers: The Past and Future of Human–Animal Relationships* (New York, 2005).

interesting to examine conceptions of "humanity" in theory than to show that no civilization really adheres to it in practice seems too hasty. "Humanity" matters, in part because it is so common in the annals of human affairs.

It is for this reason that, all along the way, different moments feature in the now large number of proposals for when the "breakthrough" to humanity was made. Snell is the paradigm of the one-time achievement approach that others have continued simply by moving the clock forwards or backwards. After the Stoics, full or partial credit for humanity has been given to: medieval spirituality, Scholastic natural law, the Renaissance, William Shakespeare, and (of course) Immanuel Kant. Jacob Burckhardt, in a vivid citation, acknowledged that *humanitas* preexisted the Renaissance, but it was only then that it was really understood. "One single result of the Renaissance is enough to fill us with everlasting thankfulness," Burckhardt exulted in one place in his classic study of the age. "The logical notion of humanity was old enough – but there the notion became a fact."[13] Harold Bloom says the same thing about Shakespeare: in his plays the "invention of the human" is staged.[14] Others view Kant's formula of humanity along similar lines (though he should more accurately have named his conception "the formula of rationality" given his constant emphasis that the power of setting ends does not solely accrue to human beings).

Sometimes these proposals are more complex, willingly connecting different moments in a story of linear acquisition: the Stoics, in the most common version, handed off a great but partial discovery to Kant for revival and completion.[15] But this approach is really just a temporalized version of Snell's approach of one-time breakthrough: extending it across history so that a series of collaborators combine to make it. For all that divides them, Snell and Veyne actually share the premise with both the historiography of one-time breakthrough and linear acquisition that there was a single moment or process of achievement of humanity – which then sets the stage for, or even covers, modern notions of human rights. It is this premise, the universal notion that human universalism is ultimately one thing, that continues to hobble the history of human rights, often presented as the conclusion and culmination of the emergence of cosmopolitanism or universalism.

---

[13] Jacob Burckhardt, *The Civilization of the Renaissance in Italy*, (trans.) S.G.C. Middlemore (New York, 1904), 354.

[14] Harold Bloom, *Shakespeare: The Invention of the Human* (New York, 1998). Bloom's prologue is entitled "Shakespeare's Universalism."

[15] Martha Nussbaum, *The Cosmopolitan Tradition* (forthcoming).

Yet on reflection, the model of one-time breakthrough (or its more complex form, linear acquisition) is deeply implausible, in part because there have been so many different candidates for when universalistic insight was finally achieved. Veyne's own suggestion that "humanity" is easy, and was therefore early, to see implies that in fact universalism is present in very different cultures in different ways – and that it is this *variety* of the articulations of human universalism, not the ease of its presence by itself, that matters most of all. In his brilliant comparative study of Latin and Sanskrit, focused on the linguistic embodiment of universalistic values, Sheldon Pollock has made the point arrestingly: "There has been not just one cosmopolitanism in history but several."[16] This suggestion, I want to propose, is a better starting point for the history of human rights.

It is a simple but fecund proposition. If it is correct, Michel Foucault was wrong that humanity is an invention of recent date; far more important was the variety of claims on its basis, and perhaps from the beginning of human culture. Similarly, Carl Schmitt was wrong that those who have always invoked humanity have always lied, concealing particular interests, for the condition of universalistic aspiration turns out to be its articulation in some particular version. Arguably, cosmopolitanisms have teemed all along, indeed competed with one another vigorously. And indeed they have done so in the heart of the tradition of "the west" – a point for which Pollock's insight needs to be adapted since he developed it through a comparison of different civilizations.

As the rest of this chapter will try to show, modernity itself is the forum for the most spectacular multiplication of rival and alternative cosmopolitan universalisms humanity may ever have witnessed. As late as the Cold War, which was a battle to the death of rival universalisms, "humanity" was crucial, but only in different versions aiming to supplement or to displace one another. (French communists named their newspaper: *L'Humanité.*) The history of human rights, in short, is not a story about "the cosmopolitan tradition," as either the one-time discovery of humanity cherished thereafter, or the slow emergence of a singular universalism, Western in origin or multiculturally forged. What is crucial is not any of the many alleged breakthroughs to "humanity" in world history. Instead it is what happened for human rights to seem, in a tradition of the 1940s and since that Snell helped found, like the only viable kind of universalism there is now.

---

[16] Sheldon Pollock, *The Languages of the Gods in the World of Men: Sanskrit, Culture, and Power in Premodern India* (Berkeley, 2006), 280. See also Carol A. Breckinridge *et al.*, (eds.), *Cosmopolitanism* (Raleigh, 2002), in which Pollock's chapter provides a brief overview of his theses.

From a very early date, legal systems have afforded "rights," notably the Roman legal system of which most branches of western law are tributaries. It may have been due to Stoic influence that occasionally the rights of the Roman legal system could be conceptualized as rooted partly in nature.[17] Before the rise of the modern state, empires from Rome on provided citizenship, or lesser forms for subjecthood, as well as the rights premised on that inclusion; indeed, they were to do so long into the twentieth century.[18] The rights of these imperial spaces were in this sense more like the rights of state inclusion, which premised entitlements on membership, than they were contemporary human rights. Some Roman language aside, however, thoroughgoing *natural* rights approaches were no older than the seventeenth century, and were a byproduct of the origins of the modern state. They were the children of the absolutist and expansionist state of early modern European history, not attempts to step outside and beyond the state. It was a spectacularly pivotal moment, given that it was to be for so long that rights were closely identified and bound up with the state – until this alliance was recently seen as insufficient.

The concept of "natural rights" did not come out of nowhere. When Hobbes first referred to the right of nature, he used the same word *ius* that once referred to the law of nature. This earlier doctrine, which arose from a combination of Stoic universalism and Christian values, had its heyday in the medieval period; its most famous version is found in St. Thomas Aquinas' thought. Yet if the idea of natural rights first emerged in the old language of natural law, it was so different in its intentions and implications as to be a different concept.

In modern times most revivalists of natural law, usually Catholics, have regarded it as a disaster for their creed that it gave way to an apostate rights-based successor. They are at least right that natural law, derived most often from God's will and thought to be embedded in the fabric of the cosmos, was the classic Christian version of universalism. For it to be displaced by natural rights it had to be made plural, subjective, and possessive. Natural law was originally one rule given from above, where natural rights came to be a list of separate items. Natural law was

---

[17] Philip Mitsis, "Natural Law and Natural Right in Post-Aristotelian Philosophy: The Stoics and Their Critics," and Paul Vander Waerdt, "Philosophical Influence on Roman Jurisprudence?: The Case of Stoicism and Natural Law," both in *Aufstieg und Niedergang der römischen Welt*, II.36.7 (1994), 4812–4900. But the meaning of *ius* in Roman law and its difference from the notion of a "subjective" claim in later legal systems is even disputed, notably by Michel Villey. See Michel Villey, "L'idée du droit subjectif et les systèmes juridiques romains," *Revue historique de droit français et étranger*, 4(23) (1946), 201–227.

[18] Jane Burbank and Frederick Cooper, "Empire, droits, et citoyenneté, de 212 à 1946," *Annales ESC*, 63(3) (2008), 495–531.

something objective, which individuals must obey because God made them part of the natural order he ordained: illegitimate practices were deemed *contra naturam* or "against nature." But natural rights were subjective entities "owned" by humanity as prerogatives. The timing and causes of the transition between natural law and natural rights have received massive attention in recent decades, in part because of an overestimation of how critical they were in the origins of today's human rights. The founding natural rights figures were, however, anything but humanitarians; on theoretical principle, they endorsed an austere doctrine that refused an expansive list of basic entitlements. If their invention of natural rights mattered as any sort of precursor, it is because natural rights were bound up with a new kind of powerful state taking off in the era. In many ways, the history of natural rights, like that of the rights of man afterwards, is the history of the very state that "human rights" would later attempt to transcend.

The case for the link revolves around the fact that the autarkic or freestanding individual of natural rights – the person whom Grotius and Hobbes saw as the bearer of the new concept – was explicitly modeled on the assertive new state of early modern international affairs.[19] That individual, like the state, tolerated no superordinate authority. It was for this reason that, as in the contest of states, natural individuals were imagined as in or close to a war to the death, qualified only by cooled hostilities, but never universal norms. Of moral precepts every man would acknowledge, Grotius and Hobbes argued, there was indeed only one: the legitimacy of self-preservation. It was self-preservation that Hobbes declared the first "right of nature," and the only such right that he saw. "The Right of Nature," Hobbes wrote, "is the Liberty each man hath, to use his own power, as he will himselfe, for the preservation of his own Nature; that is to say, of his own Life; and consequently, of doing any thing, which in his own Judgement, and Reason, he shall conceive to be the aptest means thereunto."[20] Just as the early modern state answered to no higher authority than its core need to preserve itself, so natural individuals only had one right, to fight — with a license to kill if necessary. Yet while states in competition in international affairs could do no more than postpone their standoff, Hobbes famously argued that domestic politics could only achieve peace if their feuding citizens empowered the state to rule. The argumentative goal of the first right – the motivation for introducing it into

---

[19] See esp. Richard Tuck, *The Rights of War and Peace: Political Thought and the International Order from Grotius to Kant* (Oxford, 1999), as well as David William Bates, *States of War: Enlightenment Origins of the Political* (New York, 2011).
[20] Thomas Hobbes, *Leviathan*, rev. edn, (ed.) Richard Tuck (Cambridge, 1996), 91.

political thought — was to empower the state, not to limit it. And one clear reason for justifying this empowerment was that states of the era were, aside from providing disciplinary pacification in a time of civil war at home, pursuing unprecedented colonization of worlds elsewhere.[21]

The century that followed was the scene of a wide variety of more generous visions of natural rights and duties that were not to be so strictly focused on self-preservation, and the construction of a state that would provide the blessings of discipline and security. But to the extent appeals to nature became more expansive, it is often because they refused to revolve around individualized rights alone.[22] The possibility of inventing rights beyond self-preservation depended, according to eighteenth-century natural lawyers like Swiss thinker J.-J. Burlamaqui and his American followers, on the deeper foundation of all entitlements in a robust doctrine of God-given duties.[23] It was in part through this process that some of the values incubated in diverse traditions were made natural rights – the right to private property in John Locke's famous theory, and many other items later. Notwithstanding the crafting of these more full-bodied lists of rights, however, the age of democratic revolution only furthered the very alliance between rights and the state through which rights had emerged. Now, even the first right of self-preservation meant the prince needed continuing consent – for Locke at least – and it was joined by a series of other natural entitlements. But even these momentous shifts did not change the fact that the answer to abridged rights was a move to a new sovereign or a new state rather than a move beyond sovereignty and state altogether. Further, in the revolutionary era, not just states but now nations became the formative crucible of rights, and their indispensable ally and forum – in other words, exactly what human rights as an idea and a practice would later have to set itself against.

The actual significance of the era of democratic revolution in America and France is as much in negating of the possibility of twentieth-century human rights doctrines as in making it available. Properly told, the history

---

[21] "It cannot be a coincidence," Tuck writes, "that the modern idea of natural rights arose in the period in which the European nations were engaged in their dramatic competition for domination of the world." Tuck, *The Rights of War*, 14. See also Anthony Pagden, "Human Rights, Natural Rights and Europe's Imperial Legacy," *Political Theory*, 31(2) (2003), 171–199, and Duncan Ivison, "The Nature of Rights and the History of Empire," in David Armitage, (ed.), *British Political Thought in History, Literature, and Theory* (Cambridge, 2006).

[22] Compare Knud Haakonssen, "Protestant Natural Law Theory, A General Interpretation," in Natalie Brender and Larry Krasnoff, (eds.), *New Essays on the History of Autonomy: A Collection Honoring J.B. Schneewind* (Cambridge, 2004), 95.

[23] See Morton White, *The Philosophy of the American Revolution* (New York, 1978), Chapters 4–5.

of democratic republicanism, or the narrower history of liberalism, is more about how human rights did not arise rather than how they did. One unintentional proof is how deeply nationalism has defined, not simply the rights of man, but partisan interpretations of their trajectory in the age of revolution. A century ago, the German scholar Georg Jellinek caused an intellectual contretemps by arguing for the priority of American rights-talk (which he in turn rooted in earlier German Reformation-era breakthroughs) as a source for the French Declaration of the Rights of Man and Citizen of 1789; the French were predictably unhappy with this attempt to steal their birthrights.[24] Such tawdry disputes have cropped up, from time to time, ever since. When the French were commemorating their achievements on the revolution's bicentennial in 1989, the mischievous Margaret Thatcher provoked a diplomatic sensation when she mordantly observed on French television that the French had not invented human rights but had taken them from elsewhere (and had then gone on to throw the debt overboard by descending into revolutionary terror).

In fact, the Americans – not so much in the Declaration of Independence of July 1776 as in the even earlier and much fuller-bodied Virginia Declaration of Rights of the month before and its successors in other states – did steal a march on the French by founding their polities on enumerated rights, even if they declined to do so within their national confederation.[25] Thomas Jefferson, in Paris in 1789, helped the Marquis de Lafayette draft the first proposed version of a French *Déclaration*. Even so, the sources for both American state and French revolutionary documents have remained hard to isolate. Whatever the answer, the French declaration arguably did move the politics of rights in a brand new direction in 1789's eventful summer. The French abbé Emmanuel-Joseph Sieyès – whose proposed draft superseded Lafayette's in Parisian debates – claimed as he and other revolutionaries moved towards

---

[24] Georg Jellinek, *Die Erklärung der Menschen- und Bürgerrechte: ein Beitrag zur modernen Verfassungsgeschichte* (Leipzig, 1895); Émile Boutmy, "La Déclaration des droits de l'homme et du citoyen et M. Jellinek," *Annales des sciences politiques* 17 (1902): 415–443; Georg Jellinek, "La Déclaration des droits de l'homme et du citoyen et M. Boutmy," rpt. in *Ausgewählte Schriften und Reden*, 2 vols., (ed.) Walter Jellinek (Berlin, 1911). For comment, see Otto Vossler, "Studien zur Erklärung der Menschen- und Bürgerrechte," *Historische Zeitschrift*, 142(3) (1930): 516–545; Wolfgang Schmale, "Georg Jellinek et la Déclaration des Droits de l'Homme de 1789," in *Mélanges offerts à Claude Petitfrère: Regards sur les sociétés modernes (XVIe-XVIIe siècle)*, (ed.) Denise Turrel (Tours, 1997) and Duncan Kelly, "Revisiting the Rights of Man: Georg Jellinek on Rights and the State," *Law and History Review*, 22(3) (2004): 493–530.

[25] Along with Jellinek, see Gilbert Chinard, *La déclaration des droits de l'homme et du citoyen et ses antécédents américains* (Washington, 1945).

constitutional monarchy in 1789 that the American commitment to rights remained too dependent on an antique tradition of aristocratic rights-talk stretching back to the Magna Carta, which merely reserved prerogatives "negatively" from the king rather than actually founding the polity "positively" on rights principles. In *The Federalist Papers* of the same period – written before a bill of rights for the new national government had been forced on him – Alexander Hamilton even took this antiquarian aspect of bills or declarations of rights as a reason for *not* including one in the new American Constitution: "It has been several times truly remarked," Hamilton noted, "that bills of rights are, in their origin, stipulations between kings and their subjects, abridgements of prerogative in favor of privilege, reservations of rights not surrendered to the prince."[26] If there were no prince, in other words, no enumeration of rights would be necessary.

In the event, of course, Frenchmen decided that a list of rights had to become the first principles of a constitution, and the American framers were forced to append one to their handiwork to gain public support for it. These events surely did document the meteoric rise of the notion of "the rights of man" across the second half of the eighteenth century, however it is to be explained, and whether it was self-evident to many at the time or not. Americans had typically invoked natural rights in their earlier revolution, and even by 1789 the natural framing of their assertion had faded. After Thomas Paine's defense of the French Revolution for Anglo-American republicans in *The Rights of Man* (1791), the fortunes of that new phrase were cemented across the Atlantic world and beyond. Paine's accidental variation of his translation of *droits de l'homme* as "human rights" once in his book did not, however, catch on, as it would a century and a half later.

The detailed history of rights in this turbulent period is no doubt fascinating, especially when the original French canon gave way, during the Terror of 1793, to a new declaration introducing social concern as rights for the first time. The overwhelmingly important point, however, is that the rights of the revolutionary era were very much embodied in the politics of the state, crystallizing in a scheme worlds away from the political meaning human rights would have later. In a sense, every declaration of rights at the time (and until recently) was implicitly what the French openly labeled theirs: a declaration of the rights of man *and citizen*. Rights were neither independent arguments nor countervailing forces, and were always announced at the moment of founding the polity,

---

[26] *The Federalist Papers*, (ed.) Clinton Rossiter (New York, 2003), 512 (No. 84).

and justifying its erection, and often its violence.[27] The "rights of man" were about a whole people incorporating itself in a state, not a few foreign people criticizing another one for its wrongdoings. Thereafter, they were about the meaning of citizenship. This profound relationship between the annunciation of rights and the fast-moving "contagion of sovereignty" of the century that followed not only cannot be left out of the history of rights, but has arguably been its main plot element until very recently. If so, it is far more fruitful to examine how human rights arose mainly because of the collapse of the model of revolutionary rights rather than through its continuation or revival. Not least revolution, with its non-reformist radicalism and potentially violent techniques, framed the rights of man as the era of democracy began. In glib terms, revolutionary era rights were revolutionary: the justification for the creation or renovation of a citizenship space, not the protection of "humanity."

As principles to which positive law was supposed to conform, the rights invoked by many Enlightenment thinkers and then in the revolutionary moment were in some sense above the state. But they only appeared through the state, and there was no forum above it, or at times even in it, in which to claim that the state transgressed. Indeed, once they were declared, it was not self-evident that rights would have many purposes independent of the emergence of the state. For example, they did not give rise directly to mechanisms of judicial projection to afford check against sovereign authority – even though this may seem like their obvious function today. In the United States, the now familiar practice of judicial review of legislation in the name of fundamental rights was not a foregone conclusion in 1789, when the first ten amendments were framed. And even when judicial review appeared it did not spark a rich tradition of litigation, given the initially restricted purposes of the national government. In England, it was assumed that wise opinion and tradition would protect unwritten rights, making it unnecessary to announce them, much less provide a high court to protect them. In France, meanwhile, it took more than 150 years, until after the Second World War, for the constitutional rights on which successive republics were always based at the outset to become the grounds for judicial indictment of the state.[28] What now seems like a natural assumption, that the very point of

---

[27] Compare Dan Edelstein, *The Terror of Natural Right: Republicanism, the Cult of Nature, and the French Revolution* (Chicago, 2009).

[28] On America, see, for example, Larry D. Kramer, *The People Themselves: Popular Constitutionalism and Judicial Review* (New York, 2005). On France, see, for example, Philippe Raynaud, "Des droits de l'homme à l'État de Droit," *Droits*, 2 (1985) and Alec Stone Sweet, *The Birth of Judicial Politics in France: The Constitutional Council in Comparative Perspective* (New York, 1992).

asserting rights is to restrict the activities of the state by providing a courtroom forum for their protection, was not what revolutionary rights were about. Instead, the main remedy for the abrogation of revolutionary rights remained democratic action up to and including another revolution. And while no non-governmental organizations now contemplate that extreme recourse, it was the only response imaginable at the time in the name of the rights of man.

If abstract principles were called upon in the era mainly as grounds for creating new states, they were just as important in their justification of the erection of their insurmountable external borders. Where the American states based on natural rights entered a weak confederation, while retaining local autonomy, France set the model for the modern nation-state in its achievement of centralized sovereign independence for a democratic people. Far from providing a rationale for foreign or "human" claims against states, assertions of rights were at root – and for at least a century – a justification for states to come about. Unlike the founding documents of the American states, the Declaration of Independence had no real list of entitlements in it, since it aimed primarily to achieve sovereignty externally against European encroachment.[29] As a matter of fact, rights were subordinate features of the creation of both state and nation beginning in this era, for few took the trouble to distinguish them.[30] A mere decade after the American "people" declared the autonomy of its new state to the world, Frenchmen in their own revolutionary declaration insisted "the principle of all sovereignty resides essentially in the Nation," adding for good measure that "no body and no individual may exercise authority which does not emanate expressly from it" (Art. 3). In an era in which American popular unity coalesced thanks more to bloody Indian war than to humane principles, it may have been simply true to stereotype for the French to identify their own national identity with universal morality; they saw no conflict in proclaiming the emergence of a sovereign nation of Frenchmen and announcing the rights of man as man at one and the same time. As a result, rights announced in the constitution of the sovereign nation-state – not "human rights" in the contemporary sense – were the great and fateful bequest of the French Revolution to world politics.

[29] David Armitage, *The Declaration of Independence: A Global History* (Cambridge, Mass., 2006), esp. 17–18.

[30] Cf. Istvan Hont, "The Permanent Crisis of a Divided Mankind: 'Contemporary Crisis of the Nation-State' in Historical Perspective," *Political Studies*, 42 (1994): 166–231, esp. 191–198, and J.K. Wright, "National Sovereignty and the General Will: The Political Program of the Declaration of Rights," in Dale Van Kley, (ed.), *The French Idea of Freedom* (Stanford University Press, 1994).

No doubt, the transition to the world of potentially republican states did not simply reproduce the international affairs of a world in which empire and monarchy set the standard. The French Revolution did have profound implications for the global order, immediately making several Enlightenment visions of "perpetual peace" seem within reach to a few. Yet aside from the memorably outlandish German baron Anacharsis Cloots – who joined the revolutionary National Assembly as the representative of non-French humanity, and supported aggressive warfare as a step toward truly world government – utopian visions took a form wholly compatible with the spread of national sovereignty, rather than imagining rules or rights above it.[31] In practice, when the encirclement of the revolutionary state by the armies of its European enemies forced it to spread its fire abroad in the closing decade of the eighteenth century, the republic did not move towards global law but set up "sisters" (as they were called) and toyed with some sort of concert of new republics.[32] In theory, Kant consciously rejected Cloots' radicalism, instead holding out a wholly minimal *Weltbürgerrecht* or "world citizen law" that envisaged no more than an asylum right for individuals out of place in a world of national states. True, Kant, like the Stoics, was a cosmopolitan thinker. But he was not for today's human rights, in the full-bodied protection they promise even when they rest content with an international order composed of nations.[33]

As a result, in the nineteenth century the often heartfelt appeal to the rights of man always went along with the propagation of national sovereignty as indispensable means, entailed precondition, and enduring accompaniment. If there was a rights of man *movement* in the nineteenth century, it was liberal nationalism, which sought to secure the rights of citizens resolutely in the national framework. By the end of his career, Lafayette found himself bringing the rights of man to Poland, where he assumed, like so many adherents of modern revolution, that

---

[31] Alexander Bevilacqua, "Cloots, Rousseau and Peaceful World Order in the Age of the French Revolution" (M.Phil. thesis, University of Cambridge, 2008) and Albert Mathiez, *La Révolution et les Étrangers: Cosmopolitisme et défense nationale* (Paris, 1918); on German theorizing, see Pauline Kleingeld, "Six Varieties of Cosmopolitanism in Late Eighteenth-Century Germany," *Journal of the History of Ideas* 60 (1999): 505–524 and Kleingeld, "Defending the Plurality of States: Cloots, Kant, and Rawls," *Social Theory and Practice* 32 (2006): 559–578.

[32] See Marc Bélissa, *Fraternité universelle et intérêt national (1713–1795): les cosmopolitiques du droit des gens* (Paris, 1996) and *Repenser l'ordre européen, 1795–1802: de la société des rois aux droits des nations* (Paris, 2006).

[33] Compare Martha Nussbaum, "Kant and Stoic Cosmopolitanism," *Journal of Political Philosophy* 5, 1 (March 1997): 1–25, rpt. as "Kant and Cosmopolitanism," in James Bohman and Mathias Lutz-Bachmann, (eds.), *Perpetual Peace: Essays on Kant's Cosmopolitan Idea* (Cambridge, Mass., 1997).

"the universal and particular rights of any people ... were best protected by sovereign nation-states."[34] To take the most emblematic figure, Italian Giuseppe Mazzini, the revolutionary rights of man were high ideals. "The individual is sacred," Mazzini maintained. He had "Liberty, Equality, Humanity" written on one side of the banner of his movement, Young Italy. But on the other, he emblazoned "Unity, Independence," in perfect conformity with the spreading conviction across the continent that liberty and nationality were mutually implied. Indeed, the full dependence of rights on national autonomy meant that "the epoch of *individuality* is concluded," as Mazzini firmly announced (emphasis in the original). Now, "collective man is omnipotent on the earth he treads." Without placing the nation-state first among aims, through whatever means, "you will have no name, token voice, nor rights," as he put it to his fellow Italians, "no admission to the fellowship of the peoples."[35]

Mazzini very much caught the spirit of the rights bequeathed by revolution. As a result, rights were impossible to free from the apotheosis of the state even for those who worried about revolutionary excess. French liberal thinkers like Benjamin Constant, François Guizot, and Alexis de Tocqueville anxious about popular despotism treated rights as only one element on a long list of tools liberal civilization had afforded to ensure freedom in the state. Elsewhere on the political spectrum in France, the one-time epicenter of the rights of man, the political language was strikingly abandoned in the nineteenth century, and the same thing happened everywhere.[36] For premier German philosopher G.W.F. Hegel, rights were worthwhile only "in context," in a state reconciling freedom and community.[37] In German lands before and after their unification, the partisans of liberalism were deeply statist and nationalist in their thinking and strategy of mass appeal; even when they were motivated by universal principles, they first allied themselves with the

[34] Cited in Lloyd Kramer, *Lafayette in Two Worlds: Public Cultures and Personal Identities in an Age of Revolutions* (Chapel Hill, 1996), 255–256.
[35] Citations from Lewis B. Namier, "Nationality and Liberty," rpt. in Eugene C. Black, *European Political History, 1815–1870: Aspects of Liberalism* (New York, 1967), 139–141, except for the last, from Yael Tamir, *Liberal Nationalism* (Princeton, 1995), 124. Compare Michael Walzer, "Nation and Universe," in *Thinking Politically: Essays in Political Theory* (New Haven, 2007) and C.A. Bayly and Eugene Biagini, (eds.), *Giuseppe Mazzini and the Globalisation of Democratic Nationalism, 1830–1920* (Oxford, 2008).
[36] Tony Judt, "Rights in France: Reflections on the Etiolation of a Political Language," *Tocqueville Review* 14, 1 (1993): 67–108. See also Norberto Bobbio, "Diritti dell'uomo e del cittadino nel secolo XIX in Europa," and other essays in Gerhard Dilcher, et al., (eds.), *Grundrechte im 19. Jahrhundert* (Frankfurt, 1982).
[37] See Steven B. Smith, *Hegel's Critique of Liberalism: Rights in Context* (Chicago, 1991).

Rechtsstaat ideal of princely bureaucracy, and later shared in the conviction that the mild internationalism of Kant's era had passed in favor of the absolute supremacy of the national project. The rights that Germans argued over in the revolutionary year of 1848 were for this reason civil rights linked to citizenship boundaries; and their paeans to the coming of liberty were bound up with outbursts of nationalist chauvinism.[38] In this, they were unique only in details, their "national liberalism" fitting with that of all who invoked rights everywhere else.

The alliance with state and nation was not some accident that tragically befell the rights of man: it was their very essence, for the vast bulk of their history. It is most plausible to think that the shift in the direction of statism and nationalism in the nineteenth century occurred on the basis of congenital features of rights talk. After the era of revolution, the right of collective self-determination, as it would come to be called in the twentieth century, would offer the obvious framework for citizen entitlements. And this framework was to resonate until living memory, notably during the post-Second World War decolonization of the globe. If revolutionary self-rule inspired so many during the nineteenth century and after, it was thus not because their examples had secured "universal human rights" directly. Rather, their appeal lay in emancipation from monarchical despotism and backward tradition in the French case and postcolonial liberation from empire and the creation of state independence in the American one.

As Hannah Arendt understood, the centrality of the nation-state as the crucible for rights is of understandable appeal, if the first order of business is to provide citizenship spaces even at the price of political borders. Indeed, the subordination of rights to the nation-state may have been the main historical reason that rights became less salient the more the nineteenth century passed. It must have become clearer and clearer as time passed that not the assertion of abstract principles but the achievement of specific citizenship was what truly mattered. Once justified as given by God or nature, rights-talk more and more acquired a statist or "positivist" rationale everywhere it percolated. The rights of man, as Arendt phrased it, were "treated as a sort of stepchild by nineteenth-century political thought and . . . no liberal or radical party in the twentieth century . . . saw fit to include them in its program . . . If the laws of

---

[38] See Herbert A. Strauss, *Staat, Bürger, Mensch: die Debatten der deutschen Nationalversammlung 1848/1849 über Grundrechte* (Aarau, 1947); cf. Brian E. Vick, *Debating Germany: The 1848 Frankfurt Parliamentarians and National Identity* (Cambridge, Mass., 2002); for some texts, Heinrich Scholler, (ed.), *Die Grundrechtsdiskussion in der Paulskirche: eine Dokumentation* (Darmstadt, 1973).

their country did not live up to the demands of the Rights of Man, they were expected to change them, by legislation ... or through revolutionary action."[39] However human in basis, rights were national political achievements first and foremost.

Along with capitalism, the nation-state has probably been the single most emancipatory force in world history – though like capitalism, the modern-nation state has also been an agent of great immiseration and destruction. Whatever one thinks of them, both have been the central engines of the proliferation – even the conceivability – of rights. Both are universalistic in their foundations, or at least were in the origins of conceptual defenses they attracted. Just as capitalism and nationalism are very different from one another, the concept and practices associated with the contemporary enterprise of international human rights are departures from the state as the self-sufficient forum of universalistic values.

In the terms I have developed in this chapter, the history of rights itself, then, provides a vivid example in which no one-time breakthrough or linear acquisition occurred. Instead, contemporary human rights from their origins on have broken with the primary meaning of rights in modern times. In effect, natural rights and then the rights of man, with their statism and often nationalism, deserve to be compared with the human rights that succeeded and eventually displaced them. As much continuity as one might seek between them, they are competing and alternative universalisms in their spirit and consequences.

An important proviso, of course, is that alternative and indeed antagonistic universalisms can share particular norms, and even overlap substantially. To take one example, the norm against human killing (always with permissible exceptions) is to be found in every known human culture. To take another, the competing cosmopolitanisms of the Cold War shared a great deal, beginning with their emancipatory visions of political freedom and their commitment to industrial modernity as the vehicle through which it was supposed to be achieved. But no one would claim that, because they have a zone of overlap, capitalism or even social democracy in the west coincided with the principles or practices of communist empire. The rise of one alternative presupposed the fall of the other.

In a similar vein, the universalism of the Enlightenment and revolutionary eras clearly does bear some affinity to contemporary forms of cosmopolitanism summed up in the commitment to international human

---

[39] Hannah Arendt, *The Origins of Totalitarianism*, 3rd edn (New York, 1968), 293.

rights. Yet what the Enlightenment put forward as "the immortal rights of man" was nevertheless part of a strikingly distinct political project from contemporary human rights (which, in fact, were born out of a criticism of revolution). The rights of man were utopian, and evoked emotion: "Who will dare to avow that his heart was not lifted up," Johann Wolfgang von Goethe exclaimed in 1797, "when the new sun first rose in its splendor; when we heard of the rights of man, of inspiring liberty, and of universal equality!"[40] Yet unlike later human rights, they were imaginatively and practically bound up with the construction, through revolution if necessary, of state and nation. It is now the order of the day to supplement that state forum for rights, but until recently the state was their sole and essential crucible.

As Sheldon Pollock might have put it, there has been not one cosmopolitanism in the history of rights but several. And the example is generalizable. If human rights departed so fundamentally from what have typically been regarded as their immediately prior avatars within the tradition of western rights-talk, then it seems implausible to continue to believe that they did not depart in even deeper ways from all the universalisms that have teemed across the annals of civilization. Euripides, it seems, did not invent human rights after all. We did.

---

[40] J. W. von Goethe, *Hermann and Dorothea*, (trans.) Thomas Conrad Porter (New York, 1854), 97.

Part IV

Rights and power

12   Second-generation rights as biopolitical rights

Pheng Cheah

This chapter is a preliminary attempt to grapple with the implications posed by the proliferation of different regimes of human rights – commonly described as second- and third-generation human rights – to the concept of human rights itself, especially its normativity. One common argument is that the proliferation of different types of human rights attests to the genuinely infinite and open-ended normativity of human rights as an ideal project because it shows a prodigious capacity for accommodating multiple universalisms that contest and compete with each other. This would lead to a gradual refining of human rights so that they can attain the greatest degree of universality possible in a current historical conjuncture. In this chapter, I suggest that regimes of human rights that focus on positive duties to fulfill human needs radically put into question the rational–normative structure of human rights because it puts their juridical form into communication with something else – the biological or natural dimension of human life – that deforms and even explodes this juridical form. We see this deformation in some of the negative consequences that mark the implementation of second-generation rights. I suggest that we can better account for these consequences by understanding these rights in terms of biopolitics.

Second-generation human rights: the mistaken opposition of sovereignty and human rights

Despite the clear indication of the structural connection between universal human rights and positive law in the stipulation of the preamble of the Universal Declaration of Human Rights that "human rights should be protected by the rule of law," the juridical form of modern human rights has often been called into question on the grounds that their normative validity is extra-legal and precedes and transcends sovereign states because they are "equal and inalienable rights of all members of the human family" that are grounded in "the inherent dignity" of all human beings. Accordingly, it is customary to point out that modern human rights are influenced by ideas about natural liberties from the modern philosophy of natural rights, whereby rights are liberties (*jus*) that are prior to laws (*lex*), which imply obligation and, therefore, coercion and compulsion from a sovereign authority.[1] Alternatively, when being human is determined in terms of reason rather than nature, it is argued that modern human rights are not conferred by the state because they are moral rights and their normativity stems from what is morally right according to the character of human beings as creatures of reason.

This conventional analytical distinction between (state) sovereignty and human rights is confusing, for at least three reasons. First, the natural power to preserve one's own nature can lead to acquiescence to law. Spinoza is clearest on the co-extensiveness of natural right and sovereignty. The right of Nature as a whole and the natural right of every individual is grounded in the power of God as an absolutely free being, that is, as sovereign.[2] Hence, sovereignty in the narrow sense of political sovereignty, which is the most common usage of the term, derives from the sovereign power of God as manifested in the power of a people. The people is a collective being that acts "as if by one mind" and it arises in order to facilitate the individual's power over nature through mutual assistance. Hence, even though the right and power of a people is of a different order from the natural right of individuals, it grows out of the right of individuals. Far from encroaching upon the right of individuals, the right of the state actualizes the right of individuals because both are grounded in the sovereign right of Nature:

The right of the state or of the sovereign is nothing more than the right of Nature itself and is determined by the power not of each individual but of a people which is guided as if by one mind ... [T]he individual citizen does

---

[1] Thomas Hobbes, *Leviathan* (Harmondsworth: Penguin, 1961), I.14, 189: "Right, consisteth in liberty to do, or to forbeare; Whereas Law, determineth and bindeth to one of them: so that Law, and Right, differ as much, as Obligation, and Liberty; which is in one and the same matter inconsistent."

[2] Baruch Spinoza, *Political Treatise*, (trans.) Samuel Shirley (Indianapolis: Hackett, 2000), Chapter 2 [3], 38: "God's right is nothing other than God's power in so far as that is considered as absolutely free, it follows that every natural thing has as much right from Nature as it has power to exist and to act. For the power of every natural thing by which it exists and acts is nothing other than the power of God, which is absolutely free." See also Chapter 2 [4], 38: "By the right of Nature, then, I understand the laws or rules of Nature in accordance with which all things come to be: that is, the very power of Nature. So the natural right of Nature as a whole, and consequently the natural right of every individual, is coextensive with his power. Consequently, whatever each man does from the laws of this own nature, he does by the sovereign right of Nature, and he has as much right over Nature as his power extends."

nothing and possesses nothing by right beyond what he can defend by common decree of the commonwealth.[3]

The political sovereign is thus not a negative force that restricts or constrains the natural right of individuals. It is instead a positive force because nature itself is understood as power and, therefore, in terms of sovereignty.

Second, the tradition of liberal political philosophy maintains the link between sovereignty and the natural rights of individuals by giving sovereignty the anthropologistic form of the human individual who possesses inalienable rights because he is a sovereign person. Accordingly, the apparent conflict between individual rights and the sovereign state is merely a conflict between two different sovereignties, the sovereignty of the state and that of the individual, from which political sovereignty derives. As Thomas Paine puts it, "the fact therefore must be that the *individuals themselves*, each in his own personal and sovereign right, *entered into a compact with each other* to produce a government: and this is the only mode in which governments have a right to arise, and the only principle on which they have a right to exist."[4]

Third and more generally, the apparent opposition between modern human rights and sovereignty is misleading because although we conventionally identify the latter with the territorial state, sovereignty, as we know from Bodin among others, is a theological concept and the state is only a forgotten metaphor for God as an absolute being.[5] The structural analogy between God and the political sovereign operates in both directions. Augustine characterized God as a sovereign authority: "Authority is, indeed, partly divine and partly human, but the true, solid and sovereign authority is that which is called divine."[6] In Bodin's writings, however, the sovereign prince (political authority proper) is repeatedly described as the earthly image of God. "Since there is nothing greater on earth, after God, than sovereign princes, and since they have been established by Him as His lieutenants for commanding other men, we need to be precise about their status [*qualité*] so that we may respect and

---

[3] Ibid., Chapter 3 [2], 48.
[4] Thomas Paine, *Rights of Man* (Harmondsworth: Penguin, 1985), 70, emphasis in the original.
[5] Political theology refers to the fundamentally theological character of the political sphere, especially that of political sovereignty. See Carl Schmitt, *Political Theology: Four Chapters on the Concept of Sovereignty*, (trans.) George Schwab (Cambridge, Mass.: MIT Press, 1985), 36.
[6] St. Augustine, *Divine Providence and the Problem of Evil*, in *The Happy Life, Answer to Skeptics, Divine Providence and the Problem of Evil, Soliloquies, The Fathers of the Church* series, (trans.) Ludwig Schopp, Denis J. Kavanagh, Robert P. Russell, and Thomas F. Gilligan (Baltimore, Md.: Catholic University of America Press, 2008), 304.

revere their majesty in complete obedience, and do them honor in our thoughts and in our speech. Contempt for one's sovereign prince is contempt toward God, of whom he is the earthly image."[7]

Consequently, the concept of sovereignty can be extended to characterize humanity and its powers, as it undoubtedly is in the modern discourse of the rights of man, where it is precisely the sovereign character of our ontological constitution as beings with reason and dignity that makes humanity the bearer of rights that can be asserted beyond the territorial borders of states. As Jacques Derrida rightly observes, the very form of a right implies the politico-theological concept of sovereignty, which it extends beyond the territorial state, sharing and dividing sovereignty in the process. "The Declaration of Human Rights is not ... opposed to, and does not limit, the sovereignty of the nation-state in the way a principle of nonsovereignty would oppose a principle of sovereignty ... [I]t is one sovereignty set against another. Human rights pose and presuppose the human being (who is equal, free, self-determined) as sovereign. The Declaration of Human Rights declares another sovereignty; it thus reveals the autoimmunity of sovereignty in general."[8] In other words, human rights are the sovereign self-determination of reason, expressed in, embodied by, and exercised by humanity as a collective subject. They supplement state sovereignty with another, more universal, higher sovereignty. This other sovereignty assumes the juridical figure of right with its connotations of lawfulness and the power to confer legitimacy to the state.

It follows from this deeper connection between sovereignty and human rights that human rights derive from and refer to the positive powers and capacities of humanity. Juridical instruments for the protection of specific human rights are the means for furthering these powers. They provide the institutional setting for enhancing and maximizing these capacities. Understanding human rights as derived from powers may help resolve the conundrum posed by economic, social, and cultural

---

[7] Jean Bodin, *On Sovereignty*, (ed. and trans.) Julian H. Franklin (Cambridge University Press, 1992), Book 1, Chapter 10, 46. See also, Book 1, Chapter 10, 50: "For the notion of a sovereign (that is to say, of someone who is above all subjects) cannot apply to someone who has made a subject his companion. Just as God, the great sovereign, cannot make a God equal to Himself because He is infinite and by logical necessity (par demonstration necessaire) two infinites cannot exist, so we can say that the prince, whom we have taken as the image of God, cannot make a subject equal to himself without annihilation of his power," and Book 1, Chapter 8, 45: "For if justice is the end of law, law the work of the prince, and the prince the image of God; then by this reasoning, the law of the prince must be modeled on the law of God."

[8] Jacques Derrida, *Rogues: Two Essays on Reason*, (trans.) Pascale-Anne Brault and Michael Naas (Palo Alto: Stanford University Press, 2005), 88.

rights, namely, their apparent contradiction with an individual's freedom *vis-à-vis* the sovereign state. Second-generation rights are commonly distinguished from the first-generation rights of civil and political liberties because of their positive character. Because the latter protects individuals from state incursion on their freedom and autonomy, they have a negative character. In contradistinction, economic, social and cultural rights (ESCR) prescribe positive duties to a state that are owed to individuals to see that basic human needs are fulfilled. However, if we regard human rights as not being in contradiction with sovereignty but instead as instances of its expression and extension, then we can say that where sovereign humanity is not (yet) institutionally embodied in a world state, different institutional forms of sovereignty and the rights they enable are "nested" in one another, so to speak. Instead of assuming that human rights require the transcendence of the state, one would acknowledge the necessity and efficacy of the state form in protecting human rights.

This schema of interrelated levels of sovereignty and rights is one way of explaining the compatibility of different regimes of human rights such as the right to self-determination, social and economic rights, civil and political liberties, and the right to development. Such compatibility is implied in the holistic understanding of rights as indivisible and interdependent, for example, as articulated in Art. 6(2) of the Declaration of the Right to Development: "All human rights and fundamental freedoms are indivisible and interdependent; equal attention and urgent consideration should be given to the implementation, promotion and protection of civil, political, economic, social and cultural rights." We can then understand the positive character of ESCR in terms of the structural alignment of human rights and sovereignty. First, the progressive character of their full realization indicates that these rights, like all human rights, need to be created through the rational work of collective sovereign human endeavor. Second, ESCR partake of sovereignty in the narrower political institutional sense. They are externally linked to state sovereignty at the level of their implementation.

Of course, this external connection between human rights and state sovereignty can also compromise their alleged higher lawfulness because they risk being infected by particularistic state imperatives. This is another instance of the autoimmunity of sovereignty. But the main point here is that the association with state sovereignty is the concrete unfolding of the internal link between human rights and sovereignty. This internal link also marks civil and political liberties if they are concrete and actual instead of a mere moral "ought," *das Sollen*, as Hegel would have said. As Philip Alston, former chair of the UN Committee on Economic, Social and Cultural Rights, observes: "the reality is that the full realization of civil and political rights is heavily dependent both on the availability of resources and the development of the necessary societal structures. The suggestion that realization of civil and political rights requires only abstention on the part of the state and can be achieved without significant expenditure is patently at odds with reality."[9] The full realization of human rights must then be understood as a collective political project of making human community, whereby concrete institutional ties of right that bind humanity are created that facilitate humanity's self-recognition, namely, the mutual recognition among all its members of their human status, that they all belong to and are part of sovereign humanity.

The connection between second-generation rights and sovereignty that I have suggested may seem contradictory given their socialist provenance.[10] As is well known, Marx articulated a scathing critique of the universal form of human rights as an abstraction that cannot lead to concrete equality because it is an ideological reflection of the bourgeois juridical form of the private, egoistic right to property. In fact, however, Marx retained the outline of the tenacious idea of sovereignty despite his critique of the juridical form of rights and his broader critique of the state as the superstructural instrument of bourgeois society. His critique of the structural deficiency of liberal conceptions of human rights is underwritten by the idea of sovereignty precisely because it is grounded in an account of fundamental needs and their role in the actualization of humanity. Socialized humanity, the cosmopolitan society of associated producers who will govern the world created after the revolution by rationally regulating the metabolism with nature so that universal human needs are fulfilled, is nothing other than a deterritorialized sovereign, the world sovereign who governs world political economy. Marx's theory of human needs can be developed into a socialist reformulation of rights beyond the system of private property and commodity exchange and is arguably an important theoretical basis for ESCR. We can say that socialist states subsequently gave fuller determination to socialized sovereign humanity through the juridical form of second-generation rights. Their enshrinement in socialist constitutions

---

[9] Philip Alston and Gerard Quinn, "The Nature and Scope of States Parties' Obligations under the International Covenant on Economic, Social and Cultural Rights," *Human Rights Quarterly*, 9(2) (1987), 156–229, at 172.

[10] Second-generation rights are generally held to derive from socialist ideals of the late nineteenth and early twentieth centuries and the rise of the European labor movement. Because they express the goals of socialist society, they were championed by Soviet states and enshrined in socialist constitutions.

distinguished them as concrete rights from the merely abstract civil and political rights of the bourgeois individual.

Biopolitical rights: the sovereignty of juridical form in question

I have suggested that both the bourgeois liberal conception of human rights and the Marxist reformulation of human rights presuppose sovereignty. Indeed, we can say that the juridical form of right as epitomized by the modern conception of human rights is the contemporary shape of sovereignty. Understood in this way, different human rights regimes can be critically assessed in terms of the particularity or universality of the rights in question. What makes ESCR fundamentally problematic is that as rights that are based on the fulfillment of needs, they undermine the figure of sovereignty and its juridical form insofar as needs arise from a dimension of existence – that of life – that cannot be saturated by human self-determination in its attempt to achieve the universal satisfaction of needs. Simply put, as a living species, humanity cannot be completely self-determining because there cannot be any ultimate human sovereignty over life.

In making the above argument, I am departing from a good deal of excellent jurisprudential thought on how second- and third-generation rights as new human rights become acknowledged in international law through the recognition and adequate justification of needs and the creation of new instruments that protect these newly visible rights. In essence, these rights have a structure in which a need is spliced onto or fused with a juridical mode of legitimation, i.e. justification. Philip Alston succinctly outlines the process by which a need gradually evolves into a specific human right in international law:

> The process by which a specific right becomes a part of international law is a lengthy one involving, inter alia, the perception and articulation of a need, the mobilization of support in favour of satisfaction of the need, and widespread acceptance of both the validity of the need and the responsibility of another party for its satisfaction ... It is sufficient to note that the lengthy period of gestation thus required provides ample protection against the prospect of a need becoming a right without adequate justification.[11]

The process of acknowledgment/creation of new human rights indicates that a right is a recognized human need that is supported by adequate

---

[11] Philip Alston, "Human Rights and Basic Needs: A Critical Assessment," *Revue des Droits de l'homme*, XII (1–2) (1979), 19–67, at 38.

justification. It is only through the process of justification that a recognized need becomes endowed with the universality requisite to a human right. Moreover, a right must be of general import to prevent an uncontrollable increase in new rights concerned with minute specificities of human needs. "Claims for new rights," Alston adds, "should be formulated so as to cover clear and sufficiently broad subject areas. The implications of such broadly-stated rights can then be more fully spelt out through the process of international standard-setting on specific matters. The alternative is to risk an undue proliferation of human rights with attendant confusion and the dilution of the significance of rights already recognized."[12]

The emergence of second- and third-generation human rights coincided with a new focus on basic needs in the discourse of economic development.[13] The points of convergence and compatibility between these two discourses bring out clearly the ideas of needs and life at the heart of human rights discourse. As with the basic needs approach, the needs that are the basis of claims to new rights are not merely material needs but can also be psychological or spiritual. What is important for present purposes is that regardless of whether such needs are material or non-material, they are fundamental and constitutive features of living human beings. The fact that they are made to undergo a process of justification so that they can be given the rational form of universal human rights that need to be protected clearly indicates that the conception of life that tacitly underwrites human rights discourse is governed by the principle of sovereignty, more specifically, the leitmotif of the sovereign human being who can satisfy fundamental human needs through collective rational self-determination. Indeed, the two key concepts that the basic needs approach to economic development and the discourse of second- and third-generation rights share – self-determination and participation – are precisely the two fundamental characteristics of sovereign humanity.

Self-determination is the more primary of these two characteristics, so much so that it takes the form of a specific collective right (the right of

[12] Ibid., 39.

[13] On the basic needs approach, see the writings of Johan Galtung, such as Johan Galtung, "The Basic Needs Approach" [.pdf of unpublished manuscript], and Johan Galtung and Anders Wirak, "Human Needs, Human Rights and Theories of Development," in *Indicators of Social and Economic Change and Their Applications, Reports and Papers in the Social Sciences*, No. 37, UNESCO (1977), 7–34. On the link between human needs and human rights, see *Expert Meeting on Human Rights, Human Needs and the Establishment of a New International Economic Order* (Paris, 19–23 June 1978), UNESCO, SS-78/CONF.630/COL.2.

peoples to self-determination) in addition to being the ontological basis of all other human rights. Thus, the right of peoples to self-determination is regarded as one of the fundamental conditions of the enjoyment of ESCR and civil and political liberties on the grounds that this right needs to be continuously maintained after formal political independence because it has an important impact on economic, social and cultural life:

The implementation of the right of peoples to self-determination involves not only the completion of the process of achieving independence or other appropriate legal status by the peoples under colonial and alien domination, but also the recognition of their right to maintain, assure and perfect their full legal, political, economic, social and cultural sovereignty. The right of peoples to self-determination has lasting force, does not lapse upon first having been exercised to secure political self-determination and extends to all fields, including of course economic, social and cultural affairs.[14]

Moreover, in discussions prior to the International Covenants on Human Rights, the explicit mention of the right to self-determination in the United Nations Charter and its implied presence in the Universal Declaration of Human Rights, especially in the right of everyone to a nationality, was foregrounded in order to argue that it was the necessary corollary of individual freedom. It "was the source of or an essential prerequisite for other human rights, since there could be no genuine exercise of individual rights without the realization of the right to self-determination."[15] Hence, it was suggested that "the right to self-determination was the right of a group of individuals in association; it was certainly the prerogative of a community, but the community itself consisted of individuals and any encroachment on its collective right would be tantamount to a breach of their fundamental freedoms."[16] In this endless oscillation between the self-determination of sovereign humanity as the basis of all human rights and the collective right of peoples to self-determination, what we see is the unfolding of the latter as the concrete actualization of the former *qua* potentiality. This teleological unfolding is expressed in the form of a reciprocal relation that amounts to a marvelous tautological equation of the right of peoples to self-determination with the human capacity for self-determination or freedom as such: "It was said that the right of all men to freedom in all its forms, particularly the right to combine or associate

---

[14] Hector Gros Espiell, *The Right to Self-Determination: Implementation of United Nations Resolutions* (New York: United Nations, 1980), para. 47, 8, E/CH.4/Sub.2/405/Rev.1.

[15] Aureliu Cristescu, *The Right to Self-Determination: Historical and Current Development on the Basis of United Nations Instruments* (New York: United Nations, 1981), para. 30, 4, E/CN.4/Sub.2/404/Rev. 1.

[16] Ibid., para. 31, 4.

in collective entities and nations, demonstrated the close link between individual freedom and effective national sovereignty."[17]

The tautology between sovereign humanity and national sovereignty, the human capacity for freedom and the right to self-determination of a people prepares the way for the inscription of ESCR within global development discourse. Consequently, although ESCR are individual rights, national economic self-determination is the concrete context for their realization. Because the state is the chief political instrumentality of economic self-determination, state economic policy has a primary role in the protection of ESCR. A state's ability "to achieve progressively the full realization" of ESCR depends on the maximum "available resources" at its disposal.[18] In global development discourse, economic self-determination and ESCR are the mutual cause and effect of each other. The enhancement of human capacities (the realization of ESCR) is an important condition of development (achieving economic self-determination) at the same time that it is an important end of development. The problem, however, with this mutual embrace between ESCR and economic self-determination is that the latter always takes place within an uneven field of resources and, therefore, is competitive in its structure. The achievement of ESCR then becomes part of the drive to increase a country's economic competitiveness and these rights shade into and become indistinguishable from the project of cultivating human capital or "human capacity-building." The following example from a UN Economic and Social Council for Asia and the Pacific document on women and globalization illustrates clearly how human capacity-building is a means of improving the comparative advantage of a country's economy by moving to higher value-added manufacturing, the tertiary sector and knowledge-based enterprises:

The rapid changes in job-market requirements and needed skills increases the emphasis on training and life-long learning to raise workers' employability and improve access to employment. Countries need to continually invest in skills and knowledge-development and the training of their workforce in light of these changes, including advances in technology and work organization. The risks are higher for the vulnerable groups and reduce their opportunities and incentives for

---

[17] Ibid., para. 40, 7.

[18] International Covenant on Economic, Social and Cultural Rights, Art. 2(1): "Each State Party to the present Covenant undertakes to take steps, individually and through international assistance and co-operation, especially economic and technical, to the maximum of its available resources, with a view to achieving progressively the full realization of the rights recognized in the present Covenant by all appropriate means, including particularly the adoption of legislative measures" (GA res. 2200A (XXI), 21 UN GAOR Supp. (No. 16) at 49, UN Doc. A/6316 (1966), 993 UNTS 3).

training. To progress to higher levels of value-added employment (and thus towards higher incomes at the individual and aggregate levels), the population and workforce of the country must steadily improve their knowledge and skills for contributing effectively to the changing job market requirements. Human resources development or human capital formation are essential for sustaining a productive work force. Importantly, as policy attends to the development of both human and social capital, there are two elements that deserve special attention: making new information technologies available to wider segments of the population and building productive assets, especially for the poor men and women at the household level.[19]

We could, of course, denounce these goals of human capacity-building as instances of developmentalism on the grounds that global development policy is a Euro-American-centric ideology that has been willingly accepted by the developmental states of high-growth East Asia and imposed upon states in the postcolonial South. In that case, we would view sovereign humanity as being constrained and even betrayed by state sovereignty in such a way that human rights are sacrificed in the name of national economic development. But such a dismissal would be too easy. The double bind lies in the fact that while we cannot not want workers in the economic South to build their capacities because it will facilitate the full realization of their ECSR in the long run, such policies of human development can also have disastrous consequences for the very subjects whose rights are to be realized. I take as an example the rights of migrant workers from the postcolonial South. In principle, postcolonial countries wish to cultivate their populations and enhance their aptitudes. But in order to attract transnational capital flows as a means of increasing a country's resources, they also have to suspend care for some parts of their population, sometimes to the point of sacrificing their welfare in the name of development. There is greater governmental control where states consent to harsh labor conditions for local factory workers and actively promote the exportation of migrant workers who are vulnerable to abuse in host countries.

At the same time, however, because this very structure seeks to augment their capacities and to realize their rights, what we have here is not merely a repressive and entirely exploitative system but a curious machine of simultaneous enablement and limitation, where freedom and constraint, production and regulation are the very same thing. As the product-effects of a machine that simultaneously augments human capital and recognizes human rights within the framework of global capitalist development, such human rights, I suggest, can no longer be

---

[19] *Women and Globalization*, December 2003, III.22–23, www.unescap.org/esid/GAD/Publication/women-globalization.pdf.

understood solely and primarily in terms of the juridical right of sovereign humanity, the right of a humanity that is sovereign in its living being, whether this sovereignty is determined in terms of nature or reason. This is because these human rights reveal a humanity that is heteronomous in two ways. First, it is produced in its living nature and all its capacities through governmental regulation, and second, these rational calculations are themselves a response to the incalculability of life as a resource for power. In short, we can only arrive at an adequate understanding of these rights through a biopolitical analysis.

In the first volume of *The History of Sexuality*, Foucault commented on the irony that the struggle against power in the nineteenth century was based on an affirmation of the rights of man as a concrete living being when these rights such as "the 'right' to life, to one's body, to health, to happiness, to the satisfaction of needs" were merely the juridical codification of the capacities of life produced by bio-power, a type of power that exceeded and was quite different from that of sovereignty and its juridical representation as the law and right:

[A]gainst this power that was still new in the nineteenth century, the forces that resisted relied for support on the very thing it invested, that is, on life and man as a living being ... [W]hat was demanded and what served as an objective was life, understood as the basic needs, man's concrete essence, the realization of his potential, a plenitude of the possible ... [W]hat we have seen has been a very real process of struggle; life as a political object was in a sense taken at face value and turned back against the system that was bent on controlling it. It was life more than the law that became the issue of political struggles, even if the latter were formulated through affirmations concerning rights. The "right" to life, to one's body, to health, to happiness, to the satisfaction of needs, and beyond all the oppressions or "alienations," the "right" to rediscover what one is and all that one can be, this "right" – which the classical juridical system was utterly incapable of comprehending – was the political response to all these new procedures of power which did not derive, either, from the traditional right of sovereignty.[20]

Three points are important here. First, these "rights," many of which we now understand as ESCR, are only rights in a qualified sense. They distort the very form of right as conventionally understood because their true basis is in the biopolitical technologies that regulate and produce humanity and every facet of its life. Second, their biopolitical grounding also means that they are not ideological fictions, mystificatory instruments that work at the level of consciousness. They are concrete and real because they stem from the capacities and needs of bodies and

---

[20] Michel Foucault, *The History of Sexuality, Volume 1: An Introduction*, (trans.) Robert Hurley (New York: Vintage, 1980), 144–145.

populations as these have been fabricated by biopolitical technologies. Third, these rights are the codification or thematic reflection of capacities and needs. Hence, their activation is necessarily circumscribed by the biopolitical technologies that generate these capacities and needs as these are part of a given field of power or force-relations.

I propose to call such rights "biopolitical rights." Although Foucault did not use the phrase or directly address the phenomenon of bio-political rights in the two lecture series given at the Collège de France in 1977–1978 and 1978–1979, he explored how bio-power led to a different form of freedom and, by implication, a different type of right that is no longer that of a juridical subject. In the first place, Foucault argued that unlike sovereign power, the target of bio-power is not a subject whose relation to power is one of obedience or revolt. It is instead the population, whose *natural* character makes it dependent on a series of variables such that it "cannot be transparent to the sovereign's action." Hence, instead of assuming a natural continuity between the sovereign human individual and state sovereignty that becomes perverted by devel-opmentalist imperatives, what is emphasized here is how the natural character of the population, as a living datum that is subject to a set of variables, is not amenable to sovereign imperatives and, indeed, even undermines the sovereign modality of power. The population "escapes the sovereign's voluntarist and direct action in the form of the law. If one says to the population 'do this', there is not only no guarantee that it will do it, but also there is quite simply no guarantee that it can do it."[21] What is at issue here is not a matter of rational will but a matter of capacity that depends on natural variables. Although these variables can be regulated, the population's dependency on them – its heteronomy in a strict Kantian sense – cannot be eradicated or transcended through the imposition of laws from outside nature. This nature "is not something on which, above which, or against which the sovereign must impose just laws. There is not nature and then, above nature and against it, the sovereign and the relationship of obedience that is owed to him."[22] Thus, the sovereign must pay heed to and even respect this nature. It "must deploy reflected procedures of government within this nature, with the help of it, and with regard to it."[23] "With the population," Foucault observes, "we have something completely different from the

[21] Michel Foucault, *Security, Territory, Population: Lectures at the Collège de France 1977–78*, (ed.) Michel Senellart, (trans.) Graham Burchell (Basingstoke: PalgraveMacmillan, 2007), 71.
[22] Ibid., 75.   [23] Ibid.

collection of subjects of right differentiated by their status, localization, goods, responsibilities, and offices."[24]

Foucault argues that this new subject or target of power, which is constitutively immersed among other living beings, is no longer human-kind (*le genre humaine*), that subject we conventionally regard as the bearer of rights by virtue of being endowed with reason, but the human species (*l'espèce humaine*), which is one among other living species.[25] And he further adds that "the theme of man, and the 'human sciences' that analyze him as a living being, working individual, and speaking subject, should be understood on the basis of the emergence of population as the correlate of power and the object of knowledge. After all, man, as he is thought and defined by the so-called human sciences of the nineteenth century, and as he is reflected in nineteenth-century human-ism, is nothing other than a figure of population."[26] What is implied here is a radical questioning of human rights that is directed at both terms of the phrase. First, instead of taking the ontological status of human beings for granted, Foucault sketches an alternative account of the generation of humanity and humanism from biopolitical mechanisms. Second, he questions from a historical standpoint the dominance of natural rights, natural law and rationalist conceptions of human rights by arguing that "the juridical notion of the subject of right" is the necessary correlate of the theory of sovereignty whereas the human being only comes into existence when the population becomes the target of government.[27]

At the same time, the population's natural character also leads to a new form of freedom and to a different conception of rights that accompanies the rise of political economy. For the fact that the population as a natural living datum escapes the sovereign will and that the sovereign must respect and work with its nature becomes the basis of the freedom or independence of the governed *vis-à-vis* governmental power. This freedom of the governed is what I will call "biopolitical rights." The emergence of political economy, Foucault argues, inaugurates the market as a field in which the sovereign must let nature run its own course according to its own laws because the market is viewed as obeying spontaneous mechanisms, the modification of which can only lead to their perversion and distortion.[28] Consequently, the governmental form of power gradually changes to favor less government as the best form of government. This is liberal governmentality, according to which the freedom or independence of the governed, typified by *homo*

---

[24] Ibid.   [25] Ibid.   [26] Ibid., 79.   [27] Ibid.

[28] Michel Foucault, *The Birth of Biopolitics: Lectures at the Collège de France, 1978–79*, (trans.) Graham Burchell (Hampshire and New York: PalgraveMacmillan, 2008), 15–16.

œconomicus, is an indispensable component of effective government because it is the optimal way of increasing the forces of the state.

Foucault distinguishes the freedom of the governed from the revolutionary or natural law conceptualization of freedom.[29] The latter is a juridical problematic, where law is an expression of the rational will. It corresponds to the postulate of sovereign humanity I outlined above. It begins from the natural and original rights of man and defines how some of these rights were willingly ceded and exchanged in the formation of political regimes and, therefore, how the sphere of sovereignty and its governmental functions are in turn limited by law. In Foucault's words, "this approach consists in starting from the rights of man in order to arrive at the limitation of governmentality by way of the constitution of the sovereign ... It is a way of posing right from the start the problem of legitimacy and the inalienability of rights through a sort of ideal or real renewal of society, the state, the sovereign, and government."[30]

In contradistinction, the freedom of the governed is concerned with *de facto* limits to governmentality that arise from within its practices. These limits (and the law that codifies them) are the result of a separation of the sphere where public authorities can intervene from that of an individual's independence. This separation occurs and is renegotiated according to the most desirable, because useful and effective way of governing in a historically determined situation, that is, in terms of where governmental intervention would be counterproductive or even pointless because governmental power is simply incompetent in a given domain.[31] Hence, freedom is not conceived as an original possession of every individual, "as the exercise of some basic rights," but as the independence of the governed that arises because it is in the interests of good government to let the governed spontaneously pursue its own interests.[32] Accordingly, the target of government is no longer a "thick" subject with an interiority from which obedience is to be solicited but is instead a bare subject of interest, which British empiricist philosophy defines as "an irreducible, non-transferrable atomistic individual choice that is unconditionally referred back to the subject himself."[33] The subject of interests is governed by "an immediately and absolutely subjective will" instead of deep rational reflection.[34]

On the one hand, an individual's interests are dependent on outside variables and accidents that cannot be foreseen and controlled. But, on the other hand, this chaos can freely lead to a convergence of the interests of all without any conscious design. Accordingly, governmental

---

[29] Ibid., 41–42.   [30] Ibid., 39–40.   [31] Ibid., 40.   [32] Ibid., 42.   [33] Ibid., 272.
[34] Ibid., 273.

power must also shape and regulate the natural environment of its target – subjects of interest – so that it can be optimized to run its own course. Governmental power is thus entrusted with the task of creating or manufacturing the conditions for the freedom of the governed. This means that the target of power is simultaneously that which must be left to run its own course and that which is eminently governable so that it can undergo optimal spontaneous development according to its potentialities with minimal disturbance by contingent and accidental environmental factors. This is why production and regulation, freedom and constriction become one and the same.

It is, of course, not a matter of the displacement of the juridical conception of freedom and rights by biopolitical rights but a matter of analyzing what kinds of rights are claimed, asserted or being realized in a particular situation. As Foucault puts it, "with regard to the problem of what are currently called human rights, we would only need look at where, in what countries, how, and in what form these rights are claimed to see that at times the question is actually the juridical question of rights, and at others, it is a question of this assertion or claim of the independence of the governed vis-à-vis governmentality."[35] My point is that to speak of human rights in the many meanings the phrase has today because of the different regimes of human rights is to yoke together two different forms of power, that of governmentality and sovereignty. This disjunctive conjunction necessarily deforms the concept of right and radically transforms it because governmentality is concerned with the biological existence of human beings, which can no longer be adequately accounted for through the figure of rightful sovereignty. Life, unless it is understood in teleological terms, is something over which no sovereignty can be exercised for two related reasons. First, as natural phenomena, the needs of living beings are radically subject to contingency, mutability, and chance despite our attempts to regulate and minimize their exposure to accidentality through technologies and rational calculation. Second, the control we can exercise over needs is also circumscribed by their inherently differential and relational nature as the expression of living forces. Because forces are always a matter of difference rather than equality, always a matter of more or less, that is to say, of magnitude in relation to other forces, it is impossible to achieve the universal satisfaction of the needs of all members of humanity at one and the same time. This is why the biopolitical augmentation of human capacities is marked by a dynamic of simultaneous freedom and constriction.

[35] Ibid., 42.

This dynamic is the common basis of the welfare state and the idea of human capital in the neo-liberal economics of the Chicago School. Just as the welfare state involves strong government, the idea of human capital implies the governability of the subject of interests: "the person who accepts reality or who responds systematically to modifications in the variables of the environment, appears precisely as someone manageable, someone who responds systematically to systematic modifications artificially introduced into the environment . . . From being the intangible partner of *laissez-faire homo œconomicus* now becomes the correlate of a governmentality which will act on the environment and systematically modify its variables."[36]

What is important for present purposes is that this dynamic is also the basis of the constitutive link between state policies to achieve economic self-determination and the realization of ESCR. These are the two arms of the governmental production of concrete humanity. The realization of ESCR became inseparable from policies of human development that gradually gained ascendancy in the late 1970s. Such policies emphasize the importance of improving the well-being of populations to any program for global economic growth. What is especially significant about the discourse of human development is that it seeks to resolve the apparent tension between economic growth and the ideals of fairness, justice, and equity by suggesting that the cultivation of human capacities facilitates and is co-extensive with sustainable economic development. In the words of the International Development Strategy for the Third United Nations Development Decade, "the development process must promote human dignity. The ultimate aim of development is the constant improvement of the well-being of the entire population on the basis of its full participation in the process of development and a fair distribution of the benefits therefrom."[37]

I have argued elsewhere that the governmental production of humanity can have deplorable consequences, especially when the discourse of human rights intersects with the economic development policies of states in the global South.[38] Human development is the humanization of economic development. But this means that the humanity that is produced can also be deployed by states in their strategies for increasing

[36] Ibid., 270.
[37] International Development Strategy for the Third United Nations Development Decade, General Assembly, Thirty-Fifth Session, UN Doc. A/RES/35/56 (December 5, 1980), para. 8.
[38] Pheng Cheah, "The Physico-Material Bases of Cosmopolitanism," in Sigal R. Ben-Porath and Rogers Smith (eds.), *Varieties of Sovereignty and Citizenship* (Philadelphia, Pa.: University of Pennsylvania Press, 2013), 189–210.

their resources, thereby compromising and marring the human face of development. This contamination is structural to the humanity produced by global governmentality. The problem of implementing second- and third-generation human rights would need to be reconsidered from the ground up, not simply as the distortion and compromise of a set of normative ideals that express the inalienable rights and capacities of sovereign humanity but instead in terms of the very structure of biopolitical rights, in terms of the inscription of these rights in a biopolitical field that is always shifting.

13   History, normativity, and rights

Paul Patton

Appeals to right have long been an especially potent form of social and political criticism. There is something compelling about defending certain ways of acting or ways of being treated as a matter of right. To say that someone has a right to something is to say that they have a particular kind of entitlement such that others, or governments, are under an obligation to provide it or at least not to prevent their obtaining it. For this reason, the appeal to rights has played an important role in the recent history of minority struggles. Activities and relationships associated with particular forms of life, such as non-European Indigenous ways of life or non-heterosexual relationships, are often defended as rights. This form of argument can be described as a strategy of universalization in the sense that it involves presenting the activities and interests of a particular group as consistent with the activities and interests of the polity as a whole. "Rights arguments do this: they restate the interests of the group as characteristics of all people."[1]

From a normative and political point of view, the appeal to rights has fallen out of favor for many on the left in recent years. A range of theoretical arguments and pragmatic political considerations has been taken to provide good reasons to abandon "rights-talk" and appeals to rights altogether. I focus on the theoretical arguments below, particularly those drawn from the work of Foucault and Deleuze. I will argue that, in different ways, they provide grounds for an alternative response to the criticism of rights that does not abandon rights altogether, but rather the received view of rights as universal and a-historical. A common thread running through the criticism of rights is acceptance of the universality of rights. Wendy Brown summarizes this received view of the notion of rights in suggesting that:

---

[1] D. Kennedy, "The Critique of Rights in Critical Legal Studies," in W. Brown and J. Halley, (eds.), *Left Legalism/Left Critique* (Durham, NC and London: Duke University Press, 2002), 188.

rights necessarily operate in and as an ahistorical, acultural, acontextual idiom: they claim distance from specific political contexts and historical vicissitudes, and they participate in a discourse of enduring universality rather than provisionality or partiality. Thus, while the measure of their political efficacy requires a high degree of historical and social specificity, rights operate as a political discourse of the general, the generic and universal.[2]

Foucault and Deleuze offer an alternative approach since, while both are critical of certain aspects of rights discourse, they nonetheless make use of concepts of right. How is it possible to historicize liberal civil and political rights, as Foucault does, yet still appeal to particular rights? How is it possible to denounce human rights as new forms of transcendence, as Deleuze does, yet still endorse the creation of new rights? The answer to this question can only be a different concept of rights. I will argue that in different ways both Foucault and Deleuze conceive of rights as embedded in relations of power, in discursive representations of the nature and functions of power, and in structures of belief and affect that underpin the considered opinions of a people. At the same time, their ways of appealing to rights suggest that, rather than abandon the concept or the discourse of rights altogether, we should abandon the idea that rights are a-historical, a-cultural or a-contextual. Rights have long been an important vector of the "radical potential of normativity."[3] The challenge is to develop an historical conception of rights that retains the normative force of rights claims and their role in the critique of existing institutions, public policies and forms of social life.

Existence of rights

Duncan Kennedy suggests that rights claims serve the universalizing strategy of defending particular ways of acting or being treated because they function as "mediators" between the subjective domain of value judgments and the objective domain of factual judgments:

The point of an appeal to a right, the reason for making it, is that it can't be reduced to a mere "value judgment" that one outcome is better than another. Yet it is possible to make rights arguments about matters that fall outside the domain commonly understood as factual, that is, about political or policy questions of how the government ought to act.[4]

---

[2] W. Brown, *States of Injury: Power and Freedom in Late Modernity* (Princeton University Press, 1995), 97.
[3] C. Douzinas, "*Adikia*: On Communism and Rights," in C. Douzinas and S. Žižek, (eds.), *The Idea of Communism* (London and New York: Verso, 2010), 81–100 at 86.
[4] Kennedy, "The Critique of Rights," 184.

In other words, claiming that some way of acting or being treated is a right amounts to claiming that it is more like an empirical fact than a merely subjective value judgment or preference. Hence the common recourse to the language of discovery in speaking about rights: people often refer to the *acknowledgment* that a particular group possesses certain rights or the *recognition* of those rights by the law, as though the rights in question exist in some sense independently of their institutionalization in systems of law.

Many philosophers seek to explain the objective and "factoid" character of rights as well as their normative force by arguing that they are ultimately moral rights. Different theorists cash out the moral basis of rights in different ways, but many suggest that these inhere in individuals by virtue of some universal "rights-bearing" feature of human nature, such as sentience, rationality, interests or the capacity to form and pursue projects. For example, Alan Gewirth offers a transcendental argument along Kantian lines to the conclusion that all humans have a right to freedom and well-being since these are necessary presuppositions of the human capacity to form and pursue projects.[5] Whatever moral theory is taken to provide a satisfactory account of the content of rights, the result in all cases is that rights are supposed to be universal "in the sense that they derive from needs or values or preferences that every person shares or ought to share."[6] They are a-historical phenomena in the sense that, if a particular right exists for a given class of rights bearers then it has always existed.[7]

The universal and a-historical character of rights provides a clear basis for the critical function of appeals to rights. It is because rights exist independently of their recognition in law and public policy that we can criticise laws and other institutions for not recognizing rights that should be recognized, or for recognizing rights that should not be recognized. In effect, the relationship between the independent existence of rights and their critical function runs in both directions. One the one hand, the criticism of laws and constitutions for their denial of particular rights to minority groups is taken as evidence that there are rights that exist in

---

[5] A. Gewirth, "The Epistemology of Human Rights," in E. Paul, F. Miller, and J.H. Paul, (eds.), *Human Rights* (Oxford: Blackwell, 1984).

[6] Kennedy, "The Critique of Rights," 185.

[7] Gewirth provides an extreme statement of the a-historical view in speaking about human rights in the following terms: "The existence of human rights depends on the existence of certain moral justificatory reasons; but these reasons may exist even if they are not explicitly ascertained. Because of this, it is correct to say that all persons had human rights even in ancient Greece, whose leading philosophers did not develop the relevant reasons. Thus, the existence of moral reasons is in important respects something that is discovered rather than invented," Gewirth, "The Epistemology of Human Rights," 4.

some sense outside of or apart from their legal enactment. On the other hand, the existence of such rights is taken to provide a basis for criticism of existing laws and constitutions. In this manner, it could be asserted in 1987 "that black South Africans have the moral right to full representation even though this right has not been accorded legal recognition, and in saying this we mean to point to the right as a moral reason for changing the legal system so as to accord it recognition."[8]

As a descriptive claim, the view of rights as existing independently of social attitudes and practices leads to implausible results. According to this view, it makes no sense to say that new rights have come into existence or that old ones have disappeared. Changes may occur in the beliefs of people about rights and rights bearers but the possibility of change in what rights there are is ruled out. Yet this is precisely what has occurred in relation to the now widely accepted rights of Indigenous peoples to their traditional lands and ways of life in Australia, Canada, and other common law countries established by colonization. Given what we know about the theories of civilization, property entitlement, and racial hierarchy that were common in Europe between the sixteenth and nineteenth centuries, and given what we know now about the levels of ignorance with regard to Indigenous cultures that prevailed throughout this period, it is implausible to suggest that these rights always existed and that people were simply ignorant or unaware of their existence. Private opinion and public political reason alike were supported by pseudo-scientific theories about the supposed cultural inferiority of Indigenous peoples, along with ill-informed beliefs about the absence of political organization or property in land that characterized their societies. Such beliefs were relied upon to deny any entitlement on the part of Indigenous peoples to their lands or ways of life. No doubt there were dissenting views within the culture of the colonizing peoples, but these were in a minority. Such prejudicial beliefs have now largely, although not entirely, disappeared from public political culture. The removal of all forms of overt legal discrimination has made the commitment to equality stronger and more extensive. In this sense, there has been real epistemic, moral and legal change. From an historical point of view, it is more plausible to conceive of claiming rights as a complex social practice that, like all such practices, changes over time. What rights there are in a given community will change over time as its laws and public policies change, often as a consequence of changes in the beliefs, affects and other social practices of the communities.[9]

---

[8] L. W. Sumner, *The Moral Foundation of Rights* (Oxford: Clarendon Press, 1987), 13.
[9] D. Ivison, *Rights* (Stocksfield: Acumen, 2008).

Such a conception of rights as subject to historical change is consistent with the view of those "external" theorists who deny the existence of rights independently of the social recognition and protection of certain ways of acting or being treated by others.[10] On this view, whether or not individuals or groups possess rights depends on facts about how they are able to act and how they are treated within a given social milieu.[11] Different formulations are offered with regard to precisely what is required to speak of the existence of rights from such institutional or externalist perspectives. Rex Martin characterizes rights as "established ways of acting *or* established ways of being acted toward, ways of being treated."[12] Derrick Darby builds on this characterization of rights by specifying the meaning of "established" in terms of "institutional respect," where this implies some institutional mechanism for recognizing a given behavior as a matter of right and enforcing or protecting that right.[13] Different expressions of rights are consistent with this general conception of rights in terms of the established behaviors open to individuals and groups. Legal mechanisms for recognizing and maintaining or enforcing particular practices might serve as paradigm cases of institutional respect for certain ways of acting or being treated, but this does not exclude the possibility that rights might exist by virtue of less formal institutional practices. In these terms, all societies including communist societies will have rights.[14] On a global scale, human rights might be considered a work in progress as the appropriate cosmopolitan forms of

[10] See Sumner, *The Moral Foundation of Rights*; R. Martin, *A System of Rights* (Oxford: Clarendon, 1993); D. Darby, "Two Conceptions of Rights Possession," *Social Theory and Practice*, 27 (2001), 387–417; "Unnatural Rights," *Canadian Journal of Philosophy*, 33 (2003), 49–82; and *Rights, Race and Recognition* (Cambridge University Press, 2009). Susan James also draws attention to the complex social conditions required for the existence of rights as effectively enforceable claims, S. James, "Rights as Enforceable Claims," *Proceedings of the Aristotelian Society, New Series*, 103 (2003), 133–147.

[11] Darby, "Two Conceptions," 387; *Rights, Race and Recognition*, 74.

[12] Martin, *A System of Rights*, 41.

[13] Darby, "Unnatural Rights," 66; *Rights, Race and Recognition*, 85–87.

[14] Costas Douzinas notes that Marx did not dismiss rights out of hand. He goes on to suggest that communism will realize "the universal promise of rights": "Freedom will stop being negative and defensive and will become a positive power of each in union with others. Equality will no longer mean the abstract comparison of unequal individuals but catholic and full participation in a strong community. Property will cease being the limitation of each to a portion of wealth to the exclusion of all others and will become common. Real freedom and equality look to the concrete person in community, abandon the formal definitions of social distribution, and inscribe on their banners the principle 'from each according to his ability, to each according to his needs'," Douzinas, "*Adikia*: On Communism and Rights," 84–85. Leaving aside the humanist universalism of this Marxist vision of community, it is clear that it will require some institutional mechanisms for recognizing certain ways of acting as matters or right and for limiting infringements of such rights.

institutional respect for certain ways in which individuals or groups should or should not be treated are put in place.

For externalist theorists, rights are positive rights in the sense that they only exist when relevant institutional or other means of enforcement or protection of behaviors are present. However, the existence of established laws or practices that lack credible justification shows that the presence of institutional respect does not in itself constitute a right. A further important condition for an established way of acting or being acted upon to constitute a right is that it must be justified. In effect, both established ways of acting or being acted upon and the presence of acceptable justifications are separately necessary and jointly sufficient for the existence of rights. The consensus among many externalist theorists is that there must be moral justification in order for there to be a right. However, this is a difficulty insofar as the theories are supposed to apply to modern democratic societies that are characterized by a plurality of comprehensive moral views. I will return to this problem at the end of this chapter and suggest that a plausible historical conception of rights requires us to assume some form of public justification for established ways of acting or being treated by others. In this sense, a historical conception that applies to the conditions under which citizens in democratic societies collectively exercise power over one another, and that seeks to preserve the normative force of rights, will be a political rather than a moral conception.

Critique of rights

A variety of concerns have fuelled recent "scepticism and suspicion about the value of rights."[15] For legal and political practitioners, disillusionment with the political polyvalence of rights-talk came with the realization that appeals to rights can be made from all points along the political spectrum and that, when pursued through the courts, they are subject to the open textured character of all legal argumentation. The fact that appeals to rights were often inconclusive meant that legal decisions often came down to "balancing" competing claims to conflicting rights.[16] For legal and political theorists, a range of arguments drawn from Marx and Foucault fueled suspicion of rights. In his critique of Bruno Bauer's *On the Jewish Question*, Marx famously condemned the false universalism of the rights of man and citizen as these had been proclaimed at the end

---

[15] K. Baynes, "Rights as Critique and the Critique of Rights: Karl Marx, Wendy Brown, and the Social Function of Rights," *Political Theory*, 28(4) (2000), 451–468 at 452.
[16] Kennedy, "The Critique of Rights," 194–199.

of the eighteenth century. The civil rights of personal protection and political participation represented valuable but limited forms of emancipation from the constraints of religion and private property. The remaining rights of citizens, to freedom of conscience and action, to property, equality and security, were no more than the rights of the egoistic subjects of modern bourgeois society. They did not correspond to the social relations of a truly emancipated humanity. The formal egalitarianism of such rights amounted to an imaginary equality that masked an inegalitarian and egoistic social order.

Although Foucault abandoned the humanism and historical teleology implicit in Marx's condemnation of bourgeois rights, and sought to distance himself from the concept of ideology, his language in *Discipline and Punish* sometimes resembled that of Marx. For example, he suggested that the rights and duties associated with the juridico-political institutions of modern capitalist society were not simply means to protect the natural rights of individuals but also essential elements within the complex assemblage of discourses, institutions, and practices through which governmental power was exercised: "The general juridical form that guaranteed a system of rights that were egalitarian in principle was supported by these tiny, everyday, physical mechanisms, by all those systems of micro-power that are essentially non-egalitarian and asymmetrical that we call the disciplines ... The real corporeal disciplines constituted the foundation of the formal, juridical liberties."[17] The widespread adoption of disciplinary mechanisms constituted the "dark side" of the process of establishing a "formally egalitarian judicial framework" that masked the political dominance of the bourgeoisie.[18] Similarly, in his 1976 lectures, he argued that the juridico-political theory of sovereignty that had become the discursive framework of government in Europe since the Middle Ages served not only as an instrument but also as concealment for the fact and mechanisms of political domination:

This theory, and the organization of a juridical code centred upon it, made it possible to superimpose on the mechanisms of discipline a system of rights that concealed its mechanisms and erased the element of domination and the techniques of domination involved in discipline, and which, finally, guaranteed that everyone could exercise his or her own sovereign rights thanks to the sovereignty of the State.[19]

---

[17] M. Foucault, *Discipline and Punish*, (trans.) A. Sheridan (London: Allen Lane/Penguin, 1977), 222.
[18] Ibid., 222.
[19] M. Foucault, *"Society Must be Defended": Lectures at the Collège de France, 1975–1976*, (ed.) M. Bertani and A. Fontana, (trans.) D. Macey (New York: Picador, 2003), 37.

Foucault was widely regarded as having contributed to the widespread disillusionment with rights on the left. His historical analyses of kinds of subjectivity, which treated individuals as the effects of particular techniques and strategies of power, undermined the idea that there are distinctive human characteristics in virtue of which individuals possess rights.[20] He drew attention to ways in which the rights of individuals were inextricably bound up with the exercise of power over them, thereby providing theoretical support for the suspicion that appeals to rights associated with particular social identities end up by entrenching and solidifying those identities, often at the expense of "intersectional" minorities within. This raises the question whether the rights attached to particular identities "partly function to imprison us within the subject positions they are secured to affirm or protect?"[21]

Deleuze and Guattari provide a further critical perspective on rights-talk and its function in the contemporary world. In *What is Philosophy?*, they argue that human rights have come to function as axioms within the immanent axiomatic of global capital. As such, the basic civil and political rights co-exist alongside other axioms, such as those designed to ensure the security of property. As a result, when economic conditions demand the tightening of credit or the withdrawal of employment, the rights of the poor to basic social goods are effectively suspended. Deleuze and Guattari are critical of the very concept of *human* rights insofar as these are supposed to be grounded in universal features of human nature such as freedom, rationality, or the capacity to communicate. Such universal rights "say nothing about the immanent modes of existence of people provided with rights."[22] Since they presuppose a universal and abstract subject of rights, irreducible to any singular, existent figures, they are eternal, abstract, and transcendent rights belonging to everyone and no one in particular. Deleuze elaborated further on the emptiness of abstract human rights in his *Abécédaire* interviews with Claire Parnet, with reference to the problems facing an Armenian population that had been subjected to a massacre by Turks and then to a massive earthquake.[23] He objected that, when people make declarations about human rights in such situations

---

[20] B. Golder, "Foucault's Critical (Yet Ambivalent) Affirmation: Three Figures of Rights," *Social & Legal Studies*, 20(3) (2011), 283–312.

[21] Brown, *States of Injury*, 120.

[22] G. Deleuze and F. Guattari, *What is Philosophy?*, (trans.) H. Tomlinson and G. Burchell (New York: Columbia University Press, 1994), 107.

[23] Deleuze is referring to the earthquake that struck on December 7, 1988. For further comment on these passages from *L'Abécédaire*, see D. W. Smith, "Deleuze and the Liberal Tradition: Normativity, Freedom and Judgment," *Economy and Society*, 32(2)

these declarations are never made as a function of the people who are directly concerned, the Armenian society, the Armenian communities, etc. Their problem is not "the rights of man."[24]

Deleuze here contrasts the abstract and empty concept of human rights with the territorial and political rights required in order for this Armenian enclave within the former USSR to survive. In short, human rights grounded in a particular rights-bearing feature of human nature are useless because they are fixed and a-historical, unable to evolve in accordance with the requirements of a particular case.

Deleuze on the creation of rights

At the same time that he was critical of the recourse to human rights as a transcendent ground of moral and political criticism, Deleuze defended a conception of jurisprudence as the creation of rights. In conversation with Antonio Negri, he declared that what interested him was not the law or laws, nor even right or rights, but jurisprudence: "It is jurisprudence, ultimately, that creates right, and we must not go on leaving this to judges."[25] His thesis that jurisprudence creates right (*droit*) can be taken to mean, certainly, that it involves the creation of law but also, more profoundly, that it involves the creation of the right or rights that are expressed by law. He takes as an example the establishment of new rights in relation to modern biology and the biotechnologies this has made possible. In this context, for example, it might be argued that decisions about rights of access to genetic material should involve the users of fertility treatments, or that decisions about access to genetic information should involve those being subjected. or subjecting themselves, to genetic screening techniques. Such matters, Deleuze suggests, ought not be left to ethics committees or to judges but should involve those directly concerned. At this point, he comments, "we move from law into politics."[26] In other words, the new ways of acting or being acted upon made possible by modern biology are matters for jurisprudence, where this ultimately involves the political processes leading to the creation of new rights that are expressed in law. For Deleuze, these processes include the public activity of governments and political parties but also

---

(2003), 312–317 and A. Lefebvre, *The Image of Law: Deleuze, Bergson, Spinoza* (Stanford University Press, 2008), 53–59.

[24] G. Deleuze, *G comme Gauche* from *L'Abécédaire de Gilles Deleuze avec Claire Parnet*, available on video cassette (1996) and DVD (2004) from Vidéo Editions Montparnasse, Paris.

[25] G. Deleuze, *Negotiations 1972–1990*, (trans.) M. Joughin (New York: Columbia University Press, 1995), 169, translation modified.

[26] Deleuze, *Negotiations*, 170.

the background changes in the sensibilities and beliefs of individuals and populations that make changes in law and public policy possible: "everything is political, but every politics is simultaneously a *macropolitics* and a *micropolitics*."[27] While these micropolitical changes occur below the threshold of public political reason and its institutional mechanisms, they are nevertheless indispensable conditions in constitutional democracies for the establishment of new ways of acting, or ways of being treated.[28]

For Deleuze, jurisprudence was always a matter of politics, in the broad sense in which he understood the term, and not merely confined to the legal institution. In conversation with Bellour and Ewald, he described jurisprudence as the field or process through which peoples organized into constitutional states (*états de droit*) enter into becomings. In the case of peoples governed by means of such states "it is not established and codified rights that count, but everything that currently creates problems for the law and that threatens to call what is established into question."[29] Whether we consider the Civil or the Penal code, he suggests, there is no shortage of such problems confronting the law. In this context, where he is referring to rights codified in law, he declares that:

It is not codes or declarations that create law (*droit*) but jurisprudence. Jurisprudence is the philosophy of law and proceeds by singularities, by working out from singularities.[30]

By referring to jurisprudence as the "philosophy of law" Deleuze means that it should be understood to stand in relation to law in the same way that philosophy, as he understands it, stands in relation to concepts. The task of philosophy is the creation of new concepts or the modification of old ones, where concepts are supposed to give expression to pure events. For this reason, philosophy is an inherently political activity: it shapes many of the mundane events in terms of which we understand and respond to the history that unfolds around us. Philosophy provides the concepts in terms of which we describe political life and its processes.

---

[27] G. Deleuze and F. Guattari, *A Thousand Plateaus: Capitalism and Schizophrenia*, (trans.) B. Massumi (Minneapolis, Minn.: University of Minnesota Press, 1987), 213.

[28] P. Patton, "Immanence, Transcendence and the Creation of Rights," in L. de Sutter and K. McGee, (eds.), *Deleuze and Law* (Edinburgh University Press, 2012), 24–26. William Connolly offers an account of the changes in affect, sensibility and belief required for the emergence of new rights that accords with this Deleuzian concept of micro-politics. He provides helpful examples such as the kinds of changes below the level of political judgment involved in the recognition of a right to die, W. E. Connolly, "An Ethos of Engagement," in *Why I Am Not a Secularist* (Minneapolis, Minn. and London: University of Minnesota Press, 1999). James, "Rights as Enforceable Claims," also points to the importance of such conditions for the enforceability of rights.

[29] Deleuze, *Negotiations*, 153, translation modified.

[30] Deleuze, Negotiations, 153, translation modified.

For example, the concept of revolution has pursued "its immanent path" from the English through the French, American and then Soviet revolutions, each with their different ideals and aims.[31] The critical function of the concept is ensured, firstly, by the fact that, *qua* expression of a pure event, it is never exhausted by its empirical manifestations; secondly, by the fact that it relates to the milieu in which it is deployed.[32] In these terms, we can say that the concept of democracy contains at its core an idea of the equality of all who are governed, and their equal participation in decisions that affect them. This idea is expressed in the idea of a well-ordered society governed in accordance with a particular conception of justice, but not exhausted by this form of political liberalism. Deleuze's concept of "becoming-democratic" reminds us that the pure event of democracy is also expressed in a variety of ongoing efforts to give institutional expression to its core egalitarian ideals, whether in relation to decision-making, social status or the fair distribution of the material benefits of social cooperation.[33]

Deleuze and Guattari do not explicitly consider the concept of right as a philosophical concept of the same order as revolution or democracy, even though they do occasionally invoke this concept.[34] However, there is no reason why they could not regard the concept of right in the same way they regard the concepts of democracy and revolution, namely as a philosophical concept that has pursued its own immanent path from ancient Greece up to the present. In these terms, Deleuze's concept of jurisprudence would be another name for the process of "becoming-right," where this refers to the variety of means by which new ways of acting or being acted towards become established (or old ways disestablished).[35] In societies governed by law, these processes include the electoral and legislative steps that lead to new laws, as well as the judicial review and modification of existing laws. But they also include the subterranean shifts in sensibility, affect and desire that constitute what Deleuze and Guattari call "micropolitics." It is these processes that

---

[31] Deleuze and Guattari, *What is Philosophy?*, 100.
[32] P. Patton, *Deleuzian Concepts: Philosophy, Colonization, Politics* (Stanford University Press, 2010), 191.
[33] Ibid., 154–159, 191–193.
[34] Deleuze and Guattari, *What is Philosophy?*, 102–104. Patton, "Immanence, Transcendence and the Creation of Rights," 24–26. Deleuze and Parnet summed up the variety of social movements and lines of flight in relation to linguistic, ethnic, regional, sexual, youth and other minorities that challenged the capitalist economy and nation state assemblages in the 1970s as expressions of a "*right to* desire", G. Deleuze and C. Parnet, (1996), 176; *Dialogues II*, (trans.) H. Tomlinson and B. Habberjam (London: Athlone Press, 2002), 147.
[35] Patton, "Immanence, Transcendence and the Creation of Rights," 26–29.

Deleuze has in mind when he remarks that, in moving beyond judges and moral experts to consider new rights in relation to modern biology, we move from law to politics.

The concept of becoming-right allows us to reconcile Deleuze's criticism of human rights with his praise of jurisprudence. He does not oppose rights as such. Rather, he opposes the idea that there exists a definitive set of human rights grounded in some rights-bearing feature of human nature. He opposes the idea that rights are a-historical or a-contextual. Certain ways of acting or being treated "become right" under certain historical circumstances. For Deleuze, rights are like philosophical concepts in that they are situational or site-specific. Just as philosophical concepts must refer to the milieu in which they are developed or modified, if they are to be politically effective and to realize the political vocation of philosophy, so too must rights refer to the "immanent modes of existence" of the people concerned. Deleuze's preference for jurisprudence over declarations of human rights or their enshrinement in legal codes is a preference for the ongoing and open-ended micro- and macro-political processes that lead to the invention of new rights and the modification of existing laws.

Foucault and the emergence of new rights

Like Deleuze, Foucault was widely misread as an opponent of the language of rights.[36] In fact, in interviews and political essays during the late 1970s and early 1980s, Foucault often appealed to existing rights or called for the recognition of new rights. Thus, in a 1977 interview discussing the extradition of the lawyer for the Red Army Faction, Klaus Croissant, he referred to the "rights of the governed" and described these as "more precise and more historically determined than the rights of man."[37] Among the rights of the governed especially relevant to the case of Croissant, he mentioned the right to be properly defended in a court of law. However, his characterization of this right goes well beyond a mere formal or procedural right to be represented in court to include the right to a legal representative who speaks with and for the accused, not only enabling them to be heard but also seeking to protect their life, their identity and the force of their refusal.[38] As an example of appealing to

---

[36] P. Patton, "Power and Right in Nietzsche and Foucault," *International Studies in Philosophy*, 36, 43–61, repr. in B. Golder and P. Fitzpatrick, (eds.), *Foucault and Law* (Farnham: Ashgate, 2004); P. Patton, "Foucault, Critique and Rights," *Critical Horizons*, 6 (2005), 267–287; Golder, "Foucault's Critical (Yet Ambivalent) Affirmation."

[37] M. Foucault, *Dits et écrits, tomes I–IV* (Paris: Éditions Gallimard, 1994), III, 362.

[38] Ibid.

rights that are not yet widely recognised or established, in a 1981 speech in support of NGOs attempting to protect Vietnamese refugees being attacked by pirates in the Gulf of Thailand, he spoke of the rights and duties of an international citizenship that obliges us to speak out against abuses of power.[39] He suggested that it was also a duty associated with this international citizenship "to always bring the testimony of people's suffering to the eyes and ears of governments."[40] He suggested that the actions of NGOs such as Amnesty International, *Terre des Hommes* and *Médecins du Monde* had succeeded in creating a new right on the part of private individuals "to effectively intervene in the sphere of international policy and strategy."[41] In a 1982 interview on the question of gay rights, he advocated the creation of new forms of relational right that would recognize same-sex relationships.[42] In a 1983 interview on Social Security, he endorsed the idea of a right to the "means of health" and also a right to suicide.[43]

Foucault's embrace of the language of rights provides further clues to how we might understand rights as historical and contextual features of particular societies, or as features of a particular state of relations between societies, peoples, and their forms of political organization. Whereas Deleuze pointed to the micro-political processes involved in the creation of new rights, Foucault's distinctive contribution derives from his commitment to a "principle of existence" in relation to the critique of power. In a lecture given in Japan in 1978, he suggests that philosophy can play a role in support of forms of counter-power, but only on the condition that it "stops posing the question of power in terms of good and evil, but poses it in terms of existence."[44] What he means by this is that criticism of existing forms of power, or support for forms of counter-power, is effective only when it draws upon existing forms of governmental discourse. To see how this bears on the normative basis of rights, recall that in the discussion of externalist approaches to rights above I noted that there are two conditions that must be satisfied in order for a right to exist: some form of institutional respect for certain ways of acting or being acted upon and some form of acceptable justification.

---

[39] M. Foucault, *Essential Works of Foucault 1954–1984, Vol. 3, Ethics,* (ed.) J. D. Faubion, (trans.) R. Hurley *et al.* (New York: The New Press, 2000), 474.

[40] Foucault, *Essential Works,* 3, 474.

[41] Ibid., 475.For further commentary on this speech, see Patton, "Power and Right in Nietzsche and Foucault," and J. Whyte, "Human Rights Confronting Governments?: Michel Foucault and the Right to Intervene," in M. Stone, I. R. Wall and C. Douzinas, (eds.), *New Critical Legal Thinking: Law and the Political* (Abingdon: Routledge, 2012).

[42] Foucault, *Essential Works,* 1, 157–162.

[43] Foucault, *Essential Works,* 3, 365–381.   [44] Foucault, *Dits et écrits, III,* 540.

Rex Martin adds an important qualification to the justification condition when he argues that the relevant justification must be available to those for whom the right is said to exist. He argues that the normative force of rights claims means that they involve some direction of behavior, for example that others must provide or at least not impede our access to the good in relation to which we have a right. The normative direction of individuals' behavior is taken to mean that they can experience the requirement to act or to refrain from acting in certain ways as a duty. On the basis that people cannot be supposed to have duties of which they cannot be aware, he further argues that particular ways of acting or refraining from action only become rights when people can effectively become aware of the justification, given the moral views and other beliefs which they do have.[45] For this to be the case, it is not sufficient that there be some form of moral justification for the right in question, the justification must be accessible to agents on the basis of their actual moral and other beliefs:

> For obligations or duties that cannot be acknowledged in a given society, or that cannot be shown to follow, discursively, from accredited principles of conduct which are at least reflectively available to persons in that society, cannot be regarded as proper duties which could normatively bind conduct in that society.[46]

On this view, if the acknowledgment of something as a duty is blocked by beliefs about the incapacity or unworthiness of those to whom the duty would be owed, then there is no duty. This is arguably what occurred in relation to colonized peoples and slaves. If there is now widespread agreement that such people are entitled to the same rights as others, or that they are, in Rawls' phrase, "self-authenticating sources of valid claims," this is because the beliefs that underpinned their former exclusion no longer hold sway.[47] In this sense it follows for Martin that, to the extent that there is change in the principles of conduct that are reflectively available to people, there is a genuine historical dimension to the existence of rights.

However, I also noted above that for Martin and other externalist theorists the justification of rights is achieved by comprehensive moral views that are available to members of the relevant community in which those rights exist. This is a difficulty insofar as this approach is supposed to apply to the conditions of modern constitutional democratic societies

---

[45] Martin, *A System of Rights*, 45.   [46] Ibid., 78.
[47] J. Rawls, *Political Liberalism: Expanded Edition* (New York: Columbia University Press, 2005), 32.

in which there is a plurality of such moral views. Rawls points out that the plurality of comprehensive moral, philosophical and religious views is not simply an empirical consequence of immigration, colonization or cultural differences, but a defensible outcome of freedom of thought and conscience. It follows that a democratic political order and associated regime of rights cannot rely on conceptions of right that are justified by reference to particular comprehensive moral views. Disagreement would be endemic and political stability difficult to maintain. It is not evident how the forms of institutional respect required for the existence of rights would be able to be instituted as outcomes of democratic political processes. More importantly, to rely on moral justification for particular ways of treating others and being treated would fail to meet the standard of reasonableness that is a necessary condition of justice and stability for the right reasons in a democratic political community. The kind of justification required to institute public institutional protection of certain ways of acting or being treated should respect the inevitable plurality of comprehensive views. The justifications advanced in support of particular rights should involve public reasons that meet the required standards of reciprocity and reasonableness. The basic rights of citizens should be supported by reasons that citizens can offer to one another in the reasonable belief that these will be acceptable to others who might not share their own comprehensive views.

In other words, the appropriate form of justification for rights should not be moral but political in Rawls' sense of the term.[48] Neither Deleuze nor Foucault interrogates the normative basis of rights in modern constitutional democracies, even though they appeal to such rights.[49] Rawls does offer an account of the conditions under which rights are normatively justified, namely when they can be derived from a political conception of justice that meets the requirements of wide reflective equilibrium and on which there could be overlapping consensus. This is a constructivist conception of the normative basis of rights in the sense that the principles of justice can be represented as the outcome of a procedure of construction that says these are principles that all

---

[48] P. Patton, "Historical Normativity and the Basis of Rights," in B. Golder, (ed.), *Re-Reading Foucault: On Law, Power, Rights* (Abingdon: Routledge, 2012), 15–31.

[49] See above regarding Foucault's appeal to the right to legal representation in the case of Croissant. Deleuze made a similar appeal to procedural rights in his "Open Letter to Antonio Negri's Judges," where he takes issue with the lack of consistency in the charges, the acceptance of ordinary logical principles of reasoning in the examination of evidence, and the role of the media in relation to this judicial procedure, G. Deleuze, *Two Regimes of Madness: Texts and Interviews 1975–1995*, (trans.) A. Hodges and M. Taormina (New York: Semiotext(e), rev. edn., 2007), 169–172.

reasonable citizens would accept.[50] Principles of justice that meet these conditions will provide a sufficiently objective basis for judgments about which ways of acting or being treated should enjoy institutional respect. So far, however, this account of the normative basis of rights remains divorced from the actual historical conditions under which particular rights can be said to exist in a given social milieu.

At this point, Foucault offers a qualification that is helpful for the historical conception of rights and that parallels Martin's accessibility condition. He reminds us that, in order for rights to exist, they should be justifiable in terms of a common discursive framework that is available to all members of the society in question. Rights can only exist where the discursive conditions of their formulation and exercise are available to the parties involved. He relies on the "principle of existence" mentioned above with regard to the ways in which criticism of the exercise of power, often in the name of particular rights, invariably draws upon rationalities of government that are available within the prevailing political culture. This principle is evident both in his efforts as an engaged citizen advocating new or emerging rights and in his analyses of the different forms of "counter-conduct" that emerged in response to particular kinds of pastoral and political government. Thus, he argues that the precise mechanisms through which pastoral power sought to direct the conduct of individuals provided the basis for forms of counter-conduct through which some dissident subjects sought to conduct themselves differently: these included asceticism, different forms of community, mysticism, eschatology and disputes over the proper interpretation of the Scripture.[51] Similarly, in relation to the *raison d'État* conception of government that developed from the eighteenth century onwards, the different forms of counter-conduct that emerged were based upon elements of this governmentality. In some cases these took the form of claims founded on fundamental rights: to the primacy of civil society over the state, to economic truth as opposed to error, and to an "absolute" right to revolt or to revolution.[52] Against the principle of *raison d'État* that insisted on the obedience of individuals to the state, Foucault suggests, there emerged a form of counter-conduct the meaning of which was: "There must be a moment when, breaking all the bonds of obedience, the population will really have the right, not in

---

[50] Rawls, *Political Liberalism*, 89–90.
[51] M. Foucault, *Security, Territory, Population: Lectures at the Collège de France 1978–1979*, (ed.) M. Sennellart, (trans.) G. Burchell (Houndmills and New York: PalgraveMacmillan, 2007), 194–216.
[52] Ibid., 356.

juridical terms, but in terms of essential and fundamental rights, to break any bonds of obedience it has with the state."[53]

Foucault exemplifies the same principle of existence in his 1981 comments in support of the humanitarian intervention to assist Vietnamese refugees. He draws upon particular elements of historically available and effective forms of governmental reason to provide normative support for the right of private individuals to intervene in support of stateless refugees. First, he invokes the independence of the individual "members of the community of the governed" who chose to speak out against this particular dereliction of State power: the fact of being appointed by no one constitutes their right to speak.[54] Second, he invokes the explicit pact that grounds the legitimacy of government in its concern for the welfare and security of its citizens.[55] It is because the idea that government guarantees the welfare and security of citizens is an accepted element of public political reason, and because governments have the administrative means to undertake this task, that they can be held accountable for the welfare of their citizens. In turn, this mutually accepted basis of the relationship between governors and governed provides grounds on which to argue that governments should be held responsible for the suffering of people outside their borders. In language that recalls his description of the right to revolt that emerged in response to eighteenth-century government insistence on the obedience of its citizens, he argues that in the era of government that guarantees the welfare of its citizens, the suffering of individuals "grounds an absolute right to

[53] Foucault, *Security, Territory*, 356.
[54] Foucault, *Essential Works*, 3, 474. In a discussion in his 1979 lectures of the two predominant liberal ways of conceptualizing the limitation and legitimation of the powers of governments, Foucault drew attention to the two corresponding concepts of freedom: a juridical concept based on the imprescriptable rights of individuals and a utilitarian concept of freedom as "the independence of the governed with regard to government" (*The Birth of Biopolitics: Lectures at the Collège de France 1978–1979*, (ed.) M. Senellart, (trans.) G. Burchell (Houndmills and New York: PalgraveMacmillan, 2008), 42). The latter corresponded to the freedom of the moderns that Benjamin Constant considered had become all the more necessary and valuable by virtue of the development of commerce: "The Liberty of the Ancients Compared with that of The Moderns," (1819), in B. Constant, *Political Writings*, (trans. and ed.) B. Fontana (Cambridge University Press, 1988), 309–328.
[55] In an interview around the time of the Croissant *affaire* in 1977, Foucault suggested that whereas the primary function of the state was once limited to the guarantee of peace and safety behind its borders, a "territorial pact," the contemporary relationship of the state to its people is different: "Today the frontier problem hardly ever arises. The pact that the State proposes to its population is: 'You will be guaranteed.' Guaranteed against every form of uncertainty, accident, damage, risk. Are you ill? You will have Social Security! You have no job? You will have unemployment benefits," Foucault, *Dits et écrits*, III, 385.

stand up and speak to those who hold power."[56] The general principle behind his support for this intervention and the earlier historical analyses is that resistance on the part of citizens to the ways in which they are governed invariably draws upon the very conceptions of government that inform those ways of governing. Extending this principle to the justification of particular rights in modern democratic societies, we can say that Foucault reminds us that this depends on the available forms of public political reason, including conceptions of the nature and functions of government. Of course, the mere fact that certain views about government or the appropriate behavior of citizens are available does not make them right. Rawls reminds us that, in order to become right, they must be derivable from principles of justice that all reasonable citizens could accept. The universalism of this principle is limited to those for whom the right is supposed to exist. Moreover, it is not an a-historical universalizing principle of the normative basis of rights but an historical principle that derives its own normative force from the European tradition of democratic government in which it arose. It reflects an historically specific conception of political society according to which citizens are answerable to one another and to their considered judgments about what is right and just. Within this democratic tradition, some such judgments have remained relatively stable over centuries, thereby providing a sufficiently stable basis for public political reason and for certain fundamental civil and political rights. Other judgments remain contested and controversial in response to conflicting conceptions of the task of government or the shifting grounds of citizens convictions. For these reasons, the content of public political reason changes over time and the particular ways of acting or being treated that citizens can justify to one another will also be subject to change. In this sense, rights will be historical and political.

---

[56] Foucault, *Essential Works*, 3, 475.

14 "All of us without exception": Sartre, Rancière, and the cause of the Other

Bruce Robbins

How not to write the history of human rights

In an article entitled "Bleeding Humanity and Gendered Embodiments: From Antislavery Sugar Boycotts to Ethical Consumers," published in 2011 in the new and highly respected journal *Humanity*, Mimi Sheller offers an intriguing example of where the conversation has gotten on the increasingly linked subjects of human rights and humanitarianism.[1] According to Sheller, white women who participated in the anti-slavery sugar boycotts of the late eighteenth century, an early instance of what Jacques Rancière calls "the cause of the other," were really interested in asserting their superiority over black women. This is not quite what Sheller says, but I think it is a reasonable approximation. Consider: "the making of the female ethical consumer as a humanitarian actor involved techniques of differentiating the white woman from the enslaved woman, remaking (rather than dislodging) the very forms of difference that enslavement pivoted upon" (174). Here the studied abstractness of the phrasing seems calculated to avoid a direct charge of evil intentions. The differentiating of white from black women is attributed only to the "techniques," not to the white women themselves. But why should "techniques" have any intentionality at all? Who else but the white women who wielded these techniques can be held responsible? That Sheller does in fact want her reader to hold the white women responsible is suggested by the parenthetical phrase "rather than dislodging." This phrase implies that there was another option available and that the white women were free to choose it. Why didn't they opt to dislodge the forms of difference that separated them from female slaves? It's their own fault that instead they re-made the forms of difference, thus

---

[1] Mimi Sheller, "Bleeding Humanity and Gendered Embodiments: From Antislavery Sugar Boycotts to Ethical Consumers," *Humanity*, 2(2) (2011), 171–192. Page numbers in this and other cited works are given in parentheses.

defending and preserving their supposed superiority. No charge is filed, but they have nonetheless been found guilty.

This is bad writing not because it is (rather belatedly) following a Foucaultian fashion, but because it is bad thinking. And it is bad thinking of a representative kind. The white women who participated in the abolitionist movement were different from the slaves they were trying to free: they were already free, and the slaves were not. This is not something the abolitionist women could pretend out of existence. It is inconceivable, historically speaking, that their freedom, which made their action possible, would not "differentiate" them from the unfree. If the free white woman and the black enslaved woman had been equals in their historical situation, there would have been no political movement, and no need for one.[2] To argue that the white women somehow needed to insist on and re-assert their difference – "to maintain clear distinctions and hierarchies between them" (175) – is to mistake the initial circumstances of their action, circumstances of inequality, for the purpose of that action. Sheller's own purpose in adding this bit of phantasmatic teleology is clearly to undercut the supposed idealism of the white women's motives, as if they could not possibly have wanted what they thought and said they wanted. But this argument betrays a much greater idealism on Sheller's part. What else *but* immense, disappointed idealism could have led her to conclude that "there are limitations to the forms of agency, solidarity, and equality inherent in these humanitarian gestures" (187)? What else could she have possibly expected? Yes, there are "limitations" in humanitarianism generally and in the form of the boycott (which is not restricted to humanitarianism) in particular. But of what "forms of agency, solidarity, and equality" would this not be the case? All the forms by which human beings have thus far sought to liberate themselves or mitigate the hard fates assigned to their brothers and sisters, children and grandchildren – that is, all forms of progressive politics – have of course had their "limitations." Who could have imagined otherwise? The French Revolution, the Bolshevik and Maoist revolutions, the labor movement, the women's suffrage movement, the civil rights movement, the Arab Spring, Occupy: all of them have of course been partly shaped and tainted by the structures of inequality and injustice that they were contesting. Marx and Lenin and Mao were

---

[2] The same mistake is made about consumerism: Paul Glennie writes, "In each case, consumption was made morally legitimate through notions of responsible consumption." In order to demonstrate this point, Glennie would have to show that consumption seemed morally illegitimate beforehand. This seems unlikely. Paul Glennie, "Consumption Within Historical Studies," in Daniel Miller, (ed.), *Acknowledging Consumption* (London: Routledge, 1995), 183.

not among the poorest of the poor; they belonged to the educated middle class. To whom is this shocking? The existing structures of power do not instantly disappear when the first petition is drafted or the first rock is thrown. If they were not so powerful, these structures would not define what has to be contested and changed. But their power, which includes advantages in defining the terrain and terms of contestation, does not mean that the movements and revolutions that rose up against them accomplished nothing.

Again, who could have imagined otherwise?

This will sound like a rhetorical question, but it invites an actual answer. Imagining that "forms of agency, solidarity, and equality" should not have any "limitations" and setting up such hypothetically limitationless, miraculously pure forms as the relevant standard of judgment when examining the history of human rights and humanitarianism is not an arbitrary mistake. It belongs to an intellectual syndrome that ought to be familiar. Those who suffer from it speak the language of politics but, demanding above all else moral purity as judged by today's standards, are unprepared for any of the messiness of historical struggle. In the presence of actual alliances and actual allies they can only point a sternly disapproving finger. The irony is that the moralistic, a-political idealism that is the chief symptom of this self-righteous pathology is nowhere more flagrantly displayed than in the human rights movement itself.

I will return below to the example of white women who participated in the anti-slavery boycotts of the late eighteenth century, suggesting another way of linking this chapter of our past to the urgencies of our present. But for now, let me continue with the motif of idealism – both that of the advocates of human rights and humanitarianism and, more particularly, that of their critics. It is the idealism of the critics of human rights and humanitarianism that interferes more insidiously with the narrating of their history.

As the "ancient times" in its title suggests, Micheline Ishay's *The History of Human Rights: From Ancient Times to the Globalization Era* sets itself up as an advocate's inspiring story of universality.[3] Human rights are said to be "the result of a cumulative historical process that takes on a life of its own" (2), but they are also presented as effectively timeless: they exist in ancient times, already fully themselves, and from then on they are "transmitted consciously and unconsciously from one generation to another" (2). This continuous, trans-historical history is both challenged

---

[3] Micheline R. Ishay, *The History of Human Rights: From Ancient Times to the Globalization Era* (Berkeley, Cal.: University of California Press, 2004).

and carried on by Lynn Hunt's *Inventing Human Rights: A History*. Hunt places the true emergence of human rights at a much later moment: the American Declaration of Independence in 1776 and the French Declaration of the Rights of Man and Citizen in 1789.[4] In an effort to explain this emergence, Hunt talks about historical pre-conditions, in particular the development of a sense of empathy and autonomy. A particular kind of autonomous, empathetic, egalitarian self had to come into existence in order for, say, torture to come to seem unacceptable: "any account of historical change must in the end account for the alteration of individual minds" (34). "Human rights could only flourish when people learned to think of others as their equals, as like them in some fundamental fashion" (58). Human rights needed the help of principles like equality and empathy in order to come into being. Once born into the historical world, however, they function as ideals that are no longer subject to historical contingency. Hence Samuel Moyn can conclude in a review that "Hunt provides historical details about the recognition of human rights but ultimately seems to think of them as timeless."

Aryeh Neier's *The International Human Rights Movement: A History*[5] begins with the 2009 murder of Natalya Estemirova, researcher for the Russian human rights organization Memorial, and the opening story says all you need to know about the history to follow. Governments do very bad things, and good people spontaneously arise and assemble (in NGOs) to expose and protest those bad things. Human rights is not a "universalistic scheme" (4), not an ideology, not a politics, not (as Moyn suggests in his own history, *The Last Utopia: Human Rights in History*) a substitute for other visions of how society should be organized. For Neier, it is merely a natural human reaction against tyranny. In that sense, although Neier calls his book a history, what it suggests is that the history of the human rights movement cannot really be told, any more than that of tyranny itself. Like tyranny, the human rights struggle is eternal. "There is little or no prospect that this movement will fade away or decline significantly," Neier writes, "when it achieves a particular goal, as happened, for example, to the feminist movement for nearly half a century" (7). This sentence comes very close to complacency: it's as if the movement were congratulating itself on an immortality that it guaranteed in advance by defining its enemy as immortal and its own goals, therefore, as unachievable. Focused

---

[4] Lynn Hunt, *Inventing Human Rights: A History* (New York: W. W. Norton, 2007).
[5] Aryeh Neier, *The International Human Rights Movement: A History* (Princeton University Press, 2012).

exclusively on individuals and on civil and political rights, uninterested in economic, social, and cultural rights or other collective rights like the right to development, Neier's thin, minimalist program can never run out of work to do but by the same token can never do work that will make any large difference.

There has been no stronger effort to reverse the idealism of history-writing like Neier's than Moyn's *The Last Utopia*. Moyn locates the emergence of human rights in the current sense very late: in the 1970s.[6] In his version of human rights history, earlier points of origin – ancient Greece, the Enlightenment, and the post-Second World War years in which people digested news of the Holocaust – are really speaking about a different object. The object always takes its meaning from its context, and for Moyn the only relevant context for the origin of human rights as we understand them is the death of the explicitly political projects of communism and national liberation. Yet the same ambiguity that Moyn finds in Hunt also hovers over his own argument. Do human rights, once they emerge into history, become subject to historical contingency and fluctuation? Or does Moyn, like Hunt, see them as still determined by the origin ascribed to them? Contexts change, he tells us, and meanings ought to change with them. In the era of its breakthrough, Moyn says, human rights was "a minimalist utopia of anti-politics" (218). Is it still an anti-politics, a political project only in the sense that it replaces better, more genuinely political ones? Or is it now a genuinely political project in its own right and to be judged as such, perhaps positively as well as negatively?

In hesitating to embrace the latter possibility, Moyn arguably fails to attribute *enough* difference to human rights. But he also seems committed to attributing to them *too much* difference. No one would dispute his point (in his review of Hunt) that "if historians miss how different rights were in the past, they will fail even to recognize what it would take to explain rights in the present."[7] And yet the assumption on which this argument is based is worth pausing over. Is history about nothing but difference? Is its one true message the message of discontinuity? This version of history would surely block out as much as Hunt's does – to be specific, the very possibility that (as Hunt insists) human rights can be credited with political results. Hunt stresses the increasing popular revulsion from torture. On this topic, a case for progress in sensibility can

---

[6] Samual Moyn, *The Last Utopia: Human Rights in History* (Cambridge, Mass.: Harvard University Press, 2010).
[7] Samuel Moyn, "On the Genealogy of Morals," *The Nation*, March 29, 2007, http://the nation.com.

be made. Moyn comments that this emphasis "obscures structural wrongs that are less easy to see – when they sometimes also cause the body to suffer, as with the pangs of hunger or the exhaustion of work."[8] But if human rights have sometimes worked in the past to obscure structural causes of economic deprivation, does this mean that they must continue to do so, come what may? Moyn's own context-dependent understanding of rights discourse is incompatible with the notion that such discourse is constitutionally incapable of furthering the project of economic equality. Perhaps, the context having changed, human rights could indeed serve this project.[9] And if so then he, like Hunt, might have to express a cautious optimism about its worldly effects. Unwilling, it seems, to face the prospect that his chosen origin for human rights might not after all continue to determine their meaning as time goes on, Moyn digs in his heels, stubbornly resisting at the conceptual level any possible narrative of improvement. He does not acknowledge the (to my mind, real) progress on torture, nor does he ask why many of those who said they were against torture under any circumstances nevertheless did not protest loudly about Abu Ghraib. (The most likely answer, nationalism, would perhaps be inconvenient to Moyn, whose book quietly defends the nation-state against a human rights transnationalism that he sees, not without reason, as prematurely anti-nationalist.) Even the appearance of Whig history must be shunned. If the relevant facts seem for once to support a narrative of progress, then they must be instantly surrounded by other facts that do not. Does the emergence of humanitarianism seem like a good thing? It was accompanied, Moyn comments, by the invention of total war. In fact the two are "historical twins."[10] But if this is how things work, if anything that looks like progress will always be discovered to have an evil twin, then we have arrived at the undeclared moral of Moyn's history, its own evil twin: nothing ever really changes, at least not for the better.

---

[8] Moyn, "On the Genealogy of Morals."

[9] Moyn's position on this question is in fact quite nuanced: "the theoretical and doctrinal energy harnessed to the project of finding a vision of human rights adequate to global immiseration graphically illustrates the sheer distance from the landmark of their antitotalitarian invention that human rights have had to travel. The jury is clearly still out on whether a rights framework for global poverty is the right frame. But the verdict is debated only because human rights were forced to face – and it seemed believable that they might be able to face – problems that had been addressed by other schemes, and contending utopias, before," Moyn, *The Last Utopia*, 224–225. Still, isn't there something wrong both with the word "utopia" here and with the idea that different political projects must find themselves in contention instead of, say, interpenetrating each other and joining forces?

[10] Moyn, "On the Genealogy of Morals."

Moyn would surely reject this interpretation, and his book can no doubt be read otherwise. But what else is one to make of the repeated suggestion that anything resembling improvement or reform must under analysis be triumphantly revealed as another strategy of domination, or at least evilly twinned with one? Here history-as-difference flip-flops into its opposite, a vision less historical than theological. Theology seems the inevitable term when difference, which is limited to expressing variety in the regimes and techniques of domination, blurs together into sameness.[11] There is much change but nothing important ever changes. Domination itself remains, an eternal fact of things, or the eternal fact of things.[12]

One reason for beginning my argument with Mimi Sheller's essay (which appeared in the journal of which Moyn is editor) is that it offers a humble garden-variety instance of the errors that such a history will encourage. An overestimation of difference combines with a pro-grammatically anti-progressive history to generate not difference but an unbearable and indeed untenable sameness. When Sheller proposes that the eighteenth-century abolitionists wanted "to maintain clear dis-tinctions and hierarchies" between themselves and black slaves, her assumption seems to be that white people will always cling to racism and that racism therefore cannot ever go away. Racism becomes a sort of mystical quantity that can never be diminished even by one drop, a trans-historical, quasi-divine, invulnerable being that is capable of shape-shifting but can never be destroyed or lessened or even con-strained. One need not pretend that race is no longer a real issue in order to see the distortions imposed by this sort of supernaturalism.

In "Society Must Be Defended," Foucault speaks of politics as war by other means. But he speaks as if this were somehow a war in which our side never won any battles, never conquered and held any tract of once hostile ground. Such a situation cannot be properly described as a war. If war is indeed an appropriate metaphor for politics, then the possibility must be entertained of our side as well as theirs occupying and control-ling social territory. Hunt's example of intolerance for torture would be one example. Public intolerance for racism would be another. Compare

---

[11] Theological immutability is the flip-side of the worship of difference. Certain Foucaultians have placed a kind of sacred interdiction over the moments of transition between the various regimes of domination: these spaces thou shalt not try to explain. The burning pit of old-fashioned Marxist economic determinism awaits any who do not heed the commandment.

[12] Let us agree, then, not to obey the Foucaultian taboo against accounting for the transition between one regime of domination and another – and not to assume, for that matter, that domination is all you ever get.

the elementary school classrooms of today with those of fifty or one hundred years ago. From the perspective of race, are there really no changes of significance to notice? The answer may be negative, but the question must first be posed and investigated. You cannot continue to speak in the name of history while ruling out even the hypothetical possibility of something like progress.

Here I am not inviting self-congratulation. I am merely making the case for politics. If we do not accept the premise that progress is possible, then why bother? No, human rights advocates and humanitarians have not had only the highest motives. No, their actions have not had only the wished-for consequences. Those who assume they have are no more plausible than the cynics who invariably assume the reverse. The cynics are right that such projects are permeated by existing structures of power. This has to be conceded. But in conceding it, one merely repeats a proposition that ought by now to be both obvious and unobjectionable: that no politics happens in circumstances of its own making. No political action, however revolutionary, can be solely and successfully carried out by people who lack any trace of power or privilege. To demand purity from political actors is to take oneself out of politics. And to assume that those who have some self-interest in the status quo will always and necessarily act to maintain the status quo is simply to ignore the historical record.

The idea that those invested with power will want to perpetuate or increase that power, which is central to Sheller's view of the abolitionist sugar boycott, can of course be illuminating in any number of contexts: for example, much of American human rights policy during the Cold War and more recently as applied to America's foremost competitor, China. Still, it remains wrong in other instances and wrong as a general principle. And this reductive view of motive and solidarity seems especially wrong-headed as it applies to the movement for global economic justice, to whose history I now turn.

The discourse of the beneficiary

In his preface to Fanon's *The Wretched of the Earth*, published in 1961, Sartre wrote as follows: "You know well enough that we are exploiters. You know too that we have laid our hands on first the gold and the metals, then the petroleum of the 'new continents,' and that we have brought them back to the old countries. This was not without excellent results, as witness our palaces, our cathedrals, and our great industrial cities; and then when there was a threat of a slump, the colonial markets were there to soften the blow or to divert it. Crammed with riches,

Europe accorded the human status de jure to its inhabitants. With us, to be a man is to be an accomplice of colonialism, since all of us without exception profited by colonial exploitation" (25).[13]

This passage is an example of what I call the discourse of the beneficiary: a denunciation of global exploitation and inequality that is both addressed to the beneficiaries of that inequality – in this case, Sartre's fellow Europeans – and spoken by a beneficiary. The vacillation between heavy sarcasm ("excellent results") and self-indictment ("With us, to be a man") can no doubt be accounted for by the structural contradiction at the heart of this discourse: denouncing a system which one finds unbearable but to which one nevertheless continues to belong, from which one continues to derive certain benefits and privileges, and from which one may have no possibility of making a clean break. As a literary critic, I find this rhetorical situation intriguing enough to examine further. But in order for Sartre's mix of global revolutionary indignation and ethical self-flagellation to seem a promising object of analysis, it would also have be significant, and not merely for what it reveals about Sartre's psychology.[14] I would like to sketch out a case for its significance by pursuing the following series of propositions. (1) The odd qualities of Sartre's language are shared with enough other writers to allow us to speak of the discourse of the beneficiary as a full-fledged genre. (2) Although this genre cannot be properly described either as political or as humanitarian, it possesses a certain mobilizing potential that is especially worth reflecting on because (like the discourse of human rights) it works at a trans-national scale, where many have asserted there can be no such thing as a genuine politics. (3) Since it is by hiding out beyond the borders of the nation that so much economic inequality protects itself from scrutiny and revolt, a rhetorical genre that tries to adapt itself to or even merely problematizes this distance deserves to be considered a useful experiment in stretching the political, an experiment in fashioning a politics of global economic inequality. (4) However successful or unsuccessful the experiment may be judged, this proto-political discursive hybrid would therefore exemplify a more serious kind of cosmopolitanism than most of the varieties we have come to know. Human rights cosmopolitanism, which as mentioned above has not

---

[13] Jean-Paul Sartre, "Preface," in Frantz Fanon, *The Wretched of the Earth*, trans. Constance Farrington (New York: Grove Weidenfeld, 1961), 7–31.

[14] I take the term "auto-flagellation" from Noureddine Lamouchi's *Jean-Paul Sartre et le tiers monde: rhétorique d'un discours anticolonialiste* (Paris: L'Harmattan, 1996): "Certes, il y a un peu d'auto-flagellation dans cette violence verbale de l'intellectuel, obligé d'être contre son propre pays," 176. See also Paige Arthur, *Unfinished Projects: Decolonization and the Philosophy of Jean-Paul Sartre* (London: Verso, 2010).

traditionally taken economic inequality for its primary target, offers an interesting comparison.

In support of the premise that Sartre's strong words on Europe's exploitation of its colonies can indeed be taken as belonging to a rhetorical genre, let me suggest two more examples. Two decades earlier, in his essay "Not Counting Niggers" (1939), George Orwell had refused, even in the cause of anti-Fascism, "to lie about" the disparity in income between England and India, a disparity so great that, he says, an Indian's leg is commonly thinner than an Englishman's arm.[15] "One mightn't think it when one looks round the back streets of Sheffield, but the average British income is to the Indian as twelve to one. How can one get anti-Fascist and anti-capitalist solidarity in such circumstances? ... Indians refuse to believe that any class-struggle exists in Europe. In their eyes the underpaid, downtrodden English worker is himself an exploiter."[16] There is considerable evidence that Orwell himself believed this as well: the language of "all of us without exception" is to be found in much of his writing. But he does not say so, at least here. For all Orwell's confident appeals to common decency, the simultaneous co-existence of Fascist abominations, which threatened England, and colonialist abominations, which were perpetrated by England, left him with no clear ethical place to stand in a war between nations, and no unwaveringly righteous tone to adopt.

Thirty years after Sartre's preface, in a play called *The Fever*, the American writer Wallace Shawn gives an account of much the same experience when his narrator tries to make sense of the exotic phrase "fetishism of commodities." First, there is a seemingly straightforward denunciation of the global economic system:

A naked woman leans over a fence. A man buys a magazine and stares at her picture. The destinies of these two are linked. The man has paid the woman to take off her clothes, to lean over the fence. The photograph contains its history – the moment the woman unbuttoned her shirt, how she felt, what the photographer said. The price of the magazine is a code that describes the relationships between all these people – the woman, the man, the publisher, the photographer – who commanded, who obeyed. The cup of coffee contains the history of the peasants who picked the beans, how some of them fainted in the heat of the sun, some were beaten, some were kicked.

---

[15] George Orwell, "Not Counting Niggers," in *The Collected Essays: Journalism and Letters, Vol. 1*, ed. Sonia Orwell and Ian Angus (Harmondsworth: Penguin, 1970), 434–438.

[16] George Orwell, "Review of *Letters on India* by Mulk Raj Anand," *Tribune*, 19 March 1943, in Peter Davison (ed.), *The Complete Works of George Orwell, Vol. 15*, "Two Wasted Years" (London: Secker & Warburg, 1998), 33.

For two days I could see the fetishism of commodities everywhere around me. It was a strange feeling. Then on the third day I lost it, it was gone, I couldn't see it anymore.[17]

Shawn's narrator presents the act of looking through commodities to see the social relations that lie on the other side as literally unendurable, as if it delivered a sense of the world that the human eye or the human heart is simply not constructed to sustain. But the problem seems to be less the human organs as such than his own location in the system. He feels that he shares the blame with those who are beating and kicking the peasants and those who force the woman to pose in the nude, and he concludes that his own life is unjustifiable: "if it's appropriate for you to have the share of things which in fact you have, and it's appropriate for all the people who are like you all over the world to have the share that *they* have, that means that it's not *in*appropriate for all of the others to have the share that remains. You know that what you have is what you deserve, and that means that what they have is what they deserve" (59–60). "The life I live is irredeemably corrupt. It has no justification" (63).

Assuming that over these five decades there has come to exist a sizable archive of roughly similar instances, the question that follows is whether the genre's inner conflicts – in Shawn's case dramatic enough to make the text work as a theatrical monologue – are of more than diagnostic value. An unsympathetic observer might object that such statements reveal nothing more interesting than "bourgeois guilt." To this I would respond that the term "bourgeois" is in fact inaccurate, and inaccurate in a way that unveils some of the topic's deeper interest. To say that the discourse of the beneficiary applies to "all of us without exception" is to say that it applies to a great many people in the metropolis who could by no means be properly described as bourgeois. That is precisely what is new about the genre. It would of course not be unprecedented to address inequality at a global scale: "Workers of the world, unite!" does exactly that. What Marx and Engels do not do is assume, with Orwell and Sartre, a gulf of inequality separating even workers in the global North from both workers and bourgeoisie in the global South. If the assumptions of dependency and world-systems theory, which Orwell and Sartre antici-pate, sometimes seem to oversimplify the vectors of guilt at the planetary scale, they also create complications within the class system at the national or local scale, complications which are both interesting and (if we are going to come up with a politics aimed at global economic inequality) necessary to engage with.

[17] Wallace Shawn, *The Fever* (New York: Grove Press, 1991), 21.

It is arguable that this genre deserves to be considered political only negatively – that its effects are political in the palpable but disappointing sense of being counterproductive. The broader sharing of blame for global economic inequality might for example be seen as a way of slipping out from under the burden of class guilt at home. This accusation has been leveled more than once at Orwell. Or the rhetorical archive could be dismissed as politically trivial. Unlike, say, *The Communist Manifesto*, Sartre's language does not address the victims of a wrong and exhort those victims to take action to right it. On the contrary, it addresses itself to those who benefit from the wrong. This not what we ordinarily think of as effective politics. Imagine founding a political party by pointing out an injustice and then trying to recruit your membership among those who profit from that injustice. On the other hand, speech like this cannot be dismissed as mere humanitarianism. Humanitarian discourse forbids the positing of a causal logic between the situation of the haves and the situation of the have-nots. As a humanitarian, you can make your address-ees feel guilty, but you can't do so by saying, as Sartre does, that distant others are miserable because they themselves are much better off. An analysis that makes this causal link is doing something more ambitious than humanitarianism even if it is not doing the sorts of things we might expect from directly political speech, like communicating directly with the victims of economic inequality in search of a hypothetical alliance against what we have come to call globalization. And it seems worth speculating that this causality, which ramps up the tone to levels not everyone will want to hear, is also definitive of whatever specific effect this ethico-political amalgam can be shown to have.

Jacques Rancière, commenting on Sartre's preface to Fanon in an essay called "La Cause de l'autre" from the collection *Aux bords du politique* – an essay which has been strangely omitted from the English translation *On the Shores of Politics* – is skeptical as to whether statements like Sartre's deserve to count as "political."[18] Sartre's preface, Rancière writes, "was paradoxical, for it presented us with a book that was not addressed to us [that is, us Europeans]. The war of liberation of the colonized is theirs, Sartre told us. This book is addressed to them. They have nothing to do with us, and especially not with our protestations of 'beautiful soul' humanism. These are the last form of colonial falsehood that the war smashes in pieces, [a falsehood] to which the war opposes its truth. The truth of war was thus posed as the denunciation of ethics."

---

[18] Jacques Rancière, *On the Shores of Politics* (New York: Verso, 1995). Jacques Rancière, "La Cause de l'autre." First published in *Algérie-France: regards croisés, Lignes*, 30 February 1997, here quoted from *Aux bords du politique* (Paris: Gallimard, 2004).

As we saw above ("Crammed with riches, Europe accorded the human status de jure to its inhabitants"), Sartre is indeed scathingly critical of the well-meaning humanist and his merely ethical condemnation of the state's bad behavior. He writes: "Chatter, chatter: liberty, equality, fraternity, love, honor, patriotism, and what have you. All this did not prevent us from making anti-racial speeches about dirty niggers, dirty Jews, and dirty Arabs. High-minded people, liberal or just soft-hearted, protest that they were shocked by such inconsistency; but they were either mistaken or dishonest, for with us there is nothing more consistent than a racist humanism since the European has only been able to become a man through creating slaves and monsters" (26). And yet because Sartre is of course addressing European readers even when he says (wrongly) that Fanon's book is indifferent to them, the result, Rancière argues, is simply more ethics. "The paradox of this anti-ethical affirmation," Rancière goes on, "is that by excluding 'the cause of the other,' it in fact defined a relation to the war that was purely ethical and purely individual" (208–209, my translation). In other words, the discourse of the beneficiary (we have all profited by colonial exploitation) is finally not political at all but merely ethical.

The fact that for many readers Sartre's discourse continues to work quite well would seem to lend it some interesting political potential even if we agreed with Rancière that it doesn't yet count as fully or satisfactorily political. But Rancière chooses to examine French writing in support of the Algerian cause because he is trying to make the case that solidarity in such a cause can count as political. Sartre is wrong, Rancière says, in offering a (Hegelian) celebration of war as "the negation of the negation" (204), hence a definitive break with colonial identity and the conquest of a new, universal humanity or citizenship. But the more interesting question is not what war means to the Algerians; it's what anti-war politics means to the French. Is an anti-war politics, a politics that objects to war-making against another people in one's own name, really a politics at all? "How could the cause of the Algerians become our cause," Rancière asks, "other than on a moral level?" (208). His answer is that it could and did become a matter of French politics, but only because of the infamous repression of the Paris demonstration of October 17, 1961, when many Algerians who had come out in the streets were savagely beaten, drowned, and killed by other means. A complete news black-out was imposed by the French government, which sought to make its multitude of victims invisible. "For us," Rancière writes, "this meant that something had been done in our name here at home [chez nous]" (210). Rancière clearly means for the emphasis to fall less on what has been done in our name than on the fact that it was done "here at home." Other things had also been done in our name, but they were done elsewhere. Things done in other spaces presumably did not become a matter of French politics even if they were done in the name of all Frenchmen. Presumably the same would have been true, say, of the French war in Indochina.

What immediately follows in Rancière's text is a contrast between the effect of the Paris demonstration and the effect of images from Rwanda and Bosnia in the period when he was writing, the 1990s. These images "at best produce indignation" (211), Rancière says, but they do not produce politics. "Fear and pity are not political affects" (211). It is strange that Rancière is not willing to consider the possibility that what France was doing in Algeria might have produced a politics in France, even a politics of "not in our name."[19] It's as if for Rancière "our name" is not strong enough – as if events cannot become political unless they literally happen on French soil, "in French public space" (210). That's why he goes on to insist that the key element is not the war in Algeria, conducted by the military, but the twin facts that military operations in Algeria were labeled police actions and that the atrocities in the streets of Paris were indeed committed by the police.[20] Police, polis: what is central to the cause of the other is a "disidentification in relation to the French state" (212), a rupture within French citizenship. The cause of the other does not seem to involve an identification with the Algerians themselves or any other exceeding, escaping, or negating of French national belonging.

This is a very delicate matter, and I am not totally confident that I am doing Rancière justice. "As it happens," he writes in a rather complicated sentence, "there was no identification with the combatants [the Algerians], whose reasons were not ours ... But there was inclusion within a political subjectification – in a disidentification – [an inclusion] of that identity that was impossible to take on [assumer]" (213). As I read him, he is saying that the cause of the other always involves "an impossible identification" (213). His example, one page later, is the slogan "We are all German Jews" (214), an identification which does not aim to confirm or produce any real social grouping. Impossible identification is valuable because what it produces is a difference at the interior of citizenship (219), an internal alterity. It is not valuable for what it does in itself; it has no capacity to generate a new trans-national political subject. Without the

---

[19] For Americans of my generation, this will inevitably raise the question of the student movement against the Vietnam War and other movements of solidarity with victims of American foreign policy.

[20] "Politics does not declare itself in relation to war ... It declares itself in relation to the police," Rancière, "La Cause de l'autre," 211.

restrictiveness of (a given, already-existing) citizenship, which is to say the structure of an already-existing state, Rancière clearly fears that the cause of the other will slip "from politics to ethics, absorbed into duty toward those who suffer and coming finally to be accompanied by the geostrategic policing of the great powers" (218–219). Like other human rights cynics, he warns us off, not unreasonably, with the specter of ethics becoming military intervention in humanitarianism's name.

Still, Rancière does want to argue that "the cause of the other" can count as a politics. Though he neglects the cause of the other when the injustice to the other does not happen on French soil, though (for all his famous commitment to the theme of equality) he omits the themes of economic exploitation and inequality that loom large in Sartre's preface, though his overriding concern is with "the struggle against war" (208) and he does not explore the possibility that war can serve the economic self-interest of some (perhaps including some of the poor) as well as injure or limit the self-interest of those who fight in or pay for it – in spite of all this, the key point is that he does not allow politics to be defined by self-interest. He rejects the definition of politics as a community's self-interested self-preservation ("conservation de soi"). Political subjectivity, as he presents it, is never identical with group self-interest: it is only by embracing "the cause of the other" that the worker or proletarian separates off from a group identity fighting for its interests against other groups and becomes a figure for citizenship. For Rancière, in other words, disinterestedness, which seemed a reason why action taken elsewhere would not count as politics, which would thus distinguish politics from humanism or humanitarianism or simply an ethical concern for the other, is actually an unavoidable part of what makes a cause genuinely political.

Disinterestedness seems a plausible dividing line between politics, which denies it, and humanitarianism, which depends on it. Yet only a certain disinterestedness would make possible a political community across national borders, such as the anti-Nazi solidarity that Orwell desperately hoped would emerge (and yet also despaired of achieving) between the English and their Indian colonial subjects. In retrospect, Orwell's project seems ambitious but not impossible or irresponsibly utopian. One might say on the contrary that given the state of global economic inequality, it is only a political project on that extremely daunting scale that has a chance of being truly responsible.

Rancière is of course virtually unique among recent philosophers in his attention to inequality.[21] In *The Philosopher and His Poor* he argues that

---

[21] The first words of Oliver Davis' *Jacques Rancière* (Cambridge: Polity, 2010) are "Jacques Rancière, the philosopher of equality," vii.

maintaining the disparity between himself and the poor he claims to represent is definitive of Sartre's philosophy, though not Sartre's alone.[22] The problem with this view of inequality is that, like certain understandings of racism, it is always making a powerful appeal for change but is incapable of recognizing change if and when it occurs. Inequality is eternal: it is always a correct description of any given time and place because no historical movement or event is capable of diminishing it. This problem is laid out neatly, though in a slightly different vocabulary, by Oliver Marchart.[23] Marchart's term for Rancière's position is "emancipatory apriorism" (133). In his view, Rancière posits equality as a universal, then shows how in a given case it is not in fact true of the poor. Finally equality is "verified" (that is, enacted) by the political action of the poor. This means that politics for Rancière "is either egalitarian, or it is not politics" (135, emphasis mine). All politics can do is confirm a principle, equality, that comes from nowhere and remains what it was at its origin, forever sending out the same appeal. Rancière cannot explain how equality is "instituted" (143), as Marchart puts it. How the sum of equality has been added to, if and when it has been, cannot register on Rancière's instruments. One enactment cannot build on the previous one. In order to retain the purity of worker agency, Rancière cannot permit enactments of equality to accumulate, succeeding here even if they also fail there, and thus forming a historical shape that determines the conditions under which the next effort will take place. Each time, it is as if the seeker of equality had to go back and start all over again from the beginning.[24]

On the history of global egalitarianism

Those who care about the goal of equality and the prospects for realizing it in the world will want to know, *pace* Rancière, how the concept came into the world – how, when, and why demands for economic equality began to be formulated, over what obstacles they triumphed when they did, how the playing field has and has not changed, and so on. These are

---

[22] Jacques Rancière, *The Philosopher and His Poor*, A. Parker (ed.) (Durham, NC: Duke University Press, 2004).

[23] Oliver Marchart, "The Second Return of the Political: Democracy and the Syllogism of Equality," in Paul Bowman and Richard Stamp, (eds.), *Reading Rancière* (London: Continuum, 2011), 129–147.

[24] Except that the beginning is not a zero point. Efforts always begin from the principle of equality itself, which is a given and has a certain historical power. It and not something else is what calls out to be verified, and it sustains those who try to verify it. Yet it is simply posited by Rancière, an *a priori* that must necessarily remain inexplicable.

questions that could lead us to the history of the labor movement and socialism, or at a philosophical level to the (relatively recent) emergence of a concept of distributive justice.[25] Where specifically global economic equality is concerned, further factors would have to be added; the intensification of international trade would obviously have to be tracked along with colonial conquests, anti-colonial movements, communication technologies, and trans-national philanthropic and legal institutions. All or most of these would have to be invoked in order to explain how Orwell, Sartre, Shawn, and others were able to say what they said about prosperity at home being scandalously linked to misery elsewhere.

I can begin the process of historical explanation, and at the same time illustrate the understanding of history that invites me to find their voices significant, by speaking briefly about one sort of literary evidence that seems relevant here: what I call the commodity recognition scene. Commodity recognition scenes are epiphanies in which some familiar consumer good is suddenly recognized as coming from a distant place of origin and from the labor, perhaps the coerced or otherwise unpleasant labor, of the distant inhabitants. The first commodity recognition scenes I know belong to a tradition in which a male moralist points the finger at a woman in the act of consuming a luxury. An early example would be when Jonathan Swift's Gulliver observes that "this whole globe of earth must be three times gone round, before one of our better female yahoos could get her breakfast, or a cup to put it in."[26] Swift of course fails to note that what's true for a female yahoo drinking her morning tea out of a porcelain cup is equally true for yahoos who are male; they drink the same tea out of the same cups. Commodity recognition scenes emerge only when they can target the supposed consumer excesses of women – in other words, they emerge with a strong push from misogyny. And yet a misogynous recognition of distant labor is better than no recognition. Once the recognition is out there, the possibility exists for the misogyny to be subtracted from it. The materials were highly imperfect, but the recognition could be built on. And this is in fact what happened. Blamed for their luxurious consumption, many eighteenth-century women drew the conclusion that what they consumed was a political matter, and a political matter because it connected their households to the distant labor of others. Much of the labor, they then realized, was performed by slaves. Logically enough, therefore, women took the lead in the boycotts that

[25] See Samuel Fleischacker, *A Short History of Distributive Justice* (Cambridge, Mass.: Harvard University Press, 2004).

[26] Jonathan Swift, *Gulliver's Travels*, ed. Christopher Fox (Boston and New York: Bedford/ St. Martin's Press, 1995), Part IV, Chapter 6, 229.

accompanied the abolitionist campaigns of the late eighteenth century aimed at cane sugar produced by slaves. The conditions of Caribbean labor lay right there before you, as close as your teacup. One Quaker pamphlet popularized the equation of a pound of sugar with two ounces of a slave's flesh. To refuse sugar was to strike a blow against slavery. It is hard to see how such a symbolic act could not count as participation in what Rancière calls the "cause of the other."

These are of course the same women of whom Sheller speaks in the essay mentioned above. Where Sheller sees racism and white privilege, I see an internalized misogyny. For both of us, a commitment to ending slavery is accompanied and indeed enabled by unsavory and undesirable circumstances. The difference is my assumption that it is only in such a manner that historically desirable things happen – which in this case they did.

Let me give another brief example. Alongside misogynous anti-consumerism, another chapter in the development of a norm of global economic justice would deal with the welfare state. The welfare state, too, is an unlikely and unsuitable agent of cosmopolitanism: unlikely and unsuitable because it doesn't try to abolish inequality, but only to moderate its worst effects, and because it aims only at the domestic population, choosing not to acknowledge the existence of economic suffering outside the nation's borders even if, as sometimes happens, that nation is at least partly responsible for causing that suffering. Yet it is not clear that economic cosmopolitanism could have come into being in any other way. It's only the rise of the welfare state that enabled people to recognize for the first time not only the *justice of* re-distributing social resources so as to protect the victims of the market, but also the *feasibility* of doing so. From the moment when the welfare state became a more or less effective agent of re-distribution, capable of offering a safety net for the most vulnerable, if not more, from the moment when it was seen as capable to at least some degree of compensating for the inadequacies of the market within the borders of the nation, its example was also available for use at a scale beyond the nation. And much of the anti- or counter-globalization movement has drawn exactly this conclusion, calling for capitalism's "regulation" just as the anti-sweatshop has continued the work of the anti-sugar boycott.

These are by no means stories of simple cumulative progress. The abolition of slavery did not of course end exploitative labor, but it did end the boycott movement. Metropolitan consumers could not immediately imagine that "free" labor might also have to count as exploited labor. The international inequality of living standards, which was not invisible, could now be dismissed as the result of industriousness on the one side, laziness on the other. That is another reason why insights like Sartre's and Orwell's had to wait for the anti-meritocratic reasoning that eventually enabled the welfare state, which broke the Christian link between prosperity and moral worth. And why – the welfare state itself being in well-publicized danger – we are still waiting for statements like Orwell's and Sartre's to become more representative of common sense.

Rancière on human rights

By way of conclusion, let me return to human rights. Rancière's position on human rights could be predicted from his earlier account of the French struggle against French colonialism in Algeria – that it does not become political except at the moment of French police brutality in the streets of Paris. In "Who Is the Subject of the Rights of Man?" Rancière does not merely object that human rights has lent itself to the program of humanitarian interference; he proclaims that it is the very logic of human rights that they should be transformed into (military) action "on the world stage" (309).[27] The words may seem casual or random, perhaps expressing no more than legitimate outrage about the US invasion of Iraq the year before, about its ongoing consequences and about the role of human rights discourse in sweetening the public image of the killing. But Rancière insists on the shift to the planetary scale. The space of politics, he argues, has been diminishing every day, and as it diminishes rights "appear actually empty" (307). What follows is a parable of geographical expansion as an emptying out of politics. "When [rights] are of no use, you do the same as charitable people do with their old clothes. You give them to the poor. These rights that appear to be useless in their place are sent abroad, along with medicine and clothes, to people deprived of medicine, clothes, and rights. It is in this way, as the result of this process, that the Rights of Man [les droits de l'homme: the words could as properly be translated as "human rights"] become the rights of those who have no rights, the rights of bare human beings subjected to inhuman repression and inhuman conditions of existence. They become humanitarian rights, the rights of those who cannot enact them" (307).

Even the reader who shares every iota of Rancière's indignation should be wary of the parable he offers here about "abroad." "Abroad" is not only the place of more intense and absolute deprivation; it is also the place where there is no politics. Politics is replaced by humanitarianism

---

[27] Jacques Rancière, "Who Is the Subject of the Rights of Man?," *South Atlantic Quarterly*, 103(2/3) (2004), 297–310.

because the hyper-deprived are imagined as incapable of performing the sort of demand that would make rights useful. Hence demands are made in their name –this is the definition of humanitarianism – but they make no demands of their own. Human rights are symptomatic of the move from "national stages" (309) to "the world stage" (309) because, once again, Rancière has trouble imagining any political solidarity (like that between Algerians and Frenchmen fighting French imperialism) or any politics at all that is not specific to and firmly anchored in the soil of one nation. He sees the assertion of rights as the dissolution of political community. "Abroad" is neither a casual metaphor nor a bit of high sarcasm. It is the figure for a fear: the fear that dissensus, by which Rancière defines politics, might not be such a good thing after all, that it might get out of hand and end by dissolving the political community on which (as Rancière does not admit) he depends in order to limit that dissensus, to keep it manageable.

Rights, for Rancière, are not a possession; they exist only insofar as they are asserted and actively claimed. This sounds properly bracing. But while it stresses the urgency of action, it undermines that action in advance by denying that afterwards any result will remain. If the active claim of rights in one generation cannot be passed down to the next generation as a possession or legacy, if that next generation or even next set of actors must start from zero, possession-less, than what is the point of acting in the first place? Rancière sounds like a defender of democracy when he attacks democracy's attackers, but he asserts that "We do not live in democracies" (73).[28] If not, then what is there to defend? In spite of all Rancière's indignant words, his position is in effect that no moves in the direction of egalitarianism have taken and occupied territory or conferred any advantage on those who come after. In a kind of frenzy of voluntarism or presentism, the urgency of doing something now makes anything done before now disappear, including the establishment of rights, however fragile.

There is a useful contrast here with Étienne Balibar both on Algeria and on human rights. Balibar's essay "Blanchot l'insoumis (à propos de l'écriture du Manifeste des 121)", which refers to Rancière's commentary on Sartre's preface, is also centrally about the meaning of French anti-imperialism in the context of the Algerian struggle for national liberation.[29] Its emphasis, however, falls on the fact that as originally

---

[28] Jacques Rancière, *Hatred of Democracy*, (trans.) Steve Corcoran (London: Verso, 2006).

[29] Étienne Balibar, "Blanchot l'insoumis (à propos de l'écriture du Manifeste des 121)," in Étienne Balibar, *Citoyen Sujet et d'autres essais d'anthropologie philosophique* (Paris: Presses Universitaires de France, 2011), 435–461. The language of human rights does not seem

drafted (by Blanchot), the Manifesto was in fact entitled "Déclaration du droit à l'insoumission," or "declaration on the right of insubordination." The word "declaration" of course evokes the tradition that comes out of the French Revolution's Declaration of the Rights of Man and of the Citizen. It does so, Balibar adds, "not from the perspective of a revolution to come, but in the permanence of a revolution that has already been made, though always to be re-made, re-begun, re-activated" (440).

Balibar clearly and rightly shares Rancière's fear of complacency, but for him this fear has been re-framed and qualified by "the permanence of a revolution that has already been made" and that is thus firmly present, a resource that French protesters against French colonial brutality could (and did) appeal to. The revolutionary act of declaring rights, Balibar observes elsewhere, "was the anchoring point for the series of claims that, from the morrow of the Declaration, begin to base upon it their claims for the rights of women, of workers, of colonized 'races' to be incorporated into citizenship" (43).[30] There are always good reasons for thinking of rights as something to be conquered. Those who think it is enough to defend rights they already firmly possess are fooling themselves. Still, it is equally foolish to imagine that like Sisyphus we are forever damned to begin at the beginning, that in the domain of rights there is no such thing as what the French call an *acquis* – an achievement.

to have played much of a role in this or other national liberation struggles. On the contrary, it rode the wave of those struggles. Still, it is noteworthy that Sartre, who did not write this manifesto although he signed it (a brave act at the time) and is often associated with it, repeatedly used the language of human rights in his arguments in favor of the Algerian struggle of national liberation. In 1957, Sartre writes: "Colonialism denies human rights to people it has subjugated by violence, and whom it keeps in poverty and ignorance by force" (Albert Memmi, *The Colonizer and the Colonized*, in Jean-Paul Sartre, *Colonialism and Neocolonialism*, (trans.) Azzedine Haddour, Steve Brewer and Terry McWilliams, with a Preface by Robert Young and a new Introduction by Azzedine Haddour, London: Routledge, 2006 [2001], 58). The anti-rights position, Sartre writes, is taken by the colons, the French settlers who are trying to cling to their privileges as a non-Arab minority. They "detest the token universality of French institutions. Precisely because they apply to everyone, the Algerians could claim these rights" ("Colonialism as a System," in *Colonialism and Neocolonialism*, 51). If we're going to judge human rights not by what they say but by what they do in the world, then we cannot forget that the strongest voices against rights are settlers and slaveholders and shameless tyrants.

30 Étienne Balibar, "'Rights of Man' and 'Rights of the Citizen': The Modern Dialectic of Equality and Freedom," in Étienne Balibar, *Masses, Classes, Ideas: Studies on Politics and Philosophy Before and After Marx*, (trans.) James Swenson ((New York and London: Routledge, 1994), 29–59.

15   However incompletely, human

Joseph R. Slaughter

> WE have hitherto considered persons in their natural capacities, and
> have treated of their rights and duties. But, as all personal rights die with
> the person; and, as the necessary forms of investing a series of
> individuals, one after another, with the same identical rights, would be
> very inconvenient, if not impracticable; it has been found necessary,
> when it is for the advantage of the public to have any particular rights
> kept on foot and continued, to constitute artificial persons, who may
> maintain a perpetual succession, and enjoy a kind of legal immortality.[1]

In Königsberg at the end of the eighteenth century, "person" was the
basic moral unit anchoring Immanuel Kant's categorical imperative – the
name for those creatures whose "rationality" and insuperable "dignity"
"already marks them out as an end in itself."[2] In classical Greece,
"person" referred to the "face," which in Roman theater became a mask
worn by an actor, and later the actor himself. In Philadelphia in 1787, at
the US Constitutional Convention, "person" was the unit of measure that
determined the apportionment of political representation to the states,
based on a formula that counted "the whole Number of free Persons";
"all other persons" to be tallied at the discounted rate of five for three.
In 1719, on an island in the Orinoco effluence, "person" referred to
Poll, Robinson Crusoe's domesticated parrot, who "was the only Person
permitted to talk" to the shipwrecked sailor.[3] In England, during the
era of high imperialism, "person" was the legal fiction that gave life to
the business corporation (the colonial charter company) and granted
immortality to certain rights that would ordinarily "die with the [natural]
person."[4] In 1947, "person" was the "continental" concept internationalized in the draft of the Universal Declaration of Human Rights (UDHR)
that, according to Eleanor Roosevelt, started a "storm" among State
Department lawyers who insisted that it was a legal figure alien to US

[1] W. Blackstone, *Commentaries on the Laws of England* (London, 1793–1795), 467.
[2] I. Kant, *Groundwork on the Metaphysics of Morals* (Cambridge University Press, 1998), 37.
[3] D. Defoe, *Robinson Crusoe, Norton Critical Edition* (New York: W. W. Norton, 1994), 108.
[4] Blackstone, *Commentaries*, 467.

law; the storm abated in embarrassment when it was discovered that there was indeed a precedent for "person" in US law, when Supreme Court Justice Roger Taney opined for the majority in the *Dred Scott* decision in 1857 that "a slave has no juridical personality" and therefore no right to recognition anywhere as a person before the law.[5]

The formal inspiration for the opening gambit of this essay is Jorge Luis Borges' short story, *"El Zahir"* (1949), in which the narrator ("Borges") compiles an elaborate, imaginary pan-Arabic catalogue of the multiple manifestations of *Zahir*, "one of the ninety-nine names of God" that "the people (in Muslim territories) use ... to signify 'beings or things which possess the terrible property of being unforgettable, and whose image finally drives one mad'."[6] Among those fascinating things, were "a small compass," "a copper astrolabe," "the bottom of a well," and "a species of infinite Tiger ... [a painted figure] made up of many tigers fused in the most vertiginous manner."[7] One inauspicious day in June in early twentieth-century Buenos Aires, the *Zahir* appears to the narrator ("Borges") in the form of an "ordinary coin" that fascinates him to the point of incapacitation, transforming him such that although he remains, "however incompletely, Borges"[8] he is no longer "the person [he once] was."[9] In the vertiginous play of appearances in Borges' metaphysical fiction, *al-Zahir*, which the narrator translates from the Arabic as "notorious, visible," entails its opposite, *al-Batin*, which names God as hidden, invisible, concealed.[10] Himself transformed and transfixed by the metamorphic *Zahir*, the narrator is struck with the remarkable capacity to visualize both faces (*personae*) of the coin simultaneously; as he descends into madness with his new "spherical" eyesight, the narrator takes some consolation in the thought that "[p]erhaps behind the coin I shall find God."[11]

Like *al-Zahir*, "person" is itself notorious in the realm of law – a sign whose meaning everyone apparently already knows, even if there is

---

[5] E. Roosevelt, "Making Human Rights Come Alive," Speech to Pi Lambda Theta (New York: Columbia University, 30 March 1949), www.udhr.org/history/114.htm, accessed on May 29, 2001.

[6] J. L. Borges, "The Zahir," in J. L. Borges, *A Personal Anthology*, (ed.) A. Kerrigan (New York: Grove Press, 1967), 128–137 at 134. I am using two different translations of Borges' story, distinguished here by the year of publication.

[7] Borges, "the Zahir," (1967), 134–135.

[8] J. L. Borges, "The Zahir," in J. L. Borges, *Labyrinths: Selected Stories & Other Writings*, (introd.) W. Gibson (New York: New Directions, 2007), 156–164 at 156.

[9] Borges, "The Zahir," (1967), 128.   [10] Borges, "The Zahir," (1967), 134.

[11] Borges, "The Zahir," (2007), 163, 164. In Borges' story, the problem of the apparent and the hidden is an exegetical problem, and it parallels in many ways the (inter)play of appearances between the technical term "person" and the humanist term "human" in the text of international human rights law that I explore throughout this chapter.

"no created thing in the world which could not take on the properties" of a person before the law.[12] Unlike *al-Zahir*, which manifests itself (and its transfixing apparency) in only one thing and one place at any one time, "person" appears to appear everywhere at once, where the expansive "everyone" in "Everyone has the right to recognition everywhere as a person before the law" (as declared in Art. 6 of the UDHR) seems to have no limiting principle behind it in the law; that is, as John Dewey complained in 1926, "person" might mean "whatever the law makes it mean [...]; it] might be used simply as a synonym for a right-and-duty-bearing unit. Any such unit would be a person."[13] Nonetheless, like *al-Batin*, "person" is also apparently hidden behind the "human" in human rights, concealed, it seems, behind the figure of the human, which has so fascinated scholars in the humanities, social sciences, and legal studies in the past few decades that we have almost forgotten that "man" has at least ninety-nine other names. Indeed, when it comes to human rights and international law, the human presumably behind it all seems not to possess *al-Zahir*'s "terrible property" of being unforgettable.

The law seems to forget the human rather quickly, in favor of the *terminus technicus*, "person." Or, perhaps the "human being" eludes law's grasp precisely at the moment when what the ancient Greeks called "unwritten law" is transcribed, when natural law is positivized; the human disappears behind ambiguous pronouns, passive constructions, and mysterious personifications. "All human beings" may be "*born* free and equal in dignity and rights" (as the UDHR declares in Art. 1), but, to be "enjoyed," that birth-right dignity must be supplemented by other rights: thus, for example, "Everyone has the right to life, liberty, and security of person" (Art. 3) and "Everyone has the right to recognition everywhere as a person before the law" (Art. 6). Indeed, historically "human rights" is something of a misnomer, and not simply because contemporary human rights law evolved in part from the law of peoples, or law of nations. The UDHR starts with the "human being" as the titular, eponymous *subject* of human rights, but it (and the International Covenants that followed and fortified it) very quickly shifts focus to the "person" as the *vehicle* of human rights. "Person" functions as a juridical pronoun whose antecedent appears to be the human, however incompletely; but this subtle displacement of the "human being" by "the person" all but eliminated "the human" as a noun from the text of

[12] Borges, "The Zahir," (1967), 128.
[13] J. Dewey, "The Historic Background of Corporate Legal Personality," *Yale Law Review*, 35(6), 655–673 at 656.

human rights law. Perhaps behind the person, we shall find the human; perhaps behind the human, we shall find God ... or the coin.

When did we begin to think that human rights were all about us?

Human rights law is a personifying law that articulates the rights of the human being in advance of their full realization in the world and, there-fore, also in advance of the appearance of the human who could enjoy its human rights in full. Questions about what or who stands behind human rights have constantly shadowed their declaration. Who is behind such statements as "All human beings are born free and equal in dignity and rights"? And who is anticipated? Who guarantees this sort of rights-talk? Who is this creature that declares human rights, claims human rights, and bears human rights as a birth-right?

Contemporary commonsense notwithstanding, the human has not always been the obvious answer to these questions. Edmund Burke, Karl Marx, and Hannah Arendt all famously argued that the eighteenth-century bourgeois revolutions introduced a categorical split between the human and the person that is reflected in the very title of the French *Déclaration des Droits de l'Homme et du Citoyen*. The modern human rights regime, Marx argued, bifurcated and "reduc[ed] man, on the one hand, to a member of civil society, to an egoistic, independent individual, and, on the other hand, to a citizen, a juridical person."[14] Under this Westphalian paradigm, so-called human rights attached not to "man" but to the citizen, opening what Jacques Rancière has described as "an interval for political subjectiviza-tion," in which rights that go by the name of "human" are claimed, tested, and extended through political struggles.[15] The "human" of human rights is not simply given; in fact, in a strict technical sense it is the juridical figure of the "person" that gives human rights to human beings. In a less strict sense, the person gives the human of human rights to the human being. The law works in two-dimensional space, with flattened figures and pro-jected images; the "person" is just such a projection, but it is not necessarily a projection of the human being. Indeed, the *persona ficta* of the law is an empty vessel, a rhetorical figure – "not so much a trope for 'individual man' as it is a trope for a position in certain contexts," in Miguel Tamen's

[14] K. Marx, "On the Jewish Question," in K. Marx and F. Engels, *Collected Works* (London: Lawrence & Wishart, 1975), 3, 146–174 at 167.
[15] J. Rancière, "Who is the Subject of the Rights of Man?," *South Atlantic Quarterly*, 103(2/3) (2004), 297–310 at 304. In *Human Rights, Inc.* and "Enabling Fictions and Novel Subjects," I have argued that the *Bildungsroman* (the novel of coming-of-age) is the normative generic literary form that tells the story of this process of subjectivization.

suggestive description.[16] Historically, the legal category of "person" precedes the "human" of human rights;[17] juridically, the legal category of the "person" carries certain rights and duties that precede the individual, that (perhaps) await activation in – or occupation by – the human.[18]

"Person" may seem to anticipate the "human," but the interval between the two is also open to other prospective occupants. Recently some scholars and activists have expressed concern about a corporate takeover of human rights, what Anna Grear has described as "the discursive colonisation of international human rights law" by corporations.[19] Marius Emberland has documented what he calls "the human rights of companies" in his study of how the European Court of Human Rights has, in its fifty-year history, increasingly recognized rights that we typically think of as belonging only to human beings as also belonging to corporations. If the acquisition of human rights by corporations seems a scandal of late capitalism and neo-liberal economic policies, we should remember, with Upendra Baxi, that "[l]ong before slavery was abolished, and women got recognition for the right to contest and vote at elections, corporations had appropriated rights to *personhood*, claiming due process rights for regimes of property, denied to human beings."[20] Thus, while it may be "urgent to challenge the emergence of corporate legal humanity in the discourse of human rights,"[21] it seems

---

[16] M. Tamen, "Kinds of Persons, Kinds of Rights, Kinds of Bodies," *Cardozo Studies in Law and Literature*, 10(1) (1998), 1–32 at 22.

[17] Alexander Nékám observes that historically "it was a so-called artificial person, the family, and not the so-called natural person, the individual, which made its first appearance in law," A. Nékám, *The Personality Conception of the Legal Entity* (Cambridge. Mass.: Harvard University Press, 1938), 23.

[18] For detailed histories of legal personality across the Western tradition, see R. Saleilles, *De la personnalité juridique: histoire et théories: vingt-cinq leçons d'introduction à un cours de droit civil comparé sur les personnes juridiques* (Paris: A. Rousseau, 1910); G. Del Vecchio, "Right and Human Personality in the History of Thought," *The International Journal of Ethics*, 30(2) (1920); J. Dewey, "The Historic Background of Corporate Legal Personality," *Yale Law Review*, 35(5) (1926); Nékám, *The Personality Conception*; P. Stein, 'Nineteenth Century English Company Law and Theories of Legal Personality," *Quaderni Fiorentini*, 11/12(1) (1982–1983); G. A. Mark, "The Personification of the Business Corporation in American Law," *The University of Chicago Law Review*, 54(4), 1441–1483 (1987); S. A. Schane, "The Corporation is a Person: The Language of a Legal Fiction," *Tulane Law Review*, 61, 563–609 (1987); J. E. Nijman, *The Concept of International Legal Personality: an Enquiry into the History and Theory of International Law* (The Hague: T. M. C. Asser Press, 2004); A. Grear, *Redirecting Human Rights: Facing the Challenge of Corporate Legal Humanity* (New York: PalgraveMacmillan, 2010); F. Johns, *International Legal Personality* (Burlington, Vt.: Ashgate, 2010); R. Portmann, *Legal Personality in International Law* (Cambridge University Press, 2010).

[19] Grear, *Redirecting Human Rights*, 3.

[20] U. Baxi, *The Future of Human Rights* (New Delhi and New York: Oxford University Press, 2008), 263.

[21] Grear, *Redirecting Human Rights*, 205.

equally important to re-examine the role of corporations in the history of human rights and to consider how, through the vehicle of the international person, human beings may have captured (as human rights) some of the legal rights of corporations.

In the voluminous literature on its legal status, the corporation is generally described as something more than a group person made up of individual persons (as in the famous frontispiece illustrating Hobbes' *Leviathan*), like Borges' infinite Tiger made up of other tigers—a species of infinite person fused in the most vertiginous manner. Rather, the story of corporate personhood is usually told as a tale of how "an artificial being, invisible, intangible, and existing only in contemplation of law" (in US Supreme Court Chief Justice John Marshall's words) acquired a legal life of its own, becoming a juridical person in its own right.[22] By most accounts, the corporation initially gained its "artificial" legal personality by way of analogy to the "natural" human being that figured the company as an assemblage of organic body parts and drives – a collection of qualities and capacities that we ordinarily think of as features unique to human beings. The state vested this bundle of capacities in the form of the corporation with specific rights and responsibilities in order to pursue the public good. However, the enabling figure of speech that personified the corporation has since become a dead metaphor in both common language and the law.[23] We now generally regard the corporation as having a natural life of its own – just as we can hardly avoid the conceptual collapse of the metaphor that founds human rights law, the "almost inevitable conceptual convergence between the notion of the person and the notion of the human being."[24] Over the course of the nineteenth century in Europe and the United States, the business corporation came to be regarded as having an autonomous political and legal status independent from (if subordinated to) the state that originally created it, "an autonomy that demanded the respect and consequent restraint of the state."[25] This "organicist vision," writes Gregory Mark, "proved an emancipation." Indeed, in the United States, the same law that codified the emancipation of ex-slaves, granting them full legal personality under the Fourteenth Amendment to the US Constitution, also liberated the corporation. The business company was given equal protection from state power when the moral sentiment in the US

[22] Cited in I. M. Wormser, *Frankenstein Incorporated* (New York: Whittlesey House, 1931), 57.

[23] Schane, "The Corporation is a Person," 563–609.

[24] Grear, *Redirecting Human Rights*, 49.

[25] Mark, "The Personification of the Business Corporation," 1470.

Declaration of Independence that "all men are created equal" was revised into the legal statement that "No State shall ... deny to any person within its jurisdiction the equal protection of the laws."[26] The corporation now enjoys, nearly universally, at least one of the fundamental human rights articulated in the UDHR, since it has already been recognized (almost) everywhere as a person before the law.

Historically, the "orthodox positivist doctrine" of international law recognized only sovereign states as "subjects of international law."[27] Indeed, the late nineteenth- and early twentieth-century advocates of international law were adamant on this. "Every State which belongs to the civilised States ... is an International Person. Sovereign States exclusively are International Persons – i.e. subjects of International Law," insisted Lassa Oppenheim in his foundational *International Law*.[28] According to this Westphalian view, only states had legal rights and responsibilities at an international level or the capacity to promote and protect those rights through international legal means. As such, "[h]umans, individually and collectively, generally had no direct international personality" until human rights emerged after the Second World War as a legal regime that internationalized the legal and human personality of the individual.[29] Thus, the development of human rights law becomes a story of the arrival of the individual human being on the world stage as a subject of international rights and duties, a subject constituted by international law with a kind of inviolable and inalienable individual, or personal, sovereignty. Actual practice across the nineteenth and twentieth centuries, however, "shows that persons and bodies other than States are often made subjects of international rights and duties," Hersch Lauterpacht noted, arguing for an international bill of rights in the late 1940s.[30] Indeed, in the nineteenth century, colonial

---

[26] In the US context, the corporation walked through the legal door opened by the abolition of slavery and the fourteenth amendment – see S. V. Hartman, *Scenes of Subjection: Terror, Slavery and Self-Making in Nineteenth-Century America* (New York: Oxford University Press, 1997); A. Allen, "The Political Economy of Blackness: Citizenship, Corporations, and Race in *Dred Scott*," *Civil War History*, 50(3) (2004); D. Nabers, *Victory of Law: the Fourteenth Amendment, the Civil War, and American Literature, 1852–1867* (Baltimore, Md.: Johns Hopkins University Press, 2006). How the corporation achieved its progressive emancipation on the backs of women and minorities more generally by taking advantage of laws ostensibly intended to incorporate historically marginalized groups fully into the body politic deserves more study.

[27] H. Lauterpacht, "The Subjects of the Law of Nations," in H. Lauterpacht, *International Legal Personality*, F. Johns, (ed.) (Farnham: Ashgate, 2010), 174.

[28] L. Oppenheim, *International Law: A Treatise* (London: Longmans, Green & Co., 1905), 99.

[29] J. Hickey and E. James, "The Source of International Legal Personality in the 21st Century," *Hofstra Law and Policy Symposium*, 21(1) (1997), 1–18 at 9.

[30] Lauterpacht, "The Subjects of the Law," 179.

charter companies navigated the globe as international legal persons. This status is especially clear in their quasi-state capacities, as "mediate territorial sovereign[s]," to make treaties and establish governments among colonized peoples.[31] In this sense, then, the legal category not only precedes the arrival of the individual human being as an international person; the business corporation also precedes the individual human being to the international realm as a right- and duty-bearing subject. If "person" is, as Tamen said, "a trope for a position" in particular contexts, then we might say that the position within the international realm currently occupied by the human being has also already been occupied by the corporation. In other words, the business corporation might already have beaten human beings to human rights.

When we speak of the personification of the business corporation, we ordinarily imagine the company to be modeled on analogy to the human being. But, as Barbara Johnson suggested in her provocative essay "Anthropomorphism in Lyric and Law," what if the "[t]heories of rationality, naturalness, and the 'good,' presumed to be grounded in the nature of 'man,' ... [were] in reality ... taking their notions of human essence not from 'natural man' but from business corporations"?[32] It is probably true enough in the domestic scene of national law that the corporation achieved its independence by way of analogy to the human being, but, applied to the international realm, Johnson's seemingly counterintuitive provocation seems more descriptive than suggestive. If, over the course of the nineteenth century, the corporation became a full legal person at home, during that same time, through mercantile colonialism abroad, the corporation became an international person, however incompletely. In his magisterial study, *Imperialism, Sovereignty, and the Making of International Law*, Antony Anghie has demonstrated that "colonialism was central to the constitution of international law in that many of the basic doctrines of international law ... were forged out of an attempt to create a legal system that could account for relations between the European and non-European worlds."[33] The colonial charter company was more than a vehicle for the pursuit of nineteenth-century

---

[31] J. Westlake, *Chapters on the Principles of International Law* (Cambridge University Press, 1894), 192.

[32] B. Johnson, "Anthropomorphism in Lyric and Law," *Yale Journal of Law and the Humanities*, 10, 549–574 at 573.

[33] A. Anghie, *Imperialism, Sovereignty, and the Making of International Law* (Cambridge and New York: Cambridge University Press, 2004), 3. In a sense, Anghie puts things the other way around from Martti Koskenniemi in *The Gentle Civilizer of Nations: The Rise and Fall of International Law, 1870–1960* (Cambridge University Press, 2002), where international law develops to support colonialism.

colonialism. Not only was the company charged with carrying some of what we now call human rights to supposedly backwards peoples in the unenlightened parts of the earth; it was itself the bearer of some international rights now regarded as the human rights of individuals. Indeed, a collection of qualities and capacities we typically think of as uniquely human were first combined and protected at the international level in the legal personalities of charter companies. As I argue below, corporations, and especially the colonial charter companies, were recognized as international persons in advance of the human beings they ostensibly served, and, thus, as much as we need to be vigilant about the current "colonization" of international, human rights law by corporations, we need also to recognize the complex ways in which international, corporate, and human rights law are all intertwined, and how the early international law of high imperialism set the stage for the emergence of human beings as international persons in their own rights.

Floating signifiers and castaway creatures of human rights

"It is, of course, commonplace," writes Antony Anghie, "that human rights theory has been significantly shaped by an idea of possessive individualism that focuses on economic rights, most notably the right to property."[34] Not merely human rights theory, I would add, but also human rights law; and not merely an economic right to property, but also a moral individual right to a Lockean property in one's own person that is often construed as an economic right to property as such. Locke's ideas about property creation and ownership – particularly about owning property in one's self – have influenced the elaboration of human rights law from early modern articulations such as the English Bill of Rights (1689), the French Declaration of the Rights of Man and of the Citizen (1789), and the US Bill of Rights (1789) to late modern amplifications in contemporary international law. By an elisionary calculus, in which human rights are personal rights and personal rights are property rights, individualism becomes a possession. The self becomes a form of property, and international law becomes a regime of "trade-related, market-friendly human rights."[35]

The drafters of the UDHR shared these basic possessive individualist assumptions about human nature. In this regard, the characterization of rights as properties by the USSR delegate to the UN's Third Committee

[34] Angie, *Imperialism*, 270.   [35] Baxi, *The Future of Human Rights*, xxxi.

on Social, Humanitarian, and Cultural Affairs in the Fall of 1948 reflects a fairly common sentiment: "each individual was a possessor of rights and could, therefore, insist that his rights should be recognized."[36] The category of the "person" was nominated as the legal vehicle by which the individual could claim possession of his or her rights.[37] Amid the more common references to Locke and Rousseau, Lenin and Marx, members of the Third Committee also debated the moral implications of that quintessential novelistic study of possessive individualism, Daniel Defoe's *Robinson Crusoe*, in their discussions of the text of what would become Article 29: "Everyone has duties to the community in which alone the free and full development of his personality is possible." I have elsewhere written about the curious appearance of Defoe's famous novel in the UDHR drafting debates, where it formed "the novelistic subtext of Article 29, … underwrit[ing] the law, warranting the legal image of the human personality, its sociality, and its role as the medium through which the reconciliation of the [desires of the] individual and [the demands of] society is to be effected and expressed."[38] I make no causal claims about the relation between the reading of a novel and the drafting of the law, but the literary image of the castaway Crusoe, with its myth of economic individualism and possessive self-sufficiency, has held powerful sway over theories of the subject in the Euro-American intellectual traditions – from Rousseau's recommendation in *Émile*, through Marx's illustration of a simple equation between labor and use-value, to the Belgian–USSR disputation in the Third Committee over whether *Crusoe* demonstrated that "the individual could attain the full development of his personality only within the framework of society."[39] I will approach *Robinson Crusoe* from a slightly different angle than the thematic meaning that concerned the drafters of the UDHR, because Defoe's narrative interest in the intertwined problems of property and personality creation make it possible to read a history of human rights through the discursive forms that constitute juridical personality in the novel. Contemporary international human rights law may be modeled on (or may articulate) a particular theory of "economic man," but *homo economicus*, at least in Defoe's narrative sketch of modern

---

[36] United Nations, *Third Session, Proceedings of the Third Social and Humanitarian Committee* (Lake Success, NY: Third Committee, 1948), 227.

[37] My sense from the drafting debates is that each of the delegates had "some other person in mind" when they agreed to the juridical language of "personality," Slaughter, 2007), 57. In other words, the term "person" worked as a kind of empty signifier, in which each of the delegates could hear echoes of their own moral tradition of human dignity. Consensus was facilitated by misunderstandings and failed translations.

[38] Slaughter (2007), 54.   [39] United Nations, *Third Session*, 660.

rationalism and self-possession in the figure of Crusoe, was himself inflected by an emerging theory of corporate personhood. In his analysis of "the personification of the business corporation in American law," Gregory Mark concludes with the intriguing observation that by the early twentieth century "the business corporation had become the quintessential economic man."[40] At the other end of the history of corporate personification and on the other side of the Atlantic, in Defoe's early eighteenth-century novel, the textual forms that so-called rational self-interest takes overlap with the emerging textual technologies of corporate creation, management, and account-keeping. In other words, many of the discursive forms of personal accounting by which *homo economicus* takes narrative and textual possession of the self in the novel are marked by their simultaneous employment as forms of corporate chartering and bookkeeping.

Crusoe's well-known obsessions with contracts and account-keeping – and Defoe's representation of the texture of those obsessions – make it possible to perceive the outlines of a discursive history of legal personality that tracks from the emergence of economic individualism and corporate capitalism through mercantile colonialism and the "civilizing mission" to the appearance of the human individual and human rights as proper subjects of international law. The textual evolution of international human rights law is entangled with (and inseparable from) the documentary legal developments that made charter-company colonialism possible in the nineteenth century. Many of the juridical technologies that evolved to sustain the legal and international personality of the corporation (and later the human individual) are prefigured in Defoe's fable about economic man's self-constitution on the colonial frontier – an isolated realm where there seems to be no interval (or gap) between the "natural personality" of the human individual and the "artificial personality" of the corporate or juridical person. Indeed, Defoe's novel suggests that the imaginary figure of economic man (already, at its puted birth) was, quintessentially, a business corporation – a business "man." Specifically, I want to argue that economic man was created in the image of the colonial charter company.

This was all a Fiction ... yet it had its desired Effect

In his immensely influential, *The Rise of the Novel*, Ian Watt famously cited *Robinson Crusoe* as his primary textual evidence of the deep linkages among the novel genre, industrial capitalism, and modern (Lockean)

---

[40] Mark, "The Personification of the Business Corporation," 1483.

individualism.[41] The generic innovations of Defoe's novelistic study of the psychology of *homo economicus* combines popular forms of Protestant confessional autobiography with the mercantilist development of double-entry book-keeping, the formal accounting of profits and losses that Max Weber regards as central to the rise of economic rationalism. In fact, more than merely reflecting "a central theme in the modern social order," as Watt writes, Crusoe's obsessions with documentation, account-keeping, and (personal) inventory-taking become textual principles of narrative itself.[42] Thus, as much as Crusoe's journal serves as spiritual confession, it is also, quite simply, a corporate ledger in which the self is inked in red and black. Crusoe asserts his self-possession through a narrative of invoice, in which taking a written inventory of the self becomes a mode of production that turns raw thoughts and self-apperceptions into useful personal goods. After landing on the deserted island, Crusoe pauses to take stock of his "Condition, and the Circumstances I was reduc'd to," and "to set the good against the Evil, that I might have something to distinguish my Case from worse; and I state it very impartially, like Debtor and Creditor, the Comforts I enjoy'd, against the Miseries I suffer'd."[43] He puts his "Affairs in Writing," making his case in columns:

EVIL.	GOOD.
I am cast upon a horrible desolate Island, void of all Hope of Recovery.	But I am alive, and not drown'd, as all my Ship's Company was.
I am singl'd out and separated, as it were, from all the World to be miserable.	But I am singl'd out too from all the Ship's Crew to be spar'd from Death;
. . .	. . .
I have no Soul to speak to, or relieve me.	But God wonderfully sent the Ship in near enough to the Shore, that I have gotten out so many necessary things as will either supply my Wants, or enable me to supply my self even as long as I live.[44]

Crusoe also applies this rational principle of impartial accounting to the composition of his journal. Here is his narrative from his first days on the island:

---

[41] I. Watt, *The Rise of the Novel: Studies in Defoe, Richardson and Fielding* (1957) (University of California Press, 2001), 60.
[42] Ibid., 63.   [43] Ibid., 43.   [44] Ibid., 49–50.

September 30, 1659. I, poor, miserable *Robinson Crusoe*, being shipwreck'd, ... came on Shore on this dismal unfortunate Island, ... all the rest of the Ship's Company being drown'd, and my self almost dead... At the Approach of Night, I slept in a Tree for fear of wild Creatures, but slept soundly tho' it rain'd all Night.

October 1. In the Morning I saw to my great Surprise the Ship had ... driven on Shore again much nearer the Island, which as it was some Comfort on one hand ..., so on the other hand, it renew'd my Grief at the Loss of my Comrades ...[45]

The diary, like the double-entry account, counterposes the losses and gains: he's miserable but alive; fearing but sleeping soundly; grieving but comforted. This calculating narrative invoices the experience of daily life as a balancing of the books. More than a simple stock-book, as Marx has it in the first volume of *Capital* – that "contains a list of the objects of utility that belong to him, of the operations necessary for their production; and lastly, of the labour-time that definite quantities of those objects have, on an average, cost him"[46] – the "Journal of every Day's Employment" narrates personal existence and experience in the legalistic mode of corporate account-keeping.[47] Over the course of the journal, Crusoe emerges as the Lockean subject of his labors through a mode of narrative invoicing that accounts the self-possessive individual into existence, by accounting for the various costs (physical, mental, spiritual, psychological, administrative, and textual) of self-making.[48]

In Crusoe's account of himself, the textual modes of personal self-expression and moral self-possession are fully entangled with those of legal affidavits and corporate ledgers. In fact, in Crusoe's journal, what we ordinarily think of as private diary language begins in the mode of a public legal testament that asserts the integrity of the subject: "I, ... *Robinson Crusoe*, [of poor mind and miserable body,] being shipwreck'd ..." However, his testamentary account soon yields to an economic double-entry logic that weighs credits against debits. Each biographical event in Crusoe's life is registered twice (and, in fact, throughout the novel, often twice again), creating, as Weber says of the corporate bookkeeping method, "the fiction ... that different departments within an enterprise ... conduct exchange operations with each other."[49] In other words, Crusoe's narrative mode of account-keeping creates, or registers,

[45] Watt, *The Rise of the Novel*, 52.
[46] K. Marx, *Capital: A Critique of Political Economy* (Chicago: C. H. Kerr, 1907), 77.
[47] Defoe, *Robinson Crusoe*, 51.
[48] M. Seidel, *Robinson Crusoe: Island Myths and the Novel* (Boston, Mass.: Twayne, 1991), 79.
[49] M. Weber, *Economy and Society* (Berkeley, Cal.: University of California Press, 1978), 92–93.

a kind of split personality, an infinite person made up of other persons. As I will argue below, Crusoe accounts for a surplus of personality that manifests itself in three forms that each seems to have a characteristic textual mode of expression and personification: as a territorial sovereign, as a castaway individual (subject to that sovereignty), and as a corporate enterprise.

Defoe uses the word "person" on remarkably few occasions in *Robinson Crusoe*, and it often appears in its then most pedestrian sense, signifying the physical body and aspect of the human being: "the Captain knew the Persons and Characters of all the Men in the Boat, of whom he said, that there were three very honest Fellows."[50] Defoe distinguishes here the incarnate forms of the individual (Persons) from what we might think of today as the abstract moral qualities of personality (Characters), but even in this pedestrian use of "person," the term already marks these mutinous sailors as subjects of the law; "he [the Captain] told them [the mutineers] . . . that the Island was inhabited, and that the Governour was an *English* Man; that he might hang them all there, if he pleased; . . . Though this was all a Fiction . . ., yet it had its desired Effect."[51] There is, of course, no formal government and no formal legal system on Crusoe's island, but the mere creation of the fiction of their existence has the desired effect of personifying its potential subjects as creatures of the law, creatures constituted by and answerable to the law in its imposing abstraction. Indeed, throughout the novel, the category of "person" appears as a trope for a position within legalistic contexts that holds the place of a creature to come – a creature capable of legal representation, of being represented (and making representations) within the terms of Crusoe's improvised island regime. Thus, for example, Crusoe's domesticated parrot, Poll, is a person within his fantastical dominion: "there was my Majesty the Prince and Lord of the whole Island; I had the Lives of all my Subjects at my absolute Command. I could hang, draw, give Liberty, and take it away, and no Rebels among all my Subjects. . . *Poll*, as if he had been my Favourite, was the only Person permitted to talk to me."[52] Crusoe "grants" Poll legal personality and imagines his speech as freedom exchanged for his subjection; Poll is given the liberty of language in return for subjecting himself to Crusoe's commands. In this regard, it is worth noting the difference between Poll's "legal" status and that of Friday, who is a slave taken from the native population. While Crusoe names both, even fondly calling his "savage" "my *Man* Friday," Friday himself never seems to acquire full personhood.

[50] Defoe, *Robinson Crusoe*, 187.   [51] Ibid., 193.
[52] Ibid., 108.

The interval between Man and Person, in Friday's case, seems greater than that between Parrot and Person.

In Defoe's fiction, legal personality, on and off the island, is a vessel that carries certain rights and duties; personhood is grantable, revocable, portable, and transferable. In the scene where the law takes hold of the mutineers, hailing them to Crusoe's summons, the fictional appeal to sovereign authority has other personifying effects. Until this point, in his island isolation Crusoe has imagined himself "King and Lord of all this Country indefeasibly," with a "Right of Possession," having mixed his labor with the land;[53] "I was Lord of the whole Manor; or, if I pleas'd, I might call myself King or Emperor over the whole Country which I had Possession of. There were no Rivals. I had no Competitor, none to dispute Sovereignty or Command with me."[54] Over animals, savages, and selves, Crusoe simply claims sovereignty, but with the appearance of other people on the island, his "Right of Possession" no longer seems so inalienable, nor his Sovereignty undisputed. And so, when this self-declared King of the Island presents himself to the mutineers, they are told that "I was the Person the Governour had order'd to look after them, and that it was the Governour's Pleasure they should not stir any where, but by my Direction; ... so that as we never suffered them to see me as Governour, so I now appear'd as another Person." [55] Crusoe is no longer the person he once was; he no longer embodies sovereignty in the person of the Governor. Instead, he assumes its plenipotentiary mask in the form of another person, a representative (or functionary) of the imaginary sovereign's authority, creating the fiction that he transacts business between two parts of himself. Or, rather, then, he embodies the person of the sovereign *and* he *also* embodies a person of sovereignty's dispersed functions, occupying an office opened by positing the fiction of the sovereign. There is a kind of double-entry logic to Crusoe's (multiple personality) ruse: authority is debited on one side of the account to be credited on the other. Crusoe is here two persons at once: the island sovereign, as well as the individual castaway who works in the name of the sovereign (who derives his legal personality from the sovereign) and who is, according to this fiction, himself subjected to the sovereign's command. In the figure of "another Person," Crusoe presents himself to the sailors with something like "mediate sovereignty" – the derivative status, according to John Westlake, of the colonial charter company in early international law.[56] The Sovereign being Crusoe's fiction, this delegated person, too, is a fiction.

[53] Ibid., 73.   [54] Ibid., 94.   [55] Ibid., 195.
[56] Westlake, *Chapters*, 192.

If Crusoe's performance makes clear that his political sovereignty is a fiction, in other cases Crusoe's sovereign authority is clearly the effect (rather than the source) of documentary arrangements with other persons. When Crusoe rescues a shipwrecked Spaniard, whose shipmates are marooned nearby on the coast of South America, Crusoe gives him "leave to go over to the *Main*, to see what he could do with those he had left behind":

I gave him a strict Charge in Writing, Not to bring any Man with him, who would not first swear in the Presence of himself and of the old *Savage*, That he would no way injure, fight with, or attack the Person he should find in the Island, ... but that they would stand by and defend him against all such Attempts, and wherever they went, would be entirely under and subjected to his Commands.[57]

"[A]ny Man" may become a person under Crusoe's command, but Crusoe himself becomes simply "the Person" on the island, a kind of empty signifier that leaves open the particular legal capacities – rights and duties – that will be filled in by the terms of the agreement. "[T]his should be put in Writing, and signed with their Hands," Crusoe insists, although the lack of ink, having exhausted his supply on the diary, produces some anxiety over his sovereign status: "How we were to have this done, when I knew they had neither Pen or Ink; that indeed was a Question which we never asked." These sorts of subjugating oaths, which Crusoe contracts with a number of accidental visitors, operate according to a kind of recognition principle by which one sovereign *recognizes*, "with constitutive effect," the sovereignty of another; this is the traditional logic of international law, whereby states "become subjects ... only by virtue of being granted [legal personality]... by already existing States acting in the free unfettered exercise of their discretion."[58] In other words, Robinson Crusoe acquires his sovereign personality – and is effectively capacitated to act "like a King" – through the constitutive effects of others' (forced) recognition.

These sorts of oaths are also the forms that colonial charter companies used not only to subjugate native peoples but also, in effect, to acquire international personality of their own. Ordinarily, the constitutive recognition of effective political sovereignty or personality would seem to require a person of equal capacity, already capacitated as a sovereign subject and therefore capable of granting recognition. (Or, at the very least, the speech act of recognition would itself seem to confirm that capacity in the person signing the treaty.) According to Anghie,

---

[57] Defoe, *Robinson Crusoe*, 179.
[58] Lauterpacht, "The Subjects of the Law of Nations," 176.

this "recognition doctrine" was one of the historical ways that international legal analysts "account[ed] for the metamorphosis of a non-European society into a legal entity,"[59] but these subjugation treaties, through which the signer "would be entirely under and subjected to his Commands" (in Crusoe's proposed language), come with an important difference from the normative recognition models in traditional theories of international law. The following is an example of the fill-in-the-blank forms used by the Royal Niger Company to acquire land, mining concessions, and governmental rights in West Africa at the end of the nineteenth century:

We, the undersigned Chiefs of _____, with the view to the bettering of the condition of our country and people, do this day cede to the Royal Niger Company, for ever, the whole of our territory extending from _____.
     We also give to the said Royal Niger Company full power to settle all native disputes arising from any cause whatever, and we pledge ourselves not to enter into any war with other tribes without the sanction of the said Royal Niger Company.

. . .

the said Royal Niger Company (Chartered and Limited) bind themselves not to interfere with any of the native laws or customs of the country, consistently with the maintenance of order and good government.

. . .

Done in triplicate at _____ this _____ day of _____, 188_____.[60]

The emptiness of the sovereign signifier "Chief" – a person capacitated to do chiefly things within a particular context – is dramatically illustrated here by the empty space of the fill-in-the-blanks. And yet, that blank space is invested with the authority to "give to the said ... Company" full sovereign powers of "order and good government." In this model of international affairs, sovereign powers cannot substantiate their own sovereignty and must seek the recognition of others.

While those who sign as "Chiefs" (whether actual Chiefs or no[61]) are, through the treaty, effectively recognized at an international legal level with chieftain sovereignty, they are, in effect, recognized (constituted and capacitated) precisely in order to relinquish that sovereignty. This function contrasts sharply with the revolutionary work of "Declarations of

---

[59] Anghie, *Imperialism*, 75.   [60] Andrea and Overfield, 319–320.
[61] Given that the treaties required a sovereign's signature, an occasional effect of these contracts was the creation of "chiefs" where there were none before or the elevation to "chiefs" of people who were not, by local arrangements, authorized by the community.

Independence," as Jacques Derrida has described them, which constitute "the people" as democratic popular sovereigns.[62] The people who sign such declarations, Derrida observes, "do not exist as an entity, the entity does not exist before this declaration, not as such. If it gives birth to itself, as free and independent subject, as possible signer, this can hold only in the act of the signature."[63] The signature also "invents the signer" in the colonial charter company treaties, but it invents the signer as a sovereign only to dispossess the signer of precisely the sovereignty that seems to be acquired and affirmed in the signature. It may be true, as some legal historians such as Charles Alexandrowicz have argued, that many non-European peoples acquired some form of international legal personality through charter company colonialism, but the formal documentary mode by which they "enter[ed] into th[at] system negated the rights which they were supposed formally to enjoy upon admittance."[64] The colonial treaties, like Crusoe's oaths, invent the signer only to disinvent and divest the signer of the capacity to sign treaties. Also like the oaths, such treaties gave the charter companies much of their effective international legal personality.[65] Thus, under the recognition doctrine, at least at the international level, the colonial corporations were effectively the creations of "savages."

The colonial enterprise acquires a certain international personality and sovereignty at the expense of the natives (who nonetheless are also recognized, in effect, with a fainter kind of subordinate international personality and sovereignty). If we understand this contractual encounter scene to be originary of international personality in the colonial context, we can see the simplest (perhaps paradigmatic) version of the international sovereignty–subjection arrangement played out

---

[62] In *Human Rights, Inc.*, I discuss how this autogenic structure of incorporation found in the eighteenth-century declarations becomes the rhetorical form of self-evidence that grounds the UDHR, 63–72.

[63] J. Derrida, "Declarations of Independence," in J. Derrida, *Negotiations: Interventions and Interviews, 1971–2001*, (ed.) J. Rottenberg (Stanford University Press, 2002), 46–54 at 49.

[64] Anghie, *Imperialism*, 87.

[65] In Charles Alexandrowicz's judgment, these "delegated sovereign rights, which vested external legal capacity in a Company and allowed it to act in the international field, to conclude treaties, transact rights and obligations, [and] acquire territory," made colonial corporations "State-like," anticipating "the twentieth century when States ceased to be the only legal person in international law," C. H. Alexandrowicz, *The European–African Confrontation: A Study in Treaty Making* (Leiden: Sijthoff, 1973), 41–42. Treaty-making capacity is regarded as a hallmark of traditional international legal personality. See especially, M. F. Lindley, *The Acquisition and Government of Backward Territory in International Law: Being a Treatise on the Law and Practice Relating to Colonial Expansion* (New York: Negro Universities Press, 1969); Lauterpacht, "The Subjects of the Law of Nations," 82–83; and Oppenheim, *International Law*, 22–24.

symbolically between Crusoe and Friday: "At last he lays His Head flat upon the Ground, close to my Foot, and sets my other Foot upon his Head ...; ma[king] all the Signs to me of Subjection, Servitude, and submission imaginable,"[66] which Crusoe takes to mean that Friday is "swearing to be my Slave for ever."[67] Friday trades his natural liberty for his life, in exchange acquiring other liberties. He "Signs" away his self-sovereignty in exchange for things that look like human rights. Here's how Crusoe describes his political order after Friday, Friday's father, and the Spaniard have submitted perfectly to his authority:

> My island was now peopled, and I thought my self very rich in Subjects; ... How like a King I look'd. First of all, the whole Country was my own meer Property; so that I Had an undoubted Right of Dominion. *2dly*, My People were perfectly subjected: I was absolute Lord and Lawgiver; they all owed their Lives to me, and were ready to lay down their Lives, *if there had been Occasion of it*, for me. It was remarkable too, we had but three Subjects, and they were of three different Religions. My Man *Friday* was a Protestant, his Father was a *Pagan* and a *Cannibal*, and the *Spaniard* was a Papist: However, I allow'd Liberty of Conscience throughout my Dominions.[68]

Crusoe can think himself "very rich in Subjects" through a conflation of occupation and possession, and he constitutes his international sovereign personality on the property relations he establishes with his Subjects. In return for "perfect subjection," those Subjects have claims on the sovereign – especially Liberty of Conscience, but also rights to life, speech, and personal property. These are liberties that we now think of as human rights (and that, as we shall see, were borne by nineteenth-century colonial charter companies). The contractual logic of Crusoe's kingdom suggests that the human rights holder (as opposed to the sovereign) is precisely that creature who has signed away the human rights she or he presumably already enjoys – in other words, the human rights holder is a creature who has signed away its "natural" rights in order to enjoy them positively as a person before the law.

Crusoe holds onto his precarious sovereignty on the island through various legal agreements, but when he returns to England he, too, must submit himself for subjection to the sovereign law of the land in order to regain his personal rights. Thus, Crusoe answers the call of the law, which here is made stronger by economic self-interest: "he made me enter my Name in a Publick Register, with his Affidavit, affirming upon Oath that I was alive, and that I was the same Person who took up the Land for the Planting the said Plantation at first."[69] Crusoe signs away

[66] Defoe, *Robinson Crusoe*, 149.   [67] Ibid., 147.
[68] Ibid., 174.   [69] Ibid., 204.

his sovereign prerogatives for civil (or human) rights that had only recently been affirmed in the English Bill of Rights. He has to give up his multiple personalities to become again an English subject and to acquire his right to recognition as a person before the laws of England. "[A]s there was no Proof of my being dead,"[70] Crusoe's properties and personal capacities (to hold and transfer property, to enter into contracts) had been divided among trustees, partners, and the government, which "claim'd the Administration [of his plantation], as being the Effects of a Person not to be found, which they call'd *Civil Death*."[71] Official recognition of his lost English personality returns not only his capacity to act as a legal subject within the British dominion; it also returns his material possessions, which have continued to amass in his absence. "Man" is mortal; "person" is not. The property effects of his person persist (for all legal intents and purposes), even if the body is presumed dead. In this sense, Defoe's fantasy of "a kind of legal immortality" for Crusoe turns the castaway into a kind of corporation, a *persona ficta* "who may maintain perpetual succession," keeping "particular rights ... on foot and continued," as William Blackstone described the juridical innovation of the corporate personal form under British law.[72]

The effects of a person not to be found

If there is a kind of double-entry accounting logic to rights in Defoe's text – liberty is subtracted from the "natural" side to be added to the "positive" – perhaps this is not simply because human rights derive from and describe a model of possessive individualism that makes human rights a species of property rights; rather, the model of possessive individualism personified in *homo economicus* was already a form of "corporate humanity."[73] Crusoe is himself a kind of proto-corporation, comprised of multiple personalities whose various capacities are distributed among different departments, which (in this business fiction) conduct exchange operations with each other. Crusoe effectively occupies three positions at once: the individual Enlightenment monadic subject, imagined capable of self-government; the sovereign monarchic subject, in whom legislative functions and executive authority reside; and a corporate subject, in whom certain limited rights and responsibilities

---

[70] Defoe, *Robinson Crusoe*, 202.   [71] Ibid., 204.

[72] Blackstone, *Commentaries*, 467.

[73] Anna Grear uses the term "corporate humanity" to describe the quality of (juristic) life that corporations are gradually acquiring by enlisting human rights law to challenge the sovereign authority of state regulation.

are vested as a functionary enterprise of sovereignty. Crusoe is corporate in a larger sense as well, since these multiple personalities and capacities are all incorporated within a single individual. In his composite person-ality, with his manifold capacities, Crusoe looks less like the unified, self-knowing, self-sufficient subject of Enlightenment fiction and more like a corporate human – a fictional creature that usually bears the name "economic man" but who, given the dispersal of his personal capacities among discrete internal departments, might better answer to "business man."

Crusoe seems to embody some of the primary qualities and inter-national legal capacities that will come to mark the colonial charter company in the nineteenth century, at the historical beginnings of con-temporary international law. Beyond operating according to principles of economic rationalism, Crusoe has other qualities that we ordinarily think of as characteristic of corporations. He has, in his civil death, a kind of legal immortality that seems almost magical in its effects, in the economic and legal benefits attained even in his absence. He lives a kind of company life, with his sovereign functions dispersed among his multiple personalities, so that each one of them seems to have limited liability for its actions, since its activities always derive their authority from "another Person" within the Crusoe enterprise. Any sovereignty he can claim is a mediate sovereignty; even his personal and political sovereignties (he concludes, while contemplating his condition) ultim-ately derive from the "Person ... [who] made all Things,"[74] whose "Sovereignty" Crusoe "was not to dispute," since God has "a judicial Right to condemn me."[75] And yet, functionally, Crusoe obtains an effective international legal personality in relation to the groups with whom he interacts on his island by leveraging the ambiguities and authority carried in the juridical pronoun "person." The *persona ficta* of law has real estate and effects.

Crusoe himself is also a carrier of human rights in ways that colonial charter companies were later charged, as vehicles of the civilizing misson, with bearing human rights to the "natives." Indeed, many of the things that we have come to regard as human rights were first set afoot (or afloat) at the international level with the colonial charter companies. The rights that Crusoe guarantees to his subjects – namely, life, liberty of conscience, and personal property – are, not coincidentally, the same rights that colonial corporations in the era of high imperialism would be asked to "protect and favor" among the natives. This human rights

---

[74] Defoe, *Robinson Crusoe*, 156.   [75] Ibid., 114.

missionary charge was detailed both in the charters of the colonial companies and in the early international law of imperialism and free trade. For example, the General Act of the Conference of Berlin (1885), which set the formal legal terms for the division of African territory among European colonial powers, provides a humanitarian alibi for corporate exploitation:[76]

All Powers exercising rights of sovereignty or an influence in the Said territories engage themselves to watch over the conservation of the indigenous populations and the amelioration of their moral and material conditions of existence and to strive for the suppression of slavery and especially of the negro slave trade; they shall protect and favor without distinction of nationality or of worship, all the institutions and enterprises religious, scientific or charitable, created and organized for these objects or tending to instruct the natives and to make them understand and appreciate the advantages of civilization ... Liberty of conscience and religious toleration are expressly guaranteed to the natives as well as to allegiants and to strangers. The free and public exercise of all forms of worship... shall not be subjected to any restriction or hindrance. (Art. 6; 13)

If, in the US context, corporations walked their rights through doors opened by ex-slaves and the Fourteenth Amendment to emerge as full legal persons, in the international realm the abolition of the slave trade and slavery in Africa provided similar legal pretexts for the acquisition of the colonial charter company's international personality.[77] Parties to the Berlin Treaty additionally pledged that "Strangers shall enjoy there without distinction, for the protection of their persons and their goods, the acquisition and transmission of their movable and immovable property ..., the same treatment and the same rights as the allegiants" (Art. 5). Under the General Act, property rights were not explicitly

---

[76] The Conference of Berlin brought together major European imperial powers with interests in Africa in order to respond to a crisis over competing territorial claims caused (in part) by colonial charter companies vested with independent power to conclude treaties with the "natives" – that is, by problems created when corporations acted as (semi-)autonomous international persons. For a good history of the conference, see S. E. Crowe, *The Berlin West African Conference, 1884–1885* (London: Longmans, published for the Royal Empire Society, 1942).

[77] Defoe's novel does not challenge the legitimacy of slavery as an institution. In fact, Crusoe is shipwrecked while pursuing illegal slaving in West Africa. Jenny Martinez has argued that nineteenth-century anti-slavery courts were the first international human rights legal institutions. If we accept this argument, then we must also acknowledge that human rights and international law are not simply the byproducts of imperial encounters; they were, in fact, twin engines of nineteenth-century European colonialism. In other words, international law and human rights developed, at least in part, to regulate the exploitation of non-European peoples. For an excellent argument on humanitarianism as colonial alibi, see G. Gott, "Imperial Humanitarianism: History of an Arrested Dialectic," in B. E. Hernández-Truyol, (ed.), *Moral Imperialism: A Critical Anthology* (New York University Press, 2002).

guaranteed to the "indigenous populations" – which would be an especially egregious example of European missionary hypocrisy, given that the force of the international treaty was to set the legal terms for the "rightful" dispossession of the natives' properties – but such provisions were typical of the company charters.

"[R]ights of sovereignty" were generally exercised over "the Said territories" through colonial companies, whose charters, in addition to sanctioning economic activities, normally granted to the enterprise "all rights, interests, authorities, and powers for the purposes of government, preservation of public order, protection of said territories or otherwise," as the Royal Niger Company's Charter has it.[78] Furthermore, in addition to claiming that "the condition of the natives ... would be materially improved, and the[ir] civilization ... greatly advanced,"

The Royal Niger Company (Chartered and Limited) ... agreed ... not to encroach on or to interfere with any private property ... [to] abolish by degrees any system of domestic servitude existing among the native inhabitants ... [and] not in any way [to] interfere with the religion of any class or tribe of the people of its territories.[79]

The charters and treaty are primarily concerned with economic matters, with property and trade rights, even if these are given a moral charge of advancing the "condition of the natives"; "The commerce of all nations shall enjoy complete liberty," proclaims the General Act in Art. 1. (If commerce, in this context, is primarily personified in the form of the charter company, can the corporation's rights to "life ... and security of person" (UDHR Art. 3) be far behind the "liberty" it already enjoys at the international level?) Both the charters and the treaty overlay moral (or human) rights on the economic rights of the companies, allegiants, strangers, and natives. From this perspective, it is the basic economic rights of these entities – including the rights of the natives as potential future free-traders – that seem to qualify them for special moral protections: life, liberty of conscience, and property in the self. Indeed, at least in the case of nineteenth-century company colonialism, Africans enter the emerging regime of international law (through citation in the corporate charters, reference in agreements such as the General Act, and signature in the company treaties) as a bundle of trading interests and property rights – collectively as corporate tribal units,

---

[78] Reprinted in A. F. Mockler-Ferryman, *Up the Niger* (London: George Philip & Son, 1892), 294.
[79] Ibid., 292–295.

individually as economic man – to whom certain basic human rights are therefore also due.

Like Crusoe, the colonial charter companies were simultaneously functionaries of sovereignty and functional sovereign international persons of their own. In this regard, corporations carried something like international human rights; they were charged with promoting and protecting some of the most basic human rights that we now recognize, and they were themselves the bearers of international personality that we now see as a hallmark of the human rights regime. In this twofold sense, colonial charter companies were bearing human rights around the world by the late nineteenth century, more than fifty years before the human being as such (that is, not shrouded in the personhood of some other official state capacity) was formally recognized as a bearer of international human rights. In other words, the business corporation was a subject of international human rights, however incompletely, before the human being became a subject of human rights and an international person in its own right, however incompletely.

The corporation also preceded the human being to international human rights in another sense as well. The late personification of the human being as a subject of international human rights law shares a discursive history with the legal personification of the corporate form. Initially, corporations were chartered by Royal or state authority; that is, they were *granted* their legal personalities, which were charged with specific itemized rights and duties. Over the course of the long nineteenth century, as corporations went from being treated as completely artificial legal persons to being regarded as real creatures, the personifying regulatory mechanisms changed accordingly. The grant system gave way to registration procedures, by which corporations simply filed for recognition of their legal personality and rights. Corporations changed from being mere objects of law (who "could do only those things specifically allowed by its charter") to being subjects, who "could do anything not specifically prohibited to it."[80] Thus, rather than being treated merely as a creature of the state, the emancipated corporation claimed to need (human rights) protection from it. In the legal history of the personification of the corporation, the person is granted, before being taken for granted.

At the international level, it seems that the human being is on a figurative path paved in advance, at least partially, by the colonial charter company. "[W]hat is the real position of individuals in

---

[80] Mark, "The Personification of the Business Corporation," 1455.

International Law?" asked Oppenheim in his 1905 treatise.[81] "[I]ndividuals are never subjects but always objects," was the standard answer; "It is through the medium of their nationality only that individuals can enjoy benefits from the existence of the Law of Nations."[82] Today, after more than sixty years of human rights law-making, Hersch Lauterpacht's dream of a "declaration [that] would amount to constituting individuals subjects of international law" has more or less been realized, since human beings are increasingly treated as international legal persons in their own right.[83] In the legal history of the personification of the international human being, the person is granted, before being taken for granted ... Or, at least that is the idea behind a legal regime that declares that "All human beings are born free and equal in dignity and rights" (UDHR Art. 1), while acknowledging that this would entail that everyone be recognized "everywhere as a person before the law" (Art. 6). The UDHR has an anticipatory tenor, imagining "the advent of a world in which human beings shall enjoy freedom of speech and belief [liberties that Crusoe and colonial charter companies permitted] and freedom from fear and want" (Preamble) – a world in which the "the natural human being will have become the [self-substantiating] international human rights person."[84] In this sense, the person of human rights is an artificial creature (a *persona ficta*) that the international regime of human rights intends to realize. Given the history of the legal liberation of the corporate form, it may be that the business corporation, having beaten the human being to its human rights, has already outcompeted human beings for both their natural resources *and* rights.

My objective in telling a story of international human rights law through the imaginative vision of a novel is not to offer another true history of human rights, in which the corporation and capitalist colonialism are discovered to be its true unacknowledged sources. Nor do I mean to valorize literature over history and the law, even if the literary (forming something like a compound lens with legal history) can lend us a kind of Borgesian "spherical eyesight" that enables us to visualize a more complex picture of human rights law than might be legible from any single traditional disciplinary viewpoint. I am reading *Robinson Crusoe* as a fabulous documentary of some of the primary textual forms (or legal instruments) by which individuals and corporations historically acquired personal sovereignty, international personality, and human rights in

---

[81] Oppenheim, *International Law*, 344.   [82] Ibid., 345.

[83] Lauterpacht, 'The Subjects of the Law of Nations," 190.

[84] Joseph R. Slaughter, *Human Rights, Inc.: The World Novel, Narrative Form, and International Law* (New York: Fordham University Press, 2007), 80.

order to remind us that the human rights personification of the human being has a discursive genealogy that is entangled with the legal life of the corporation and imperial capitalism – and, more importantly, therefore, that figuring the human being through the vehicle of the person in international law remains a risky business, since its occupants and destination are far from certain.[85] In entertaining Barbara Johnson's provocative idea that some of "what have been claimed to be the essential characteristics of man" may "have in fact been borrowed from the nature of the corporation,"[86] I hope to trouble the dominant smooth teleological histories that tell simplistic stories of the triumph of human rights, drawing a straight line from the French Revolution (or even classical Greek democracy) to the formation of the United Nations. However, I also intend to problematize the current alarming stories about the corporate corruption of human rights which, in their turn, risk reifying a naive version of international law and human rights, as if there were a simpler antediluvian time before corporate capitalism, when protecting and promoting human rights were innocent business. The business corporation may indeed precede the human being in human rights, and some basic provisions of contemporary human rights law may have first been borne at the international level by the colonial charter company and articulated in so-called free-trade agreements, but we court a kind of collective amnesia if we forget (or ignore) the messy roles of capitalism and imperialism in the formation and perpetuation of human rights and international law. Moreover, we risk reducing human rights to a mere culture of sentimentalism if we forget ourselves (like the narrator in Borges' story), becoming singularly fascinated by the human in human rights and lose sight of the legal fiction and technical figure of the person – the functional subject of law who walks rights around in the world.

---

[85] Anna Grear's admonitions in *Redirecting Human Rights* would lead to similar conclusions. Because the conceptual ambiguities contained in the concept of personality have real legal effects and social consequences, John Dewey urged "eliminating the idea of personality until the concrete facts and relations involved have been faced and stated on their own account," "The Historic Background of Legal Personality," *Yale Law Review*, 35(6) (1926), 673.

[86] Johnson, "Anthropomorphism in Lyric and Law," 572.

16 Welcome to the "spiritual kingdom of animals"

Slavoj Žižek

The German expression *rückgängig machen*, usually translated as "annul, cancel, unhitch," has a second more precise meaning: to undo something retroactively, to make it as if it had not taken place. The comparison between Mozart's *Figaro* and Rossini's Figaro operas makes this action immediately clear. In Mozart, the emancipatory political potential of Beaumarchais' play survives the pressure of censorship – think only of the finale, where the Count has to kneel down and ask for forgiveness before his subjects (not to mention the explosion of the collective "Viva la liberta!" in the finale of Act 1 of *Don Giovanni*). The breathtaking achievement of Rossini's *Barber* should be measured by this standard. Rossini took a theatrical symbol of the French bourgeois revolutionary spirit, and totally de-politicized it, changing it into a pure *opera buffa*. No wonder the golden years of Rossini were between 1815 and 1830. These were the years of reaction when the European powers tackled the impossible task of the *Ungeschehenmachen* (making-it-not-happen) of the previous revolutionary decades. This is what Rossini did in his great comic operas: he tried to bring back to life the innocence of the pre-revolutionary world. Rossini did not actively hate or fight the new world. He simply composed as if the years 1789–1815 did not exist. Rossini was therefore right to (almost) stop composing after 1830 and to adopt the satisfied stance of a *bon vivant* making his *tournedos* – this was the only properly ethical thing to do. His long silence is comparable to that of Jean Sibelius and, in literature, to Arthur Rimbaud and Dashiell Hammett.

Insofar as the French Revolution is the Event of modern history, the break after which "nothing was the same," one should raise the question: is this kind of "undoing," of "dis-eventalization," one of the possible destinies of every Event? It is possible to imagine the attitude of the fetishist split towards an Event: "I know very well there was no Event, just the ordinary run of things, but, perhaps, unfortunately, none-theless ... [I believe] there was one?" An even more interesting case would be: is it possible for an Event to be denied not directly but retroactively? Imagine a society which fully integrates into its ethical substance the great modern axioms of freedom, equality, democratic rights, and the duty to provide for education and basic healthcare for all its members, a society which renders racism and sexism simply unacceptable and ridiculous. There is no need to argue against, say, racism, since anyone who openly advocates it is immediately perceived as a weird eccentric who cannot be taken seriously. But then, step by step, although this society continues to pay lip service to these axioms, they are *de facto* deprived of their substance. Here is an example from the ongoing European history: in the summer of 2012, Viktor Orban, the Hungarian Rightist Prime Minister, said that in Central Europe a new economic system must be built:

> and let us hope that God will help us and we will not have to invent a new type of political system instead of democracy that would need to be introduced for the sake of economic survival . . . Cooperation is a question of force, not of intention. Perhaps there are countries where things don't work that way, for example in the Scandinavian countries, but such a half-Asiatic rag-tag people as we are can unite only if there is force.[1]

The irony of these lines was not lost on some old Hungarian dissidents: when the Soviet Army moved into Budapest to crush the 1956 anti-Communist uprising, the message repeatedly sent by the beleaguered Hungarian leaders to the West was "We are defending Europe" – against the Asiatic Communists, of course. After Communism collapsed, the Christian–conservative government presented western multi-cultural consumerist liberal democracy as its main enemy and called for a new more organic communitarian order to replace the "turbulent" liberal democracy of the previous two decades. This is the latest instalment of the saga of designating the Enemy as the coincidence of the opposites. The "plutocratic–Bolshevik plot" (the (ex-)Communists) and the liberal "bourgeois" democrats are perceived as the two faces of the same enemy. No wonder Orban and some of his allies repeatedly express their sympathies for the Chinese "capitalism with Asian values," looking to "Asian" authoritarianism as the solution against the ex-Communist threat.

We can find examples of the same paradox in the army. From my own experience of military service in 1975, I remember how the old infamous Yugoslav People's Army was homophobic to the extreme – when someone was discovered to have homosexual inclinations he was instantly turned into a pariah, treated as a non-person, before being

---

[1] Quoted from www.presseurop.eu/en/content/news-brief/2437991-orban-considers-alternative-democracy.

formally dismissed. Yet, at the same time, everyday army life was excessively permeated by a homosocial atmosphere. How is this weird coincidence of opposites possible? The mechanism was described by Robert Pfaller:

As Freud observed, the very acts that are forbidden by religion are practiced in the name of religion. In such cases – as, for instance, murder in the name of religion – religion also can do entirely without miniaturization. Those adamantly militant advocates of human life, for example, who oppose abortion, will not stop short of actually murdering clinic personnel. Radical right-wing opponents of male homosexuality in the United States act in a similar way. They organize so-called "gay bashings" in the course of which they beat up and finally rape gays. The ultimate homicidal or homosexual gratification of drives can therefore also be attained, if it only fulfills the condition of evoking the semblance of a counter-measure. What seems to be "opposition" then has the effect that the x to be fended off can appear itself and be taken for a non-x.[2]

What we encounter here is a textbook case of the Hegelian "oppositional determination": in the figure of the gay basher raping a gay, the gay encounters himself in its oppositional determination. Tautology or self-identity appears as the highest contradiction. This inherent inconsistency of the ideologico-legal order is at its most conspicuous in China. How do official Communist theorists react when confronted with the all too obvious contradiction, of a Communist Party which still legitimizes itself in Marxist terms, but renounces Marxism's basic premise, that of workers' self-organization as a revolutionary force in order to overthrow capitalism? One suspects that all the resources of the legendary Chinese politeness are mobilized. It is considered impolite to directly raise (or insist on) these questions. This resort to politeness is necessary, since it is the only way to combine what cannot be combined: to enforce Marxism as official ideology while openly prohibiting its central axioms, which would cause the collapse of the entire ideological edifice rendering it meaningless. The result is that, while certain things are clearly prohibited, this prohibition cannot be publicly stated, but is itself prohibited. It is not merely prohibited to raise the question of workers' self-organization against capitalist exploitation as the central tenet of Marxism, it is also prohibited to publicly claim that it is prohibited to raise this question.[3] In this way, we violate what Kant called the

---

[2] Robert Pfaller, "The Potential of Thresholds to Obstruct and to Facilitate: On the Operation of Displacement in Obsessional Neurosis and Perversion" (unpublished paper, 2002).

[3] What one usually gets from theorists is a private admission that, of course, this is contradictory, but that, nonetheless, such a contradictory ideological edifice *works*, and works spectacularly: it is the only way to ensure fast economic growth and stability in China. Need we add that this is the "private use of reason" at its purest?

"transcendental formula of public law": "All actions relating to the right of other men are unjust if their maxim is not consistent with publicity." A secret law, a law unknown to its subjects, would legitimize the arbitrary despotism of those who exercise it – compare with this formula the title of a recent report on China: "Even what's secret is a secret in China."[4] Troublesome intellectuals who report on political oppression, ecological catastrophes, or rural poverty, receive years in prison for betraying state secrets. The catch is that many of the laws and regulations that make up the state-secret regime are themselves classified, making it difficult to know how and when they are in violation.

This secrecy of the prohibition itself serves two different purposes, which should not be confused. Its commonly admitted role is to universalize guilt and fear: if you do not know what is prohibited, you cannot even know when you are violating a prohibition, which makes you potentially guilty all the time. Except of course at the climax of the Stalinist purges when effectively everyone could be found guilty and people knew when they were doing something that would annoy those in power. The function of prohibiting prohibitions is thus not to give rise to "irrational" fear, but to let the potential dissidents (who think they can get away with their critical activity, since they are not breaking any laws, but only doing what laws guarantee – freedom of speech or of the press – know that, if they annoy those in power too much, they can be punished at the power's will. In ex-Yugoslavia, the infamous Article 133 of the penal code could always be invoked to prosecute writers and journalists. It criminalized any text that falsely presented the achievements of the socialist revolution or that *might arouse tension and discontent among the public* for the way it dealt with political, social, or other topics. This last category is obviously not only infinitely plastic, but also conveniently self-relating. The fact that you are accused by those in power means that you have indeed "*aroused tension and discontent among the public.*" I remember asking a Slovene politician how he could justify such a law. He smiled and, with a wink, told me: "Well, we have to have some tool to discipline those who annoy us without worrying about legal niceties."

But prohibiting prohibitions has also the crucial function of *maintaining appearances*. We know how absolutely crucial appearances were in Stalinism. The regime reacted with total panic whenever there was a threat that appearances might be disturbed. The Soviet media had no black chronicles, no reports on crimes and prostitution, no mention of workers or public protests. This prohibiting of prohibitions is far from

---

[4] See "Even What's Secret is a Secret in China," *The Japan Times* (June 16, 2007), 17.

being limited to Communist regimes however. It is operative also in today's "permissive" capitalism. A "postmodern" boss insists that he is not a master but just a coordinator of our joint creative efforts, the first among equals. There should be no formalities among us, we should address him by his nickname, he shares a dirty joke with us. But in all this, he remains our master. In this situation, relations of domination function through their denial. We are not only obliged to obey our bosses, we are also obliged to act as if we are free and equal, as if there is no domination – which, of course, makes the situation even more humiliating. Paradoxically, in such a situation, the first act of liberation is to demand from the master to act as such. One should reject false collegiality from the boss and insist that he treats workers with cold indifference and distance, as a master. No wonder all this sounds vaguely Kafkaesque – Kafka effectively wrote that "it is an extremely painful thing to be ruled by laws that one does not know,"[5] thereby bringing out the implicit superego obscenity of the famous legal principle that "ignorance [of the law] is not an excuse."[6] Jacques Derrida is fully justified in emphasizing the self-reflexivity of the prohibition with regard to the Law – the Law not only prohibits, it is itself prohibited:

The law is prohibition: this does not mean that it prohibits, but that it is itself prohibited, a prohibited place ... one cannot reach the law, and in order to have a rapport of respect with it, one must not have a rapport with the law, one must interrupt the relation. One must enter into relation only with the law's representatives, its examples, its guardians. These are interrupters as much as messengers. One must not know who or what or where the law is.[7]

In one of his short fragments, Kafka himself pointed out how the ultimate secret of the Law is that it does not exist – another case of what Lacan called the inexistence of the big Other. This inexistence, of course, does not simply reduce the Law to an empty imaginary chimera. It rather makes it into an impossible Real, a void which nonetheless functions, exerts influence, causes effects, curves the symbolic space. In today's political space, the most extreme case of such a Law is found in North

---

[5] Franz Kafka, "The Problem of Our Laws," in *The Complete Stories* (New York: Schocken Books 1995), 437.

[6] The EU pressure on Greece in 2011 and 2012 to implement its dictates fits perfectly what psychoanalysis calls superego. Superego is not an ethical agency proper, but a sadistic agent which bombards the subject with impossible demands, obscenely enjoying the subject's failure to comply with them; the paradox of the superego is that, as Freud saw clearly, the more we obey its demands, the more we feel guilty. Imagine a vicious teacher who gives his pupils impossible tasks, and then sadistically jeers when he sees their anxiety and panic. This is what is so terribly wrong with the EU demands/commands: they don't even give a chance to Greece, her failure is part of the game.

[7] Jacques Derrida, *Acts of Literature* (New York: Routledge 1992), 201.

Korea where patriarchy is effectively undermined in an unexpected way. Here are the words of North Korea's most popular political song:

> Ah, Korean Workers' Party, at whose breast only
> My life begins and ends
> Be I buried in the ground or strewn to the wind
> I remain your son, and again return to your breast!
> Entrusting my body to your affectionate gaze,
> Your loving outstretched hand,
> I cry out forever in the voice of a child,
> Mother! I can't live without Mother![8]

This is what the excessive mourning after Kim's death signals: "I can't live without Mother!" As a further proof, here are the two entries ("mother" and "father") from a North Korean *Dictionary of the Korean Language* (1964):

MOTHER: (1) The woman who has given birth to one: Father and mother; a mother's love. *A mother's benevolence is higher than a mountain, deeper than the ocean.* Also used in the sense of "a woman who has a child": *What all mothers anxiously want is for their children to grow up healthy and become magnificent red builders.* (2) A respectful term for someone of an age similar to one's own mother: *Comrade Platoon Leader called Dŏngmani's mother "mother" and always helped her in her work.* (3) A metaphor for being loving, looking after everything, and worrying about others: *Party officials must become mothers who ceaselessly love and teach the Party rank and file, and become standard-bearers at the forefront of activities.* In other words, someone in charge of lodgings has to become a mother to the boarders. This means looking carefully after everything: whether someone is cold or sick, how they are eating, and so on. (4) A metaphor for the source from which something originates: *The Party is the great mother of everything new. Necessity is the mother of invention.*
FATHER: the husband of one's birth mother.[9]

Maybe this is the reason why the leader's wife was not mentioned in public till the third Kim. The Leader was hermaphroditic, with the the feminine features dominating. Is this in contradiction with North Korea's "military first" policy, with ruthless disciplining and drilling of soldiers? I believe that these are two sides of the same coin. The figure of the mother we are dealing with here is the so-called "non-castrated" omnipotent devouring mother. Apropos of the real mother, Jacques-Alain Miller noted that "not only is there an unsatisfied mother but also an all-powerful one. And the terrifying aspect of this

---

[8] Quoted from www.theatlantic.com/magazine/archive/2004/09/mother-of-all-mothers/3403/.
[9] B.R. Myers, *The Cleanest Race* (New York: Melville House 2011), 6.

figure of the Lacanian mother is that she is all-powerful and unsatisfied at the same time."[10] Therein resides the paradox: the more "omnipotent" a mother appears, the more unsatisfied (which means lacking) she is: "The Lacanian mother corresponds to the formula *quaerens quem devoret*: she looks for someone to devour, and so Lacan presents her then as the crocodile, the subject with the open mouth."[11] This devouring mother does not respond to the child's demand for a sign of love. As such she appears omnipotent: "Since the mother does not respond, ... she is transformed into real, that is to say, into power ... if the Other does not respond, he is transformed into a devouring power."[12] This is why the feminized features discernible in the official portraits of the two Kims are not accidental:

Kim /Il Sung/ was more a mother to his people than a stern Confucian patriarch: he is still shown as soft-cheeked and solicitous, holding weeping adults to his expansive bosom, bending down to tie a young soldier's bootlaces, or letting giddy children clamber over him. The tradition continues under Kim Jong Il, who has been called "more of a mother than all the mothers in the world." His military-first policy may come with the title of general, but reports of his endless tour of army bases focus squarely on his fussy concern for the troops' health and comfort. The international ridicule of his appearance is thus as unfair as it is tedious. Anyone who has seen a crowd of Korean mothers waiting outside an examination hall will have no difficulty recognizing Kim's drab parka and drooping shoulders, or the long-suffering face under the pillow-swept perm: this is a mother with no time to think of herself.[13]

Does North Korea then stand for something like the Indian Kali – the benevolent/murderous goddess – in power? One should distinguish between two levels. The superficial level of manly–military discourse with the Leader as "General," with *Juche* as idea of self-reliance, with humanity as a master of its destiny, is sustained by a deeper level, that of the Leader as a maternal protector. This is how Myers formulates the basic axiom of North Korean ideology: "The Korean people are too pure blooded, and therefore too virtuous, to survive in this evil world without a great parental leader."[14] Is this not a nice example of Lacan's formula of paternal metaphor, of the Name-of-the-Father as a meta-phoric substitute for the desire of the mother? The Name-of-the-Father (Leader/General) stands above the mother's protective/destructive

---

[10] Jacques-Alain Miller, "Phallus and Perversion," *lacanian ink*, 33, 23.
[11] Jacques-Alain Miller, "The Logic of the Cure," *lacanian ink*, 33, 19.
[12] *Op.cit.*, 28.
[13] Quoted from www.theatlantic.com/magazine/archive/2004/09/mother-of-all-mothers/3403/.
[14] Myers, *The Cleanest Race*, 9.

desire.[15] One of the New Age commonplaces is that the West is too much dominated by the male/paternal principle of domination, discipline and struggle. To re-establish balance, we should reassert the feminine principle of loving care and protection – however, cases of "hard" female politicians from Indira Gandhi to Margaret Thatcher should make us think twice. Today the predominant form of the social bond is no longer sustained by a patriarchal Master. Even "totalitarianism" is not the discourse of the Master. The tragic experience of many revolutions in which the overthrowing of the old Master ended up in a much more murderous terror should not lead us to advocate a return to paternal symbolic authority as the only way out of the self-destructive deadlock of the late capitalist narcissistic protean self. This self involves its own "dis-eventalization" masked as progress, its own reduction of a man to human animal. Let me give an example.

In August 2012, it was reported that from December 2012 tobacco companies would no longer be allowed to display their distinctive colors, brand designs, and logos on cigarette packs in Australia. To make smoking as unglamorous as possible, the packs will come in a uniformly drab shade of olive and feature graphic health warnings and images of cancer-riddled mouths, blinded eyeballs, and sickly children.[16] This is a kind of *Selbst-Aufhebung* of the commodity-form: no logo, no "commodity-aesthetics" which should seduce us into buying the product. On the contrary, the package of the product openly and graphically draws attention to its dangerous and harmful qualities and thus provides reasons against buying it. This anti-commodity presentation of a commodity is not a novelty. It accounts for the allure of "cultural" products like paintings or music which are "not strictly a commodity; it is … worth buying only when the pretence that it is not a commodity can be successfully maintained."[17] Here, the antagonism between commodity and

---

[15] Are then – to put it bluntly – North Koreans incestuous psychotics who reject entering the symbolic order? The answer is no – why? Because of the distance towards the symbolic order proper which persists even in official ideological texts. That is to say, even North Korea's official ideological discourse ("Text," as Myers calls it) does not engage in direct divinization of the Leader; instead, the divinization is elegantly attributed to "naïve" western visitors fascinated by the Leader's wisdom: "while the Text likes to draw bemused attention to outsiders, including Americans and South Koreans, who allegedly regard Kim Il Sung as a divine being, it never makes such claims for him itself" (Myers, *The Cleanest Race*, 111). Is this not a clear case of "subject supposed to believe," of the naïve other onto which our own belief is transposed?

[16] http://news.yahoo.com/australian-court-oks-logo-ban-cigarette-packs-004107919-finance.html.

[17] Charles Rosen, *Schoenberg* (London: Fontana/Collins 1975), 77.

non-commodity reverses the way the logo-less cigarettes work. The superego injunction is "you should be ready to pay an exorbitant price for this commodity precisely because it is much more than a mere commodity." In the case of logo-less cigarettes, the raw use value is deprived of its form – in a similar way, discount stores sell logo-less sugar, coffee, sweets. In the case of a painting, the logo itself "sublates" use value, and price seems to determine value, as Marx already noted.

But does this direct "pragmatic contradiction" really take us out of commodity fetishism? Does it not rather provide yet another example of the fetishist split signaled by the well-known phrase *je sais très bien, mais quand même*? A decade ago a German publicity poster for Marlboro cigarettes had their standard cowboy-figure directly pointing down towards the obligatory note "Smoking is dangerous for your health!" and the added words "*Jetzt erst rechts!*," which can be loosely translated as "Now things are getting serious!" The implied meaning is clear. Now that you know how dangerous smoking is, you can prove that you have the courage to go on smoking! In other words, the attitude solicited in the targeted subject is: "I know very well the dangers of smoking, but I am not a coward, I am a true man and, as such, ready to take the risk and remain faithful to my smoking commitment." This way, smoking effectively becomes a form of consumerism: I am ready to consume cigarettes "beyond the pleasure principle," beyond the petty utilitarian considerations about health. And is not this dimension of lethal excessive enjoyment at work in every publicity or commodity appeal? Are all utilitarian considerations (this food is healthy, it was organically grown, it was paid under fair trade conditions, etc.) not just a deceptive surface containing a deeper superego injunction: "Enjoy! Enjoy to the end, irrespectively of consequences"? The Australian "negative" packaging brings out the superego injunction which was here all the time. A smoker, buying the "negatively" packed cigarettes will hear beneath the negative message the silent present and pressing voice of the superego. This voice will answer his question: "If all these dangers of smoking are true – and I accept they are – why am I then still buying the package?"

This superego pressure is not limited to consumerism. It acquires different guises, some of them with catastrophic socio-ethical consequences. The documentary *The Act of Killing* (Final Cut Film Production, Copenhagen) premiered in 2012 at the Telluride film festival and was also shown at Toronto International Film Festival. *The Act of Killing*, directed by Joshua Oppenheimer and Christine Cynn, provides a unique and deeply disturbing insight into the ethical deadlock of global capitalism. The film shot in Medan, Indonesia, in 2007, reports a case of extreme cruelty. It is about Anwar Congo and his friends, who are now respected politicians, but were gangsters and death squad leaders playing a key role in the 1966 killing of around two and a half million alleged Communist sympathizers, mostly ethnic Chinese. *The Act of Killing* is about "killers who have won, and the sort of society they have built." After their victory, their terrible acts were not relegated to the status of the "dirty secret," the founding crime whose traces are to be obliterated. On the contrary, the perpetrators boast openly about the details of their massacres – the way to strangle a victim with a wire, the way to cut a throat, how to rape a woman in a most pleasurable way. In October 2007, Indonesian state TV produced a talk show, *Freemen*, celebrating Anwar and his friends. In the middle of the show, after Anwar says that their killings were inspired by gangster movies, the beaming moderator turns to the cameras and says: "Amazing! Let's give Anwar Congo a round of applause!" When she asks Anwar if he fears the revenge of the victims' relatives, Anwar answers: "They can't. When they raise their heads, we wipe them out!" His henchman adds: "We'll exterminate them all!," and the audience explodes into exuberant cheers ... But what makes *Freemen* extraordinary is the level of reflexivity between documentary and fiction – the film is, in a way, a documentary about the real effects of living a fiction:

> To explore the killers' astounding boastfulness, and to test the limits of their pride, we began with documentary portraiture and simple re-enactments of the massacres. But when we realized what kind of movie Anwar and his friends really wanted to make about the genocide, the re-enactments became more elaborate. And so we offered Anwar and his friends the opportunity to dramatize the killings using film genres of their choice (western, gangster, musical). That is, we gave them the chance to script, direct and star in the scenes *they had in mind when they were killing people.*[18]

Did they reach the limits of the killers' "pride"? They touched it some-what when they asked Anwar to play the victim of his tortures in a re-enactment. When a wire is placed around his neck, he interrupts the performance saying "Forgive me for everything I've done." But this was a temporary lapse, which did not lead to a deeper crisis of conscience. His heroic pride immediately took over again. The protective screen which prevented a deeper moral crisis was probably the cinematic screen. As in their real killings and tortures, the perpetrators experienced their activity as an enactment of their cinematic models – they played a role in

---

[18] Quoted from the publicity material of Final Cut Film Production.

their massacres, imitating a Hollywood gangster, cowboy or even a musical dancer. This enabled them to experience reality as a fiction. They were great admirers of Hollywood and had started their career as organizers and controllers of the black market in cinema tickets.

Here the "big Other" enters twice, in *The Killers* that modeled their crimes on the cinematic imaginary, but also in the much more important social moral vacuum. What kind of symbolic texture, or set of rules drawing the line between what is publicly acceptable and what is not exists in a society where even the minimal level of public shame is suspended, and the monstrous orgy of torture and killing can be publicly celebrated even decades after it took place, not even as a extraordinary necessary crime for the public good, but as an ordinary acceptable pleasurable activity? But we should not put the blame either on Hollywood or on the "ethical backwardness" of Indonesia. The starting point should rather be the dislocating effects of capitalist globalization which, by undermining the "symbolic efficacy" of traditional ethical structures, creates such a moral vacuum.[19]

The status of the "big Other" deserves a closer analysis here. Let me compare *The Act of Killing* to an incident which drew a lot of attention in the United States a few decades ago. A woman was beaten and slowly killed by a violent perpetrator in the courtyard of a big apartment block in Brooklyn, New York. Some seventy witnesses saw what was happening from their windows, but not one called the police..Why not? As the later investigation established, the main reason was that every witness thought someone else already had or would soon call the police. This evidence should not be moralistically dismissed as mere excuse for moral coward-ice and egotistic indifference: this is another function of the big Other, not as Lacan's "subject supposed to know," but as what one could call "the subject supposed to call the police." The fatal mistake of the witnesses of the slow Brooklyn killing was to misread the symbolic (fictional) function of the "subject supposed to call the police" as an empirical claim, wrongly concluding that there must be at least one who

---

[19] More generally, how can (relatively) decent people do horrible things? To account for this, one should turn around the standard conservative anti-individualist view according to which social institutions control and contain our individual, spontaneous evil tendencies to follow ruthlessly our destructive and egotist strivings: what if, on the contrary, we as individuals are (relatively) decent, and institutions have to apply all their subterfuge to make us do horrible things? The role of institutions as agents of mediation is crucial here: there are things I would never be able to do directly, in first person, but if I leave it to my agents to do it for me I can pretend not to know what is going on. How many humanitarians invest their money in housing projects in Dubai which employ modern versions of slave work – and, of course, they (can pretend that they) don't know about it, that it was done by their financial advisers, etc.

effectively did call the police. They overlooked the fact that the function of the "subject supposed to call the police" is operative even if there is no actual subject who enacts it.[20]

Does this mean that, through the gradual dissolution of our ethical substance, we are simply regressing to individualist egotism? Things are much more complex. We often hear that our ecological crisis is the result of our short-term egotism. Obsessed with immediate pleasures and wealth, we forgot the common Good. However, it is here that Walter Benjamin's notion of capitalism as religion becomes crucial. A true capitalist is not a hedonist egotist. On the contrary, he is fanatically devoted to his task of multiplying his wealth, ready to neglect his health and happiness, not to mention the prosperity of his family and the well being of the environment. There is no need to evoke some high-ground moralism and trash capitalist egotism. Against perverted capitalist dedi-cation, it is enough to evoke a good measure of simple egotistical and utilitarian concerns, what Rousseau called the natural *amour-de-soi* which requires a highly civilized level of awareness. Or, to put it in the terms of Alain Badiou, but contrary to what he implies, capitalist subjectivity is not that of the "human animal," but a call to subordinate egotism to the self-reproduction of Capital.

Self-interested egotism is not the brutal fact of our societies but its ideology is – the ideology philosophically articulated in Hegel's *Phenom-enology of Spirit* towards the end of the chapter on Reason, under the name of "*das geistige Tierreich*" – the "spiritual kingdom of animals." This is Hegel's name for modern civil society in which human animals are caught in self-interested interaction. As Hegel put it, the achievement of modernity was to allow "the principle of subjectivity to attain fulfillment in the self-sufficient extreme of personal particularity."[21] The reign of this principle makes civil society the domain in which autonomous human individuals associate with each other through the institutions of free market in order to satisfy their private needs. All communal ends are subordinated to private interests. What matters for Hegel here is the opposition of private and common, as perceived by Mandeville or Smith on whom Hegel as well as Marx relied. Individuals perceive the common as a domain that serves their private interests. But in pursuing their

---

[20] One can even imagine an empirical test for this claim: if one could recreate a circumstance in which each of the witnesses were to think that he or she were alone in observing the gruesome scene, one can predict that despite their opportunist avoidance of "getting involved in something that isn't your business," a large majority of them would have called the police.

[21] G.W.F. Hegel, *Elements of the Philosophy of Right* (Cambridge University Press 1991), para. 260.

narrow goals, they effectively serve the communal interest. The properly dialectical tension emerges when we become aware that the more individuals act egotistically the more they contribute to the common wealth. The paradox is that when individuals want to sacrifice their narrow private interests and directly work for the common good, it is the common good that suffers. Hegel loves to tell historical anecdotes about a good king or prince whose very dedication to the common good brings his country to ruins. Hegel's philosophical novelty was to further determine this "contradiction" along the lines of a tension between the "animal" and the "spiritual." The universal spiritual substance, the "work of all and everyone," emerges as the result of the "mechanical" interaction of individuals. The very "animality" of the self-interested "human animal" (the individual participating in the complex network of civil society) is the result of the long historical process of the transformation of medieval hierarchic society into modern bourgeois society. It is thus the very fulfillment of the principle of subjectivity – the radical opposite of animality – which brings about the reversal of subjectivity into animality.

Traces of this shift can be detected everywhere today, especially in the fast-developing Asian countries where capitalism exerts a brutal impact. Bertolt Brecht's "The Exception and the Rule", a learning play written in 1929–30, tells the story of a rich merchant who, with his porter or "coolie," crosses the Yahi Desert (yet another of Brecht's fictional Chinese places) to close an oil deal. When the two get lost in the desert and their water supplies are running low, the merchant mistakenly shoots the coolie, thinking he was being attacked, when the coolie was actually offering him some water he still had left in his bottle. Later, the merchant is acquitted by the court. The judge concludes that the merchant had every right to fear a potential threat from the coolie. He was therefore justified in shooting him in self-defense regardless of whether there was an actual threat. Since the merchant and his coolie belong to different classes, the merchant had every reason to expect hatred and aggression. This is the typical situation, the rule, while the coolie's kindness was an exception. Is this story yet another of Brecht's ridiculous Marxist simplifications? No, judging from the following report from contemporary China:

In Nanjing, half a decade ago, an elderly woman fell while getting on a bus. Newspaper reports tell us that the 65 year old woman broke her hip. At the scene, a young man came to her aid; let us call him Peng Yu, for that is his name. Peng Yu gave the elderly woman 200RMB (at that time enough to buy three hundred bus tickets) and took her to the hospital. Then, he continued to stay with her until the family arrived. The family sued the young man for

136,419 RMB. Indeed, the Nanjing Gulou District Court found the young man to be guilty and ordered him to pay 45,876 RMB. The court reasoned, "according to common sense," that because Peng Yu was the first off the bus, in all probability he had knocked over the elderly woman. Further, he actually had admitted his guilt, the court reasoned, by staying with the elderly woman at the hospital. It being the case that a normal person would not be as kind as Peng Yu claimed he was.[22]

Is this incident not exactly parallel to Brecht's story? Peng Yu helped the old lady out of simple compassion and decency. But since such a display of goodness is not "typical" nor the rule ("a normal person would not be as kind as Peng Yu claimed he was"), it was interpreted by the court as a proof of Peng Yu's guilt, and he was appropriately punished. Is this a ridiculous exception? Not so, according to the government newspaper the *People's Daily* which, in an online opinion poll, asked a large sample of young people what they would do if they were to see a fallen elderly person: "87% of young people would not help. Peng Yu's story echoes the surveillance of the public space. People will only help when a camera was present." What such a reluctance to help signals is a change in the status of public space. The street has become an intensely private place and seemingly the words "public" and "private" no longer make sense. Being in a public space does not entail only being together with other unknown people, In moving among them, I am still within my private space, and I am not engaged in interaction with or the recognition of others. The space of my coexistence and interaction with others counts as public only if covered by security cameras.

Another sign of this change can be found at the opposite end, the recent trend towards public sex in hard-core pornography. An increasing number of films show people engaged in sexual acts in heavily frequented public spaces, such as public beaches, inside a bus or train, at train stations, or in the open space of a shopping mall. A large majority of people who pass by (pretend to) ignore the scene – a few throw a discrete glance at the couple, even fewer make a sarcastic or obscene remark. It is as if the copulating couple remained in a private space, so that we should not be concerned by their intimacies.

This brings us back to Hegel's "spiritual animal kingdom." Who behaves like this, passing by dying fellows in blessed ignorance or copulating in front of others? Animals, of course. This fact in no way entails the ridiculous conclusion that we are somehow "regressing" to the animal level. The animality with which we are dealing here – the ruthless egotism of each individual pursuing his/her private interest – is

---

[22] Michael Yuen, "China and the Mist of Complicated Things" (text with author).

the paradoxical result of the most complex network of social relations (market exchanges, social mediation of production) and of the fact that individuals are blinded because this complex network points towards its ideal ("spiritual") character. In a civil society structured by the market, abstraction rules more than ever in history. In contrast to nature, the market competition of "wolves against wolves" is thus the material reality of its opposite, of the "spiritual" public substance which provides the background and base for this struggle among private animals.

It is often said that as a result of total exposure to the media, to the culture of public confessions and to instruments of digital control, private space is disappearing. One should counter this commonplace with the opposite: it is the *public* space proper which is disappearing. The person who displays on the web his/her naked images or intimate data and obscene dreams is not an exhibitionist. Exhibitionists intrude into the public space, while those who post their naked images on the web remain in their private space and are just expanding it to include others. The same applies to Anwar and his colleagues in *The Act of Killing*. They are privatizing the public space in a manner more threatening than economic privatization.

On humanitarianism and human rights

Against this background, the lie of the "humanitarian" War on Terror can be easily discerned in its ambiguous attitude towards suffering. The occasional excessive indifference towards suffering, even and especially when it is widely reported and condemned, gives the impression that the outrage at suffering turns us into its immobilized fascinated spectators. Recall, in the early 1990s the three-year-long siege of Sarajevo, with the population starving, exposed to permanent shelling and sniper fire. Although the media were full of pictures and reports, why did the UN forces, NATO or the United States not attempt even a small act of breaking this siege, or of imposing a corridor through which people and provisions could circulate freely? It would have cost nothing. A little serious pressure on the Serb forces would have terminated the prolonged spectacle of encircled Sarajevo exposed to excessive terror. The only credible answer to this enigma has been proposed by Rony Brauman who, on behalf of the Red Cross, coordinated the help to Sarajevo. The presentation of the Sarajevo crisis as "humanitarian," the recasting of the political–military conflict into humanitarian terms, was sustained by the eminently *political* choice of taking the Serb side in the conflict. Especially ominous and manipulative was the role of French President Mitterrand:

The celebration of "humanitarian intervention" in Yugoslavia took the place of a political discourse, disqualifying in advance all conflicting debate ... It was apparently not possible, for François Mitterrand, to express his analysis of the war in Yugoslavia. With the strictly humanitarian response, he discovered an unexpected source of communication or, more precisely, of cosmetics, which is a little bit the same thing ... Mitterrand remained in favor of the maintenance of Yugoslavia within its borders and was persuaded that only a strong Serbian power was in the position to guarantee a certain stability in this explosive region. This position rapidly became unacceptable in the eyes of the French people. All the bustling activity and the humanitarian discourse permitted him to reaffirm the unfailing commitment of France to the Rights of Man in the end, and to mimic an opposition to Greater Serbian fascism, all in giving it free rein.[23]

From this specific insight, one should make the move to the general level and problematize the depoliticized humanitarian politics of "human rights" as the ideology of military interventionism serving specific economic and political purposes. As Wendy Brown comments in response to Michael Ignatieff, such humanitarianism "presents itself as something of an antipolitics – a pure defense of the innocent and the powerless against power, a pure defense of the individual against immense and potentially cruel or despotic machineries of culture, state, war, ethnic conflict, tribalism, patriarchy, and other mobilizations or instantiations of collective power against individuals."[24] However, the question is somewhat different: "What kind of politicization do those who intervene on behalf of human rights set in motion against the powers they oppose? Do they stand for a different formulation of justice or do they stand in opposition to collective justice projects?"[25] It is clear that the US overthrowing of Saddam Hussein, legitimized in the terms of ending the suffering of the Iraqi people, not only was motivated by other politico-economic interests (oil), but also relied on a determinate idea of the political and economic conditions that should open up the perspective of freedom to the Iraqi people: western liberal democracy, guarantees of private property, the inclusion into the global market economy, and so on. The purely humanitarian anti-political politics of merely preventing suffering thus effectively amounts to the implicit prohibition of elaborating a positive collective project of socio-political transformation.

---

[23] Rony Bauman, "From Philanthropy to Humanitarianism," *South Atlantic Quarterly*, 103 (2/3) (2004), 398–9 and 416.
[24] Wendy Brown, "Human Rights as the Politics of Fatalism," 453.
[25] Ibid., 454.

At an even more general level, one should question the opposition between the universal, pre-political human rights, which belong to every human being "as such," and the specific political rights of the citizen. In this vein, Étienne Balibar argues for the "*reversal* of the historical and theoretical relationship between 'man' and 'citizen'; which proceeds by "explaining how *man is made by citizenship* and not citizenship by man."[26] Balibar refers to Hannah Arendt's insight apropos the twentieth-century phenomenon of refugees: "The conception of human rights based upon the assumed existence of a human being as such, broke down at the very moment when those who professed to believe in it were for the first time confronted with people who had indeed lost all other qualities and specific relationships – except that they were still human."[27] This line of argument leads directly to Agamben's notion of *homo sacer* as a human being reduced to "bare life." In a properly Hegelian paradoxical dialectics of universal and particular, it is precisely when a human being is deprived of his particular socio-political identity which supports his determinate citizenship, that he, in one and the same move, is no longer recognized and/or treated as human. In short, the paradox is that one is deprived of human rights precisely when one is effectively, in one's social reality, reduced to a human being "in general," without citizenship, class, or profession. When one effectively becomes the ideal bearer of "universal human rights" which belong to the person "independently of" her profession, sex, citizenship, religion or ethnic identity, one is no longer human.

We thus arrive at a standard "postmodern," "anti-essentialist" position, a kind of political version of Foucault's idea that sex is generated by a multitude of practices of sexuality. "Man," the bearer of human rights, is generated by a set of political practices which materialize citizenship. But is this enough? Jacques Rancière has proposed a very elegant and precise solution of the antinomy between human rights (belonging to "man as such") and the politicization of citizens.[28] Human rights cannot be posited as an unhistorical "essentialist" beyond with regard to the contingent sphere of political struggles or as the universal "natural rights of man" exempted from history. At the same time, they should also not be dismissed as a reified fetish, as the exclusive product of concrete historical processes and citizen politicization. The gap between the universality of human rights and the political rights of citizens is not a

---

[26] Balibar, "Is a Philosophy of Human Civic Rights Possible?," 320–1.
[27] Hannah Arendt, *The Origins of Totalitarianism* (New York: Meridian 1958), 297.
[28] See Jacques Rancière, "Who is the Subject of the Rights of Man?," *South Atlantic Quarterly*, 103(2/3) (2004), 297–310.

gap between the universality of man and a specific political sphere. It, rather, "separates the whole of the community from itself," as Rancière put it in a precise Hegelian way.[29] Far from being pre-political, "universal human rights" designate the precise space of politicization proper: they amount to *the right to universality as such*, the right of a political subject to assert its radical non-coincidence with itself in its particular identity and to posit itself – precisely insofar as it is the "supernumerary" subject, the "part with no part," the one without a proper place in the social edifice – as an agent of universality as such. The paradox is thus very precise and symmetrical to the paradox of universal human rights as the rights to inhumanity. *At the very moment we try to conceive political rights of citizens without the reference to universal "meta-political" human rights, we lose politics itself*, i.e. we reduce politics to a "post-political" negotiation of particular interests.

What, then, happens to human rights when they are reduced to the rights of *homo sacer*, of those excluded from the political community, reduced to "bare life" – i.e. when they become of no use, since they are the rights of those who, precisely, have no rights, are treated as inhuman? Rancière proposes here an extremely salient dialectical reversal:

[W]hen they are of no use, you do the same as charitable persons do with their old clothes. You give them to the poor. Those rights that appear to be useless in their place are sent abroad, along with medicine and clothes, to people deprived of medicine, clothes, and rights. It is in this way, as the result of this process, that the Rights of Man become the rights of those who have no rights, the rights of bare human beings subjected to inhuman repression and inhuman conditions of existence. They become humanitarian rights, the rights of those who cannot enact them, the victims of the absolute denial of right. For all this, they are not void. Political names and political places never become merely void. The void is filled by somebody or something else … if those who suffer inhuman repression are unable to enact Human Rights that are their last recourse, then somebody else has to inherit their rights in order to enact them in their place. This is what is called the "right to humanitarian interference" – a right that some nations assume to the supposed benefit of victimized populations, and very often against the advice of the humanitarian organizations themselves. The "right to humanitarian interference" might be described as a sort of "return to sender": the disused rights that had been sent to the rightless are sent back to the senders.[30]

In the predominant western discourse, the "human rights of the third world suffering victims" *give rise to the* right of the western powers to intervene – politically, economically, culturally, militarily – in countries of their choice in order to defend human rights. It reminds us of Lacan's

---

[29] Rancière,"Who is the Subject," 305.   [30] Ibid., 307–9.

formula of communication, in which the sender gets back from the receiver–addressee his own message in its inverted – that is true – form. In the reigning discourse of humanitarian interventionism, the developed west is effectively getting back from the victimized third world its own message in its true form. As soon as human rights become depoliticized, the discourse dealing with them becomes moral and references to the pre-political opposition of Good and Evil are mobilized. Today's "new reign of Ethics"[31] clearly discernible in Michael Ignatieff's work, relies on a violent gesture of depoliticization, of denying political subjectivity to the victimized other. As Rancière pointed out, liberal humanitarianism *à la* Ignatieff unexpectedly meets the "radical" position of Foucault or Agamben. The Foucauldian–Agambenian notion of "biopolitics" presented as the culmination of the entire western thought ends up getting caught in a kind of "ontological trap" in which concentration camps appear as a kind of

ontological destiny: each of us would be in the situation of the refugee in a camp. Any difference between democracy and totalitarianism grows faint and any political practice proves to be already ensnared in the biopolitical trap.[32]

When, in a shift from Foucault, Agamben identifies sovereign power and biopolitics – according to him the two overlap in our generalized state of exception – he precludes the possibility of the emergence of political subjectivity. However, the rise of political subjectivity takes place against the background of a certain limit of the "inhuman." The paradox of the inhumanity of the human deprived of citizenship remains. The "inhuman" pure man is a necessary excess of humanity over itself, humanity's "indivisible remainder," a kind of Kantian limit-concept of the phenomenal notion of humanity. In the same way that Kant's sublime Noumenal appears as pure horror when we come too close to it, man "as such," deprived of all phenomenal qualifications, appears as an inhuman monster, something like Kafka's *Odradek*. The problem with human rights humanism is that it covers up this monstrosity of the "human as such," presenting it as a sublime human essence.

The Marxist symptomatic reading can convincingly demonstrate the particular content that gives the specifically bourgeois ideological spin to the idea of human rights. For the Marxist critique of ideology, universal human rights are effectively the rights of the white male private owners to exchange freely on the market, exploit workers and women, and exert political domination. This identification of the particular content that hegemonizes the universal form is, however, only half of the story.

---

[31] Rancière, "Who is the Subject," 309.   [32] Ibid., 301.

The crucial other half asks a much more difficult supplementary question: how did the form of universality emerge? In what specific historical conditions does abstract universality become a fact of social life? In what conditions do individuals experience themselves as subjects of universal human rights?

Marx's analysis of "commodity fetishism" is the key to answering these questions. When commodity exchange predominates, individuals relate to themselves and to the objects they encounter in their daily lives, as contingent embodiments of abstract universal notions. What I am, my concrete social or cultural background, is experienced as contingent, since what ultimately defines me is the "abstract, universal capacity to think and to work." All objects that can satisfy my desire are experienced as contingent, since my desire is conceived as an "abstract" formal capacity, indifferent towards the multitude of particular objects that may – but never fully do – satisfy it. This is evident in relation to the "professions." The modern idea of "profession" implies that I experience myself as an individual who is not directly 'born into' his social role – what I will become depends on an interplay between the contingent social circumstances I find myself in and my free choice. Today's individual has a profession, be it electrician, professor, or waiter; it would be meaningless to claim that a medieval serf was a peasant by profession. The crucial point is that in certain social conditions – those of commodity exchange and global market economy – "abstraction" becomes a direct feature of actual social life, of the way concrete individuals behave and relate to their personal fate and social surroundings.

Marx shares here Hegel's insight. Universality becomes "for itself" only insofar as individuals no longer fully identify the core of their being with their particular social situation, only insofar as they experience themselves as "out of joint" with regard to this situation. The concrete, effective existence of the universal is an individual without a proper place in the social edifice. Universality becomes "for itself," fully active, only in those individuals who lack a proper place in it. The mode of appearance of abstract universality, therefore, its entry into actual existence, is an extremely violent move of disrupting the preceding organic poise.

It is not enough to make the well-known Marxist point that a gap separates the ideological appearance of the universal legal form and the particular interests that effectively sustain it. We should immediately add at this level, the counter-argument, made, among others, by Lefort and Rancière: the form is never "mere" form. It has its own dynamism, which leaves its traces in the materiality of social life. The bourgeois "formal freedoms" set in motion "material" political demands and practices, from trade unions, to feminism, and anti-racism. Rancière is right to emphasize the radical ambiguity of the Marxist notion of the "gap" between formal democracy and the economic reality of exploitation and domination. One interpretation presents it as a symptom of the distance between the "appearance" of equality and freedom (what Étienne Balibar has called "equaliberty") and the social reality of economic, social, or cultural inequality. In this approach, the form of universal rights is a necessary but illusory form of expression of the concrete social content of universal exploitation and class domination. But a much more radical interpretation accepts that the "appearance" of equaliberty has an effectiveness of its own, which sets in motion the progressive "politicization" and re-arrangement of socio-economic relations. Lévi-Strauss' term "symbolic efficiency" is of help here. The appearance of equaliberty is a symbolic fiction which possesses actual efficiency of its own.

One does not only begin with the authentic articulation of a life-world experience which is then re-appropriated by those in power to serve their particular interests and impose on their subjects to make them docile cogs in the social machine. Much more interesting is the opposite process, in which something that was originally an ideological edifice imposed by rulers is taken over by the subordinates and becomes a means for articulating their grievances. Recall the classic case of the Virgin of Guadalupe in early colonized Mexico. With her appearance, Christianity, which up to that point had acted as the imposed ideology of the Spanish colonizers, was appropriated by the indigenous population and became a symbol of their terrible plight. This is perhaps the way human rights work today for the exploited and dominated people of the world.

Index